To Grandma &
Grandpa With Love

About Island Press

Since 1984, the nonprofit Island Press has been stimulating, shaping, and communicating the ideas that are essential for solving environmental problems worldwide. With more than 800 titles in print and some 40 new releases each year, we are the nation's leading publisher on environmental issues. We identify innovative thinkers and emerging trends in the environmental field. We work with world-renowned experts and authors to develop cross-disciplinary solutions to environmental challenges.

Island Press designs and implements coordinated book publication campaigns in order to communicate our critical messages in print, in person, and online using the latest technologies, programs, and the media. Our goal: to reach targeted audiences—scientists, policymakers, environmental advocates, the media, and concerned citizens—who can and will take action to protect the plants and animals that enrich our world, the ecosystems we need to survive, the water we drink, and the air we breathe.

Island Press gratefully acknowledges the support of its work by the Agua Fund, Inc., Annenberg Foundation, The Christensen Fund, The Nathan Cummings Foundation, The Geraldine R. Dodge Foundation, Doris Duke Charitable Foundation, The Educational Foundation of America, Betsy and Jesse Fink Foundation, The William and Flora Hewlett Foundation, The Kendeda Fund, The Forrest and Frances Lattner Foundation, The Andrew W. Mellon Foundation, The Curtis and Edith Munson Foundation, Oak Foundation, The Overbrook Foundation, the David and Lucile Packard Foundation, The Summit Fund of Washington, Trust for Architectural Easements, Wallace Global Fund, The Winslow Foundation, and other generous donors.

Wildlife and Society

The Science of Human Dimensions

Wildlife and Society

The Science of Human Dimensions

Edited by

Michael J. Manfredo

Jerry J. Vaske

Perry J. Brown

Daniel J. Decker

and Esther A. Duke

Society and wildlife in the twenty-first century : human dimensions of natural resources management / Michael J. Manfredo ... [et al.].
p. cm.
Includes bibliographical references.
ISBN-13: 978-1-59726-407-5 (cloth : alk. paper)
ISBN-10: 1-59726-407-5 (cloth : alk. paper)
ISBN-13: 978-1-59726-408-2 (pbk. : alk. paper)
ISBN-10: 1-59726-408-3 (pbk. : alk. paper)
1. Wildlife management—Social aspects. 2. Wildlife conservation—Social aspects. I. Manfredo, Michael J.
SK355.S62 2008
333.95'416—dc222008007473

Printed on recycled, acid-free paper ⊛

Design by Joan Wolbier

Manufactured in the United States of America

10 9 8 7 6 5 4 3 2 1

Table of Contents

Acknowledgments

The editors and contributing authors thank the Western Association of Fish and Wildlife Agencies and the Arizona Game and Fish Department for their financial support of this book. Immense thanks are also extended to the Warner College of Natural Resources: Colorado State University, Cornell University, the University of Montana, the National Wildlife Federation, the Wildlife Society, and Routledge: Taylor & Francis Group for their generous contributions to this project. We also thank Barbara Dean at Island Press for her support of this book and for her expert guidance.

CHAPTER 1

Introduction: Perspectives on the Past and Future of Human Dimensions of Fish and Wildlife

Perry J. Brown

From fear to full stomachs, from curiosities to art, fish and wildlife are a part of the human psyche. We have chased and been chased by wildlife throughout our sojourn on the Earth. With primitive weapons and modern cameras we have approached fish and wildlife and all that they bring to our lives. But despite our forever association with wild animals, the emergence of an academic field of human dimensions of fish and wildlife is relatively recent. Over the past fifty years this field has emerged, evolved, and taken root.

Before we dissect the field into all its component parts, we will present an overview of its emergence and some of its evolutionary highlights, and we will give perspective to its future. One fundamental premise is that people are interested in and care about fish and wildlife, and it is their relationships to animals and their habitats that are critical to sustaining animal diversity and the benefits arising from our association with these critters.

Americans' burgeoning use of the outdoors following World War II set the stage for the study of human dimensions of fish and wildlife to emerge. To be sure, before the 1950s in the United States naturalist and scientific writers were beginning to note the relationships between people and wildlife, both the pleasures and the controversies. Aldo Leopold, for example, clearly pointed us to the social and political world of wildlife management. But during the 1950s, as more and more people poured into our national parks and monuments, national forests, fish and wildlife refuges, and private recreational lands and forests, human dimensions issues became more and more prominent. Recognition of this changing use of the American landscape was institutionalized in the establishment of the Outdoor Recreation Resources Review Commission ([ORRRC], 1958), initiation of massive development programs of both the National Park Service (Mission 66, 1956) and the U.S. Forest Service (Operations Outdoors, 1957), and new laws affecting use and management of wildlands such as the Multiple Use Sustained-Yield Act (1960), the Wilderness Act (1964), and the Wild and Scenic Rivers Act (1964).

For a glimpse of this use of the outdoors, we can look at the statistics on fishing and hunting produced for the ORRRC and for later *National Surveys of Fishing, Hunting, and Wildlife-Associated Recreation.* From a baseline in 1960 of 260 million fishing occasions, ORRRC projected that by 2000 there would be over 520 million occasions (ORRRC 1962). The U.S. Fish and Wildlife Service reported that we had taken 454 million fishing trips by 1991, indicating that we were well on the way to meeting the prediction (U.S. Fish and Wildlife Service 1991). Similarly for hunting, ORRRC used a 95-million-occasion baseline and projected participation at 174 million occasions by 2000 (ORRRC 1962), yet in 1991 we had already exceeded the projection with 214 million trips (U.S. Fish and Wildlife Service 1991). In the consumptive wildlife areas of fishing and hunting, use was skyrocketing; adding to that were the growing urban and nonconsumptive uses of fish and wildlife.

Three groups of human dimensions scientists began to respond to the issues of growing use and interest in fish and wildlife. Biologists and naturalists were called upon to provide insight to policy makers responsible for fish and wildlife management. A classic case of this was the work of the Craighead brothers, who reviewed bear management in Yellowstone National Park in relation to human encounters with bears and some of the management practices that were causing problems for both bears and management (Craighead, Sumner, and Mitchell 1995). Economists such as those at Utah State University also responded with studies of the use and value of wildlife, especially by hunters and fishers (Wennergren 1964, 303; 1967). Finally, an emerging group of noneconomic social scientists became engaged in trying to characterize both the users and the phenomenon of human relationships with wildlife (Hendee and Potter 1971). From these early efforts sprung what we now characterize as the human dimensions of fish and wildlife.

In the early 1970s, human dimensions study got a real boost when John Hendee and Clay Schoenfeld developed a human dimensions session at the 38th North American Wildlife and Natural Resources

Conference and then published the nineteen papers that were presented (Hendee and Schoenfeld 1973). These papers stretched from defining and evaluating recreation quality to assessing elk behavior in relation to human activities such as cattle grazing, recreation, and traffic. Human dimensions sessions were organized at subsequent North American Wildlife and Natural Resources Conferences, thus stimulating a vital field of inquiry.

As we moved through the 1970s and early 1980s scientists were expending considerable effort on various topics of the human dimensions of fish and wildlife. For example, in Wisconsin Tom Heberlein and his students were actively applying sociological principles and theories to the field; in Colorado Doug Gilbert was exploring wildlife and other natural resource communications, and Jack Hautaluoma and Perry Brown were exploring the psychological dimensions underlying big-game hunting; in Arizona Bill Shaw was leading us to an understanding of why some people oppose hunting; and at Yale Steve Kellert was teasing out the various values underlying people's relationships to fish and wildlife (e.g., Gilbert 1971; Shaw 1977, 19; Kellert 1976; Hautaluoma and Brown 1978, 271). Economists were continuing to explore the nature of nonmarketed resources with fish and wildlife as prime examples (e.g., Wennergren 1967).

Once we began to notice that more and more people were entering the field, fourteen of us from around the country agreed to meet in Minneapolis at the Minnesota Valley National Wildlife Refuge in the early 1980s to explore how we might organize to promote the field. The outcome was the Human Dimensions of Wildlife Study Group. This group immediately began gathering members, started a quarterly newsletter, and became the focal point for organizing meetings and symposia. The group was important in developing a language around human dimensions of fish and wildlife and in giving the emerging group of human dimensions graduate students a home for their energy and interests.

Other human dimensions activities were under way as well, many of them focused on parks and recreation and on public policy regarding natural resources. Some of the same people involved in the fish and wildlife work were involved in these realms, but there were other people as well. Thus, a significant collection of human dimensions of natural resources scientists was developing. The culmination of this activity was the first conference devoted to social science in natural resources, held at Oregon State University in 1986 and hosted by Don Field and

Perry Brown. A wide variety of social scientists studying a wide variety of topics, including the human dimensions of fish and wildlife, attended the conference, which now occurs somewhere in North America every other year. The conference became truly international in 1997 when Mike Manfredo organized the first non–North American version of the conference in Belize. This conference also occurs every other year but outside North America, attracting many researchers from around the world.

Another significant conference that occurred in the mid-1980s dealt with the topic of valuing wildlife (Decker and Goff 1987). Many of the academic and agency scientists involved in developing the field of human dimensions of wildlife made presentations at this New York meeting, and the resulting book is a wonderful compilation of ideas the scientists were investigating at that time.

The International Association for Society and Resource Management and its journal, Society and Natural Resources, and another journal, *Human Dimensions of Wildlife*, first published in 1996, eventually replaced the Human Dimensions of Wildlife Study Group. This evolution was natural, demonstrating the maturity that the field was developing across the broad area of natural resources and the environment.

During this period of development, an active congressional natural resource and environment agenda, coupled with some activities in individual states, spurred the need for human dimensions work. The Multiple Use Sustained-Yield Act (1960), the McIntire-Stennis Cooperative Forestry Research Act (1962), the Wilderness Act (1964), the Land and Water Conservation Fund Act (1965), the Water Quality Act (1965), the National Historic Preservation Act (1966), the Wild and Scenic Rivers Act (1968), the National Trails System Act (1968), the National Environmental Policy Act (1969), the Clean Air Act Amendments (1970), the Endangered Species Act (1973), the Resources Planning Act (1974), the National Forest Management Act (1976), the Federal Land Policy and Management Act (1976), and state environmental policy, wildlife, recreation, and parks legislation all set the stage for important human dimensions research and study and the incorporation of many voices in natural resources decisions and management.

Especially in response to much of this legislation we began to ask questions about integration in natural resource management and how we might integrate social information with biophysical information. The general feeling was that social assessments were not being used since they simply were sections of plans and reports that were separate from other sections dealing with resources and management. What social scientists, biologists, and resource managers had failed to do was to identify where we were working within planning and management models. Most social information fits on the demand side of the planning equation. Although the demand side certainly is relevant for identifying what and how we need to inventory and manage on the supply side, most of us have training and information on the supply side, and that bias exacerbated the problem of using social information in natural resource planning and management. We tried to integrate demand-side information with supply-side information, but it did not work. Social factors drive resource management as demand and policy variables, not as supply variables. Thus, we were struggling with not only what to integrate but also how to integrate. As separate chapters whose fit was undefined and as products from researchers who advocated human dimensions considerations but made little effort to demonstrate their relevance and practicality, social information was generally lost to the decision-making system. That did not make social information any less relevant; it simply rendered such information less useful because people did not know what to do with it.

This became a big issue in the controversy surrounding the spotted owl and development of the Northwest Forest Plan. In the 1990s, when the issues were more bold and recognized as more complex than previously thought, nearly everyone began to talk about the need for human dimensions information, pronouncing that "we know that social values drive our decisions." But actions do not always follow talk. FEMAT (Forest Ecosystem Management Assessment Team), for example, brought social scientists to the table, but their work seemed more like window dressing than the base for understanding the forest management issues and potential resolution of them in the U.S. Pacific Northwest. Although we learned a lot from FEMAT, raised some significant questions, and developed some new technologies for social analysis, the Columbia River Basin and other megastudies repeated the fundamental problem of not recognizing the relevance of social information. Again, social scientists assembled important human dimensions information and developed some technologies for its analysis and display (especially spatial technologies), but it appears that they were constantly in a battle to work their way into the dominant biological, supply-side paradigm guiding assessments and plans.

Currently, there is widespread recognition that we need to hear many relevant voices; that human dimensions information is important for defining resources and identifying what to inventory and manage; and that human dimensions information is important to understanding how people can participate in natural resource decisions.

The many voices enfranchised since the 1980s give urgency to our work as social scientists and human dimensions practitioners. As we have moved from a model of natural resource management in which an elite called the shots to a much more collaborative and diffuse model, our work has become more critical. The book *Nature and the Human Spirit* (Driver et al. 1999) is convincing about the many relevant voices with fascinating and important perspectives. And human dimensions is the scientific arena that will uncover these perspectives.

As we have moved into the twenty-first century many of the same themes continue for human dimensions study, but it seems there now is more recognition of the profound changes that are under way in our administration and management of natural resources, and maybe in many other ways that we govern ourselves. These changes, and those to come, have made human dimensions information a necessity for fish, wildlife, and other natural resource management. This information is not a luxury. We need information on the who, what, where, when, and why for all those interested in or affected by natural resource decisions anytime we are allocating and managing natural resources.

With the many voices of interested and affected people, with the complexity of the decisions that need to be made, and with the long-term consequences associated with most decisions, how can we not know what is perceived, preferred, and required and that what we do has impact on people? As we discovered in the 1970s and '80s, we also need to develop techniques for people to effectively voice their observations and concerns, to affect collaboration in planning and decisions, and to provide continuing involvement long past the initial decisions.

Finally, we need to dedicate ourselves to helping others learn how to use human dimensions information. We can learn a lot and we can slowly let our learning seep into fish and wildlife decisions, but the pace of change in natural resources does not allow us such luxury. What we learn needs to be used now, and it is on our backs to help people see the relevance of the information and ideas we generate. It is our job to work with administrators and managers to challenge and support their decisions and to help them learn how to listen to people and to process human dimensions information.

Lessons from Our History

This brief history suggests a convergence of several important events and people who effectively led us to where we are today. This is likely always the case as fields of science emerge and evolve, but some emerge and evolve faster and more efficiently than others, and the fifty years or so of human dimensions emergence seems particularly fast. Here are a few of the important lessons over this fifty-year period.

First, managers, policy makers, and scientists must recognize that people are important in sustaining fish and wildlife. They must recognize that animals, their populations and habitats, will not be sustained, even if we have all the biological and physical knowledge we can ever obtain, unless people want fish and wildlife and are willing to make policies and sacrifices to sustain them. Thus, sustaining and managing fish and wildlife will depend on people, which means that managers must understand these people and their relationships to fish and wildlife. As managers and policy makers have recognized this fact, they have stimulated development of human dimensions science.

Second, there is a time when the issues and the people are ripe for a field of science to emerge. In the United States it was necessary to have growing interest in fish and wildlife, or crises associated with their management, to lead us toward the questions we needed to ask. In response to these questions, the human dimensions of natural resources surfaced and became linked to the biological information that managers and policy makers were already using.

Third, patience is needed; fields of science evolve as issues unfold and as capacity to do more and more complex science develops. From the small group that began human dimensions research, even before it had that label, the cadre of people working in the field has grown considerably, their skills have sharpened, and their perspectives have multiplied. The emergence of new issues has brought new people and new perspectives into the cadre over time, and these new issues have led us to consider different biological questions along with the human dimensions questions.

Fourth, the commitment and compassion of those involved is necessary, and they need to sustain this commitment and compassion for a long time. Today's old-timers such as John Hendee, Tom Heberlein, Bill Shaw, Steve Kellert, Jim Applegate, Tommy Brown, Perry Brown, and a few others have remained involved for decades, a few of them even in retirement. With the next generations of professionals such as Dan Decker, Mike Manfredo, Jerry Vaske, Mike Patterson, Tara Teel, and many others, we have been fortunate in building a field of science and drawing to it many from the social science disciplines.

Fifth, organizational leadership and ability are needed, and we have also been fortunate in having people such as Don Field and Mike Manfredo who are masters at developing scientific journals and who had ideas and the initiative to carry them forward for meetings and symposia. Other people had administrative ability and political savvy to advance organizations and ideas where it counts financially.

Sixth, communication devices are instrumental in building networks and exchanging information. There may be many forms of these devices, but for us, newsletters and journals were prominent. In the future we might expect that Web sites and electronic newsletters will substitute for the paper we mailed to people.

Seventh, our field would not have grown without the development of university programs, especially at the doctoral level, since much of the human capacity for human dimensions work is developed through university education. Centers such as those developed at Cornell University and Colorado State University have been particularly valuable in bringing focus to research and outreach aspects of the human dimensions of fish and wildlife management. They also have helped stimulate the development of human dimensions units in the state fish and wildlife agencies. As universities were embracing the need for human dimensions expertise, study, and capacity building, government agencies and NGOs were beginning to recognize that they too needed human dimensions expertise on staff to complement their biological expertise and thus have hired many of the products of university programs.

Eighth, people working in human dimensions of natural resources such as the pioneers listed earlier may come from different disciplines and backgrounds, but they share a passion for fish and wildlife and their sustainability. These relationships were formed between them early in the development of human dimensions science.

One might be able to find other lessons from our experience, but these eight were instrumental along the evolutionary path that we took. They form a package of ingredients to understand our success.

What Might the Future Hold?

One of the significant changes to affect fish and wildlife management and policy is the decidedly urban nature of the human population. This is true not only in the United States, where over 80 percent of the population lives in urban places, but also in the rest of the world, where over 50 percent of the population lives in urban places. For these populations, connections to the land, when they exist, are often different from those of agrarian societies. For example, the proportion of people engaged in hunting and fishing is declining, while the complexities of ecological relations and the human dependency on healthy and clean environments are being recognized by more people. Those who are engaged in human dimensions science in fish and wildlife have the responsibility to tease out how urban people define fish and wildlife resources, how they perceive the use and value of these resources, and what are acceptable and unacceptable means of managing these resources.

Many human dimensions scientists are likely to be called upon to participate in conservation education activities, advising educators about fish and wildlife and helping them devise means for learning about these resources and their importance to people. Other human dimensions scientists will be enmeshed in advising policy makers about the importance of these resources and how they might be managed. The science-policy interface thus will become less distinct, and scientists will need to be vigilant not to compromise their science and become part of the partisan advocacy lobby.

The burgeoning urbanization of the world suggests an approach to the human dimensions of fish and wildlife that is not readily inherent in the management perspectives that have dominated U.S. human dimensions research. Drawing on the synthesis perspectives of anthropology and geography, scientists have more fully considered and investigated social issues of indigenous rights, poverty, governance, and social justice. This has led to study of phenomena such as human-wildlife conflicts, ecotourism, illegal harvesting and trade, comanagement, wildlife and human health, and the effects of wildlife on the development of culture and human spirit. These issues are likely to be prominent in our future and will represent a new focus, a new theoretical underpinning, and a new set of inquiries for human dimensions researchers.

Since the 1960s many voices have been legitimized in natural resource decision-making processes, and human dimension scientists will need to attend to these voices. From what was an elite system of decision making about the management and use of natural resources, including fish and wildlife, a far more pluralistic and democratic system has been forged, bringing a much more diverse set of ideas and actors into the arena, including many ethnic and local voices (Brown 1995). This calls for human dimensions scientists and practitioners to move past mere public input to develop means for active participation by the various interests.

These voices, especially the local ones, have been increasing our attention to issues of community and collaboration. Fish and wildlife are very much local resources—things that people see and cherish. As we have moved toward a more participatory democracy, especially at the local level, human dimensions scientists have been called upon to develop effective means of local participation and to develop means of regional and national, and sometimes international, participation in the face of strong local participation. They have been called upon to examine the various collaborative schemes that have been developing and to help determine when they are and when they are not effective. As we consider appropriate arrangements for governance of fish and wildlife, and public lands in general, a rich field of human dimensions science is before us.

As with all life we often become surprised at the way events unfold and we can seize opportunities if we are attentive. Warming of the earth is challenging our countries, societies, and natural resources management in ways not experienced before, and fish and wildlife are not immune from it. Human dimension scientists will have plenty to investigate and understand. For example, many of our parks and protected areas, which are refuges for our wildlife and their habitats, are islands in the midst of larger landscapes that include towns and cities, multiple-use forests and grasslands, the headwaters of rivers, municipal watersheds, and other critical spaces. These protected areas will experience changes in plant and animal composition and changes in hydrologic regimes just as will the surrounding lands. While these changes are occurring, human populations surrounding them will be involved in dealing with wildfire, invasive species, attacks from bugs and pathogens, and urbanization. They will want to be involved but will be perplexed about what is happening to these special places and to the animals that they support. Human dimensions scientists are likely to be in the middle of helping societies understand how environments are adapting to climate change that is occurring on a scale that has not been observed in modern times. They will be involved in identifying appropriate and acceptable responses to these changes and the many policies that will evolve.

Water and energy development will present particular challenges for the future existence of fish and wildlife. Governments will press for changes in resource management as they confront changes in policy for water and energy use. That water and energy developers will need to consume more and more land to extract resources will be exacerbated by growing human populations and by climate change. We are currently seeing some of the effects of such development in the coal-bed methane areas of northeastern Wyoming and southeastern Montana, where habitat of the greater sage grouse (*Centrocercus urophasianus*) is particularly affected. Understanding what is happening and how people and their governments are reacting to changes will be a major undertaking for human dimensions scientists. Understanding how we might mitigate some of the negative effects of change will also be a challenge for these professionals.

Finally, a growing interest in the relationship between fish and wildlife and their neighbors is emerging. As we become more urban and as our urban fringes encroach on more and more wildlife habitat, the issues of neighbors become larger. Deer eating flowers and gardens and mountain lions eating domestic cats and dogs, and sometimes attacking humans, are issues. But the issues are not just urban–centered because they occur in rural areas as well. The issue of bison exiting Yellowstone National Park and what we do about them is a human dimensions issue as is the pest nature of wildlife in urban areas. There are myriad policy and management responses to these issues of neighbors, which human dimensions scientists will likely discuss. As we consider these neighbors, when we think of fish and wildlife, we often think of food and other staples of life while other people think of their economic potential through tourism. And for others, fish and wildlife are considered for employment and enjoyment. No matter which perspective one takes, or all of them together, just how neighbors participate in the benefits of fish and wildlife is a significant issue that will occupy more and more time of human dimensions professionals.

Exploring the Human Dimensions of Fish and Wildlife

This history and prediction about the future of the human dimensions of fish and wildlife is an introduction to the many dimensions of this important field. In the chapters that follow, written by many of the most prominent human dimensions scientists are the many faces of human dimensions science. Issues of values and demographics; the culture of wildlife management; working with communities; legal and institutional factors; wildlife conflicts and diseases; managing wildlife viewing, privatization, and trade; and communications are addressed along with several other topics. The human dimensions of fish and wildlife is a field that has developed rapidly, but it has much more development to come. With issues of urbanization and growing world population, with movement toward participatory democracy, with the enfranchisement of a wider range of voices, with accelerated climate change, with demand for energy development, and with many other issues confronting societies, there will be a rich future for the human dimensions of fish and wildlife.

Literature Cited

Brown, P. J. 1995. Forestry yesterday and tomorrow: Institutional assumptions and responses. XIX William P. Thompson Memorial Lecture. Flagstaff: Northern Arizona University.

Craighead, J. J., J. S. Sumner, and J. A. Mitchell. 1995. *The Grizzly bears of Yellowstone: Their ecology in the Yellowstone ecosystem, 1959–1992.* Washington, DC: Island Press.

Decker, D. J., and G. R. Goff, eds. 1987. *Valuing wildlife: Economic and social perspectives.* Boulder, CO: Westview Press.

Driver, B. L., D. Dustin, T. Baltic, G. Elsner, and G. Peterson, eds. 1999. *Nature and the human spirit.* State College, PA: Venture Publishing.

Gilbert, D. L. 1971. *Natural resources and public relations.* Bethesda, MD: Wildlife Society.

Hautaluoma, J. E., and P. J. Brown. 1978. Attitudes of the deer hunting experience—a cluster analytic study. *Journal of Leisure Research* 10:271–87.

Hendee, J. C., and R. R. Potter. 1971. Human behavior and wildlife management: needed research. In Transactions of the 36th North American Wildlife and Natural Resources Conference, 383–96. Washington, DC: Wildlife Management Institute.

Hendee, J. C., and C. Schoenfeld, eds. 1973. *Human dimensions in wildlife programs.* Washington, DC: Wildlife Management Institute.

Kellert, S. R. 1976. *Perceptions of animals in American society.* New Haven, CT: Behavioral Sciences Study Center, Yale University.

Outdoor Recreation Resources Review Commission (ORRRC). 1962. *Outdoor recreation for America.* Washington, DC: U.S. Government Printing Office.

Shaw, W. 1977. A survey of hunting opponents. *Wildlife Society Bulletin* 5:19–24.

U.S. Fish and Wildlife Service. 1991. *National survey of fishing, hunting, and wildlife-associated recreation.* Washington, DC: U.S. Department of the Interior.

Wennergren, E. B. 1964. Valuing non-market priced recreational resources. *Land Economics* 40:303–14.

———. 1967. *Demand estimates and resource values for resident deerhunting in Utah.* Logan: Utah State University Agricultural Experiment Station Bulletin 469. The publisher is the Ag Exp. Station at USU; this pub is #469 in their series.

PART I

Social Factors Creating Change in Fish and Wildlife Conservation

The future of human coexistence with wildlife is unfolding in day-to-day, issue-to-issue decisions made by humans. As human populations around the world continue to expand, reconciling nature conservation with human needs and aspirations is imperative. This book, *Wildlife and Society: The Science of Human Dimensions,* is designed to address the myriad issues that arise as people and wildlife struggle to coexist in a healthy and sustainable manner. Through an exploration of contemporary issues, the book highlights the relevance of human dimensions (HD) of fish and wildlife work across the globe. It provides a theoretical and historical context for the field of human dimensions of fish and wildlife as well as a demonstration of tools, methodologies, and idea sharing for practical implementation and integration of HD practices. Written by leading researchers, the chapters in *Wildlife and Society: The Science of Human Dimensions* document the progress of key topics in human dimensions of fish and wildlife and offer a multifaceted presentation of this truly interdisciplinary field.

Chapter 1 provided an introduction to the field of human dimensions of fish and wildlife management and research. This introduction included a review of the development of this field over the past fifty years. The chapter also presented key lessons learned from this history and followed those lessons with identification and discussion of several emerging issues and opportunities such as the decidedly urban nature of human populations, changes in decision-making approaches, communities and collaboration, climate change, and water and energy development.

Part I explores some key social factors that create change in fish and wildlife conservation. Social factors refer to a system of common life attitudes, orientations, or behaviors that take the interests, intentions, or needs of other people and animals into account. Interactions among people and between people and wildlife are relations of mutual dependence. Fish and wildlife management is a public sector system developed by communities to define relationships and minimize conflicts between people and animals. The public sector strives to meet the need for governance for the good of all. Ever-changing social factors define fish and wildlife management needs. Increased public involvement in wildlife management, shifting values about wildlife, and other changes have impact on wildlife management.

Chapter 2 explores the social and demographic changes in the United States that influence fish and wildlife management. The long-term well-being of fish and wildlife resources depends on a broad range of stakeholders. Understanding these different segments of society and the changes occurring in the social and demographic fabric of the nation is critical to planning, management, and policy development. Although these issues are critically important in the United States, they will ultimately create similar challenges throughout the world as organizations respond to twenty-first century management needs.

Chapter 3 explores trends in human thought and societal organization that affect human-wildlife relationships and wildlife conservation. Shifting values toward wildlife affect wildlife-related attitudes and behaviors at the individual level. At the societal level, this shift appears to be related to conditions of modernization and its effect on day-to-day life. Chapter 3 also examines the potential causal link between forces of modernization and trends in broad societal-level thought. Forces of modernization affect these trends within the confines of different cultural and religious contexts. The trends suggest a changing future for wildlife management agencies in the United States. At the international level, these changes set the stage for differing perspectives on issues involving human-wildlife conflict.

Chapter 4 considers the role of conservation nongovernmental organizations (NGOs) in building the infrastructure necessary for successful fish and wildlife management in developing countries. To secure the rights of local people to manage local resources (e.g., wildlife), organizations like the Wildlife Conservation Society focus their efforts on increasing local democratic governance skills. This chapter explores the relationships between successful natural resource management and participatory democracy.

Global climate change has governments and the private sector working to build stronger global environmental partnerships. Chapter 5 examines the effect of global climate change on wildlife and wildlife management. Climate change poses a challenge to humankind and a threat to all living beings on a scale that is beyond any other environmental issue faced in human history. Human dimensions researchers need to work across economic and cultural boundaries to communicate climate change issues in a meaningful way.

Overall, Part 1 provides a context for understanding how and why fish and wildlife management is changing and is changed by society. Parts 2 through 4 build upon this context by exploring the integration of social science practices into management policy and actions and by examining the implications of these practices for contemporary fish and wildlife management. This book provides a platform for improving fish and wildlife management activities at the local, national, and international levels through the integration of appropriate social science tools.

CHAPTER 2

Social and Demographic Trends Affecting Fish and Wildlife Management

Michael A. Schuett, David Scott, and Joseph O'Leary

Outdoor recreation activities and resources make up an important lifestyle component in the United States. Participation in outdoor recreation defines, in part, who we are as individuals while providing people innumerable benefits (Manning 1999). Likewise, our system of national parks, national forests, and wildlife refuges preserves our cultural and natural heritage and defines who we are as Americans (Nash 2001). However, the long-term well-being of our parks and natural and cultural resources will forever depend on their being relevant to young and older Americans alike. Since the 1960s, the popularity of traditional outdoor recreation activities like fishing and hunting has plummeted, signaling a change in how Americans use and view the natural environment.

This chapter begins by summarizing past, current, and future participation rates in fishing, hunting, and wildlife-associated recreation, examining several sociodemographic variables. The chapter then discusses three key factors that we believe are likely to have impact on current and future participation in these activities: (1) population growth and urbanization in the United States, (2) the changing racial and ethnic composition of the United States, and (3) constraints to participation. In conclusion, the chapter discusses the implications of these factors for management and provide suggestions for future research.

We would like to thank the Center for Socioeconomic Research and Education at Texas A&M University for technical assistance.

Participation Trends in Hunting, Fishing, and Wildlife-Associated Activities

Since the 1960s, local, state, and federal governments have sought to gauge Americans' activity participation and use of natural resources in order to learn more about current and future demand. This is important as resource managers seek to balance the interests and needs of visitors and the protection of cultural and natural resources for future generations (Manning 1999). One important source of data is the *National Survey of Fishing, Hunting, and Wildlife-Associated Recreation*. Since 1955, at approximately five-year intervals, the U.S. Fish and Wildlife Service has conducted in-depth surveys of Americans to better understand participation in wildlife-related activities. We have compiled participation data from the survey for fishing (table 2.1), hunting (table 2.2), and wildlife watching away from home (table 2.3) for 1980, 1985, 1991, 1996, 2001, and 2006. We have also broken down participation rates by gender, age, race, and population size of residence. Collectively, these data provide a useful snapshot of how Americans' involvement in fishing, hunting, and wildlife watching has changed over the last generation.

What is striking about these data is just how much participation in wildlife-related activities has plummeted over time. In 1980, about one-quarter of Americans said they fished at least once a year. In 2006, only 13 percent of Americans reported they had gone fishing one or more times that year. A similar pattern is evident for hunting. In 1980, one out of ten Americans said they hunted; in 2006, only 5 percent of Americans reported they hunted. Participation in wildlife watching away from home dropped from 17 percent in 1980 to 10 percent in 2006. These figures show, in very stark terms, that participation in wildlife-related activities among Americans is on the decline.

The survey also shows that declines are greatest for Americans who are younger and living in large urban areas. Participation rates in fishing, hunting, and wildlife watching away from home in 2006 is about half of what they were in 1985. Overall declines in participation in fishing and wildlife watching among younger Americans are particularly dramatic. Table 2.1 shows that a little more than one-quarter of Americans who were eighteen to twenty-four years of age in 1980 said they had gone fishing. In 2006, only 10 percent of eighteen- to twenty-four-year-olds said they had gone fishing. Table 2.3 shows even greater declines in wildlife watching for this same age group (21 percent to 5 percent). However, increases in wildlife watching from 2001 to 2006 were evident for those over age twenty-five and especially in the thirty-

TABLE 2.1 **U.S. Participation in Fishing, 1980-2006**

	1980 %	1985 %	1991 %	1996 %	2001 %	2006 %
TOTAL	**25**	**26**	**19**	**17**	**16**	**13**
SEX						
Men	36	37	28	27	25	20
Women	15	16	10	9	8	6
AGE						
16 and 17	29	31	23	20	17	13
18 to 24	26	27	20	16	13	10
25 to 34	31	32	23	21	19	13
35 to 44	29	31	22	22	21	17
45 to 54	24	24	18	20	17	15
55 to 64	20	21	16	15	16	14
65 and older	12	13	9	9	8	7
RACE						
White	26	27	20	19	18	15
Black	14	13	10	10	7	6
Other	17	18	11	11	8	7
POPULATION SIZE OF RESIDENCE						
Large MSA* (1 million or more)	—	20	14	14	12	10
Medium MSA (245,000 to 999,999)	—	25	19	18	17	13
Small MSA (50,000 to 249,999)	—	27	22	21	22	19
Outside MSA	—	33	25	25	24	21

Source: National Survey of Fishing, Hunting, and Wildlife-Associated Recreation
*MSA = Metropolitan Statistical Area

five to fifty-four age group. This upswing demonstrates a possible shift in activity interest for those over twenty-five years of age.

Tables 2.1 through 2.3 show that participation in fishing, hunting, and wildlife watching is lowest among Americans living in large urban areas. Moreover, rates of participation have dropped faster for Americans living in larger cities than elsewhere. This is particularly true for fishing (table 2.1). In 1985, 20 percent of Americans living in cities of one million or more said they went fishing. In 2006, only 10 percent of

TABLE 2.2 **U.S. Participation in Hunting, 1980-2006**

	1980 %	1985 %	1991 %	1996 %	2001 %	2006 %
TOTAL	**10**	**9**	**7**	**7**	**6**	**5**
SEX						
Men	20	18	14	13	12	10
Women	2	2	1	1	1	1
AGE						
16 and 17	15	14	10	9	8	6
18 to 24	14	11	9	7	6	4
25 to 34	13	12	9	8	7	5
35 to 44	9	11	9	9	8	7
45 to 54	7	9	8	8	7	6
55 to 64	3	7	6	6	6	6
65 and older	3	3	3	3	3	3
RACE						
White	11	10	8	8	7	6
Black	3	2	2	2	1	1
Other	4	3	2	3	2	2
POPULATION SIZE OF RESIDENCE						
Large MSA* (1 million or more)	—	5	4	3	3	4
Medium MSA (245,000 to 999,999)	—	8	6	7	6	3
Small MSA (50,000 to 249,999)	—	10	9	9	10	5
Outside MSA	—	16	15	15	13	9

Source: National Survey of Fishing, Hunting, and Wildlife-Associated Recreation
*MSA = Metropolitan Statistical Area

Americans living in these cities said they went fishing. Participation in fishing, hunting, and wildlife watching continues to be highest among Americans living in smaller cities and rural areas.

In general, future projections to 2050 for hunting, fishing, and wildlife watching show declines for most age groups and in some regions of the country (Bowker, English, and Cordell 1999). As a proportion of the overall population, hunting participation will decline by 11 percent, the larger declines (35 percent) occurring in the Pacific Coast

TABLE 2.3 **U.S. Participation in Wildlife Watching Away from Home, 1980-2006**

	1980 %	1985 %	1991 %	1996 %	2001 %	2006 %
TOTAL	**17**	**16**	**16**	**12**	**10**	**10**
SEX						
Men	19	17	18	12	11	11
Women	16	16	14	11	9	9
AGE						
16 and 17	16	17	14	9	9	3
18 to 24	21	17	14	8	6	5
25 to 34	25	23	21	13	11	13
35 to 44	18	21	20	16	13	26
45 to 54	15	13	16	15	12	23
55 to 64	11	11	12	11	11	19
65 and older						
RACE						
White	19	18	18	13	11	11
Black	5	4	4	2	2	3
Other	11	7	9	7	5	5
POPULATION SIZE OF RESIDENCE						
Large MSA* (1 million or more)	—	15	13	11	9	9
Medium MSA (245,000 to 999,999)	—	17	16	12	10	10
Small MSA (50,000 to 249,999)	—	16	18	13	13	12
Outside MSA	—	18	19	14	13	13

Source: National Survey of Fishing, Hunting, and Wildlife-Associated Recreation
*MSA = Metropolitan Statistical Area

and southern regions of the United States. However, participation increases are projected for the Rocky Mountains (20 percent) and for nonwhite populations. For fishing, national participation is expected to increase by 36 percent, the Rocky Mountain region experiencing the highest increase (57 percent). Last, for wildlife-watching activities, participation increases of 61 percent are expected, the largest increases occurring in the South.

Factors Affecting Participation in Hunting, Fishing, and Wildlife-Associated Activities

Multiple factors contribute to activity participation changes that will have impact on the future use and management of fish and wildlife areas. This section discusses several explanations for participation changes in hunting, fishing, and wildlife-associated recreation.

Population Growth and Urbanization in the United States

Among the key factors that will affect recreation activity participation and the management of fish and wildlife areas is population change. The population of the United States now stands at over 300 million and is projected to increase to 363 million by 2030. It is important to note that this increase is not taking place evenly throughout the country; population growth in the Northeast and the Midwest is expected to be stagnant compared with large projected increases for the South and the West (fig. 2.1).

The balance of human use and land management can be increasingly controversial as competing interests are challenged to sustain economic growth and maintain habitat conservation. In the western and southern United States, population growth and housing develop-

Figure 2.1 **Projected Population in U.S. by Region from 2000–2030**

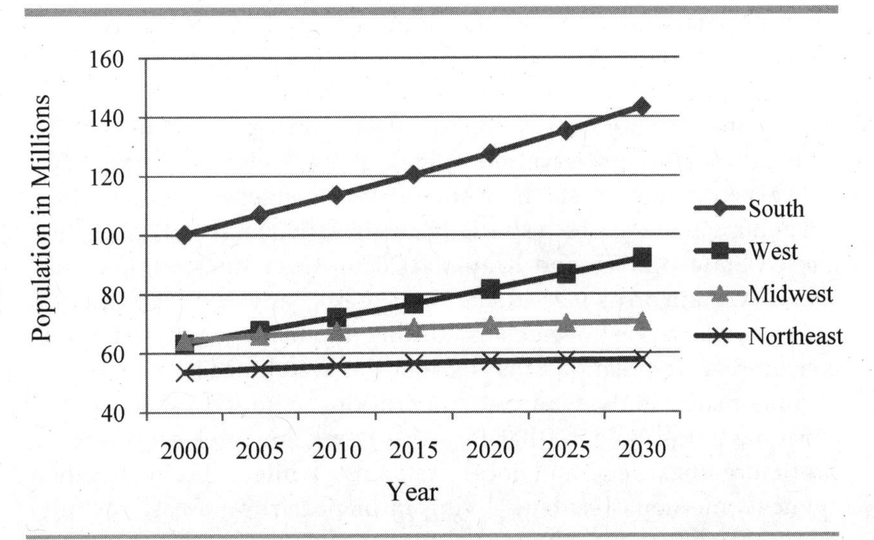

Source: U.S. Census Bureau 2007

ment must compete with other land uses such as energy extraction, mining, and logging. Land development has increased by 34 percent from 1992 to 1997 and may double in the next twenty-five years (Alig, Kline, and Lichtenstein 2004). Over time continued urbanization, loss of habitat, and land use change have modified the natural landscape in the United States, thus affecting places to recreate (Alig, Butler, and Swenson 2000; Alig et al. 2004; Kline 2006) and the types of outdoor recreation activities people engage in.

Research shows that residents are increasingly living in areas of the wildland-urban interface (WUI) where urban development meets the rural landscape (Dwyer and Childs 2004). This type of encroachment has impacts on parks and forests as well as prairies and farmlands. Development and urbanization can eliminate areas for hunting, fishing, and wildlife-associated recreation. This issue is especially a problem for those who recreate on private lands; once private recreation areas such as ranches for hunting are gone, existing places to recreate become limited or crowded. Urbanization can also be problematic for property rights infringement (Johnson 2001).

Given the impacts of urbanization, managers are finding it beneficial and necessary to work with more stakeholders in developing community-based management and minimizing conflicts (Raik et al. 2005). Stakeholders (e.g., environmental groups, recreation user groups, businesses, and NGOs) are engaging in sustaining the viability of protected natural areas through increased public involvement and other formalized options such as participation on advisory committees (Lafon et al. 2004; Weber 2003). Newcomers as well as seasonal homeowners are becoming involved in issues about wildlife management and preservation (Clendenning, Field, and Kapp 2005). However, "culture clash" may emerge with longer-term residents as development increases, especially in growth areas of the western United States (Smith and Krannich 2000). Over time conflicts may arise in certain areas if residents want public lands managed less for consumptive recreation such as hunting and managed more for nonconsumptive recreation such as wildlife watching. Managers will become increasingly challenged in working with a diverse cadre of concerned stakeholders that includes recreation user groups, nonprofit organizations, and local residents, while adhering to their agency's mission. Residents living in or near rural areas, amenity-rich locations, and public lands will continue to be engaged in balancing open space preservation, resource management, and

FIGURE 2.2 **Projected Population in U.S. by Race and Ethnicity from 2000–2030**

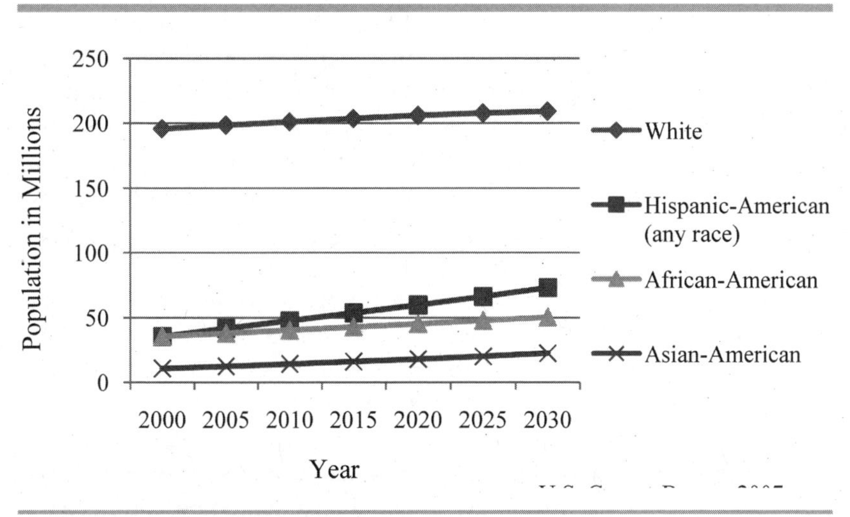

Source: U.S. Census Bureau 2007

recreation use as the American countryside becomes more developed and continues to draw those seeking a better quality of life (Weber 2003).

The Changing Racial and Ethnic Composition of the United States

Over the last few decades, the United States has become more racially and ethnically diverse. In 2005, approximately 30 percent of the U.S. population included nonwhites and/or people of Hispanic origin (U.S. Bureau of the Census 2007). People of Hispanic and Asian ancestry are among the fastest-growing population groups in the United States, accounting for a large portion of overall population growth. From 1990 to 2000, both Hispanic Americans and Asian Americans grew by about 50 percent, compared with only 10 percent for whites and 17 percent for African Americans. Projected growth for Hispanic Americans and Asian Americans in the next generation will increase dramatically. For example, in 2000 the national Hispanic American population was 35.6 million; it is projected to increase to 73 million by 2030 (fig. 2.2). In 2007, 303 U.S. counties or about one in every ten counties in the nation (3,141 total) had a population that was more than 50 percent minority.

Constraints to Participation

Using data from the 2001 survey, Leonard (2007) reported that time constraints are by far the most important factor that people mention when they explain why they quit hunting and fishing. Forty-seven percent of Americans who had quit fishing said they did so because they did not have enough time. Similarly, 43 percent of Americans said they stopped hunting because they did not have enough time. Leonard reported that time constraints are most acute among nonwhites, people with high levels of income and education, people who live in large cities, and people between the ages of twenty-five and forty-four.

There are a variety of other constraints to participation beyond lack of time, including costs, work, lack of access, and poor health. Given the changing nature of the population throughout the United States, it is important to understand how constraints limit participation and preferences among racial and ethnic minorities. Currently, people of color hunt, fish, and participate in a wide range of other outdoor recreation activities at a rate far lower than their white counterparts (tables 2.1–2.3). People of color are also far less likely than whites to visit state parks, national parks, and national forests. Cultural values, economic factors, and discrimination and harassment help explain why many members of minority groups do not visit parks, hunt, fish, or participate in many other forms of outdoor recreation (Allison 2000; Floyd 1999). A summary of research findings shows the following:

- Many members of minority groups regard some outdoor recreation activities as culturally "irrelevant," meaning that nonparticipation is partly due to lack of interest.
- Members of ethnic and racial minorities are also far more likely than whites to have lower levels of education and income. Thus, low participation in wildlife-related outdoor recreation activities by members of minority groups partly is related to a lack financial resources to travel and purchase recreation equipment.
- Prejudice and discrimination in public places are common incidents experienced by many members of minority groups. Anticipation of harassment may actually discourage members of minority groups from using parks and outdoor recreation areas away from home.
- Constraints to participation are aggravated by the frequent shortage of employees at park and recreation agencies who

have the same physical characteristics of the population at large. Park managers, planners, and rangers may lack skills to effectively relate to minority visitors; consequently, minority visitors may be less likely to go to these places.

The long-term well-being of natural resources in the United States depends on making recreation sites and protected areas accessible and relevant to a broad range of constituents. This issue will become increasingly urgent as ethnic and racial minorities increase their share of the U.S. population and learn to experience and appreciate our parks, forests, and water areas.

Implications and Future Research

In summary, this chapter is about change and its influence on activities that are part of the fabric of American life. Participation rates for hunting, fishing, and wildlife-associated recreation have declined over the last generation. Overall future participation projections are modest; however, participation increases are expected in the growth areas of the South and the West and by nonwhite populations. Factors influencing a decline in participation include population growth and urbanization, changing racial and ethnic composition, and constraints to participation. For those who are actively engaged in the use and management of fish and wildlife areas, activity participation will dictate where resources are allocated, how areas are managed, what places are visited, and whether or not future generations will be able to use and appreciate them. From the user perspective, those who continue to participate in these outdoor recreation activities may find fewer places to go to visit and more crowded areas, and they may have less free time for these activities. Managers of areas for hunting, fishing, and wildlife-associated recreation may need to make the recreation experience more accessible and relevant for diverse visitors and work with stakeholders who want to be more involved in natural resource decision making.

Future research on participation will need to expand so that more detailed data are available about those who engage in these outdoor activities *as well as* those who drop out and possibly reengage (Fedler and Ditton 2001). As populations shift, individuals can become more interested in outdoor activities as they move to new areas, both urban and rural. At the same time, people can become less interested in outdoor recreation when communities become crowded and users substitute for other recreation activities (Ditton and Sutton

2004). Changes in participation patterns over time in urban and rural areas will also need more investigation.

Research about anglers, hunters, and wildlife watchers should be targeted to examine how agencies are responding to a diverse population and potential changes in visitation and management of these recreation areas. Because the population of nonwhites is expected to increase, it is important to understand more fully their perceptions of wildlife and the role of wildlife in their lives. It is also important to understand how agency policies and programs facilitate and/or stymie interest and participation in fishing, hunting, and wildlife watching.

As for places where people go to recreate, land use change, fragmentation, and development will continue to be key issues for residents, users, and managers alike. These factors raise additional research questions on the cumulative effects of development on habitat (Theobald, Miller, and Hobbs 1997). Additional studies are needed in monitoring recreation use in the WUI and its impact on public lands (Schuett et al., 2007). Resource managers will need to educate new and existing residents about living near protected areas, both public and private. This issue can be a challenge for managers given tighter federal and state budgets and less staff. Hopefully, this type of environmental education will make citizens more informed and foster a land ethic for future generations. In conclusion, adults and, most important, our children must become more aware of the significance of using and caring for our natural resources. User groups, resource managers, policy makers, scientists, and local residents need to work together to balance human needs with ecological sustainability if we aspire to use and conserve our fish and wildlife areas into the next millennia.

Literature Cited

Alig, R. J., B. J. Butler, and J. J. Swenson. 2000. Fragmentation and national trends in private forest lands: Preliminary findings from the 2000 renewable resources planning assessment. In *Proceedings from the Fragmentation 2000 Conference,* 34–45. Annapolis, MD.

Alig, R. J., J. D. Kline, and M. Lichtenstein. 2004. Urbanization on the US landscape: Looking ahead in the 21st century. *Landscape and Urban Planning* 69:219–34.

Allison, M. T. 2000. Leisure, diversity and social justice. *Journal of Leisure Research* 32:2–6.

Bowker, J. M., D. B. K. English, and H. K. Cordell. 1999. Projections of outdoor recreation participation to 2050. In *Outdoor Recreation in American Life*, ed. H. K. Cordell, 323–50. Champaign, IL: Sagamore Publishing, 1999.

Clendenning, G., D. R. Field, and K. J. Kapp. 2005. A comparison of seasonal homeowners and permanent residents on their attitudes toward wildlife management on public lands. *Human Dimensions of Wildlife* 10:3–17.

Ditton, R. B., and S. G. Sutton. 2004. Substitutability in recreational fishing. *Human Dimensions of Wildlife* 9:87–102.

Dwyer, J. F., and G. M. Childs. 2004. Movement of people across the landscape: A blurring of distinctions between areas, interests, and issues affecting natural resource management. *Landscape and Urban Planning* 69:153–64.

Fedler, A. J., and R. B. Ditton. 2001. Dropping out and dropping in: A study of factors for changing recreational fishing participation. *North American Journal of Fisheries Management* 21:283–92.

Floyd, M. F. 1999. Race, ethnicity and use of the national park system. *Social Science Research Review* 1:1–23.

Johnson, M. P. 2001. Environmental impacts of urban sprawl: A survey of the literature and proposed research agenda. *Environment and Planning*, 33:717–35.

Kline, J. D. 2006. Public demand for preserving local open space. *Society and Natural Resources* 27:645–59.

Lafon, N. W., S. L. McMullin, D. E. Steffen, and R. S. Schulman. 2004. Improving stakeholder knowledge and agency image through collaborative planning. *Wildlife Society Bulletin* 32:220–31.

Leonard, J. 2007. Fishing and hunting recruitment and retention in the U.S. from 1990 to 2005. *Addendum to the 2001 National Survey of Fishing, Hunting, and Wildlife-Associated Recreation*. Arlington, VA: U.S. Fish and Wildlife Service.

Manning, R. E. 1999. *Studies in outdoor recreation: Search and research for satisfaction*. Corvallis: Oregon State University Press.

Nash, R. 2001. *Wilderness and the American mind*, 4th ed. New Haven, CT: Yale University Press.

Raik, D. A., B. T. Lauber, D. J. Decker, and T. L. Brown. 2005. Managing community controversy in suburban wildlife management: Adopting practices that address value differences. *Human Dimensions of Wildlife* 10:109–22.

Schuett, M. A., J. Lu, D. Fannin, and G. Bowser. 2007. The wildland urban interface and the National Forests of East Texas. *Journal of Park and Recreation Administration 25:6–24.*

Smith, M. D., and R. S. Krannich. 2000. Culture clash revisited: Newcomer and longer-term residents' attitudes toward land use, development, and environmental issues in rural communities in the Rocky Mountain West. *Rural Sociology* 65:396–421.

Theobald, D. M., J. R. Miller, and T. N. Hobbs. 1997. Estimating the cumulative effects of development on wildlife habitat. *Landscape and Urban Planning* 39:25–36.

U.S. Bureau of the Census. 2007. State and county quick facts. http://quickfacts.census.gov/qfd/states/00000.html.

Weber, E. P. 2003. *Bringing society back in grassroots ecosystem management, accountability, and sustainable communities.* Cambridge, MA: MIT Press.

CHAPTER 3

Understanding Global Values toward Wildlife

Michael J. Manfredo, Tara L. Teel, and Harry Zinn

Every culture's relationship with wildlife is a response to universal human needs (e.g., food, protection, reproduction), and across cultures, both differences and similarities exist in how these needs have been met. Cross-cultural study of human-wildlife relationships reveals these differences and similarities, providing important information for wildlife managers who increasingly operate in a global context. In this chapter we offer a global perspective on human relationships with wildlife that are expressed through wildlife values. We approach this topic in four steps. First, we discuss multiple social science approaches to understanding the concept of values. Second, we explore the possibility of a genetic foundation for human-wildlife relationships. Third, we differentiate the concepts of values, ideology, and value orientations, the human cognitions acquired through cultural learning that are central to attaining a cross-cultural understanding of human-wildlife relationships. Finally, we introduce the hypothesis that modernization is affecting human-wildlife relationships by spawning the reemergence of a mutualism value orientation toward wildlife as societies move through preindustrial, industrial, and postindustrial phases.

Diverse Social Science Perspectives on Human Values

In the early 1980s, the U.S. Pacific Northwest witnessed an abrupt decline in salmon runs. Salmon harvest seasons were dramatically reduced, and as a result, recreational charter fishing was limited. Charter boat captains were faced with exploring alternative sources of business (e.g., bottom fishing or whale watching) or going out of business. Many chose the latter strategy, and for the people directly involved, this occurrence was deeply disruptive and life changing. From a broader perspective, however, this situation is routine in natural resource management; a social structure emerges around a natural resource; then, as availability of and/or demand for the resource changes, the social structure is also forced to change and adapt. The interdependency of society and the natural environment can be viewed in this way as a complex and dynamic entanglement without an easily identifiable start and with an uncertain future trajectory.

This salmon decline in the Northwest can provide a means to illustrate different social science approaches to exploring values toward wildlife. One approach would be to elicit the *individual stories* of people involved. These stories might express different individuals' feelings about the effects of change on their lives, their views of the ocean and salmon, and the causes of this situation. The stories would stand on their own as evidence describing the change phenomenon. We might also glean from these stories the rich symbolism that emerges from our entanglement with the salmon resource (e.g., the association of salmon with qualities of strength, beauty, and power). Another research approach might focus on the *attitudes of groups of people* affected by the situation. It might, for example, explore charter boat captains' attitudes toward alternative forms of business, or attitudes toward new agency regulations. This approach may reveal the importance of social identity in understanding why the captains hold on to certain types of occupations in the face of economic disaster. A third approach might examine the *effects of salmon decline on coastal communities* by documenting the decline's impact on tourism, on the composition of social groups and social networks, on the distribution of power, and on land tenure and wealth in these places and the economic impacts on communities. A fourth approach might explore the *impact of salmon decline on political institutions* involved in salmon management. In particular, how well do the various levels of government and their interrelationships (e.g., state and federal wildlife agencies, multistate/multinational agency coalitions) reflect contemporary societal values, and how do relationships change with conditions of scarcity?

Each of these social science approaches might also consider the *multicultural nature of human-salmon relationships* in the Pacific Northwest where tribal nations have court-established rights in decisions about salmon allocation. A large, court-ordered increase in the proportion of salmon runs allocated to native tribes in the 1970s reflects important values of a society that previously focused on effective extraction of resources and elimination of competition for those resources from "outside groups." Multinational cooperation and competition among the United States, Canada, and Japan over commercial harvest represents another multicultural aspect of the situation, one that might be explored by studying power relationships as revealed by international laws and treaties, domestic laws, and the impacts of legal mandates on resource rights, catch rates, stakeholder conflict, and resource overharvest.

At still another level, we might look at how, worldwide, *broader economic, demographic, and technological changes* affect the situation. How, for example, does the widespread presence of relatively low-cost and highly effective fishing technologies affect catch? More broadly, how can we draw linkages to this issue from a longer chain of societal events; from advancements in technology to massive changes in occupational sectors and modes of economic production, to the emergence of social movements (e.g., environmentalism), to a widespread shift in public values, to a clash between consumptive and protection-oriented views toward natural resources, to more specific debates inherent in the salmon allocation issue? How do we account for all of these linkages and also relate them to changes in the natural environment? Further, how do we marry this broader, societal-level view with other approaches discussed previously?

This example illustrates the varied social science perspectives on natural resource issues. Our point, however, is to emphasize that there are many highly informative views on the topic of wildlife values, all useful, all important. None alone tells the whole story, and a thorough understanding demands multiple perspectives. They can be contrasted on the basis of their different scales (e.g., time, element of focus, geographic), different social science theoretical traditions (e.g., psychology, sociology, political science), and diverse methodologies.

The purpose of our chapter is to provide a framework and a context for exploring global patterns of similarities in human values toward wildlife. As we look for these broad generalities, we recognize that there is something historically and situationally unique about the ways different cultures regard wildlife. For example, when Douglas (1990) discusses the importance of the pangolin to the fertility cult of the Lele of Central Africa, she references many specifics that would apply only to that culture. At the same time, we endorse the search for broader generalizations. For example, when Douglas concludes that the consumption of certain meats among the Lele symbolizes social class distinctions, we wonder about patterns of differential food consumption across social classes in other cultures, why these patterns occur, and how generalizable they are.

A cross-cultural understanding of wildlife values has important managerial implications. To illustrate, consider the following management situations:

- Management of migratory species (e.g., waterfowl) often requires cross-cultural collaboration.
- Cross-cultural collaboration will also increasingly be necessary to combat global environmental problems, including the acceleration of human-wildlife conflict and climate change.
- A growing trend in wildlife conservation is for developed nations to attempt to intervene to protect biodiversity in developing nations. Today, conservation NGOs from developed countries reach into virtually all areas of the globe.
- We are increasingly a mobile society, and day to day, wildlife managers in all countries deal with multiple cultural perspectives. Different views of the wildlife resource might exist, for example, among foreign visitors and recent immigrants, or among diverse segments within a population.

In all of these cases, we contend that mutual understanding of wildlife values is a good starting point for successful discussions and actions. The most difficult issues are where basic values conflict. Understanding the role of those values in discussing a conservation issue is key. Moreover, with globalization and modernization, values toward wildlife are likely to change. How will that impact the roles and challenges of wildlife management? To contribute to greater understanding in these areas, we look for commonalities in response to wildlife across cultural groups. We first ask what evidence exists to suggest biologically prepared responses that may explain cross-cultural similarities. We then discuss the potential for examining commonalities and change in human-wildlife relationships across cultures via the concepts of values, ideology, and value orientations.

A Genetic Foundation for Human Thoughts about Wildlife?

At the most basic level, we can ask whether or not there appear to be any panhuman tendencies in response to wildlife. E. O. Wilson (1993), in his biophilia hypothesis, proposed a strong, biologically fashioned human attachment to wildlife and natural environments. While there is scant scientific evidence to support Wilson's advocacy claim of a human *need* for an intimate association with natural environments, there is little doubt that our genetic makeup has been shaped profoundly by our interactions with wildlife. For example, current male tendencies toward aggression have been explained as the remnants of selection for traits that resulted in more effective hunters (Wrangham and Peterson 1996). At the same time, human social and communal tendencies have been explained as the result of selection due to human social groups' survival advantages in the face of predation by other species (Hart and Sussman 2005).

Some researchers have explored the mechanisms by which our genetically determined dispositions may affect our reactions to wildlife. One explanation focuses on the way in which heritability prepares humans to learn more quickly, and forget more slowly, in situations involving wildlife. Experiments examining "biophobia" suggest that this happens, for example, when people are presented with threatening stimuli such as snakes and spiders from the natural environment (Ohman 1986). Other writers have suggested that wildlife automatically draws human attention because of the evolutionary advantage posed in signaling safety or danger (Katcher and Wilkins 1993). The jerky motion of an injured animal or an animal running to escape a predator would signal danger, whereas the smooth, continual motion of animals in a more tranquil state (e.g., waterfowl swimming, deer feeding) would signal safety.

Two additional topics involving human universal response to wildlife are anthropomorphism and totemism (Mithen 1996). Anthropomorphism is the tendency to project human characteristics on nonhuman animals. It is a widespread and pervasive human predisposition that has been cast as the archenemy of objectivity in the Cartesian sciences. Despite this view, recent theory suggests that anthropomorphism resulted from natural selection because it served to improve humans' hunting abilities (Mithen 1996). In addition, anthropomorphic art found in cave drawings is interpreted as providing evidence of complex human thought that emerged just 40,000 YBP (years before present). Today, the tendency to ascribe human characteristics to wildlife may be contributing to a widespread shift in human values toward wildlife, as we shall see in a later section of the chapter.

Totemism is a term used to describe a worldview in which one's existence is closely intertwined with the natural environment. It has been found in virtually all hunter and gatherer societies. With totemism, people believe they have descended from, and are related to, a particular plant or animal species (Mithen 1996). People who identify themselves as part of a specific totemic clan (e.g., a bear clan) feel a strong obligation to other kin in the clan. The totemic animal (or plant) becomes the clan emblem; it is seen as both kin and a godlike ancestor. Totemism's widespread existence in human society has long attracted the interest of anthropologists. Lévi-Strauss proposed that totemism underlies the panhuman tendency to engage in analogical reasoning and suggested that we look at the organization of animals for deriving explanations of human society (Willis 1990). Similarly, Douglas (1990) proposed that we explain wildlife behavior and the natural world based on what we believe about ourselves (which suggests that totemism and anthropomorphism may be linked).

What can we conclude about the effects of genetics on human values toward wildlife? Wildlife have been central actors in shaping the attraction and avoidance tendencies in humans. It seems likely that we have been genetically prepared to learn quickly about wildlife. Features of our societal organization appear to reflect the unique role of wildlife in shaping human understanding of the environment. Still, our genetically prepared tendencies certainly do not predetermine our values toward wildlife, a topic we will explore in the remaining sections of this chapter.

Culturally Shaped Human Thoughts about Wildlife: Values, Ideology, and Value Orientations

Theory suggests that, at the individual level, behavior toward wildlife is dictated by beliefs and affective responses. Beliefs are information we hold as true. Affect refers to the "feeling" states we experience, including positive or negative moods and/or emotions. Beliefs and affect are the building blocks of many key concepts in psychology, including attitudes, norms, and values. Attitudes are evaluations expressed with some degree of favor or disfavor toward anything that emerges in our consciousness (e.g., entities, issues, behaviors), whereas norms are beliefs about what others expect us to do (Ajzen and Fishbein 1980). Together, attitudes and norms are the proximate causes of individual behavior, such as avoiding, petting, or feeding wildlife. But across many situations, attitudes and behaviors are also guided by values.

Values

Values hold a unique and central place in our cognitive structure. They are enduring beliefs about desired end states and appropriate modes of conduct (Rohan 2000; Schwartz 2004). Other characteristics of values include the following:

- Values form slowly over many experiences. They are shaped through learning during one's youth and change very little throughout one's adult life.
- Values are superordinate guidelines for what to think and do. They direct human behavior through their influence on attitudes and norms, giving consistency to thought and action across time and situations.
- Values are critical elements in the transmission of culture from one generation to the next.
- Values are culturally directed ways of meeting the existence needs of individuals and the cohesion needs of society.

Various theorists have proposed panhuman value typologies that are applicable to exploring human-wildlife relationships. Schwartz's (2004) typology has attained a prominent place in contemporary values literature and been applied in a select few cases to understanding human-wildlife relationships (see Manfredo 2008, in press). Findings suggest that values related to conformity, tradition, security, and self-enhancement support utilitarian views toward wildlife, while values related to openness to change and self-transcendence support more protectionist, aesthetic, and mutualist views toward wildlife.

Ideology

Ideology is considered a broader and more inclusive concept than values. It has been equated with the notion of worldview. By Pratto's (1999) definition, ideology includes beliefs about social stereotypes, principles of resource allocation, role prescriptions, origin myths, citizenship rules, and other ideas that define groups. Schwartz's (2006) recent work has recognized the importance of this concept, particularly in cross-cultural comparisons. He has identified three bipolar dimensions that represent "cultural ideals." Embeddedness versus autonomy involves thought regarding relationships between the person and group; hierarchy versus egalitarianism addresses the ways in which people act to preserve the social fabric; and harmony versus mastery addresses issues of how to manage relationships with the social and natural world.

Ingold (1994) introduced a proposal that addresses how cultural ideology and perceptions of self direct human-wildlife relationships, which, according to his view, reflect the nature of interpersonal human relationships within a society. In hunter and gatherer societies, for example, an egalitarian ideology was present. People were perceived in roles of equality, and wildlife were seen as "fellow inhabitants of the same world" (18). Wildlife would "present themselves" to hunters, and if hunters behaved wastefully or greedily, the wildlife would not return in the future. With pastoral societies a domination ideology emerged. Hierarchies that formed among people were also present in human-animal relationships. Herdsmen controlled animals and had responsibility for their care and authority over their use. This domination ideology underlies the stark separation between humans and nature that is characteristic of contemporary developed societies and facilitates the belief that it is humans' role to exercise mastery over wildlife.

Value Orientations

Clyde Kluckholn (1951) introduced the concept of value orientations. For him, value orientations represent "unity thema," or ethos that capture the personality of a cultural group. His research in the southwestern United States illustrated this concept, revealing that Mormons were oriented toward mastery over nature, Spanish Americans were oriented toward subjugation to nature, and Navaho were oriented toward harmony with nature. Kluckholn's work guided Manfredo and Teel (2008, in press), who propose that value orientations reflect the influence of ideology on an individual's values and thereby help explain individual variation in attitudes and behaviors. For example, two different people might hold with equal importance a value related to humanitarian treatment of all living things. Yet this value might motivate one person to kill an injured animal quickly and another person to attempt to save its life. The difference in response is rooted in how the value is oriented. A domination or mastery orientation could result in the former behavior, while an egalitarian or mutualism orientation might contribute to the latter.

Manfredo and Teel propose that these two value orientations direct a significant amount of thought about wildlife in North America. A *domination wildlife value orientation* reflects the extent to which an individual (or group) holds an ideological view of human mastery over wildlife. Tests of this concept reveal that the stronger one's domination orientation, the more likely he or she will be to prioritize human well-being over wildlife, accept actions that result in death or other intrusive control of wildlife, and evaluate treatment of wildlife in utilitarian terms. A *mutualism wildlife value orientation*, in contrast, views wildlife as capable of living in relationships of trust with humans, as life-forms having rights like those of humans, as part of an extended family, and as deserving of caring and compassion. Those with a strong mutualism orientation are more likely to engage in welfare-enhancing behaviors for individual wildlife (e.g., feeding and nurturing abandoned or hurt animals), less likely to support actions resulting in death or harm to wildlife, and more likely to view wildlife in human terms, with personalities and characteristics like those of humans.

A recent application of these concepts demonstrated their utility in understanding the foundation for stakeholder conflict on wildlife-related issues (Manfredo and Teel 2008, in press). Further, it suggested that wildlife value orientation shift, from domination to mutualism, is occurring as a result of modernization (characterized by increasing income, education, and urbanization) in the western United States. These findings raise questions about whether or not the rise of mutualism in human-wildlife relationships is accompanying modernization in other parts of the world. We turn to this topic of value shift in the remaining section of our chapter.

Global Shift in Values and Wildlife Value Orientations

Though an individual's values change little during adulthood, the values of a cultural group can change intergenerationally in response to changes in the prevailing conditions and needs of the society. Culture shift theory proposes that societal thought (including ideology, values, attitudes, etc.) is part of an intricate web of interactions, shaped by forces of technology, demography, modes of economic production, institutions, and the environment. As change occurs in one part of the web, it produces change in other areas. Building upon this theoretical tradition, Inglehart and Welzel (2005) proposed that, on a global scale, societies are experiencing predictable shifts from traditional/religious values during preindustrial periods to secular/rational values during industrial periods to an emphasis on self-expression and belongingness values in postindustrial periods. Modernization and its effects on the prevailing need states within a society, they argued, are driving this shift. According to these authors, as improvements in economic well-being alleviate concerns for subsistence needs, belongingness and other higher-order needs take precedence. This in turn spawns the emergence of a new set of values more reflective of altered need states. Support for their proposal is provided by longitudinal data from the World Values Survey (Inglehart and Welzel 2005), which shows that modernization is accompanied by an increase in the proportion of people with postmaterialist values (focused on self-expression and belongingness) relative to the proportion with materialist values (focused on physical and economic security). Cross-cultural research reported by Schwartz and Sagie (2000) reinforces this argument, indicating that developed nations score higher on universalism values (similar to postmaterialist values) than developing nations (Schwartz and Sagie 2000).

Manfredo and Teel (2008, in press) propose the reemergence of a mutualism wildlife value orientation in the United States as a result of these modernization forces. The mutualism of this postindustrial society is linked to an egalitarian ideology that is married with elements of domination. This modern-day view can be contrasted with the mutualism of hunter and gatherer societies where a subjugation-to-nature ideology was prevalent. The contemporary mutualism value orientation fits a lifestyle where:

- Modernization forces have eliminated reliance upon wildlife as a source of food or material.
- People tend not to learn from direct experience with wildlife in their day-to-day lives; instead, information about wildlife is obtained through indirect sources (e.g., media, stories, learning from others) in which wildlife are often portrayed as anthropomorphized representations.
- Wildlife are perceived less as resources or threats and more as part of one's social environment. In particular, wildlife are perceived as potential companions, a view that has been facilitated by the pervasive human tendency to anthropomorphize along with a rise in the need for belongingness.

Empirical data from nineteen states in the western United States are consistent with the proposal that modernization is associated with growth in mutualism wildlife value orientations (Manfredo and Teel 2008, in press). Is this a phenomenon unique to the United States, or is it a shift toward mutualism occurring globally as a function of modernization? A group of researchers recently explored this question in five countries (China, Estonia, Mongolia, the Netherlands, and Thailand) using a qualitative methodology (see Teel, Manfredo, and Stinchfield 2007). Findings did indeed support the possibility of a global shift by providing evidence of a mutualism orientation in other countries and suggesting a greater predominance of this orientation in postindustrialized nations like the Netherlands. Moreover, findings provide impetus for future research to more fully examine the association between mutualism and modernization and its implications for wildlife management at a global level.

Conclusion

The concept of value orientations (the orientation of values by ideology) poses a useful approach for exploring human relationships with wildlife cross-culturally. Its application would help depict cross-cultural differences and also help in understanding how societal thought regarding wildlife may change and how this change can affect the success of wildlife conservation efforts. As an example, consider the case of a shift from domination to mutualism wildlife value orientations in the western United States discussed in this chapter. The domination orientation, pervasive in the early twentieth century, served as the foundation for the wildlife profession that emerged during that period. A principal task of managers was, through regulations and enforcement, to maintain populations of animals with a harvestable surplus. In this regard, their charge was very much like that of a commander, summoning troops of hunters to deal with populations of animals. With the rise of mutualism and the expansion of human development into wildlife habitat, human-wildlife conflict has emerged as a leading concern of the wildlife profession. Dealing with this conflict is typically focused on individual animals in situations where stakeholders are concerned about their personal interactions with wildlife (e.g., animals raiding a garden, a predator wandering into a neighborhood, an animal falling through the ice of a pond and struggling to survive). The role of management in this case is very much like that of police, enforcing relationships among people and wildlife, ensuring that "bad" or needy wildlife and people are dealt with. This is just one effect that the rise of mutualism may be having on the task of wildlife management in the United States. Our understanding of the role and importance of values information in wildlife management will continue to expand as we engage more researchers and more perspectives in this area of study.

Literature Cited

Ajzen, I., and M. Fishbein. 1980. *Understanding attitudes and predicting social behavior.* Englewood Cliffs, NJ: Prentice-Hall.

Douglas, M. 1990. The pangolin revisited: A new approach to animal symbolism. In *Signifying animals: Human meaning in the natural world*, ed. R. G. Willis, 25–36. London: Unwin Hyman.

Hart, D., and R. Sussman. 2005. *Man the hunted: Primates, predators, and human evolution.* New York: Westview Press.

Inglehart, R., and C. Welzel. 2005. *Modernization, cultural change, and democracy: The human development sequence.* New York: Cambridge University Press.

Ingold, T. 1994. From trust to domination: An alternative history of human-animal relations. In *Animals and human society: Changing perspectives*, ed. A. Manning and James Serpell, 1–22. New York: Routledge.

Katcher, A., and G. Wilkins. 1993. Dialogue with animals: Its nature and culture. In *The biophilia hypothesis*, ed. S. R. Kellert and E. O. Wilson, 173–200. Washington, DC: Island Press.

Kluckholn, C. 1951. Values and value orientations in the theory of action. In *Toward a general theory of action*, ed. T. Parsons and E. A. Shils, 388–433. Cambridge, MA: Harvard University Press.

Manfredo, M. 2008, in press. *Who cares about wildlife: Social science concepts for understanding human-wildlife relationships and other conservation issues.* New York: Springer Press.

Manfredo, M., and T. Teel. 2008, in press. Integrating concepts: Demonstration of a multi-level model for exploring the rise of mutualism value orientations in post-industrial society. In *Who cares about wildlife: Social science concepts for understanding human-wildlife relationships and other conservation issues*, ed. M. Manfredo. New York: Springer Press.

Mithen, S. 1996. *The prehistory of the mind.* London: Thames and Hudson.

Ohman, A. 1986. Face the beast and fear the face: Animal and social fears as prototypes for evolutionary analyses of emotion. *Psychophysiology* 23:123–45.

Pratto, F. 1999. The puzzle of continuing group inequality: Piecing together psychological, social, and cultural forces in social dominance theory. *Advances in Experimental Social Psychology* 31:191–263.

Rohan, M. 2000. A rose by any other name? The values construct. *Personality and Social Psychology Review* 4(3):255–77.

Schwartz, S. 2004. Basic human values: Their content and structure across cultures. In *Vialores e Trabalho*, ed. A. Tamayo and J. Porto. Brasilía: Editora Universidade de Brasilía.

———. 2006. A theory of cultural value orientations: Explication and applications. *Comparative Sociology* 5:136–82.

Schwartz, S., and G. Sagie. 2000. Value consensus and importance: A cross-national study. *Journal of Cross-cultural Psychology* 31(4):465–97.

Teel, T., M. Manfredo, and H. Stinchfield. 2007. The need and theoretical basis for exploring wildlife value orientations cross-culturally. *Human Dimensions of Wildlife* 12:297–305.

Willis, R., ed. 1990. *Signifying animals: Human meaning in the natural world.* London: Routledge.

Wilson, E. O. 1993. Biophilia and the conservation ethic. In *The biophilia hypothesis*, ed. S. R. Kellert and E. O. Wilson, 31–41.Washington, DC: Island Press.

Wrangham, R., and D. Peterson. 1996. *Demonic males: Apes and the origins of human violence.* Boston: Houghton Mifflin.

CHAPTER 4

The Emergence of Conservation NGOs as Catalysts for Local Democracy

John Fraser, David Wilkie, Robert Wallace, Peter Coppolillo, Roan Balas McNab, R. Lilian E. Painter, Peter Zahler, and Isabel Buechsel

In principle, every government manages the distribution of resources under its jurisdiction for the shared benefit of its people. However, based on the current state of the wild, and the rampant state-permissioned environmental degradation of the biosphere, it has become apparent that the centralized government administration of natural resources has failed, even in countries under democratic rule. As a result, wildlife conservation NGOs have emerged to redress this failure by promoting new public processes that are embedded in the local rural communities that depend on natural resources in order to ensure more effective protection of wildlife and wildlife habitat. Unfortunately, many of these communities do not have either the governance structures or the experience necessary to manage the biodiversity in their midst. They also tend to be disenfranchised from the seats of state power and are in need of a strong advocate to support their skill development, knowledge of how to manage their resources for sustainability, and patriation of management authority. Through the following case study, we will demonstrate how one global NGO, the United States–based Wildlife Conservation Society (WCS), is helping local groups that have been excluded from land-tenure rights, have no tradition of collaborative management, or hold cultural traditions that do not recognize wildlife or natural resources as property to be managed, to develop democratic systems that can be more effective at protecting wildlife and wild places.

NGOs have been part of the government process since the advent of democracy, although their form has become more formalized over the last two centuries. A short history of WCS, where the authors of this chapter work, reveals that the state of ecological degradation has been the focus of NGO activity for over one hundred years (e.g., Hornaday 1913; Osborn 1948). It also reveals that the solutions to this international problem were embedded in the human dimensions of conservation, such as the need for increased literacy about sustainable management and promotion of a conservation ethic, as was the case for the sponsorship of the field guide series *Our Pacific World,* intended to protect wildlife in the Pacific islands where American GIs were stationed (Osborn 1945). Since that book's publication, NGOs such as WCS have increased their participation in primary conservation biology research around the world and in the development of international wildlife policy. Today, some large international NGOs have become household names, and most have researchers based in areas of conservation concern where traditional communities survive on the wildlife and products from natural resource areas.

The shared knowledge and the social relationships that have developed between traditional communities and community-based NGO staff in these same areas have allowed these NGOs a unique opportunity to participate as significant social actors in the advancement of democratic governance structures. This chapter examines how WCS exemplifies this social action that is helping local communities to assert control over their regional wildlife habitats in order to protect what remains of the wild.

Field of Social Action

Wildlife conservation requires collaborative management strategies that take into account how individuals choose to use or extract flora and fauna from landscape systems. In particular, fragile systems require adherence by individuals to a common code of conduct that will protect species and natural resources from overextraction. This shared-use practice is essentially an agreement to suppress self-interest in favor of collective participation in the management of shared public goods or assets such as wildlife. Unfortunately, trade economies advance community well-being through converting the community's natural resources to commodities, leading to the oft-referenced tragedy of the commons because a common rule of law is lacking.

Lack of democratic process skills permits state or powerful private interests to assume ownership, control, and management of the rural wildlife and natural resources on which those outside the network of patronage depend. Political assessments have shown that separation of asset ownership from the people living near the resources causes greater economic security concerns than other factors because the asymmetry of central management ignores the lives of those living directly from those resources (Obi 2005). These concerns suggest an increased need for new governance systems that will allow local communities to manage their own natural resources in a manner that is transparent, accountable, and involves local people in the collaborative decision making, essentially, the elements that constitute strong democracy (Barber 1984). Unfortunately, many local people lack democratic self-government skills because their household-level trading practices have not afforded them experience with transparent representative governance; they may have misconceptions about the importance of transparency and accountability in civil society, and lack of practice in establishing and enforcing norms (Bienen and Herbst 1996). This is particularly a problem for people living in poverty and outside the network of patronage that is held near to centers of governance (Bhalla and Lapeyre 1997). This isolation from political power permits environmental degradation and species loss to be concealed until after community well-being is compromised (Kousis 1998).

Ostrom (1990) has argued that common-pool resources can be collectively managed if monitoring and supply challenges are resolved. Prabhu (2001) notes that national government as the unrestricted owner who controls natural resources is a change from the local traditions in which resources were treated as common local property managed in structures similar to Ostrom's theory. But claims of ownership do not inherently confer resource rights unless they are acted upon (Ostrom and Schlager 1996), suggesting that lack of clarity to landownership may account, in part, for why government process or local communities have undermined conservation management plans.

Ostrom and Schlager's (1996) taxonomy of the degrees of ownership rights associated with possessions (table 4.1), is a useful framework for analyzing how NGOs are engaged in helping communities develop a more nuanced understanding of what is required for long-term sustainability management of wildlife and habitat control. Ostrom and Schlager's taxonomy illustrates that individuals with only the right-of-access and the right-to-withdraw-resources do not have a vested interest in sustainability because the resources for these people have only a commodity value. Management control and the right to exclude others from withdrawing resources have been exerted by central governments, but assertion of these rights is potentially subject to abuse because it is hard to control natural resources if people living in the area do not adhere to the rule of law or have no vested interest if the system becomes degraded. Identity attachment or the right to feel alienated from possessions is potentially the most resilient right because the loss of an asset is also associated with feelings of alienation. In the case of local wildlife where ownership can be contentious, household provisioning through hunting as free-agent traders may be perceived as a right that can usurp the collective interest and undermine any top-down plan that places limits on hunting or trapping. In these cases, only adherence to a rule of law that supports sustainable, shared-resource use for the common good will ensure the long-term resilience of natural resources management plans.

Our experience suggests that national-level democratization and governance efforts may not filter down fast enough to the rural households living in remote areas of rich biodiversity to protect the wildlife and biodiversity that are critical to local livelihoods and global patrimony. We propose that ownership of these communities' natural resources may not be apparent, even though these people may have exercised their rights of access, withdrawn assets, and believed that they can be alienated from these possessions, because these local communities have not taken advantage of their ability to manage or exclude others from withdrawing assets from their lands. It is in this context that NGOs have emerged as social actors who can help local communities to build experience with democratic processes in order to protect what remains of the wild.

TABLE 4.1 **Degrees of Ownership Rights**

	OWNER	PROPRIETOR	CLAIMANT	AUTHORIZED USER	AUTHORIZED ENTRANT
Access	√	√	√	√	√
Withdrawal	√	√	√	√	
Management	√	√	√		
Exclusion	√	√			
Alienation	√				

Source: Ostrom, E., & E. Schlager. 1996. The Formation of Property Rights. In S. Hana, C. Folke, & K. Maler (Eds.). Rights to Nature: Ecological, Economic, Cultural, and Political Principles of Institutions for the Environment. Washington, DC: Island Press.

Conservation and Social Actors

In practice, wildlife conservation requires that people limit their take of depleted resources from natural systems, even if they feel entitled to deplete these resources for personal gain. It is the case that individuals *will* act to protect natural resources when such actions are in their own interests, as would be the case in a society that deems an individual's interest to be in conflict with the interests of society and if that society is willing and able to impose sufficient sanctions on an individual to ensure compliance with society's interests. Leach, Mearns, and Scoones (1999) examined how various social actors assume entitlement to natural resources based on their ability to enforce regularized patterns of behavior between individuals and groups—in essence, how social actors lay claim to Ostrom and Schlager's (1996) different bundles of rights. In applying their analysis to community-based natural resource management projects, Leach, Mearns, and Scoones concluded that the capacity to negotiate power and control will tend to favor the social actors who already have access to power. They suggested that NGOs were uniquely positioned as social actors to advance community-based natural resource management because NGOs have the expertise to augment disenfranchised small community groups in their negotiations for power, NGOs share some common interests with these communities, and NGOs can achieve their goals through mutually beneficial partnerships that help local communities attain direct stewardship over the natural resources to which they have prior claims (Robinson 2007).

Aiding Communities in Asserting Their Management Rights

Since the 1960s, local people have harvested the understory xate (*Chamaedorea* spp.), a local name for a variety of palm fronds found in the forests of eastern Guatemala for many years, in order to supplement their income and as a form of insurance to pay for unforeseen expenses such as emergency medical treatment. These fronds were traditionally sold to middlemen who transported them to exporters who in turn sold the fronds to the international market as "green background" or filler for floral arrangements in the United States and Europe. Xate harvesting historically occurred under an open access regime, with few barriers to entry. The harvesters had traditionally asserted the right to withdraw xate but had not recognized their right to collaboratively manage the resource.

Recent surveys of xate in the forest of the Petén have shown that all three species of xate are declining in density and that overharvesting for the commercial trade is the likely cause. One reason that xate trade is unsustainable is that buyers typically purchased all fronds from harvesters regardless of quality, subsequently sorting through the bundles to discard all damaged, unmarketable fronds. Buyers incentivize harvesters to strip the plant of its leaves regardless of quality, resulting in a decrease in flowering and fruiting, occasionally the senescence of individual palms, and through time, a progressive depletion of the species throughout the forest.

As part of a collaboration commencing in 1998, WCS's full-time staff in the Petén assisted the Organización Manejo y Conservación (OMYC) in the village of Uaxactún and the Rainforest Alliance in instituting a new trading system for xate that pays harvesters only for high-quality fronds that will receive a price premium through the OMYC's new "green" marketing agreement brokered with Continental Greens Ltd of Houston, Texas. This new system is designed to provide harvesters with an economic incentive to cut only quality fronds, leaving unmarketable fronds on the palm to assist its photosynthesis. For this system to work, *xateros* (palm harvesters) must agree to harvest only quality fronds and to sell them to the OMYC xate bodega where quality controls are enforced and fronds are sold only to Continental Greens. This new process asserted a higher level of right, by supporting a management regime on behalf of the community..

A second level of right of ownership, the right to exclude others, was a key principle to protecting the community's resources. Continuing to gather all fronds and selling damaged ones to other traders, and allowing non-Uaxactún harvesters into the community forest, would cause the new trade system to fail. WCS staff realized from the beginning that helping the Uaxactún community to develop a new democratic, transparent, accountable, and effective governance system for the commercial trade of xate was the key to conserving wild palms in the forest and to ensuring this sustainable source of revenue to support local livelihoods. Shifting toward a democratic, shared-ownership regime from an open-access, household-level trading practice, however, required mentoring and skill development for the community. The new collaborative management program was one of the first occasions where households in Uaxactún came together as a community to develop and enforce agreed-upon norms for access to and withdrawal of a community resource. In the first twenty-six months since the program started, six successive management committees of the xate bodega failed to manage effectively. By 2007, the community, in collaboration with its NGO advisors, determined that it needed more transparency and more accountability in the management of the xate trade and decided to hire a university forestry graduate to manage its program.

Following the initial mentoring period and experiments in democratic management and ownership, the OMYC is now implementing a xate management plan with the approval of the Guatemalan government, is asserting its ownership rights with independent middlemen, and hired an accountant to audit the financial management of the operation. The conservation NGOs helped this community identify a community ownership right, mentored the process, and offered technical expertise that brought together a group of households into a single unit. This evolving process is helping the people of Uaxactún gain practical knowledge of the importance of establishing transparent and accountable governance systems, knowledge that can be applied to other natural resources or community enterprises.

Aiding Communities in Developing Shared-Resource Management Practices

Our work has also shown that NGOs are also uniquely positioned, as embedded social actors, to help rural communities expand their democratic skills, because NGOs share rural families' interests in sustaining the resources on which everyone depends and are also familiar with the legal processes required to ensure that local-level, democratic decision making is legally recognized under state or regional laws. In the Ruaha landscape of central Tanzania, WCS has worked to empower communities and economically incentivize wildlife conservation on village lands. This has been accomplished primarily through creation of a "Wildlife Management Area" which patriates wildlife-management authority from central government to an association of twenty-one villages. Perhaps most important though, the WMA revenue is also received locally, so the benefits of conservation are recognized and realized by the people responsible for protecting and living with wildlife.

In the past, hunters negotiated individually for hunting licenses from the Ministry of Natural Resources and Tourism, leaving villagers and village governments with no formal voice in determining who hunted or even whether village lands would be available to which hunters. As a result, hunters were compliant in paying fees to the ministry that issued the licenses, but they neglected to pay the associated local fees to the villages where they hunted.

Asserting the right of local control over access to natural resources, however, was limited by the onerous legal requirements necessary for being recognized as a management authority, requirements that were far beyond the capacity of the village governments acting independently. WCS's local conservation staff worked with the village association, known as MBOMIPA (Matumizi Bora Malihai Idodi na Pawaga, or Sustainable Use of Wildlife in Idodi and Pawaga), as a trusted partner that could technically support the patriation of management by producing collaborative land use planning recommendations, resource inventories, zone-planning recommendations, and management mentoring. In addition to technical support, WCS staff served as trusted mediator between investors and resource users. While WCS, as a conservation NGO, sought to benefit wildlife, its role as social actor helped to build good democratic governance skills that were central to the successful wildlife management strategy.

In 2007, MBOMIPA gained the authority to manage its area and is answerable to its constituent twenty-one village governments. Following collaborative discussions with WCS staff, the village governments insisted that a new and more ethical hunting company come to the area, that higher fees be charged, and that fees be paid in advance. This collaborative process also helped the village governments determine to set aside specific areas for phototourism to equitably provide more local jobs per visitor and more revenue per hectare for the stakeholder villages. In the first year of local management, hunting revenue increased eightfold, despite a 75 percent decrease in the area hunted. These changes resulted from creating a locally representative management authority that was accountable to the stakeholders most strongly affected by their decisions.

New democracies require investment in skill development, and MBOMIPA continues to learn how to improve its governance structures. For example, the twenty-one villages participating in MBOMIPA represent over fifteen ethnic groups with differing horticultural and livestock-keeping practices. The two subsistence options conflict over common access to land because livestock keepers and horticulturalists either are unaware of or disregard each other's traditional land tenure. During the dry season of 2005, the livestock keepers began using the Wildlife Management Area for livestock grazing, undermining the community-determined management strategy. WCS intervened by calling a village meeting for both types of land users to discuss the problem. During these facilitated discussions, it came to light that large portions of the set-aside grazing area had been cleared for agriculture. The clearing was inconsistent with the land use plans prepared as part of the Wildlife Management Authorization process facilitated by WCS. While the livestock keepers were included in that process, it became clear that they were marginalized in the day-to-day management of village government and chose to take their chances invading the wildlife area rather than challenge their village peers.

While developing skills in democratic management and decision making is difficult, the MBOMIPA project offers a useful case study on how patriation of shared management authority at a local stakeholder level can aid in the practice with transparency and enforcement of the rule of law, the role of peer pressure in assuring the advancement of wildlife protective social norms, and the place of NGOs in capacity development for emerging, local democratic self-governments.

Helping Communities to Control Wildlife Extraction and Habitat Degradation

NGOs also appear to be uniquely capable of helping rural communities negotiate effectively with more powerful and experienced actors and providing technical advice through the process of developing more effective representative governance in cases where land tenure is not recognized. In Bolivia, WCS Greater Madidi Landscape Conservation Program has worked with the Tacana people since 2000 in the development and implementation of a management plan for their traditional territories that neighbor and partially overlap Madidi National Park (Painter, Wallace, and Gomez 2006). As a conservation NGO, WCS sought to help promote a local constituency for conservation with a broad range of jurisdictional groups in the Madidi region to protect the rich sources of wildlife and associated biodiversity within and surrounding a globally significant continuous swathe of protected areas in Bolivia and southern Peru (Painter, Wallace, and Gomez 2006). The low population density, the desegregation of jurisdictional actors, the incongruence between these jurisdictions regulatory concerns, and lack of clarity to land-tenure and environmental entitlements had previously created opportunities for nonresident land speculators to assert ownership and dominion over lands traditionally used by the communities.

Following a WCS presentation regarding the potential community-based natural resource management in the region, CIPTA (Concejo Indígena del Pueblo Tacana, the Tacana People's Indigenous Council), the Tacana representative organization, formally requested a broader partnership that included assistance in the legal process for land titling in the region and parallel assistance in the design and implementation of an overall management vision for the TCO. Bolivia's Land Reform Law of 1996 permitted legal consolidation of indigenous collective land under an indivisible title; however, CIPTA and the twenty Tacana communities within the Tacana TCO were not able to adequately accompany and participate in this process owing to insufficient resources and the complexity of the legal process. The two-pronged approach adopted by the partnership ensured that CIPTA and the Tacana communities were as focused on building a participatory and overall sustainable long-term development vision for the Tacana TCO (CIPTA-WCS 2002) as they were on gaining legal ownership over their territorial demand and the renewable natural resources therein.

By 2004, the Tacana had secured land title for 372,000 hectares, and the CIPTA-WCS partnership has since concentrated on implementing overall territorial management mechanisms, building a larger portfolio of natural resource management projects, and shifting attention to the legal status of the second Tacana territorial claim in the Greater Madidi Landscape. The partnership has developed a series of methodologies and tools that facilitate the management of the traditional territory, from natural resource access and use regulations to participatory microzoning of the TCO, to the installation of administrative capacity in CIPTA and a series of communal and supracommunal productive associations. Many of these processes effectively established CIPTA as the representative agency that could patriate the community's collaborative ownership rights and develop community support for a resilient wildlife management plan for the region.

The CIPTA-WCS partnership has included many community-level activities, and CIPTA has taken responsibility for policies and major decisions regarding the land-titling process and management of the traditional territory, with full participation of the twenty constituent communities. This approach has not only guaranteed transparency and legitimacy in decision making and ensured capacity building that has stretched far beyond the outstanding cadre of young and absolutely committed leaders of the CIPTA directorate, but it has also provided a cornerstone to the development of over twenty communal and supracommunal productive associations across the TCO that are involved in the sustainable management of a series of natural resources, including native bee honey production, spectacled caiman harvest, commercial fishing, and experimental harvests of ornamental fish. Perhaps most strikingly, this recently established democratic system is developing new activities with formally approved management plans from the relevant national body, as well as adhering to the Natural Resource Access and Use Regulation of the Tacana TCO, with CIPTA as their democratically elected representative.

WCS's bottom-up approach to territorial planning and management in combination with capacity building at the community level is creating local demand for more transparent and democratic governance at other local government levels. Because WCS has a landscape vision for wildlife conservation and as such has developed management planning and implementation processes with many overlapping jurisdictions within the landscape, the CIPTA-WCS partnership has also included capacity-building and integration mechanisms with the Madidi protected area. This has helped crystallize the Tacana's natural sympathy with the objectives of Madidi and on several occasions has resulted in strategic and concrete support for the National Protected Area Service in the face of invasions from politically motivated actors and illegal timber harvesters.

Conclusion

Many valuable natural resources, such as water, wildlife, and forests, exist within communal or common-pool areas, and their effective management cannot be achieved without collective action. These resources have three qualities that make them an ideal foundation for building democracy: (1) local people often directly depend on them for their survival, (2) individuals are interested in managing these resources because they have economic value, and (3) these resources cannot be managed effectively by individuals working independently; they require collective management by the larger community. Avoiding depletion of common-pool natural resources is clearly critical for the welfare and economic development of the vast majority of the world's poor families. The need for effective natural resource management can easily be understood by even the most isolated communities, while the mechanism for proper management—democratic principles of collective decision making—is not as easily comprehended.

A key lesson learned from our case studies is that wildlife conservation can be achieved by helping communities develop skills with democracy at local, regional, and national levels. Moreover, the processes and institutions through which access and use rights to natural resources are secured and administered at the local level are the first exposure many subsistence-level rural communities in developing countries have to democratic, transparent, and accountable systems of governance and can lead to more resilient wildlife management plan implementation.

The WCS examples have also shown that development of democratic self-management for wildlife and environmental protection is not without risk. As a democratic self-government emerges, its leadership may not act transparently, the majority may vote for shared short-term gain over sustainability, or the leadership may choose to engage in unsustainable practices because of countervailing economic interests. However, long-term empowerment of collective decision making still offers the greatest opportunity for developing social agreements that can self-police in a manner that can prevent individual traders from degrading wildlife for personal gain.

NGOs like WCS have emerged as social actors that can facilitate the advancement of local democratic institutions that can more effectively manage natural resources and promote long-term conservation. To manage communally shared natural resources and ensure equitable sharing of benefits from these resources, local institutions need mentoring in the principles of democracy in order to patriate their ownership and define and enforce resource use norms that limit access to and meter use of their wildlife and natural resources. By combining local (bottom-up) and national (top-down) approaches, democratic governance systems will evolve more quickly and sustain themselves, allowing economies to grow, wildlife and other natural resources to be managed effectively, livelihoods to improve, and democracy to flourish.

Literature Cited

Barber, J. 1984. *Strong democracy.* Berkeley: University of California Press.

Bhalla, A., and F. Lapeyre. 1997. Social exclusion: Towards an analytical and operational framework. *Development and Change* 28:413–33.

Bienen, H., and J. Herbst. 1996. The relationship between political and economic reform in Africa. *Comparative Politics* 29:23–42.

CIPTA-WCS 2002. Estrategia de Desarrollo Sostenible de la TCO-Tacana con Base en el Manejo de los Recursos Naturales. 2001–2005. La Paz, Bolivia.

Hornaday, W. T. 1913. *Our vanishing wildlife.* New York: Clark and Frits.

Kousis, M. 1998. Ecological marginalization in rural areas: Actors, impacts, responses. *Sociologia Ruralis* 38:86–108.

Leach, M., R. Mearns, and I. Scoones. 1999. Environmental entitlements: Dynamics and institutions in community-based natural resource management. *World Development* 27:225–47.

Obi, C. I. 2005. *Environmental movements in sub-Saharan Africa: A political ecology of power and conflict.* Programme Paper Number 15. Geneva: United Nations Research Institute for Social Development.

Ostrom, E. 1990. *Governing the commons: The evolution of institutions for collective action.* Cambridge: Cambridge University Press.

Ostrom, E., and E. Schlager. 1996. The formation of property rights. In *Rights to nature: Ecological, economic, cultural, and political principles of institutions for the environment,* ed. S. S. Hanna, C. Folke, and K.G. Mäler, 127–56. Washington, DC: Island Press.

Osborn, F., ed. 1945. *The Pacific world: Its vast distances, its lands and the life upon them, and its peoples.* Washington, DC: Infantry Journal.

———. 1948. *Our plundered planet.* New York: Little, Brown.

Prabhu, P. 2001. Shoot the horse to get the rider: Religion and forest politics in Bentian Borneo. In *Indigenous traditions and ecology: The interbeing of cosmology and community,* ed. J. A. Grim. Cambridge, MA: Harvard University Press.

Painter R. L. E., R. B. Wallace, and H. Gomez. 2006. Landscape conservation in the Greater Madidi Landscape in northwestern Bolivia: Planning for wildlife across different scales and jurisdictions. Case study 12.2. In *Principles of conservation biology,* 3rd ed., ed. M. J. Groom, G. K. Meffe, and C. R. Carroll, 453–58. Sunderland, MA: Sinauer Associates.

Robinson, J. A. 2007. Recognizing differences and establishing clear-eyed partnerships: A response to Vermeulen and Sheil. *Oryx* 41:443–44.

CHAPTER 5

Imagining the Future: Humans, Wildlife, and Global Climate Change

Douglas B. Inkley, Amanda C. Staudt, and
Mark Damian Duda

Climate change is an enduring, significant, and complex problem facing humans and wildlife. It is now well established that the Earth has warmed over the past century, due mostly to the emissions of greenhouse gases from human activities (Intergovernmental Panel on Climate Change 2007), and that this warming has had impacts on wildlife and their habitats in important ways (Root et al. 2003; Inkley et al. 2004; Parmesan 2006). More serious climate impacts on wildlife are expected this century, especially if significant steps are not taken to reduce greenhouse gas emissions and to help wildlife cope with changing conditions. As stated by National Wildlife Federation president Larry Schweiger (2006), "Like it or not, global warming will be the defining issue of the 21st century."

Human-Caused Climate Change Is Affecting Wildlife

Emissions of carbon dioxide (CO_2) from fossil fuel burning have increased atmospheric CO_2 to 383 parts per million (National Oceanic and Atmospheric Administration 2007), higher than anytime in at least 650,000 years, during which the value did not exceed about 300 parts per million (Siegenthaler et al. 2005). This increase is responsible for most of the global mean temperature increase of about 0.76°C (1.4°F) in the twentieth century (Intergovernmental Panel on Climate Change 2007). Other observed climate changes related to the emission of greenhouse gases include shifts in precipitation and wind patterns, more pronounced droughts and heat waves, and increased intensity of tropical cyclones. Associated with climate change, during the last century the Earth experienced widespread melting of snow and ice, rising sea levels, decreasing ocean salinity, and increasing ocean acidification (Intergovernmental Panel on Climate Change 2007). The terms *climate change* and *global warming* are often used interchangeably. Herein, we use climate change and in so doing reference increasing temperatures and other changing climate parameters. We use global warming when the referenced source uses that term as a general reference to all aspects of the changing climate.

Meta-analyses of published peer-reviewed papers demonstrate that observed changes in phenology, such as earlier springs and later falls, as well as in distribution, such as northward movement of species' ranges in the Northern Hemisphere, are consistent with expectations from climate change (Parmesan 2006; Root et al. 2003). Furthermore, these changes are disrupting predator/prey and plant/insect interactions.

In North America, impacts of climate change on fish, wildlife, and their habitats are increasingly apparent. Since the mid-1980s, drought and warmer temperatures have caused a four- and sixfold increase in the incidence and the size, respectively, of major fires in western forests (Westerling et al. 2006). In Nevada, especially large wildfires in summer 2006 necessitated implementation of emergency regulations to reduce pronghorn populations to levels commensurate with remaining habitat (Griffith 2006). Researchers point to increasing temperatures as the reason that the moose population of northwestern Minnesota has declined by more than 90 percent in twenty years (Smith 2006). Massive coral bleaching events and die-offs due to increasing water temperatures have occurred worldwide, including the continental shelf of North America (Hoegh-Guldberg 1999).

Possible Climate Futures and Implications for Wildlife

Estimates of future warming range from about 1.1°C to 6.4°C (2.0–11.5°F) by 2100, depending upon the levels of future greenhouse gas emissions (Intergovernmental Panel on Climate Change 2007). However, no matter what steps are taken to reduce emissions, it is projected that we are committed to at least about 0.6°C (1.1°F) warming in this century due to the greenhouse gases that have already been emitted. The Intergovernmental Panel on Climate Change (2007) projects that sea level will rise 0.18 to 0.59 meters (10 to 23 inches) by the end of the twenty-first century, although more recent observations of rapid ice melting in Greenland and Antarctica suggest that these projections are too low (Rahmstorf 2007).

Future climate change will have profound impacts on wildlife, especially if changing climate conditions are outside a species' historical tolerance range, such that it cannot adapt quickly enough to accommodate the new climate conditions or cannot move to more suitable habitat because of natural or human-built barriers. Sophisticated global climate models project potential future climate conditions, which have been connected to possible species extinctions, habitat loss, and other impacts on wildlife (e.g., see fig. 5.1).

Let's imagine two different futures for wildlife. In the first scenario, greenhouse gas emissions are allowed to continue increasing unabated over the next century, allowing CO_2 levels to reach about 650 parts per million and global mean temperatures to increase by about 2.2°C (4°F) above current levels by 2100. In this scenario, up to half of all species worldwide will be committed to extinction (Thomas et al. 2004). In North America, the prairie pothole region, which serves as a major breeding ground for waterfowl, would be diminished by 38 to 54 percent due largely to drier conditions (Parry et al. 2007). Streams and rivers across North America would also warm up, reducing habitat for cold-water fish by about a quarter (O'Neal 2002; Preston 2006). These habitat changes would pose major challenges for fish and wildlife.

If instead we limit greenhouse gas emissions to achieve CO_2 levels in the atmosphere at about 450 parts per million with associated temperature increases to less than 1.3°C (2°F) above today, the impacts on wildlife will be significantly less dire. In this scenario, there will still

FIGURE 5.1 Temperature change since 1900 based on surface observations and two projections of future climate

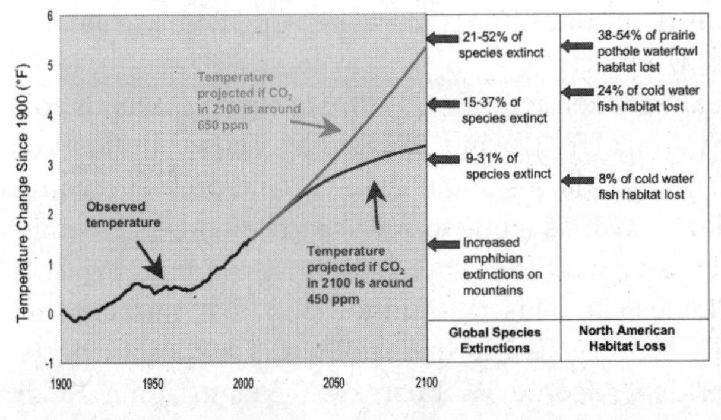

Temperature change since 1900 based on surface observations (blue line) and two projections of future climate (pink line: higher greenhouse gas emissions; green line: lower greenhouse gas emissions). Two columns on right indicate projected impacts on wildlife for different temperature increases (IPCC 2007).

Source: IPCC 2007

be some extinctions, such as amphibians in mountainous regions that already have been occurring (Pounds et al. 2006), but the overall fish and wildlife losses are projected to be much less. For example, only some 8 percent of cold-water fish habitat would be lost in North America (O'Neal 2002; Preston 2006). Although the impacts will be less, it is important to note that ecosystems will change even in this more optimistic scenario of less warming. Concerted efforts will still be required to ensure that wildlife species are best able to survive.

Human Attitudes on Climate Change

A public survey in 2003 examining environmental concerns found climate change ranked sixth behind water pollution, destruction of ecosystems, toxic waste, overpopulation, and ozone depletion (Curry, Ansolabehere, and Herzog 2007). But by 2006 climate change had become the top environmental concern (Curry, Ansolabere, and Herzog 2007). Furthermore, polls of the U.S. public in spring 2007 indicate that a strong majority of the population is convinced that climate change is real (table 5.1).

In light of the public concern about climate change, it is not surprising that there is also widespread support for taking action to address climate change (see table 5.1). Solutions could include limiting greenhouse gas emissions by fostering development of alternate fuels, setting emissions standards for business and industry, or imposing mandatory controls on greenhouse gas emissions. In addition, Gallup (2007) found broad support for various actions that individuals could take, ranging from using fluorescent lightbulbs in the home (69 percent agreed that they should be doing so) to buying a hybrid car (62 percent) to "spending several thousand dollars to make your home as energy efficient as possible" (78 percent).

Support for taking action to address climate change extends to a primary constituent group of fish and wildlife agencies: hunters and anglers. A strong majority believes that it is an "urgent problem requiring immediate action," such as steps to reduce greenhouse gas emissions and protect fish, wildlife, and habitat (National Wildlife Federation 2006) (table 5.2). This is significant in that hunters and anglers are generally conservative in their political viewpoint; sportsmen voted for President George W. Bush over Senator John Kerry almost two to one in the 2004 presidential election (National Wildlife Federation 2006). Furthermore, the results suggest that hunters and

TABLE 5.1. **Results from Selected Polls on Global Warning, 2007**

POLL	GLOBAL WARMING VIEWS	GOVERNMENT ACTION VIEWS
January 30-31, 2007 Fox News/Opinion Dynamics Corp. (2007) poll of 900 registered voters nationwide	**82%** believe that global warming exists.	N/A
March 11-14, 2007 Gallup poll of 1,009 adults nationwide (Saad 2007)	**59%** think that the effects of global warming have already begun to happen.	N/A
April 5-10, 2007 Washington Post-ABC News-Stanford University (2007) poll of 1,002 adults nationwide	**84%** think that the world's temperature probably has been going up slowly over the past 100 years.	**49%** think that the federal government should do much more to deal with global warming, and 20% think that it should do somewhat more.
March 19-22, 2007 Center for American Progress poll of 500 registered voters nationwide (Podesta, Weiss, and Nichols 2007)	**76%** believe that the effects of global warming are apparent now.	**60%** believe that we must take action now or it will be too late to stop global warming.
April 20-24, 2007 CBS News/New York Times (2007) poll of 1,052 adults nationwide	**49%** believe that global warming is having a serious impact now. **36%** believe that global warming will have an impact in the future.	**52%** think that global warming should be a high priority for government leaders.

anglers would be receptive to actions by fish and wildlife agencies to address climate change impacts to fish and wildlife resources.

Human Attitudes on Wildlife

Why do humans care about wildlife? To professionals involved in wildlife conservation, it seems so natural to be passionate about wildlife that we may give little thought to why we care or simply attribute it to childhood experiences in the out-of-doors. Wilson (1984) hypothesized

TABLE 5.2. **Results from a Nationwide Poll of Hunters and Anglers on Global Warming**

DO YOU AGREE OR DISAGREE THAT . . .	RESPONSE
global warming is currently occurring.	76% agree
global warming is primarily caused by pollution from burning fossil fuels.	56% agree
global warming is a serious threat to fish and wildlife.	71% agree
global warming is an urgent problem requiring immediate action.	67% agree
the United States should reduce its emissions of greenhouse gases like carbon dioxide that contribute to global warming and threaten fish and wildlife habitat.	78% agree
Congress should pass legislation that sets a clear national goal for reducing global-warming pollution with mandatory timelines because industry has already had enough time to clean up voluntarily.	75% agree
legislation to address global warming should include funding to protect fish, wildlife, and their habitat from the impacts of global warming.	76% agree

Source: National Wildlife Federation 2006. Nationwide opinion survey of hunters and anglers. Conducted by Responsive Management. www.targetglobalwarming.org/files/Toplines_National_FINAL.pdf.

that the drive to conserve wildlife extends from a deep-rooted connection of humans to wildlife, termed *biophilia*. This instinctive bond or connection between humans and wildlife is, according to the hypothesis, essentially an innate human preference for things in nature. Although the biophilia hypothesis is controversial (Kellert and Wilson 1993), what is clear is that humans care about the environment, wildlife, and wildlife conservation. In a nationwide study conducted by Yale University (2004), an overwhelming majority (95 percent) of Americans said that, in comparison to other issues, the environment was important to them, and more than half indicated that the environment was *very* important. Furthermore, a substantial percentage (13 percent) said the environment was the *most* important issue.

It is also clear that the public enjoys wildlife as part of a healthy environment. Studies in the northeastern and southeastern United States found that overwhelming majorities (91 percent and 90 percent, respectively) of respondents indicated that it was *very* important to them to know that wildlife exists in their state (Responsive Management 2003, 2005). Furthermore, various surveys of residents' opinions on the proposed reintroduction of wolves, panthers, and grizzly bears in their states demonstrated overwhelming public support (Responsive Management 1998).

Sportsmen and sportswomen have demonstrated their concern for fish and wildlife many times by persuading Congress to enact legislation funding wildlife conservation. These laws included the Migratory Bird Hunting and Conservation Stamp Act of 1934 ("Duck Stamp Act"), the Federal Aid in Wildlife Restoration Act of 1937 ("Pittman-Robertson"), and the Federal Aid in Fisheries Restoration Acts of 1950 and 1984 ("Dingell-Johnson" and "Wallop-Breaux," respectively). Combined, these four acts alone have generated more than $11 billion from sportsmen and sportswomen for conservation purposes (U.S. Fish and Wildlife Service 2007).

Public concern about the disappearance of wildlife led to enactment of the Endangered Species Act in 1973. Now, over thirty-five years later, the continuing passion for wildlife conservation was demonstrated by the response to the U.S. Fish and Wildlife Service's 2007 proposal to list the polar bear as a threatened species owing to declining sea ice from climate change. The U.S. Fish and Wildlife Service received about 600,000 comments (2007a), most in support of listing the polar bear (Woods 2007), even though most respondents likely never will see a polar bear in the wild.

Motivation for Action: Intersection of Conservation and Human Self-Interest

In addition to an innate love for wildlife, the conservation movement grew out of the understanding that a healthy environment is essential for the well-being of humans. For example, widespread public concern over the impacts of polluted air and water on humans and ecosystems led the United States Congress to enact in the 1970s a number of important laws, including the Clean Air Act (1970) and the Clean Water Act (1972, 1977). Similar recognition of the potential harm to humans and wildlife from climate change is a driving force behind calls for action today.

In 2005, the Wildlife Society adopted the position statement "Global Climate Change and Wildlife," calling for reductions in greenhouse gas emissions and for professional wildlife managers to take actions to help wildlife survive climate change. The American Geophysical Union and the American Meteorological Society, the two professional societies to which most U.S. climate scientists belong, have issued strong position statements on climate change. The U.S. National Academy of Sciences joined the scientific academies of ten other nations in 2005 to affirm that climate change is happening, humans are causing the observed changes, and actions are needed to reduce greenhouse gas emissions and enable humans and wildlife to adapt to some changes that will be inevitable.

Diverse groups have added their voices to the call for action on climate change. The U.S. Climate Action Partnership (USCAP) includes twenty-six large international corporations and six nongovernmental conservation organizations that together are calling on the federal government to enact mandatory legislation to reduce greenhouse gas emissions by 60 to 80 percent by 2050 (U.S. Climate Action Partnership 2007). Many companies cite their financial well-being as a reason to be proactive in their approach to climate change, seeing the opportunities of new green markets as well as the potential liabilities associated with continuing with business as usual. The faith community—including organizations representing Evangelical Christian, Roman Catholic, Jewish, and other religions—have argued that humankind has a responsibility to be good stewards of the Earth and to address international and intergenerational social justice issues.

The increasing engagement among diverse constituencies that have not traditionally been interested in climate change underscores that the issue is no longer the domain of narrow interest groups. Hunters and anglers, business leaders and church leaders, scientists and environmentalists, and liberals and conservatives all share an innate affection for wildlife, a sense of responsibility for stewardship of the Earth, and the recognition that the future of humankind could be profoundly affected if steps are not taken to address climate change.

Conservation Actions for Wildlife in a Changing Climate

The practical implications of the nexus among humans, climate change, and wildlife are complex but fall into three primary categories. First, the global climate changes that have already occurred are having an impact on fish and wildlife resources and will continue to do so. Wildlife professionals can mitigate these impacts by taking actions to help fish, animals, and their habitats survive climate change. Second, reducing greenhouse gas pollution can minimize the total impact of climate change on wildlife. Finally, natural ecosystems are an important reservoir of carbon in plants and soils. Strategic efforts to conserve these areas can prevent this organic material from decaying and releasing CO_2 into the atmosphere. Likewise, appropriate habitat restoration can remove CO_2 from the atmosphere.

Helping Wildlife Survive Climate Change

A report by the Wildlife Society (Inkley et al. 2004) describes eighteen actions wildlife managers can implement now to help wildlife survive climate change, even when the potential impacts of climate change to a specific species or area are not precisely known. Their recommendations include:

> **Maintain healthy, connected, genetically diverse populations.** Small isolated populations are more prone to local extirpations. Although managers already encourage healthy populations, climate change increases the importance of meeting this goal.
>
> **Reduce nonclimate stressors on ecosystems.** Reducing other human-induced stressors such as toxic pollution and habitat loss will minimize negative impacts synergistic with climate change and increase the resiliency of habitats and species to the effects of climate change.
>
> **Prevent and control invasive species.** Rapidly changing climates disturb habitats, thereby increasing opportunities for invasive species to spread. Extensive monitoring and control will be necessary to limit the negative impacts of invasive species.
>
> **Help wildlife cope with unexpected weather events.** As climate changes, the response of wildlife and their habitats may be surprising; therefore, natural resource management must be flexible.
>
> **Reduce the risk of catastrophic fires.** Although fire is a natural part of many ecosystems, climate change has led to more frequent fires and more damaging catastrophic fires (Westerling et al. 2006). Managers can use prescribed fires and other techniques to reduce fuel load and the potential for catastrophic fires.
>
> **Protect coastal wetlands and accommodate sea level rise.** Managers can defend against the negative impacts associated with sea level rise through conservation easements and the

acquisition of inland buffer zones to provide areas for habitats and wildlife to shift inland.

Adjust yield and harvest models. As fish and wildlife populations respond to climate change, their productivity and sustainability may increase or decrease. Managers will need to adapt yield and harvest regulations in anticipation and response to these changes.

Consider climate change models as well as historical data when making projections. Managers must be aware that, because the climate is changing, historical climate, habitat, and wildlife conditions are not reliable indicators of future conditions. Projections and planning should take into account expected changes in climate.

Employ monitoring and adaptive management. Owing to uncertainty concerning climate change, wildlife managers must anticipate the impacts on wildlife and use monitoring data to quickly adjust management techniques and strategies.

Look for new opportunities. Managers must be ready to anticipate and take advantage of new opportunities. For example, if climatic conditions leave existing agricultural areas unusable for agriculture, they could become important wildlife conservation areas.

Reducing Global Greenhouse Gas Emissions

Addressing climate change requires extensive changes in the way humans generate and use power. Energy use has grown exponentially (fig. 5.2) since the beginning of the Industrial Revolution, and carbon-based fuels (oil, coal, natural gas) have provided 80 percent of today's energy supply (Nakicenovic, Grubler, and MacDonald 1998). Governments can lead the way by reducing these emissions through legislation and by adopting new energy policies in their own operations. Conservation agencies can and should demonstrate to other government agencies means by which they can reduce agency greenhouse gas emissions in the course of their official duties and actions.

Reducing carbon emissions requires development of more-efficient power generation from fossil fuel sources, as well as the use of noncarbon-based alternative energy sources. Extensive research and development are under way to further develop solar and water power, biofuels, wind-generated energy, nuclear fusion and fission, and geothermal energy sources. Wildlife professionals will need to pay attention to minimizing or mitigating the impacts on wildlife of alternative energy sources. For example, Arnett and colleagues (2007) caution that development of wind power should consider impacts on wildlife, including mortality of birds and bats, as well as the habitat disruption and fragmentation associated with building new sites.

Energy must also be used more efficiently as a part of the overall strategy to reduce greenhouse gas emissions. Opportunities for increased efficiency are available in transportation, manufacturing, building practices, and consumer choices for appliances, lighting, and other electrical devices. Numerous federal, state, and business initiatives are either in place or being considered to promote energy efficiency. Conservation agencies also can reduce their emissions and at the same time possibly reduce costs by exploring ways to reduce everyday power usage. Just two of many possible options are replacing incandescent lightbulbs with compact fluorescent bulbs that consume nearly 70 percent less energy or using vehicles and motors with higher fuel efficiency.

Sequestering Carbon through Habitat Conservation and Restoration

Sequestering atmospheric CO_2 in plants and soils is a third category of conservation actions that can help reduce greenhouse gas levels in the atmosphere, while at the same time providing important benefits for wildlife. Significant amounts of CO_2 and other greenhouse gases can be

FIGURE 5.2 **World primary energy source by supply**

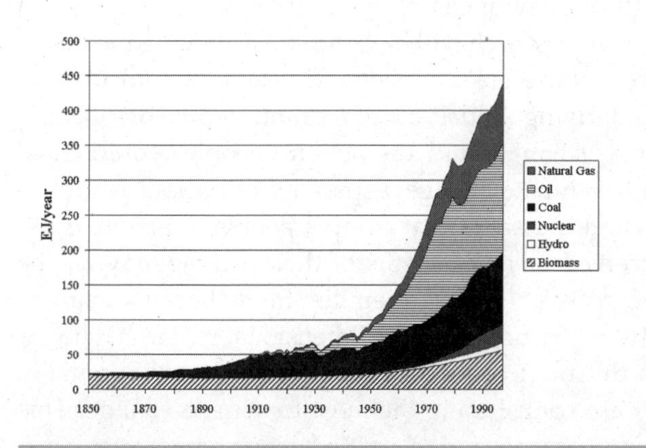

Currently over 30 billion tons of CO_2 are emitted to the atmosphere from fossil fuel burning each year. As a result, atmospheric CO_2 levels have risen more than 30% from 280 ppm to 383 ppm in the last two centuries.

Source: Nakicenovic et al. 1998

released into the atmosphere when natural forests, prairies, and wetlands are altered either for agricultural uses or for development. Restoring these lands to their natural ecosystems can allow them to begin removing CO_2 from the atmosphere through photosynthesis. Conservation agencies have an important role to play in identifying opportunities to enhance carbon sequestration through land conservation and restoration.

Human Dimension Research Needs

Herein we have demonstrated the role of humans in causing rapid climate change, the need to reduce greenhouse gas emissions, some management actions that can be taken to help wildlife survive in a changing climate, and the belief of the majority of Americans that the issue must be addressed. Climate change is now a social issue with the challenge of transforming the scientific facts and prevailing concerns into meaningful actions that reduce greenhouse gas emissions to requisite levels.

There are two aspects of the climate change issue that make it particularly challenging for individuals to move from concern to action. These are the global scope of the issue and the longtime lag between action and results. However, these challenging aspects are not unique to climate change. The ban of chlorofluorocarbons (CFCs) overcame the facts that they were used worldwide and that the first signs of a statistically detectable decrease in the ozone hole will likely not be evident until at least the 2020s (Newman et al. 2006). However, addressing climate change is more challenging because climate change will require action by everyone as individuals rather than implementation primarily by industry, as was the case with CFCs.

Human dimensions research will be critical in achieving meaningful reductions in greenhouse gas emissions. Research should include assessment of the underlying values, attitudes, and knowledge people hold regarding climate change, and the actions people would most likely take to minimize climate change. Especially important is understanding the factors and messages that compel people to action, especially when the perceived or real benefits of their actions may not be realized for decades or even within their lifetimes. Because climate change is a worldwide issue, human dimensions research should include not only North America, but also global populations, especially in the countries that are contributing the most to climate change. This would assist in finding ways to compel unified action across vastly different economic levels and cultures to reduce global warming pollution.

Conclusion

We believe that climate change is the greatest environmental challenge for humankind and the greatest threat to wildlife since the evolution of humans. The future for humans and wildlife alike depends on individual and worldwide action to reduce greenhouse gas pollution to minimize rapid climate change caused largely by the burning of fossil fuels. At the same time, concerted actions by fish and wildlife managers will be necessary to help wildlife survive those climate changes that are already inevitable.

The challenge for humankind, in the interest of current and future generations, and in the interest of wildlife conservation, is to address climate change *now*. Compelling factors for addressing climate change are self-interest, humankind's innate attraction for wildlife, and most people's concern for the environment, as evidenced by polls indicating a desire to conserve wildlife, even when that may mean some limitations on human activities. For human dimensions research, the challenge is finding out what makes climate change real to people and motivates the majority to act together, lest climate change become the ultimate "tragedy of the commons."

Literature Cited

Arnett, E. B., D. B. Inkley, D. H. Johnson, R. P. Larkin, S. Manes, A. M. Manville, J. R. Mason, M. L. Morrison, M. D. Strickland, and R. Thresher. 2007. Impacts of wind energy facilities on wildlife and wildlife habitat. *Wildlife Society Technical Review 07-2*. Bethesda, MD: Wildlife Society.

CBS News/New York Times. 2007. Americans' views on the environment. April 26. www.cbsnews.com/htdocs/pdf/042607environment.pdf.

Curry, T. E., S. Ansolabehere, and H. J. Herzog. 2007. A survey of public attitudes towards climate change and climate change mitigation technologies in the United States: Analyses of 2006 results. http://sequestration.mit.edu/pdf/LFEE_2007_01_WP.pdf.

Fox News/Opinion Dynamics Corp. 2007. Opinion Dynamics Poll 2 February 07. www.foxnews.com/projects/pdf/020207_global_warming_web.pdf .

Gallup. 2007. Gallup's pulse of democracy: Environment. www.galluppoll.com/content/default.aspx?ci=1615&pg=1.

Griffith, M. 2006. Huge wildfires prompt emergency hunt of wildlife in Nevada. *Las Vegas Sun*, September 3.

Hoegh-Guldberg, O. 1999. Climate change, coral bleaching and the future of the world's coral reefs. *Marine and Freshwater Research.* 50:839–66.

Inkley, D. B., M. G. Anderson, A. R. Blaustein, V. R. Burkett, B. Felzer, B. Griffith, J. Price, and T. L. Root. 2004. Global climate change and wildlife in North America. *Wildlife Society Technical Review* 04-2. Bethesda, MD: Wildlife Society.

Intergovernmental Panel on Climate Change (IPCC). 2007. *Climate change 2007: The physical science basis.* Contribution of Working Group I to the Fourth Assessment Report of the Intergovernmental Panel on Climate Change, ed. S. Solomon, D. Qin, M. Manning, Z. Chen, M. Marquis, K. B. Averyt, M. Tignor, and H. L. Miller. Cambridge and New York: Cambridge University Press.

Kellert, S. R., and E. O. Wilson. 1993. *The biophilia hypothesis.* Washington, DC: Island Press.

Nakicenovic, N., A. Grubler, and A. MacDonald, eds. 1998. *Global energy perspectives.* Cambridge: Cambridge University Press.

National Oceanic and Atmospheric Administration (NOAA). 2007. Trends in Atmospheric Carbon Dioxide–Mauna Loa. www.esrl.noaa.gov/gmd/ccgg/trends.

National Wildlife Federation. 2006. Nationwide opinion survey of hunters and anglers. Conducted by Responsive Management. www.targetglobalwarming.org/files/Toplines_National_FINAL.pdf.

Newman, P. A., E. R. Nash, S. R. Kawa, S. A. Montzka, and S. M. Schauffler. 2006. When will the Antarctic ozone hole recover? *Geophysical Research Letters* 33 L12814.

O'Neal, K. 2002. Effects of global warming on trout and salmon in U.S. streams. Washington, DC: Defenders of Wildlife and Natural Resources Defense Council.

Parmesan, C. 2006. Ecological and evolutionary responses to recent climate change. Annual review of *Ecology, Evolution, and Systematics* 37:637–69.

Parry, M. L., O. F. Canziani, J. P. Palutikof, P. J. van der Linden, and C. E. Hanson, eds. 2007. *Climate change 2007: Impacts, adaptation and vulnerability.* Contribution of Working Group II to the Fourth Assessment Report of the Intergovernmental Panel on Climate Change. Cambridge: Cambridge University Press.

Podesta, J., D. J. Weiss, and L. Nichols. 2007: Americans urgently want action on energy independence and global warming. Center for American Progress, April 18. www.americanprogress.org/issues/2007/04/environment_poll.html.

Pounds, J. A., M. R. Bustamante, L. A. Coloma, J. A. Consuegra, M. P. L. Fogden, P. N. Foster, E. La Marca, et al. 2006. Widespread amphibian extinctions from epidemic disease driven by global warming. *Nature* 439:161–67.

Preston, B. L. 2006. Risk-based reanalysis of the effects of climate change on U.S. cold-water habitat. *Climatic Change* 76:91–119.

Rahmstorf, S. 2007. A semi-empirical approach to projecting future sea-level rise. *Science* 315:368–70.

Responsive Management. 1998. Wildlife and the American mind: Public opinion on and attitudes toward fish and wildlife management, ed. M. D. Duda, S. J. Bissell, and K. C. Young. Harrisonburg, VA: Responsive Management.

———. 2003. Public opinions on fish and wildlife management issues and the reputation and credibility of fish and wildlife agencies in the Northeast United States. Harrisonburg, VA: Responsive Management.

———. 2005. Public opinions on fish and wildlife management issues and the reputation and credibility of fish and wildlife agencies in the southeastern United States. Harrisonburg, VA: Responsive Management.

Root, T. L., J. T. Price, K. R. Hall, S. H. Schneider, C. Rosenzweig, and J. A. Pounds. 2003. Fingerprints of global warming on animals and plants. *Nature* 421:57–60.

Saad, L. 2007. Did Hollywood's glare heat up public concern about global warming? Concern about global warming is up slightly over past year. Gallup News Service. www.galluppoll.com/content/?ci=26932&pg=1.

Schweiger, L. 2006. Speech presented at Campaign for America's Future: Take Back America, National Wildlife Federation, Washington, DC, June 12.

Siegenthaler, U., T. F. Stocker, E. Monnin, D. Lüthi, J. Schwander, B. Stauffer, D. Raynaud, J. M. Barnola, H. Fischer, V. Masson-Delmotte, and J. Jouzel. 2005. Stable carbon cycle climate relationship during the late Pleistocene. *Science* 310(5752):1313–17.

Smith, D. 2007. The mystery of the disappearing moose. *National Wildlife* 45(2):46–50.

Thomas, C. D., A. Cameron, R. E. Green, M. Bakkenes, L. J. Beaumont, Y. C. Collingham, B. F. N. Erasmus, et al. 2004. Extinction risk from climate change. *Nature* 427:145–48.

U.S. Climate Action Partnership. 2007. A call for action: Consensus principles and recommendations from the U.S. Climate Action Partnership: A business and NGO Partnership. www.us-cap.org.

U.S. Fish and Wildlife Service. 2007. www.fws.gov/duckstamps, http://federalasst.fws.gov/wr/fawr.html, http://federalasst.fws.gov/sfr/fasfr.html.

U.S. Fish and Wildlife Service. 2007a. News Release, U.S. Fish and Wildlife Service Extends Comment Period on Polar Bear Research, October 2, 2007. www.fws.gov/news/NewsReleases/showNews.cfm?newsId =61CFD2A8-AE27-DE0D-70CA1F1A770C5420.

Washington Post–ABC News–Stanford University. 2007. Environment trends. April 20. www.washingtonpost.com/wp-srv/nation/polls/postpoll _environment_042007.html.

Westerling, A. L., H. G. Hidalgo, D. R. Cayan, and T. W. Swetnam. 2006. Warming and earlier spring increase western U.S. forest wildfire activity. *Science* 313:940–43.

Wilson, E. O. 1984. *Biophilia*. Cambridge, MA: Harvard University Press.

Woods, B. 2007. Personal communication with authors.

Yale University, Center for Environmental Law and Policy and the School of Forestry and Environmental Studies. 2004. *The environmental deficit: Survey on American attitudes on the environment*. New Haven, CT: Yale University.

PART II

Building the Social Component into the Philosophy of Wildlife Management

Advancements in the science of human dimensions (HD) of fish and wildlife management have occurred over the past forty years, but actual wildlife management practices have not always kept pace. Part I of this book was concerned with defining the social science aspects of wildlife management and how human social structures interact with the natural world. Part II elaborates on the methods and tools that are used to integrate HD science into wildlife management.

Organizational change is often necessary in any successful human enterprise. Chapter 6 explores past, present, and future developments in the field of wildlife management. By investigating changes in wildlife management culture throughout history, we can better understand contemporary paradigm shifts and the integration of human dimensions into wildlife management agencies.

Chapter 7 examines case studies from Europe where ecological and social sciences have been integrated to deal with human-wildlife conflicts. The chapter describes the framework developed for these projects, applies the framework in a variety of socioeconomic and management settings, and discusses the lessons learned. These European case studies illustrate how HD science can improve existing managerial systems and suggest mechanisms for improving human-wildlife coexistence.

Chapters 8, 9, and 10 provide a critical look at attempts to integrate social and ecological sciences approach in Asia, Africa, and South America.

Comanagement (chapter 8), community-based conservation (chapter 9), integrated conservation and development projects (chapter 9), and integrated assessment (chapter 10) are examined. These approaches offer potentially useful alternatives to traditional protectionist-style management. Both the successes and the pitfalls of each approach are explored. These approaches offer hope that persistent issues such as bushmeat poaching in the Amazon and reconciling environmental conservation in impoverished communities might be addressed in new and innovative ways. Defining success in these complex situations, however, is problematic; chapters 8 and 9 provide valuable insights into how biodiversity protection is interlinked with ethical and economic issues in a rapidly changing world.

Chapter 10 calls attention to the fact that humans are part of the natural landscape and should not be viewed as external to ecosystems. This chapter explores socioecological systems as complex adaptive systems using a systems approach with a focus on resilience and flexibility rather than stability as indicators of healthy systems. A computer modeling approach is used to develop integrated assessments that better predict the outcomes of various management plans. These tools can help managers to work with communities.

People must continue to coexist with other living beings to maintain a healthy biosphere. The following chapters provide an overview of how scientists, nonprofit organizations, and government agencies are working within this conceptual framework to help human societies coexist with wildlife in the twenty-first century.

CHAPTER 6

The Changing Culture of Wildlife Management

Larry M. Gigliotti, Duane L. Shroufe, and Scott Gurtin

This chapter will use the concept of paradigms to view the development of wildlife management in North America. We will start with some definitions of the term *paradigm*. Thomas S. Kuhn (1962), author of *The Structure of Scientific Revolutions*, used the term in two different senses. Kuhn says that at one level "it stands for the entire constellation of beliefs, values, techniques, and so on shared by the members of a given community" while at another level "it denotes one sort of element in that constellation, the concrete puzzle-solutions which, employed as models or examples, can replace explicit rules as a basis for the solution of the remaining puzzles of normal science" (175). In this chapter we also tend to blur the use of paradigms between these two levels, although most of our examples reflect the second.

For another definition, Joel A. Barker presents another definition of paradigm in his 1992 book, *Paradigms: The Business of Discovering the Future*, that is a more practical guide for understanding how to be successful within a paradigm and during paradigm shifts. He provides the following definition: "A paradigm is a set of rules and regulations (written or unwritten) that does two things: (1) it establishes or defines boundaries; and (2) it tells you how to behave inside the boundaries in order to be successful" (32). More specifically in this chapter, we use paradigm to describe both how the wildlife profession as a whole views and frames wildlife problems and issues and the acceptable range of solutions, methods, and tools used to address wildlife problems and issues. We also use a simple definition for *culture* that is similar to our definition for paradigms: the guiding beliefs and philosophies for a wildlife agency.

This chapter explores the development of wildlife management in North America in broad, sweeping generalities using a paradigm. Since most wildlife management is state directed, our discussion is broad because we recognize that state wildlife agencies have developed at different rates, particularly in their use and applications of human dimensions. The main purpose of this chapter is to examine how paradigms work both to advance the wildlife profession and to pose as a barrier to new ideas, using some basic paradigm shifts in the wildlife profession as examples.

Wildlife Values in North America: Setting the Stage for Management

As defined by Aldo Leopold (1933), "game management is the art of making land produce sustained annual crops of wild game for recreational use" (3). A concept of wildlife management did not arrive on the shores of North America with the early European settlers. We imagine that the early European settlers in North America were astounded by the abundance of natural resources and especially wildlife. Long before the Europeans arrived in North America, they had "subdued" the "wildness" of the European continent (Robinson and Bolen 1984). Most large predators were extirpated or only remained in remote and limited patches of mountainous and forested lands. Much of the land was reshaped to favor domestic flocks, and where they existed, wild game animals, such as deer, rabbit, grouse, and foxes, were the property of the nobility who owned the land. Thus, the lower social classes, who made up the majority of early immigration to North America, associated little value with wildlife.

The first explorers and traders to North America found the land "densely populated" with people possessing impressive villages and agriculture (Mann 2005). Early visitors described "extensive fields of maize, beans and squash." The Native Americans were eager to trade with the newcomers but did not permit extended stays or settlement. However, that early contact with the newcomers introduced new diseases to the Native Americans that killed significant numbers, thus reducing the Native Americans ability to resist the European settlers. According to Mann (2005), the abundance of wildlife in the new land may have been largely due to the sharp decline in the native peoples. This viewpoint is in sharp contrast to the idea that American wildlife was largely unaffected by humans before the arrival of Columbus.

European settlers arrived with a "dominance" paradigm for wildlife use (Huth 1990). Some people attribute this dominance paradigm to Judeo-Christian traditions expressed in the book of Genesis where God's commandment to man is to "be fruitful and multiply" and "have dominion over the earth and all animals" (Robinson and Bolen 1984). Many people have used this as justification for unchecked exploitation of the earth's resources, but others have pointed out that dominion also implies responsibility. Reinforcing the first perspective, the first Europeans experienced what appeared to be unlimited abundance of wildlife and freedom from the nobility. This dominance paradigm in the context of abundant wildlife and personal freedom set the stage for the beginnings of wildlife management.

What is most impressive about this period in history relative to wildlife is the speed in which this land of "unlimited" resources was conquered. People came to North America in huge numbers, the human population grew and expanded westward at an ever-increasing rate, and resource exploitation was fueled by the industrial age. As more and more examples of degraded landscapes and depleted wildlife populations became evident, a conservation ethic began to emerge. The realization that people could so quickly deplete such an abundance of wildlife was a dramatic lesson for the settlers.

A Brief History of Wildlife Management: Evolving Paradigms

The First Paradigm

Wildlife management was thus a solution to a problem, that of declining wildlife populations. The first paradigm in the field of wildlife management was hunting regulations and enforcement of those restrictions. Controls on hunting were recognized fairly early in North America. According to Leopold (1933, 16), "the dominant idea in America until about 1905 was to *perpetrate*, rather than to improve or create hunting . . . restriction of hunting could 'string out' the remnants of the virgin supply, and make them last a longer time." By the time of the American Revolution, twelve of the thirteen colonies had enacted closed seasons on certain species as well as several other restrictive regulations (Leopold 1933). Wildlife agencies were formed and began hiring game wardens. A warden system appeared in Massachusetts and New Hampshire about 1850. Leopold (1933) provides a good account of the beginnings of restrictive regulations in America. Restrictive regulations became the established process for solving the problem of overharvest of wildlife. A profession therefore became necessary to support this new paradigm, and state wildlife agencies soon grew to a sizable staff of wardens along with increasingly restrictive regulations.

How Do Paradigms Work?

As a problem is identified a dominant way of viewing the problem and its solution becomes established. To be effective, a paradigm must successfully solve many of the problems and become established as a recognized solution. Professions are established to perfect and advance the solution, and soon an industry (agency) is developed to maintain this profession. Those problems that are not solved by a paradigm are simply set aside as the professionals apply their solutions to the problems that can be solved. The solvable problems are eventually remedied, while more difficult problems grow in importance. Unfortunately, while the original paradigm was successful in solving a select set of problems, it can become a barrier to creative thinking. Professionals who owe their success to their paradigm may be threatened by new ways of thinking that may require new knowledge and skills they currently do not possess, and those in power positions can effectively block or delay new paradigms from developing. Threats to an established order are one reason why change is often so difficult for wildlife agencies. One result is that new paradigms often develop from outside an established profession because of these blocks to new thinking.

The Next Paradigm

In spite of the successes in wildlife management, restrictive regulations alone failed to halt the accelerating decline in game in the face of increasing demand. Leopold wrote in 1933, "The set of ideas which served to string out the remnants of the virgin game supply, and to which many conservationists feel an intense personal loyalty, seems to have reached the limit of its effectiveness. Something new must be done" (411). The new paradigm became that of "improving upon nature," and with it came new solutions, knowledge, skills, and associated wildlife professionals (Leopold 1993). The most significant component of this new paradigm was recognition of science as a major tool for achieving this new goal.

The scientific management paradigm as a guiding philosophy for wildlife management did not occur overnight. Leopold credits Theodore Roosevelt with recognizing the importance of science in wildlife management around 1910, but it took many years before a significant proportion of biologists were staffing wildlife agencies. Many authors have credited Leopold with the establishment of science as the foundation for wildlife management when he published his book *Game Management* in 1933. One reason for the slow application of science was that it took time to identify and conduct research before science could be comfortably used to guide wildlife management. As Leopold (1933, 20) says: "The early attempts to apply biology to the management of game as a wild crop soon disclosed the fact that science had accumulated more knowledge of how to distinguish one species from another than of the habits, requirements, and inter-relationships of living populations. Until recently science could tell us, so to speak, more about the length of a duck's bill than about its food, or the status of the waterfowl resource, or the factors determining its productivity."

Leopold (1933) identified the following general progression of management approaches under this new paradigm for wildlife management:

1. Predator control
2. Reservation game lands (e.g., parks, forests, refuges, etc.)
3. Artificial replenishment (restocking and game farming, including introductions of exotics)
4. Environmental controls (control of food, cover, special factors, and diseases)

As these ideas developed, restrictive regulations remained a valuable management tool under this paradigm.

This new wildlife management paradigm provided an opportunity to take a fresh look at many of the wildlife problems that were not solved by simple application of restrictive regulations. We imagine, however, that in many cases as biologists began to infiltrate state wildlife agencies, established game wardens grew concerned about the new direction the agency seemed to be headed and perhaps even felt threatened when people with new skills and knowledge began to play larger roles in decision making in the agency.

According to Leopold (1933, 413), "one of the most important aspects of the transition has been its effect on the pre-existing 'untrained' men." Leopold (414) states that "the game manager must eventually acquire what is called 'the scientific point of view.'" The transition in wildlife management to the use of science meant that many "untrained" workers already in various positions had to, by various methods, pick up the necessary skills and knowledge. "The untrained men unable to accomplish this process of self-education have tended to drop out" (Leopold 1933, 413).

Leopold (1933, 411) states that two approaches to making policy are the following: (1) abstract logic and (2) use of factual information or experimentation, that is, use of the scientific method. "The old habit of determining policy in the abstract still persists. It must be broken down . . . the experimental approach to policy decision is a permanent thing." We have devoted a considerable amount of space in this chapter to a review of Leopold's classic *Game Management* because he provides a very good description of wildlife management in its early development stage and its first significant paradigm shift.

What Happened after Leopold?

As with any new paradigm, great advances and wildlife management success stories followed as new skills and knowledge were applied to that growing list of "unsolvable" problems that were set aside under the old paradigm. Colleges and universities responded by developing a variety of courses to train future technicians and biologists who would fill new positions at wildlife agencies. Over time a considerable amount of scientific knowledge was accumulated and was readily available for guiding future wildlife management decisions.

The paradigm shift that included wildlife biologists as a significant portion of wildlife agencies led to significant advances in wildlife management, but problems still existed that could not be solved by wildlife science. As with any paradigm, more complex problems were often pushed aside as practitioners devoted time to making progress under the current paradigm. In many cases the "unsolvable" problems were not even considered as wildlife problems because they were considered "people" problems and dismissed as problems that were outside the responsibility of the wildlife agency.

Another factor that likely contributed to a blind spot for "people" problems was the relatively high trust in government up to about the mid-1960s (Alford 2001). Wildlife agencies had abundant clout to experiment with various wildlife management techniques or strategies that they felt would best serve the public. This long period of freedom to make decisions for the public established a tradition of biologists being in control and created feelings of superiority, and science-based management was hard to refute because there were "experts" working to solve wildlife management problems.

Beginnings of a New Paradigm: The Human Dimensions

One could argue that the human (societal) factor has always been recognized as a key component of wildlife management; however, for the early history of wildlife management, say, before 1960, it would be difficult to find more than a mention that the human factor is important. Leopold (1933) devotes only the last page and a half in *Game Management* to the topic of "social significance of game management," making a profound statement that while a game manager's job is to manipulate animals and vegetation to produce a game crop, his or her ultimate goal is "to bring about a new attitude towards the land" (420). However, his only prescription for achieving this goal was for game managers to provide examples of good game management.

Until the 1960s, wildlife management's main focus was to provide game for hunters and anglers. Most wildlife managers at that time were also hunters and anglers so they had a tradition of working together and significant empathy for hunters and anglers. However, by the late 1960s it became apparent that nonconsumptive wildlife interests were increasing. Leopold devoted only two pages to the topic of "management of other wild life" in *Game Management* (403), noting that it is important "that the greatest possible variety of them [nongame wildlife] exist in each community" for the enjoyment of the average citizen. His prescription for doing this was to follow the same pattern he outlined for game management—identify the species/populations to be increased, conduct scientific research, then manipulate the environment and other necessary factors to increase their numbers. Because of the wildlife profession's historic focus on the hunting and fishing public, wildlife managers did not have particularly high standing with these new nonconsumptive stakeholders. To these "new" stakeholders, the concept of management was taking on a flavor of something that was "unnatural." This was also about the same time as overall trust in government began to decline (Alford 2001). People were demanding more input into decisions by government and more accountability from government. An antihunting movement began at about this time that was especially worrisome to state wildlife agencies funded by the sale of hunting and fishing licenses.

Not only were new challenges to the current paradigm coming from nontraditional stakeholders (in many cases these were people whom the wildlife professionals did not consider as stakeholders), but also many people issues began arising among traditional stakeholders. Since most wildlife managers were also hunters and anglers, they believed they knew what hunters and anglers wanted. However, hunters and anglers were becoming less satisfied with decisions made by wildlife agencies and began to challenge them. It was becoming apparent that wildlife professionals did not have a completely accurate understanding of the desires, preferences, and demands of their customers, and sometimes they did not have a good understanding of who their customers were. For example, the concept of recreational specialization and creation of numerous special interest groups focused on a specific species (e.g., Ducks Unlimited, Trout Unlimited, Pheasants Forever, etc.) or method (bow hunter groups, fly-fishing clubs, etc.) probably created as much or more controversy associated with various agency decisions as did issues surrounding nontraditional stakeholders.

Of interest here is what happens to people vested in the current paradigm when challenged by a new paradigm. The most prevalent response is to "circle the wagons," gathering all the successful practitioners together to mount a credible defense. It seems ironic that a profession that based its success on the application of science seems to have fallen back on the "habit of determining policy in the abstract." The statement that "the public just doesn't know all the facts" characterized the entrenched practitioners. The belief was that these controversial issues were the result of an uneducated public and that what was needed was to focus on education as a solution to getting back to the way things were. It was about this time (the 1970s and later) that information and education (I&E) programs were infused into state wildlife agencies.

While I&E strategies were valuable steps for reaching Leopold's (1933, 420) ultimate goal of bringing about "a new attitude towards the land," it was not the magic bullet envisioned by wildlife professionals to resolve the controversial issues of the time. The problem seemed as much the fault of wildlife professionals not understanding their publics as it was their publics' lack of information.

There is no official start date for when human dimensions became recognized as a significant component of wildlife management deserving of scientific research funds and recognition in the wildlife literature. However, an article by Hendee and Potter at the Thirty-sixth North American Wildlife and Natural Resources Conference in 1971 seemed to have sparked a flood of human dimensions research. Some excerpts from the introduction of their paper entitled "Human Behavior and Wildlife Management: Needed Research" are provided here:

> Most game managers profess that wildlife management is also people management, with the human element possibly

> dominant. . . . Highly scientific research on human behavior aspects of wildlife appeared scarce on our literature review. . . . The highly regarded *Journal of Wildlife Management*, from 1960 to 1970, had only 6 contributions on people-wildlife topics out of 698 total articles. Thus, despite extensive magazine and conference comment on human behavior aspects of wildlife, rigorous social-wildlife research is scarce. . . . More research is needed on human behavior aspects of wildlife.

Throughout the 1970s many human dimensions authors cited Hendee and Potter as their reason for conducting their research. Today the need for human dimensions information is well recognized, but in the 1970s researchers needed an overarching justification for conducting human dimensions research, and the Hendee and Potter article often provided that justification.

The paradigm shift in wildlife management began when scientific methodology was applied to the human component of wildlife management decisions. It would seem that this would be an easy paradigm shift for a profession that based success on the application of science, but the model and lessons from Leopold concerning the early application of science to game management can help us understand the difficulties during the birth of the discipline of human dimensions of wildlife management. While human dimensions research began during the 1960s and increased steadily during the 1970s and 1980s (Manfredo 1989), very little application of human dimensions by state wildlife agencies had occurred by the 1990s (Gigliotti and Decker 1992).

One reason for the lag in application of human dimensions by wildlife managers is very similar to Leopold's lament that while they had a lot of "descriptive" scientific data on various wildlife species, the scientists were not focused on "management"-type questions. This was also true of early human dimensions research, which tended to be very descriptive but not well focused on issues that would help wildlife managers. While this descriptive phase of human dimensions was necessary for the growth and development of the field of human dimensions, it also meant that human dimensions was largely viewed as an academic discipline for the remainder of the twentieth century.

The evolution of paradigms provides a good understanding of the lag between the introduction of human dimensions as a science and its acceptance and application in wildlife management. First, the wildlife management discipline had many wildlife professionals who were successful under the paradigm of restrictive regulations. Under this old paradigm, the human element was not ignored as decisions were still made, but those decisions were based on "speculation, supposition and conjecture" (Duda, Bissell, and Young 1998). A shift in the paradigm required established professionals to relinquish some power or prestige, which did not and still does not occur easily for many people. In his 1992 book, *Paradigms: The Business of Discovering the Future*, Barker would say that this was an excellent opportunity for a leader to capitalize on the new paradigm. A smart leader would have hired people with human dimensions education and skills to take advantage of a new paradigm and the new issues and problems that could be addressed.

Another way to examine the birth of human dimensions is to examine how the wildlife profession measured success. In a general sense the field of human dimensions began when a few researchers and managers asked a simple question: "Why do people hunt and fish?" This was considered a silly question because under the dominant paradigm it was accepted that people hunted and fished in order to harvest game. A public agency needs some method to measure success, and its measure of success is often related to its management paradigm. Since managers first saw their role as providing game to hunt and fish to catch, their first measure of success was game harvested.

However, over time (particularly after World War II) hunting and fishing participation began to increase as more and more people had time for recreation, and as a result the amount of game harvested started to decrease. Wildlife managers were now faced with a paradox. According to their evaluation, success was decreasing, yet participation in hunting and fishing was increasing. Their paradigm would have predicted that participation should drop off. Given the fact that participation did not drop, managers changed their role to that of providing "recreation" rather than game in the bag or creel. Their measure of success then became days-a-field.

In spite of the days-a-field measure of success, wildlife managers never really gave up on game bagged as being important but instead assumed that game bagged was still critical to satisfaction, although either the *amount* of game bagged was not as important as they first assumed or the relationship between amount of game bagged and satisfaction changed over time. Thus, people were willing to hunt or fish longer in order to get game, and therefore days-a-field was a "better" measure for the agency given that the agency could show improvement. Eventually, managers came to realize that the days-a-field measure was not very well correlated with satisfaction, and satisfaction gets back to the question of why do people hunt and fish. Answers to this question led to a multiple satisfaction approach to wildlife use introduced by Hendee (1974), which recognized that many satisfactions are derived from hunting and fishing and that providing a wide range of these benefits will add to the satisfactions people can derive from wildlife management. This multiple-satisfactions approach created the first need for human dimensions information, to better understand the needs and desires of hunters and anglers.

The Current Status of Human Dimensions in Wildlife Management

In 1998, Gigliotti identified that in spite of significant growth and progress of academic human dimensions research and many milestones in the human dimensions discipline, "little of this science found its way into the decision-making process of the wildlife agencies it was originally designed to benefit." A decade later the statement is still true, although much progress has been made. More agencies are hiring human dimensions professionals, and today's wildlife professionals are more likely to have a minimal exposure to some human dimensions courses during their education. However, additional progress is needed. Human dimensions includes more than conducting a survey to learn about stakeholders or to identify the various beliefs, values, and opinions concerning an issue. It represents a way of doing business (Manfredo, Decker, and Duda 1998). Human dimensions information and understanding must be applied in the process of making wildlife management decisions along with biological, ecological, fiscal, and political considerations. It involves a new way of thinking about the public's right to be involved in decisions that affect it. As is often the case at agencies, a lone human dimensions staff person, if they have one, is only minimally able to make effective use of human dimensions information.

To be effective, it seems that wildlife agencies need to diffuse human dimensions information throughout the agency. But how can wildlife agencies provide existing staff with the necessary tools and techniques needed for successful applications of a human dimensions philosophy? One pilot project developed by Colorado State University in cooperation with the Western Association of Fish and Wildlife Agencies (WAFWA) was designed for this very problem. This program was extensive, involving four one-week instructional periods on campus, using readings and course assignments while off-site, and requiring each participant to design and complete a project that had utility to his or her agency. Programs like this will help agencies better integrate the potential benefits of the human dimensions discipline.

The human dimensions discipline is now fairly well established academically, and most wildlife agency leaders recognize the importance of human dimensions. However, more progress needs to be made to fully achieve the integration of human dimensions into wildlife management decisions. The good news is that human dimensions has reached a point at which it likely will be fully incorporated and effectively utilized by wildlife agencies. There is a well-established academic research base including many colleges and universities teaching students and conducting research, a growing partnership between universities and wildlife agencies, increasing numbers of private human dimensions consultants, and, most important, a growing eagerness by wildlife agencies to obtain and use human dimensions information to help tackle controversial issues. As agencies begin using human dimensions tools and techniques, they will add new knowledge and skills and wildlife managers will become proficient at solving the set of people-related problems that have troubled the wildlife profession in the past.

The Changing Culture of Wildlife Management: Being Receptive to New Paradigms

Wildlife management has gone through some significant cultural changes since its beginning, and the pace of change is accelerating. History has taught us that change is usually for the good and that change is usually inevitable. The smart approach is to anticipate paradigm shifts and take advantage of the benefits they offer rather than expend efforts to maintain the status quo. By studying how wildlife agencies have struggled with past paradigm shifts, we hope to be better prepared for future challenges. For example, understanding why it took so long for the wildlife profession to accept and use human dimensions in spite of the recognition that people management was an essential component of wildlife management may help the profession to be more receptive to new paradigms.

The following three examples of paradigm shifts are occurring or may occur in the wildlife profession. Each example will have human dimensions as a component. If embraced, the shift will likely occur more easily. Much like the application of wildlife science, human dimensions is a common thread through which all management issues are connected. Society continues to grow and continues to change. Human dimensions is the key in ensuring that agencies are in step with the publics they serve.

Ecosystem Approach

State wildlife agencies began with the sole purpose of providing game and fish for hunters and anglers, and even today that remains their main function. While states now have a few staff or even a section devoted to threatened and endangered (T&E) species and even nongame in general, the approach to management still follows Leopold's general prescription of single species management. Wildlife managers generally know how to increase numbers of a species or population and how to measure success, and if people issues are the roadblock to achieving success, they now have the tools and techniques from the human dimensions discipline to draw upon. However, this approach, which was so successful for game management and for a limited number of threatened and endangered species, will not work for the combined assemblage of species found in an area. Maintaining wildlife diversity and functioning ecosystems will require a different approach. Using an ecosystem approach to wildlife management represents a paradigm shift for wildlife agencies. According to Scalet (2007), this shift is occurring at a faster rate within university wildlife and fisheries academic programs than state wildlife agencies.

Climate Change and Global Warming

Global climate change is already having an impact on wildlife, but what role will state wildlife agencies play in an issue that seems so large in scope and complicated? Will state agencies be content to simply document the decline in wildlife in their state in the hope that their effort will stimulate action, or will agencies take a more involved role of implementing change? With the exception of migratory species, the paradigms of state wildlife agencies have been limited by state boundaries. Even with migratory species, the focus is still on managing habitats and regulating hunters, albeit on a regional rather than a state basis. Will state wildlife agencies change their paradigm to take on a global issue?

New Funding Sources

State wildlife agencies have traditionally been funded by the sale of hunting and fishing licenses and taxes on hunting and fishing equipment. Will state wildlife agencies continue to depend on hunters and anglers, or will they expand their paradigm to include other wildlife stakeholders? Some agencies have crossed the hunter/angler boundary and obtained alternate funding through general taxes, although most states are still struggling with this paradigm shift.

Literature Cited

Alford, J. R. 2001. We're all in this together: The decline of trust in government 1958–1996. In *What is it about government that Americans dislike?* ed. J. R. Hibbing and E. Theiss-Morse, 28–46. Cambridge: Cambridge University Press.

Barker, J. A. 1992. *Paradigms: The business of discovering the future.* New York: HarperCollins.

Duda, M. D., S. J. Bissell, and K. C. Young. 1998. *Wildlife and the American mind.* Harrisonburg, VA: Responsive Management.

Gigliotti, L. M. 1998. Human dimensions and the next quarter century: An agency professional's perspective. *Transactions of the North American Wildlife and Natural Resources Conference* 63:293–303.

Gigliotti, L. M., and D. J. Decker. 1992. Human dimensions in wildlife management education: Pre-service opportunities and in-service needs. *Wildlife Society Bulletin* 20(1):8–14.

Hendee, J. C. 1974. A multiple-satisfactions approach to game management. *Wildlife Society Bulletin* 2(3):104–13.

Hendee, J. C., and D. R. Potter. 1971. Human behavior and wildlife management: Needed research. *Transactions of the North American Wildlife and Natural Resources Conference* 36:383–96.

Huth, H. 1990. *Nature and the American: Three centuries of changing attitudes.* Lincoln: University of Nebraska Press.

Kuhn, T. S. 1962. *The structure of scientific revolutions.* Chicago: University of Chicago Press.

Leopold, A. 1933. *Game management.* New York: Charles Scribner's Sons.

Manfredo. M. J. 1989. Human dimensions of wildlife management. *Wildlife Society Bulletin* 17:447–49.

Manfredo, M. J., D. J. Decker, and M. D. Duda. 1998. What is the future of human dimensions of wildlife? *Transactions of the North American Wildlife and Natural Resources Conference* 63:278–92.

Mann, C. C. 2005. *1491: New revelations of the Americas before Columbus*. New York: Vintage Books.

Robinson, W. L., and E. G. Bolen. 1984. *Wildlife ecology and management*. New York: Macmillan.

Scalet, C. G. 2007. Dinosaur ramblings. *Journal of Wildlife Management* 71(6):1749–52.

CHAPTER 7

Toward a Framework for Integrating Human Dimensions in Wildlife Management

Irene Ring

Conflicts between biodiversity conservation and other human activities are increasingly widespread and can have severe impact on rural livelihoods and the success of conservation measures (Woodroffe, Thirgood, and Rabinowitz 2005). Changes in civil society's attitudes and the success of conservation management have resulted in wildlife prospering again, returning to areas from where they had disappeared and even spreading to new habitats, such as the great cormorant in Europe. In other parts of the world, human pressure on wildlife is still increasing. Developments in wildlife management have brought forth new concepts and tools (e.g., Clark, Curlee, and Reading 1996; Treves et al. 2006; Woodroffe, Thirgood, and Rabinowitz 2005) that allow us to study and resolve these conflicts and to seek to create favorable conditions for both wildlife and humans. Such strategies, however, demand an integration of different ecological and social sciences. Although human dimensions research is increasingly becoming an integral part of wildlife decision making (Vaske, Shelby, and Manfredo 2006), linking natural and social scientific disciplines for integrative biodiversity research remains a major challenge (Jentsch et al. 2003; Gilbert and Hulst 2006). This chap-

---

The project "Development of a procedural framework for action plans to reconcile conflicts between the conservation of large vertebrates and the use of biological resources: Fisheries and fish-eating vertebrates as a model case" (with project acronym FRAP standing for Framework for Reconciliation Action Plans) was funded under the EU Fifth Framework Program.

ter disentangles the human dimensions of wildlife management by focusing on two essential issues. First, it argues that a systematic yet problem-oriented integration of social scientific disciplines is a crucial factor in effective science-based wildlife management. Second, bridging science and society is a transdisciplinary prerequisite for successful long-term wildlife management. This implies effectively involving relevant actors, interest groups, and affected people in wildlife decision making. Integrative biodiversity research is especially important when dealing with human-wildlife conflicts, which forms the focus of this chapter in order to highlight the crucial role of human dimensions.

A Basic Framework for Human-Wildlife Conflict Management

Figure 7.1 presents a generic framework for integrating human dimensions in wildlife management. Each module addresses a different topic for reconciling human-wildlife conflicts (Klenke et al. forthcoming). The modules are organized in three phases, including (1) screening of the conflict (module 1), (2) assessing and analyzing the situation from an ecological, legal, economic, and social sciences perspective (modules 2–6), and (3) developing resolution strategies (modules 7–10). In the following, we concentrate on the human dimension modules of this framework.

Figure 7.1 **A framework for integrating human dimensions in wildlife management**

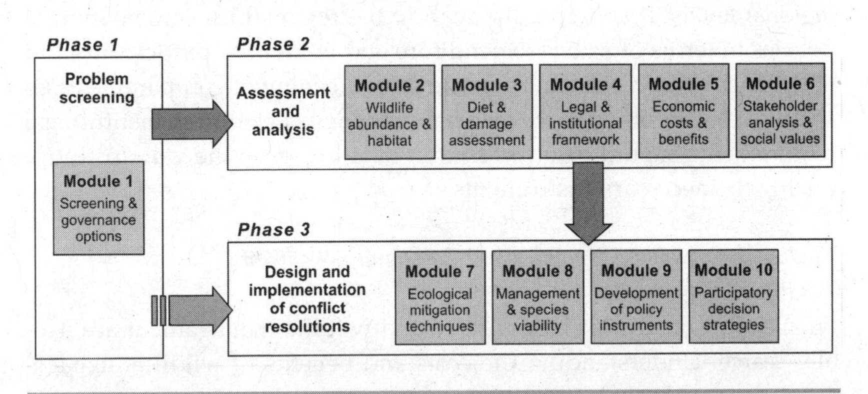

Source: adapted from Klenke et al. (forthcoming).

Module 1: Problem Screening and Governance Options

In phase 1, problem screening identifies promising governance options. Existing knowledge and major knowledge gaps are identified through expert and stakeholder interviews. This information facilitates an understanding of which modules will be most important in addressing the problem and deciding which actors, agencies, and interest groups should be involved: Module 4 identifies existing policies, relevant governmental levels (e.g., local, regional, or national), international aspects, and the major public actors. Modules 5 and 9 include a regional socioeconomic assessment and address the costs and benefits of wildlife management to different interest groups, as a basis for improving policies and developing economic incentives (e.g., payments for ecosystem services or damage compensation schemes). Modules 6 and 10 explore the views of important stakeholder groups (e.g., NGOs or professional associations) as well as educational and communications strategies currently in place, in preparation for developing participatory decision-making strategies.

Module 4: Legal and Institutional Framework

In phase 2, legal, economic, and social aspects of the conflict assessment are covered. The legal and institutional framework comprises the administrative responsibilities of wildlife management agencies. Policy instruments and their implementation are analyzed in cooperation with the relevant authorities. Inconsistencies between laws and regulations at different governmental levels should be checked (Similä et al. 2006). Depending on the problem, it may be useful to get an impression of the historical development of policy implementation. Problems with wildlife management are usually most prominent at the local and regional levels. It is helpful to analyze the regional implementation of policies in terms of public expenditure and to identify participants and nonparticipants in relevant programs. A screening of comparable cases and policies in other places is recommended. Legal and institutional requirements should be addressed in detail to pave the way for introducing the necessary instruments.

Module 5: Regional Economics and Costs and Benefits of Wildlife Management

Financial resources for biodiversity and wildlife management are usually scarce. Understanding the costs and benefits of wildlife management is crucial when identifying effective policies and measures that support wildlife management. Regional considerations must also be weighed at this stage, including an assessment of the study region's socioeconomic characteristics and the importance of the economic sectors relevant to or in conflict with wildlife management (Santos, Antunes, and Ring forthcoming).

The direct costs of wildlife management include operational and management costs (e.g., salaries, infrastructure, equipment). The total cost of wildlife management, however, also includes indirect or opportunity costs associated with the benefits foregone and the damages caused by wildlife to land users or individuals, and compensating those who bear them. Benefits may be diminished or lost through prohibited resource use due to wildlife protection. An analysis of damage caused by wildlife in physical and economic terms is essential for the development of wildlife compensation schemes (for an overview, see Haney 2007). Transaction costs influence the choice of one policy scheme over another in terms of cost-effectiveness (Schwerdtner and Gruber 2007).

On the side of wildlife benefits, use values and nonuse values are relevant (Conover 2002). Biodiversity-related values are usually derived on the basis of individual preferences and focus on single, specific services. Innovative methods increasingly value the multiple functions of ecosystem services provided by wildlife, taking into account institutional processes and arrangements across a range of different stakeholders (Turner et al. 2003). Owing to their potential for incorporating deliberative and discursive processes, group-based valuation techniques are increasingly used to elicit the economic benefits of wildlife (Lienhoop and MacMillan 2007).

Whereas the costs of wildlife management tend to be incurred at the local and regional levels, its benefits are more widespread. An important challenge consists in developing suitable institutional mechanisms and policy instruments for reconciling the local costs and global benefits of wildlife conservation and management (Perrings and Gadgil 2003; Ring 2008).

Module 6: Stakeholder Views and Social Values

This module identifies and describes relevant actors and stakeholder groups. The stakeholder analysis serves to generate an understanding of stakeholders' views, perceptions, attitudes, and values regarding wildlife and its associated problems and conflicts. A useful methodological approach is discourse analysis that focuses on existing and potential communication among stakeholders (Wilson 2004). It aims at identifying the facts, values, and interests that people associate with the conflict. Often, the views of affected local people in rural areas can differ quite considerably from those of the remote urban population that attaches value to wildlife conservation. Nevertheless, broad-based support from the general public for specific programs may ensure the sustainable financing of certain policy schemes.

In well-institutionalized human-wildlife conflicts, a stakeholder forum or committee may exist (organized by a state agency or NGO) that already gathers together relevant actors and interest groups in a participatory process at regular intervals. Here, researchers must gain the trust of the parties involved in order to build on existing processes, and inclusion of these fora is always a starting point for sound management strategies.

Module 9: Integrated Development of Policies

In phase 3, natural and social scientific results from phase 2, modules 2–6 (assessment and analysis of the conflict), are integrated in order to design and implement conflict resolution strategies (see fig. 7.1). Relevant findings from the ecological modules address the abundance of wildlife, ecological damage assessment, ecological mitigation techniques, population viability, and monitoring requirements. Ecological research results have to be integrated with those from legal, economic, and social research in order to design and improve wildlife management policies. Policy development also builds on earlier policy analysis and (regional) implementation data gathered, as well as on economic analyses regarding costs and benefits, and considers the values and attitudes of actors and stakeholder groups in conflict with wildlife. Taking into account the disciplinary findings of phase 2, policy instruments should now be evaluated in more detail with regard to (1) their effectiveness, (2) their cost-effectiveness, (3) their perception by stakeholders, and (4) their potential for including relevant actors in wildlife decision making (Ring, Schwerdtner, and Santos forthcoming).

Wildlife management policies ideally are a policy mix consisting of binding regulations, such as species protection, regulation, and derogation measures. They further involve economic incentive-based instruments to reconcile private costs and social benefits of species protection, including payments for ecosystem services and damage compensation schemes. Last but not least, activities directed at civil society are essential in wildlife management policies, although they remain somewhat neglected at times. This relates partly to communicative and educational instruments, partly to participatory decision making.

Module 10: Participatory Decision Making

A structured approach to participatory decision making in human-wildlife conflicts can be described by four steps (Rauschmayer forthcoming): (1) the conflict has to be characterized, indicating whether a participatory process is feasible and, if so, how it can be achieved, (2) an appropriate method must be chosen, (3) a decision must be made on who the process facilitator will be, and (4) the participants in the process need to be selected.

Participatory decision making always involves public agencies, sometimes at different governmental levels. The commitment of public agencies to treat seriously the outcome of a participatory process is an essential ingredient in its success. Criteria guiding the design of context-specific stakeholder involvement strategies need to be tailored to both the agencies and the stakeholders concerned (Chase, Decker, and Lauber 2004). Local knowledge and the participation of local stakeholders should not be neglected (Treves et al. 2006). In highly institutionalized conflicts participatory processes may already be in place, whereas for recent conflicts such processes may need to be set up. Participatory approaches do not always involve extensive processes or the participation of all stakeholders—or even the public. In some cases, windows of opportunity exist for participatory processes; in others, they do not. In such instances, decision-making strategies may simply involve gaining more knowledge and presenting new information about improved management practices to stakeholders. In serious conflicts, data collection and scientific work may have to be embedded in a participatory process in order to gain broad acceptance for new knowledge.

Managing the Conflicts between Fisheries and Fish-Eating Vertebrates in Europe

Setting the Scene: Model Conflicts and Regions

Improved environmental conditions and strict nature protection laws have resulted in rare or locally extinct animal species returning and increasing in numbers; this, in turn, is reigniting old conflicts between humans and wildlife. The conservation of large vertebrates, in particular carnivores or piscivores, frequently leads to intense conflicts with other human activities. This is especially the case where human food production—for example, in artificial or natural fishponds, aquaculture in lagoons, or coastal fishing—also offers attractive food resources to fish-eating vertebrates. The relationship between the conservation of Eurasian otters (*Lutra lutra*), gray seals (*Halichoerus grypus*), and great cormorants (*Phalacrocorax carbo*), respectively, and fisheries provides helpful models for these conflicts. These vertebrates cause significant damage to fisheries by preying on commercially important fish species. For each of the three model conflicts selected, two regions in different European Union (EU) member states were compared as part of the EU-funded project FRAP (Framework for Reconciliation Action Plans), which followed the generic framework presented earlier (Klenke et al. forthcoming). The comparisons included Denmark versus Italy for cormorants, central Europe (Germany, Czech Republic) versus Portugal for otters, and Finland versus Sweden for gray seals. For each conflict and region, the ecological and socioeconomic basis of the conflict was assessed, conflict mitigation strategies and their implementation were analyzed, improvements suggested, or new strategies developed.

Assessing the Model Conflicts: Legal, Economic, and Social Aspects

Regarding the *legal and institutional framework*, species protection regulation is relevant in each of the countries studied. The use of protective hunting as a mitigation measure varies from conflict to conflict and from country to country. In Denmark, the first national cormorant management plan was set up in 1992 and has gone through several revisions since then (Jepsen and Olesen forthcoming). In Sweden, a national gray seal management plan that coordinates the various policies and mitigation measures has been in operation since 2001; Finland is currently setting up a national seal management plan (Bruckmeier, Westerberg, and Varjopuro forthcoming). In Saxony, Germany, a species protection plan exists for the heavily protected otter, acknowledging the state's role in the regeneration of the otter population. Here, the focus still is on conservation measures rather than conflict management. Economic incentives and instruments based on information and training do not exist everywhere, but a few countries do use them extensively.

The legal framework at EU level was analyzed with regard to the options it offers and the limitations it imposes for member states in designing their national conflict management strategies (Similä et al. 2006). European funds are used for biodiversity conflict management in some countries but could be more extensively used in others. Fisheries funds are still largely neglected in this context. European state aid law has set limits for national compensation policies, especially in Finland.

A *socioeconomic assessment* made it possible to characterize the regions in economic terms, to evaluate the importance of fisheries in a regional context, and where possible, to assess the economic impacts of conflicts between fisheries and biodiversity conservation.

In the case of the otter conflicts, the model regions display some similarities. Both the Sado Estuary in Portugal and Upper Lusatia in Germany are part of an economically depressed region, suffering above-average unemployment rates and below-average income. Both are rural areas, where the regional economic significance of the conflict is low, even if it has some relevance at the local level (Santos-Reis et al. forthcoming; Myšiak, Schwerdtner, and Ring 2004).

There are also a number of common characteristics in the conflict between gray seals and coastal fisheries in Finland and Sweden (Bruckmeier, Westerberg, and Varjopuro forthcoming). Although the conflict is not evident on the basis of aggregate socioeconomic figures at national or regional levels, it is important at a local level. In Finland, the study region Kvarken is one of the few areas in the country where coastal fishing is still an occupation pursued by a relatively large proportion of the local population. The same holds for the Swedish model regions in Södermanland and Östergotland. After all costs such as fish losses, compensation schemes, support to seal-safe gear, monitoring of populations, R&D, and so on are considered, the seal conflict also becomes relevant in strict economic terms. Owing to a steadily increasing gray seal population (annual growth rate of more than 8 percent in the northern Baltic) and continuing economic pressure on coastal fisheries, the conflict has assumed a growing trend.

For the cormorant conflict, the regional situations differ. In Denmark, the economic importance (value) of the conflict is rather small, since the related economic activity (pound net fisheries) has very little social and economic relevance. In the future the conflict may shift from pound net fisheries to anglers, resulting in greater regional socioeconomic impacts (Jepsen and Olesen forthcoming). The cormorant conflict in the Po delta in Italy has a different socioeconomic setting. The majority of the population in the study region works in activities directly or indirectly related to fishing and aquaculture, meaning that the conflict is highly significant in socioeconomic terms. Owing to the substantial growth of the cormorant population in Europe, this conflict has also turned into a dispute at the EU level (Rauschmayer and Behrens forthcoming).

The main outcome of the *stakeholder analysis* and of stakeholders' views and attitudes was an increased sensitivity to the wide range of differences that exist at the local level between these conflicts involving fisheries and protected vertebrates (Wilson 2004, 354ff.). Critical differences emerged regarding the degree to which the conflict had already been addressed by creating conflict management institutions.

The Portuguese case is at one extreme; the FRAP project's efforts constituted a first attempt to find solutions for managing the conflict between otters and fish farms. The cases with existing national management plans for the conflict species are at the other extreme (Sweden, Denmark), indicating a high degree of formalization of the conflict. In addition to managing the conflict, the national management plans strongly influence the themes addressed in stakeholder debates (Bruckmeier, Westerberg, and Varjopuro forthcoming). Wilson (2004, 355) points out that "the Swedish and to some extent the Danish cases demonstrate how existing detailed plans carry a danger of the 'juridification' of the issue, i.e., turning it into a debate over legalisms, which can cause the exclusion of important perspectives and increased difficulties for possible reforms."

Compared with southern Bohemia in the Czech Republic, the relationship between Saxon fish farmers and the otters is relatively relaxed: otters are regarded as "belonging to the landscape" (Zwirner and Wittmer 2004). This is also thanks to a number of EU cofinanced measures introduced by the Free State of Saxony in Germany that support technical defensive measures and offer fish farmers various compensation payments (Similä et al. 2006).

In Finland, an active stakeholder forum exists, originating from a project launched in 2001 by the Kvarken Council. Its aim was to reach a common understanding of the seal's role in the region (Sava and Varjopuro 2007). Process matters, as does the inclusion of relevant stakeholders, for an important aspect of the Finnish model conflict is that the stakeholders accept most of the mitigation measures put into practice (Bruckmeier, Westerberg, and Varjopuro forthcoming).

Policy Development and Participatory Decision Strategies: Lessons Learned

The assessment of the conflicts from different disciplinary perspectives had implications regarding wildlife management and conservation policies. This holds for the evaluation of existing policies, the analysis of different regulation scenarios through modeling techniques, the development of improved instruments, as well as participatory decision strategies. Based on the results from the case studies, existing reconciliation plans have been revised (Denmark) or newly developed (Portugal), policies for conflict management have been advanced (compensation payments for otter damage in Germany), and project findings have been considered in the course of developing a national species management plan (Finland). Regarding EU policies, most direct contributions have been made to the EU Biodiversity Action Plan for the Conservation of Natural Resources (European Commission 2001), by providing a framework for action plans and by illustrating this framework for selected threatened species.

We found highly institutionalized conflicts (Denmark, Italy, Sweden, Finland, and Germany) as well as conflicts with a rather short institutional tradition (Czech Republic, Portugal). The agreed participatory actions that have been undertaken ranged from stakeholder information (Germany, Italy), contribution to a new national plan (Finland), midterm assessment of an existing national plan (Sweden), participatory improvement of reconciliation measures (Czech Republic), and elaboration of participatory decision-making strategies (Portugal) to elaboration of recommendations for improving the national cormorant management plan, while feeding in new scientific knowledge strengthening fishermen's positions that had not been taken seriously before (Denmark) (Rauschmayer 2006; Bruckmeier, Westerberg, and Varjopuro forthcoming; Jepsen and Olesen forthcoming; Poledníková et al. forthcoming). A European-level reconciliation action plan for cormorants is strongly requested by some stakeholders, though resisted by others. It was elaborated in 1997 but never adopted (Behrens, Rauschmayer, and Wittmer 2008). The approach in Portugal was exceptional, because there were no instruments targeted at the otter-aquaculture conflict. The Portuguese team used a series of workshops to develop suitable policy instruments together with stakeholders; this enabled closely related policy development with stakeholder involvement, a process still going on beyond the confines of the FRAP project itself (Santos-Reis et al. forthcoming).

One overall lesson to be learned is that biodiversity conflict management certainly needs interdisciplinary and participatory approaches to derive scientifically sound and socially relevant conflict resolutions. Despite the costs in terms of resources and time, the FRAP results showed how important continual interaction between ecological and social scientists is for developing robust biodiversity reconciliation strategies.

Transfer Potential and Challenges Ahead

Owing to its generic nature and modular structure, the framework presented here for integrating human dimensions into wildlife management can be transferred to related problems. Originally developed for large and protected vertebrate species, which compete with humans for biological resources, it is certainly applicable to human-wildlife conflicts in a broader sense.

When the framework is transferred beyond the European context, national and—depending on the federal system concerned—state regulations will certainly become more relevant. In the European Union, by contrast, species regulations such as the Habitats and Birds Directives provide a common framework for implementation by member states, as do the Common Agricultural and Fisheries Policies (Similä et al. 2006).

Conservation policies are directed primarily toward the conservation and sustainable use of biodiversity and related ecosystem services. They should be ecologically effective and socially acceptable and allocate scarce resources in a cost-effective way. However, marginalized groups require specific attention. The more low-income regions and poorer people are affected by human-wildlife conflicts, the more sustainable livelihood issues have to be integrated in the design of management strategies (Woodroffe, Thirgood, and Rabinowitz 2005). Recent literature increasingly focuses on the need to analyze the trade-off between conservation and equity objectives and calls for resolution strategies that contribute to poverty reduction and sustainable livelihoods (Landell-Mills and Porras 2002; Millennium Ecosystem Assessment 2005). Biodiversity policies have the potential to improve livelihoods if marginalized social groups, such as poor farmers or indigenous people, are potential service providers, that is, if the marginal lands where they live also have high biodiversity complementarity or provide further ecosystem services. In these cases, the trade-off between ecological, economic, and social objectives has to be made explicit, not least in order to ensure sustainable land use and the support of local communities for protected areas and wildlife conservation (Johannesen 2007).

Literature Cited

Behrens, V., F. Rauschmayer, and H. Wittmer. 2008. Managing international 'problem' species: Why pan-European cormorant management is so difficult. *Environmental Conservation.* 35(1):55–63.

Bruckmeier, K., H. Westerberg, and R. Varjopuro. Forthcoming. Baltic Sea reconciliation in practice: The seal conflict and its mitigation in Sweden and Finland. In *Human-wildlife conflicts in Europe*, eds. R. Klenke et al. Heidelberg: Springer Verlag.

Chase, L. C., D. J. Decker, and T. B. Lauber. 2004. Public participation in wildlife management: What do stakeholders want? *Society and Natural Resources* 17(7):629–39.

Clark, T. W., A. P. Curlee, and R. P. Reading. 1996. Crafting effective solutions to the large carnivore conservation problem. *Conservation Biology* 10(4):940–48.

Conover, M. 2002. *Resolving human-wildlife conflicts: The science of wildlife damage management.* Boca Raton, FL: Lewis Publishers.

European Commission. 2001. *Biodiversity Action Plan for the Conservation of Natural Resources.* Communication from the Commission to the Council and the European Parliament. COM(2001)162 final. Brussels, March 27, 2001.

Gilbert, K., and N. Hulst. 2006. *SoBio: Mobilising the European social research potential in support of biodiversity and ecosystem management. Final report.* Tilburg, Netherlands: European Centre for Nature Conservation.

Haney, J. C. 2007. *Wildlife compensation schemes from around the world: An annotated bibliography.* Conservation Science and Economics Program. Washington, DC: Defenders of Wildlife.

Jentsch, A., H. Wittmer, K. Jax, I. Ring, and K. Henle. 2003. Biodiversity: Emerging issues for linking natural and social sciences. *GAIA* 12(2):121–28.

Jepsen, N., and T. Olesen. Forthcoming. Cormorants in Denmark: Re-enforced management and scientific evidence. In *Human-wildlife conflicts in Europe*, eds. R. Klenke et al. Heidelberg: Springer Verlag.

Johannesen, A. B. 2007. Protected areas, wildlife conservation, and local welfare. *Ecological Economics* 62:126–35.

Klenke, R., I. Ring, A. Kranz, N. Jepsen, F. Rauschmayer, and K. Henle, eds. Forthcoming. *Human-wildlife conflicts in Europe: Fisheries and fish-eating vertebrates as a model case.* Heidelberg: Springer Verlag.

Landell-Mills, N., and I. Porras. 2002. How can markets for environmental services be pro-poor? Forestry and Land Use Program (FLU), London: International Institute for Environment and Development.

Lienhoop, N., and D. MacMillan. 2007. Valuing wilderness in Iceland: Estimation of WTA and WTP using the market stall approach to contingent valuation. *Land Use Policy* 24(1):289–95.

Millennium Ecosystem Assessment. 2005. Ecosystems and human well-being: Biodiversity synthesis. Washington, DC: World Resources Institute.

Myšiak, J., K. Schwerdtner, and I. Ring. 2004. Comparative analysis of the conflicts between carp pond farming and the protection of otters (*Lutra lutra*) in Upper Lusatia and South Bohemia. *UFZ Discussion Papers* 7/2004. Leipzig: UFZ Helmholtz Centre for Environmental Research.

Perrings, C., and M. Gadgil. 2003. Conserving biodiversity: Reconciling local and global public benefits. In *Providing global public goods: Managing globalization*, ed. I. Kaul, P. Conceição, K. Le Goulven, and R. U. Mendoza, 532–56. Oxford: Oxford University Press.

Poledníková, K., A. Kranz, L. Poledník, and J. Myšiak. Forthcoming. Otters causing conflicts: The fish farming case of the Czech Republic. In *Human-wildlife conflicts in Europe*, eds. R. Klenke et al. Heidelberg: Springer Verlag.

Rauschmayer, F., ed. 2006. *Recommendations for effective stakeholder interactions.* FRAP project report. Leipzig: UFZ Helmholtz Centre for Environmental Research.

———. Forthcoming. Module 10: Designing participatory decision strategies. In *Human-wildlife conflicts in Europe*, eds. R. Klenke et al. Heidelberg: Springer Verlag.

Rauschmayer, F., and V. Behrens. Forthcoming. Screening the cormorant conflict on the European level. In *Human-wildlife conflicts in Europe*, eds. R. Klenke et al. Heidelberg: Springer Verlag.

Ring, I. 2008. Biodiversity governance: Adjusting local costs and global benefits. In *Public and private in natural resource governance: A false dichotomy?*, ed. T. Sikor, 107–26. London: Earthscan.

Ring, I., K. Schwerdtner, and R. Santos. Forthcoming. Module 9: Development of policy instruments. In *Human-wildlife conflicts in Europe*, eds. R. Klenke et al. Heidelberg: Springer Verlag.

Santos, R., P. Antunes, and I. Ring. Forthcoming. Module 5: Regional economics and policy analysis. In *Human-wildlife conflicts in Europe*, eds. R. Klenke et al. Heidelberg: Springer Verlag.

Santos-Reis, M., R. Santos, P. Antunes, T. Sales-Luís, J. Gomes, D. Freitas, and L. Madruga. Forthcoming. Reconciliation of the conflict between otters and fish farmers: Lessons learned from the Sado Estuary in Portugal. In *Human-wildlife conflicts in Europe*, eds. R. Klenke et al. Heidelberg: Springer Verlag.

Sava, J., and R. Varjopuro. 2007. Asymmetries, conflicting interests and the possibilities for cooperation: The case of grey seals in Kvarken. *Journal of Environmental Policy and Planning* 9(2):165–84.

Schwerdtner, K., and B. Gruber. 2007. A conceptual framework for damage compensation schemes. *Biological Conservation* 134:354–60.

Similä, J., R. Thum, R. Varjopuro, and I. Ring. 2006. Protected species in conflict with fisheries: The interplay between European and national regulation. *Journal of European Environmental Planning and Law* 3(5):432–45.

Treves, A., R. B. Wallace, L. Naughton-Treves, and A. Morales. 2006. Co-managing human-wildlife conflicts: A review. *Human Dimensions of Wildlife* 11:383–96.

Turner, R. K., J. Paavola, S. Farber, P. Cooper, V. Jessamy, and S. Georgiou. 2003. Valuing nature: Lessons learned and future research direction. *Ecological Economics* 46(3):493–510.

Vaske, J. J., L. B. Shelby, and M. J. Manfredo. 2006. Bibliometric reflections on the first decade of human dimensions of wildlife. *Human Dimensions of Wildlife* 11:79–87.

Wilson, D. C., ed. 2004. *Discourse analysis.* FRAP project report. Leipzig: UFZ Helmholtz Centre for Environmental Research.

Woodroffe, R., S. Thirgood, and A. Rabinowitz, eds. 2005. *People and wildlife: Conflict or coexistence?* Cambridge: Cambridge University Press.

Zwirner, O., and H. Wittmer. 2004. Germany. In *Discourse analysis.* FRAP project report, ed. D. C. Wilson, 125–55. Leipzig: UFZ Helmholtz Centre for Environmental Research.

CHAPTER 8

Comanaging Wildlife in the Amazon and the Salvation of the Pacaya-Samiria National Reserve in Peru

Richard Bodmer, Pablo Puertas, and Tula G. Fang

Bushmeat hunting is an important economic activity that has been traditionally used by rural poor of the Amazon. If well managed, bushmeat hunting can provide long-term socioeconomic benefits to local communities and help conserve Amazonian biodiversity through maintaining intact rainforests. If poorly managed, bushmeat hunting will lead to the extirpation of animal populations, reduced socioeconomic benefits that rural people obtain from wildlife, and a decreased value of intact forests.

Comanaging wildlife between local communities and governmental and nongovernmental conservation institutions can be a powerful conservation strategy in the Amazon. Comanagement can enhance the sustainable use of wildlife and in turn conserve wildlife populations. Comanagement will also help implement wildlife habitat conservation

---

The authors are grateful for assistance provided by WCS Loreto staff, DICE students, Earthwatch volunteers, and Operation Wallacea and BSES students for their help during monitoring expeditions to the Peruvian Amazon. The wildlife management model was developed in collaboration with projects of the Wildlife Conservation Society (WCS) and its Amazon Landscape sites, the Durrell Institute of Conservation and Ecology (DICE), and local communities of the Amazon basin. INRENA (National Institute of Natural Resources in Peru) and the administration of the Pacaya-Samiria National Reserve must be acknowledged for their unrelenting efforts in conserving the national reserve. WCS, WWF-Peru, the Darwin Initiative, Earthwatch, Operation Wallacea, and the Gordon and Betty Moore Foundation are thanked for their financial support.

and help conserve the entire array of biodiversity. In addition, comanaging wildlife can be used to set nonhunted source areas that are in fact a type of fully protected area that concurs with the cultural and socioeconomics of the rural people.

Comanaging wildlife is currently helping to conserve Amazon forests using a management model based on the Wildlife Conservation Society's Amazon landscape sites. This model is based on extensive research on wildlife populations, human hunting practices, the cultural and economics of rural communities, and landscape-level conservation approaches.

The Wildlife Management Model

Previous research has shown important background conditions for comanaging wildlife in the Amazon. First, bushmeat is an important resource for rural people who hunt wildlife for consumption and local sale (Robinson and Bodmer 1999), and these people value the long-term socioeconomic importance of bushmeat (Bodmer, Pezo Lozano, and Fang 2004). In addition, rural people living farther from urban settlements rely more on bushmeat than those living closer to rural settlements. Areas farther from urban settlements also have greater biodiversity value than those closer to urban settlements, because those farther away have a more complete composition of biodiversity (Salovaara et al. 2003).

Research has shown that not all species are appropriate for bushmeat hunting. In the Amazon, certain wildlife species, including peccaries, deer, and large rodents have evolved life history strategies that make them less vulnerable to overhunting than other species and more appropriate as bushmeat species. Other wildlife taxa, such as lowland tapir, primates, and carnivores, are more vulnerable to bushmeat hunting and are not appropriate as bushmeat species (Bodmer, Eisenberg, and Redford 1997).

Conservation programs in the Amazon demonstrate that rural communities can successfully set up community-based wildlife management programs that reduce hunting of species not appropriate for bushmeat hunting and maintain sustainable harvests of species more appropriate for bushmeat hunting (Bodmer and Puertas 2000). However, community-based wildlife management is more successful if management plans concur with the cultural and socioeconomic reality of the communities (Bodmer 1994).

Evaluating sustainability of wildlife hunting is key to setting up community-based wildlife management in the Amazon. Over the last decade considerable effort was devoted to evaluating sustainability of bushmeat hunting in the Amazon using population harvest models, such as the unified harvest model (Bodmer and Robinson 2004). In addition, rural communities can monitor their impact on wildlife populations using hunting registers and catch-per-unit effort (CPUE) analysis (Puertas and Bodmer 2004).

Maintaining intact wildlife habitat is needed to maintain healthy wildlife populations for sustainable harvests. Destroying wildlife habitat damages wildlife populations and results in unsustainable bushmeat hunting (Bodmer and Ward 2006).

Wildlife populations go through unpredictable cycles that cause uncertainty for sustainable hunting. Socioeconomic drivers also go through unpredictable cycles that cause uncertainty about hunting pressure (Fragoso, Bodmer, and Silvius 2004), such as demand from local bushmeat markets and economic constraints on rural families. Source-sink areas buffer against biological and socioeconomic uncertainty of bushmeat hunting. Source areas are nonhunted areas adjacent to hunted (sink) areas. Wildlife emigrates out of source areas and immigrates into sink areas, if sink areas have been overhunted (Novaro, Redford, and Bodmer 2000).

The background conditions described here were used to develop a wildlife management model based on guidelines for wildlife management plans. Wildlife management plans form the basis of comanagement in many Amazonian sites. The wildlife management model allows rural communities to comanage wildlife hunting through community-based management plans, incorporating the following guidelines:

1. Develop culturally and socioeconomically acceptable community-based wildlife management plans.
2. Focus wildlife hunting on appropriate bushmeat species.
3. Prohibit or drastically reduce hunting of species not appropriate for bushmeat.
4. Set initial hunting levels using the unified harvest model.
5. Monitor hunting pressure using catch-per-unit effort (CPUE).
6. Maintain intact wildlife habitat.
7. Set nonhunted source areas adjacent to hunted areas.

Communities are inclined to set up guidelines that are culturally and socioeconomically acceptable. Implementing the guidelines ensures that wildlife populations are not overhunted and conserves animals through sustainable use. Implementing the guidelines also ensures that wildlife habitat is kept intact, helping conserve the entire range of biodiversity, not only bushmeat species. In addition, implementing the guidelines incorporates source areas as an integral part of management plans. These source areas are in fact a type of community-protected area that allows animal populations to flourish in undisturbed environments. Community protected areas not only conserve animals hunted for bushmeat, they also protect a broad array of rainforest biodiversity. But even more important, communities agree with and help defend nonhunted source areas, because they understand that some areas need protection for long-term benefits. This situation is in contrast to traditional protected areas that often exclude local people from areas that were once their traditional hunting grounds.

Comanaging Wildlife in the Pacaya-Samiria National Reserve, Peru

Because the importance of comanagement can be seen in the Pacaya-Samiria National Reserve, we will present this area as a case study for comanaging wildlife as a key conservation strategy for Amazonian forests. The Pacaya-Samiria National Reserve, situated in northeastern Peru, is one of the largest protected areas in Peru, spanning over two thousand square kilometers of tropical rainforest (fig. 8.1). The Pacaya-Samiria National Reserve is a unique flooded forest that has one of the greatest diversities of animals and plants found anywhere on Earth (INRENA 2000).

The aquatic and terrestrial wildlife of the Pacaya-Samiria National Reserve basin has recovered significantly over the last decade (Bodmer and Puertas 2007). The Samiria River has a particularly large population of river dolphins and is one of the last remaining refuges for Amazon manatee. Giant river otters are also returning, and every year more groups of otters are sighted in the rivers, lakes, and channels. There are twelve species of primates in the reserve, many of which are commonly sighted. Macaws and wading birds are abundant, as are game birds. Peccaries, deer, tapir, and capybara are also increasing. Caimans and turtles have rebounded and are now common features of the waterways.

The Pacaya-Samiria National Reserve has approximately ninety-five thousand people living in villages and towns along its boundary

Figure 8.1 **Map of the Pacaya-Samiria Nacional Reserve**

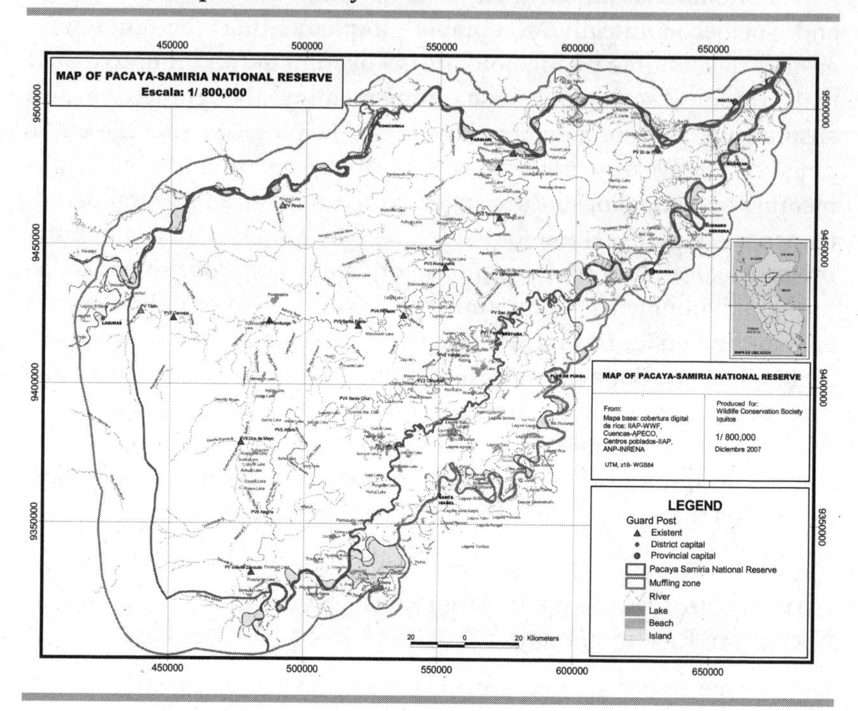

(INRENA 2000). Some of the villages lie just inside the reserve; however, there are no human settlements within the core area. Most inhabitants are Cocama-Cocamilla Indians (Puertas et al. 2000). Although their manner of dress has changed, Cocama-Cocamilla Indians still live as they did centuries ago.

History of Human Occupation in the Reserve

In the late nineteenth century several Indian groups were living along the Samiria and Pacaya rivers, including Cocama, Cocamilla, Conibos, Chamicuros, Aguanos, and Puinaguas (Raimondi 1880). Indian villages were clearly distributed throughout the two river basins, inside what is now the core area of the reserve. The human settlements within the interior of the reserve were relocated to the reserve boundary when the protected area was established in the 1940s.

A system of park guards was implemented by the reserve administration of the Peruvian government, and a set of strict controls on local people was developed during the first Management Plan period between 1986 and 1992. During this period, control on the ground was limited owing to a lack of financial resources and infrastructure. Local people were allowed to fish and hunt in restricted areas, and access was tightly controlled. Poaching was frequent despite efforts of park guards to prevent it. Poachers were largely from local communities living around the boundary of the reserve.

In 1992 a strict protectionist system was established. Park guards, who were relatively well funded through external aid from the US government, tightly controlled access to the reserve by local people. During this period, the number of poachers increased in the reserve. Likewise, animals were overhunted in the core no-use zones. In short, poaching was rampant throughout the reserve, and a higher level of conflict between reserve employees and local people became dangerous. In November 1997, a group of local people had their fishing nets confiscated by park guards. In retaliation, the fishermen, armed with machetes, attacked a park guard station, killing two young biologists and one park guard.. The news made national headlines, and the situation clearly required attention by the National Institute of Natural Resources (INRENA) in Peru.

Shortly after the attack, the head of the reserve was replaced. The new administration began to implement a strategy involving local people in comanagement of the reserve, especially for hunting and fishing. This included setting up management groups that have responsibility for managing an area of the reserve in accordance with wildlife management plans. The management groups are allowed to use a limited amount of natural resources under plans they develop with technical assistance from biologists, which require approval by INRENA and the reserve administration. The groups are given the responsibility of helping to control poaching in their area.

The Pacaya-Samiria National Reserve has clearly gone through several types of management systems. The reserve currently has a comanagement policy in which local people have responsibility for managing natural resources through comanagement and following wildlife management plans that are community based.

Impact of Comanagement

During the period of strict control, local people stated that they had no long-term vision of the reserve and feared that the reserve administration would implement even stricter measures at any moment. Their attitude was that they had to poach as much as possible, as fast as possible, since their future was uncertain.

When the park administration changed and the reserve began to incorporate local communities in comanagement, attitudes of local people also changed (Puertas et al. 2000). Local management groups were given areas to manage and were no longer considered poachers. They were able to use a limited amount of resources legally and with reserve administration approval. Many local people changed their attitude toward the reserve and began to see long-term benefits of the reserve. The reserve became part of their future plans, and there was increasing interest in getting involved. Many local people now see the socioeconomic benefits of the reserve and are themselves helping with its conservation. Hunting has decreased substantially, because poachers have become managers and because local people have kept other poachers out of their management areas (table 8.1).

Results of Comanagement in the Reserve

Animal censuses were conducted during the changes in the management policy of the Samiria River basin. Censuses of mammals and black caimans from 1995 were compared with those from 2005. The 1995 data correspond to the period of the reserve administration's strict control of local people, whereas 2005 data correspond to the period of local involvement and comanagement. Data reported herein were collected by the authors and their research teams and reported in detail elsewhere (Aquino, Bodmer, and Gil 2001; Bodmer et al. 1999; Buell 2003; Dullao 2004; Isola 2000; Moya, Pezo, and Verdi 1981; Reyes et al. 2001; Street 2004; Watson 2004). Key species for conservation that have increased in the reserve include the woolly monkey, howler monkey, white-lipped peccary, lowland tapir, black agouti, giant river otter, and black caiman (fig. 8.2).

The census results showed that animal populations in the Samiria River basin recovered significantly between the period of strict control and the period of comanagement. While this is only a correlation, we feel that the cause and effect can be justified by the changes in attitudes of local people between these two periods. The level of poaching was much greater during the period of strict control when hunting pressure was considerably greater. Local people saw no future in the reserve and considered the reserve administration as an enemy that took away their

TABLE 8.1 **Number and Percent of Animals Hunted by Community of San Martin in 1997 and 2004.**

		1997		2004	
LATIN NAME	COMMON NAME	TOTAL NUMBER HUNTED	% HUNTED	TOTAL NUMBER HUNTED	% HUNTED
MAMMALS					
Artiodactyla					
Tayassu pecari	white-lipped peccary	6	5	24	57
Tayassu tajacu	collared peccary	8	7		
Mazama americana	red brocket deer	4	3		
Perissodactyla					
Tapirus terrestris	lowland tapir	4	3		
Primates					
Alouatta seniculus	howler monkey	29	25	6	14
Ateles chameck	spider monkey	3	3		
Cebus apella	brown capuchin	10	9	1	2
Cebus albifrons	white-faced capuchin	2	2		
Pithecia monachus	monk saki monkey	3	3		
Lagothrix lagotricha	woolly monkey	17	15	2	5
Saimiri boliviensis	squirrel monkey	1	1		
Rodentia					
Agouti paca	paca	18	16	8	19
Dasyprocta spp.	black agouti	6	5	1	2
Xenarthra					
Dasypus spp.	armadillo	4	4		
TOTAL		115		42	

access to natural resources in their traditional lands. This resulted in both a rebellious attitude toward the reserve administration and a fear that future controls would be even stricter.

The conflict between local people and the reserve came to a climax when two biologists and a park guard were assassinated in retaliation

FIGURE 8.2 **The percent change in wildlife densities in the Samiria River between the period of strict protection (1995) and the period of co-management (2005).**

The baseline is set during the period of strict protection.

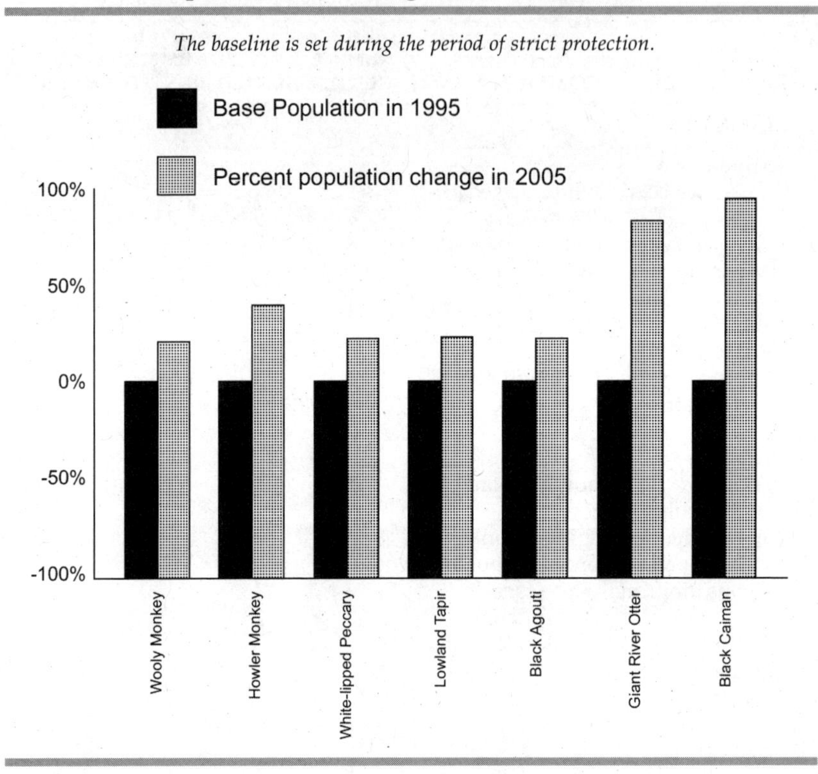

for the confiscation of fishing nets. After this incident, the strict policies of the reserve were changed and local people became involved with reserve management. As poaching activities decreased and involvement of local people in comanagement increased, animal populations have increased. There are now larger populations of most of the key wildlife species than in the recent past.

Comanaging Wildlife in Amazonia

Comanaging wildlife is clearly an important conservation strategy for the Amazon. The socioeconomic and cultural interests of local people for long-term benefits they obtain from wildlife are paramount to successful conservation. Local people are becoming the wardens of wildlife through comanagement programs throughout the Amazon. The case study of the Pacaya-Samiria National Reserve supports the notion that comanagement can work as a conservation strategy. The case study also shows that externally imposed strict protection can often fail in the long term, because it does not adequately involve participation of local people.

The wildlife management model was developed over a decade of research, conservation activities, and case studies. The wildlife management model is proving to be an important conservation strategy for the Amazon, because it conserves wildlife populations and wildlife habitats and sets up nonhunted areas all within a participatory comanagement approach that incorporates the cultural and socioeconomics of local people. The model has been used in different sites throughout the Amazon basin, both inside and outside protected areas. For example, the wildlife management model is being used as a comanagement strategy in the Kaa-Iya del Gran Chaco in Bolivia, the Tamshiyacu-Tahuayo Community Reserve in the Peruvian Amazon, the Greater Madidi Landscape in Bolivian Amazon, the Mamirauá and Amanã Sustainable Development Reserves in the Brazilian Amazon, and the Yasuni protected area landscape in Ecuadorian Amazon. The model is being implemented to ensure that wildlife use is sustainable, to maintain the economic and subsistence benefits that wildlife provide to local communities, and to preempt pressure on the protected areas. All the sites have shown that sustainable wildlife use through comanagement plans can promote conservation of forests and wildlife within the landscapes and complement protected-area conservation strategies.

The wildlife management model is also being used as a comanagement strategy for subsistence hunting in the Peruvian Amazon via a peccary pelt certification program. The peccary pelt certification program is a mechanism to add value to the peccary pelts in communities that manage their bushmeat hunting sustainably, through a process that certifies those communities that meet the standards of certification. Peccary pelts are exported to European countries where they are used in the manufacture of luxury gloves and shoes. The peccary pelt certification program is based on the wildlife management model guidelines that communities need to follow to attain certification. The guidelines are being implemented differently in each community depending on their socioeconomic and cultural needs.

The guidelines developed in the wildlife management model are also being proposed as a way to comanage wildlife in timber concessions. Many timber concessions in the Amazon hunt wildlife as a means of reducing costs of food purchases for their timbermen. This often leads to overhunting in timber concessions, resulting in unsustainable forest use and hampering timber certification. Implementing the guidelines of the management model will enable timber concessions to set up sustainable wildlife use and help ensure sustainable use of forest extraction.

Literature Cited

Aquino, R., R. Bodmer, and J. Gil. 2001. *Mamíferos de la cuenca del río Samiria. Ecología poblacional y sustentabilidad de la caza*. Lima: Junglevagt for Amazonas, AIF–WWF/DK y Wildlife Conservation Society.

Bodmer, R. E. 1994. Managing wildlife with local communities: The case of the Reserva Comunal Tamshiyacu-Tahuayo. In *Natural connections: Perspectives on community based management*, ed. D. Western, M. Wright, and S. Strum, 113–34. Washington, DC: Island Press.

Bodmer, R., C. Allen, J. Penn, R. Aquino, and C. Reyes. 1999. Evaluación del uso sostenible de la fauna silvestre en la Reserva Nacional Pacaya-Samiria, Perú. Arlington, VA: Nature Conservancy.

Bodmer, R. E., J. F. Eisenberg, and K. H. Redford. 1997. Hunting and the likelihood of extinction of Amazonian mammals. *Conservation Biology* 11:460–46.

Bodmer, R. E., E. Pezo Lozano, and T. G. Fang. 2004. Economic analysis of wildlife use in the Peruvian Amazon. In *People in nature: Wildlife conservation in South and Central America*, ed. K. Silvius, R. Bodmer, and J. Fragoso. New York: Columbia University Press.

Bodmer, R. E., and P. Puertas. 2000. Community-based co-management of wildlife in the Peruvian Amazon. In *Hunting for sustainability in tropical forests*, ed. J. G. Robinson and E. L. Bennett, 395–409. New York: Columbia University Press.

———. 2007. Impacts of displacement in the Pacaya-Samiria National Reserve, Peru. In *Protected areas and human displacement: A conservation perspective*, ed. K. H. Redford and E. Fearn, 29–33. WCS Working Papers, No. 29. New York: Wildlife Conservation Society.

Bodmer, R. E., and J. G. Robinson. 2004. Evaluating the sustainability of hunting in the Neotropics. In *People in nature: Wildlife conservation in South and Central America*, ed. K. Silvius, R. Bodmer, and J. Fragoso. New York: Columbia University Press.

Bodmer, R. E., and D. Ward. 2006. Frugivory in large mammalian herbivores. In *The impact of large mammalian herbivores on biodiversity, ecosystem structure and function*, ed. K. Danell. Cambridge: University of Cambridge Press.

Buell S. 2003. Activity levels and abundance of the Amazonian manatee, *Trichechus inunguis*, in the Pacaya-Samiria National Reserve, Peru BSc project. Loreto, Peru: Wildlife Conservation Society, Durrell Institute of Conservation and Ecology.

Dullao, T. 2004. Density and biomass of terrestial mammals in the Santa Elena region of the Samiria River. Canterbury, UK: University of Kent.

Fragoso, J., R. E. Bodmer, and K. Silvius. 2004. Wildlife conservation and management in South and Central America: Multiple pressures and innovative solutions. In *People in nature: Wildlife conservation in South and Central America*, ed. K. Silvius, R. Bodmer, and J. Fragoso. New York: Columbia University Press.

INRENA (Instituto Nacional de Recursos Naturales). 2000. *Plan maestro para la conservación de la diversidad biológica y el desarrollo sostenible de la Reserva Nacional Pacaya-Samiria y su zona de Amortiguamiento.* Lima: Instituto Nacional de Recursos Naturales.

Isola, S. 2000. Determinación de la distribución y abundancia de lobo de río (*Pteronura brasiliensis*) en la Reserva Nacional Pacaya-Samiria. Tesis presentada para optar el titulo de Ingeniero Forestal. Lima, Peru: Universidad Nacional Agraria la Molina.

Moya, L., R. Pezo, and L. Verdi. 1981. *Observaciones preliminares sobre la bioecología del lagarto blanco (*Caiman crocodylus L.*) en la cuenca del río Samiria,* 107–23. Peru: Iquitos.

Novaro, A. J., K. H. Redford, and R. E. Bodmer. 2000. Effect of hunting in source-sink systems in the neotropics. *Conservation Biology* 14:713–21.

Puertas, P., R. Bodmer, J. López, J. del Aguila, and A. Calle. 2000. La importancia de la participación comunitaria en los planes de manejo de fauna silvestre en el nor oriente del Perú. *Folia Amazónica* 11(1–2):159–79.

Puertas, P. E., and R. E. Bodmer. 2004. Hunting effort as a tool for community-based wildlife management in Amazonia. In *People in nature: Wildlife conservation in South and Central America*, ed. K. Silvius, R. Bodmer, and J. Fragoso. New York: Columbia University Press.

Raimondi, A. 1880. Foja No. 8. Mapa del Peru. Paris.

Reyes C., R. Bodmer, J. Garcia, and D. Díaz. 2001. Presión de caza y bases para el manejo de fauna con participación comunitaria en la Reserva Nacional Pacaya-Samiria. In *Manejo de fauna con comunidades rurales*, ed. C. Rozo, A. Ulloa, and H. Rubio, 49–55. Bogota, Colombia: Fundación Natura.

Robinson, J. G., and R. E. Bodmer. 1999. Towards wildlife management in tropical forests. *Journal of Wildlife Management* 63:1–13.

Salovaara, K., R. E. Bodmer, M. Recharte, and C. F. Reyes. 2003. Diversity and abundance of mammals in the Yavari valley. In *Perú: Yavari—rapid biological inventory*, ed. N. Pitman. Chicago: Field Museum.

Street, K. 2004. *The diet and abundance of three caiman species* (Caiman crocodilus, Melanosuchus niger *and* Paleosuchus trigonatus) *along the Rio Samiria, Peru*. Canterbury, UK: Durrell Institute of Conservation and Ecology, University of Kent at Canterbury.

Watson, K. 2004. *The ecological and structure of the primate in the Pacaya-Samiria National Reserve, Peru*. Canterbury, UK: Durrell Institute of Conservation and Ecology, University of Kent at Canterbury.

CHAPTER 9

Working with Communities to Achieve Conservation Goals

Catherine M. Hill

Ideas about the incompatibility of people and wilderness came to the fore during the colonial era in response to declining populations of game species prized by big-game hunters, who successfully lobbied for legislation to protect wildlife and their habitats (MacKenzie 1988). During the same period North American hunters sought to protect their native species through reducing off-take rates and the establishment of protected areas (Gray 1993). Subsequently, protected areas, such as national parks, which excluded people and livestock and outlawed resource extraction activities, became the dominant model for protection of threatened species and habitats worldwide. This preservationist approach has contributed to significant hardship and poverty among many vulnerable rural populations, particularly in developing countries (Newmark and Hough 2000). Populations living adjacent to protected areas bear the brunt of the costs (including estranged lands, restrictions on access to resources, and damage to crops, property, and human life), but receive few of the benefits, which are mainly the preserve of national institutions and governments, international researchers, scientific bodies, and tourists (Bell 1987).

Given this impact on rural populations, it is increasingly difficult to continue to uphold such principles and strategies that are likely to disadvantage further some of the world's poorest and most vulnerable people. This, combined with the high economic cost of effective protection to wildlife in parks (Leader-Williams and Albon 1988, but see Caro et al. 1998), the low economic returns from protected areas compared with alternative land use strategies (Norton-Griffiths and Southey 1995, cited in Adams and Hulme 2001), and ethical concerns over the exclusion and, in some cases, eviction of local people from parks (Neumann 1997, cited in Adams and Hulme 2001) has contributed to the declining support for this traditional approach to biodiversity protection.

Consequently, conservation ideology, and therefore policy and practice, have undergone significant changes in the last four decades. The stated mission of conservation has been revised, changing the focus of and justification for conservation programs worldwide from concentrating specifically on the protection of wildlife to one in which human well-being is an important, and sometimes prime, concern (Bell 1987). Ethical and human rights concerns as well as pragmatism and politics are brought into play, with the view that conservation policy should seek to maintain or improve people's well-being rather than render them more vulnerable to poverty (Blaikie and Jeanrenaud 1997). However, more mundane factors such as political convenience and economics have provided further incentive to forge links between conservation and development, as a way of widening opportunities to secure funding for conservation activities (Oates 1999) (Holdgate and Munro 1993, cited in Oates 1999).

The aims of this chapter are to examine how local communities are incorporated into conservation initiatives, discuss the likely effectiveness of these changing practices on biodiversity conservation, pinpoint some of the problems associated with these approaches, and identify ways to secure more effective strategies of working with communities to achieve conservation goals.

Communities and Conservation

Recognition that the support and cooperation of people neighboring wildlife habitat is necessary to promote long-term conservation success (World Conservation Union 1980, cited in Hackel 1999) has led to the development of a diverse range of approaches to engender local interest and support for conservation (but, see Brockington [2004], who argues biodiversity conservation can be achieved without local support). Broadly speaking, these new approaches can be categorized as community-based conservation (CBC) and integrated conservation and development projects (ICDPs) (Spiteri and Nepal 2006). The main precept of CBC initiatives is that promoting community participation in planning and implementing conservation projects will generate a sense of ownership of natural resources and thus accountability among communities, so encouraging sustainable resource management.

ICDPs, instead, promote community support by providing economic and social development opportunities in exchange for, or as compensation for, conservation (Newmark and Hough 2000; Hartley 1997, cited in Brockington 2002).

Communities: Who or What Are They?

The term *community* is used frequently within the conservation and development literature to define target groups of people for interventions. Often, it is assumed that a community consists of a group of people bound together by their spatial location, ethnicity, religion, language, or political system (Leach, Mearns, and Scoones 1999). These commonalities, which represent community, are assumed to promote cooperation and homogeneity of purpose and action, thus fostering equity among members. However, these assumptions do not necessarily hold for communities. Within any group of individuals, degree of access to and control over resources reflects the interplay between age, sex, livelihood, resources, hierarchy, and political structures (Agrawal and Gibson 1999; Sharpe 1998). Therefore, assuming common beliefs, needs, and thus actions among community members is naive. What constitutes "benefits" is not the same for all community members; therefore, any one benefit may not provide an adequate conservation incentive for all stakeholders (Spiteri and Nepal 2006).

Identifying the individuals who comprise a community is not always straightforward. However, inclusion or exclusion from the target community has important implications within CBC or ICDP initiatives. Inclusion or exclusion determines which stakeholders can access benefits, shapes the composition of comanagement committees, and influences representation in the decision-making process. It can result in exclusion of individuals from participation and can mask internal power relations that cause unequal distribution of costs and benefits and underrepresentation of marginalized groups in decision-making processes.

Working with Communities to Achieve Conservation Goals: How Effective Is It?

Since the 1970s CBC approaches and ICDPs have been promoted as an alternative to exclusively protectionist strategies. However, within the last two decades researchers and practitioners have questioned the efficacy of these methods in delivering effective biodiversity conservation

(Barrett and Arcese 1995; Songorwa 1999) and improving local livelihood security and well-being (Hackel 1999; Newmark and Hough 2000). An important consideration is whether such methods can address both conservation and development needs simultaneously. This raises the further point of how to define and measure "success." How success is defined will determine whether a project is considered successful or not. For example, a project promoting community use of nontimber forest products as an alternative income stream to cutting trees for timber protects forest structure, ensuring continued watershed benefits. However, competition between people and wild animal species for fruits, herbs, or rattans may be greatly increased. There is successful protection of natural resources, but this is not biodiversity conservation, because the emphasis is on reducing the impact on specific natural resources rather than on biodiversity (Hill 2002).

Delivering Biodiversity Conservation

To date, there is little empirical evidence that CBC methods or ICDPs result in effective biodiversity conservation (Hulme and Murphree 2001a), though some case studies demonstrate positive outcomes for individual species or habitats. Examples include the Community Baboon Sanctuary in central Belize, where voluntary changes in land management practices have supported an increase of approximately 50 percent in black howler monkey populations since the sanctuary's inception (Alexander 2000), and the Annapurna Conservation Area, Nepal, where vegetation surveys confirmed that land managed within the CBC area contained greater floral density and diversity compared with land outside the conservation area (Bajracharya, Furley, and Newton 2005). However, methodological problems can make it extremely difficult to show causal links between ecological change and conservation interventions, and time and resource constraints often hamper the collection of adequate data to monitor and evaluate impacts on biodiversity as part of local initiatives (Kangwana 2001).

Delivering Social and Economic Development to Local Communities

Local communities can value CBC initiatives and ICDPs for their contribution to social and economic benefits, particularly when revenue sharing or income generation occurs (e.g., Alpert 1996). However, while many projects have achieved some degree of success in delivering benefits, including development opportunities, this has not always provided satisfactory compensation for the costs of conserving wildlife, or incentives sufficient to produce the desired changes in people's behavior toward wildlife and habitats (Abbot et al. 2001; Emerton 2001; Infield and Namara 2001).

Livelihood strategies practiced by people living in relatively marginal environments are characterized by their flexibility and diverse nature, features that facilitate survival in a changeable environment (Moran 2000). This, combined with the impact of external influences such as greater inclusion within a cash-based economy or increased exposure to alternative social and cultural ideas through education or contact with outsiders, may encourage further diversification in livelihood strategies. Consequently, to assume that by gaining access to alternative income sources local communities will reduce their dependence on natural resources, rather than incorporate these alternative income streams into their already diverse livelihood activities, is not necessarily appropriate. Instead, people might be expected to maintain or even increase their previous exploitation levels in order to make the most of any new economic opportunities. Therefore, promoting strong linkages between livelihood strategies and biodiversity conservation, whereby the continued availability of valued natural resources is dependent on their successful conservation, gives user groups an incentive to (1) practice sustainable resource use and (2) prevent users external to the community from accessing valued natural resources. Again, the likely success of this strategy depends on local communities receiving a high enough return rate on their conservation investments to provide a strong incentive to adopt appropriate management practices.

Generating Positive Attitudes toward Conservation and Conservation Agencies

Perhaps the most valuable outcome of community conservation initiatives to date is their capacity to promote positive attitudes among local people toward conservation and conservation agencies (Arjunan et al. 2006; Mehta and Heinen 2001; Weladji, Moe, and Vedeld 2003). However, closer examination of the literature reveals that individual stakeholders' views reflect the degree to which they are recipients of tangible benefits (Wild and Mutebi 1997); the extent to which their specific livelihood activities or control over natural resources is affected (King 2007; Masozera et al. 2006; Scholte et al. 2006; Weladji, Moe, and Vedeld 2003); their sense of "ownership" and involvement with decision making and implementation (Alexander 2000; Bajracharya, Furley, and Newton 2005); and the degree to which management and conflict resolution processes incorporate local cultural structures and norms (Lepp and Holland 2006; Zimmerman et al. 2001). This further illustrates that different stakeholders hold different views and perspectives, and their concerns reflect, at least in part, changes in their own likely access to and control over particular resources.

Future Developments

CBC approaches and ICDPs have proved largely disappointing in their capacity to deliver effective long-term biodiversity conservation and development to rural populations in the developing world. Their main contribution is their capacity to promote more positive attitudes toward wildlife and the project of conservation rather than necessarily the specific initiative. Consequently, they have the capacity to provide an effective mechanism for improving relationships between wildlife authorities, conservation agencies, and local people. The challenge now is to develop and refine these approaches to secure better outcomes for biodiversity and communities.

Addressing Some of the Shortfalls of CBC Initiatives and ICDPs

Identifying and Delineating Communities

A greater clarity and understanding of the social complexities of communities needs to be incorporated into project design to facilitate more equitable distribution of resources, greater transparency within benefit-sharing and decision-making processes, and a recognition that benefits need to have significant value to provide communities with real incentives to adapt their behavior. Moreover, there is often a need to reassess situations over time. For example, where there is immigration into an area, the boundaries of who is included within any existing community initiative might need revising. If immigrant groups are not included within the target community, they may sabotage existing programs, either intentionally through direct action (Dzingirai 2003) or indirectly through increased impact on local natural resources (Oates 1995). However, there can be resistance from existing community members to including "outsiders" because they increase the pool of recipients for benefits, reducing the average share. Recognizing that communities are not static, homogeneous groups of people but diverse entities with a membership that changes is an important step. How this is incorporated into the mechanisms of long-term projects is likely to be challenging but needs to be addressed more effectively in the future.

The Magnitude and Guarantee of Benefits to Communities

Gaining access to natural resources rather than protecting them, and accessing benefits generated by interventions, are often reported as being local people's primary interest in participating in CBC and ICDP schemes (Mugisha 2002, cited in Lepp and Holland 2006; Masozera et al. 2006). A common interpretation is that local people are not interested in conservation, though whether this is really the case is hard to determine. However, where livelihood security is, or becomes, relatively precarious, people's decisions about natural resource use reflect the need to respond to short-term or immediate crises, rather than secure long-term availability. In addition, community members most likely to express the strongest support for CBC enterprises or ICDPs are those who have the least to lose (King 2007; Wild and Mutebi 1997), suggesting that development opportunities provided by current projects are often not adequate to offset costs to all community members. Consequently, ensuring that benefits created are of an appropriate level to provide real incentives for community members to actively participate in conservation is vital.

Projects that derive revenue for communities through sport hunting or wildlife viewing are vulnerable to the effects of war, civil insurrection, currency fluctuations, and tourist choice, all factors outside the community's control (Masozera et al. 2006). Where cash crops are introduced to reduce local dependence on natural resources or offset costs of conservation initiatives, communities and individuals can experience sudden income decline because of changing commodity markets, as happened to coffee and cocoa growers around Korup National Park, Cameroon (Alpert 1996). Under such circumstances, even where benefits are directly and explicitly linked with biodiversity conservation outcomes, local people may have to make up the shortfall in their household income by increasing their reliance on natural resources. Flexibility and the capacity to reassess and, where necessary, revise approaches are important. It should therefore be recognized that CBC initiatives and ICDPs may not always function satisfactorily in the long-term, so it is important, where possible, to take account of this during planning and implementation.

Transparency and Management Systems

Problems arise if community members perceive an inequitable distribution of benefits (Kellert et al. 2000), benefits received do not match expectations (Abbot et al. 2001; Alexander 2000), benefits received are not considered adequate to offset the costs (Emerton 2001), or benefits are not selectively directed toward those individuals bearing the brunt of the costs (Abbot et al. 2001; Walpole and Goodwin 2000). Many of these issues are associated with, or exacerbated by, a lack of transparency within benefit-sharing and decision-making processes, which weakens trust between the different stakeholders. Corruption and participation in illegal resource utilization can occur at all levels from villagers to government officials and international agencies (Polansky 2003). Ensuring strong linkages between the various stakeholder groups and implementing powerful systems of checks and balances to ensure that no one individual or group has excessive authority would help address these issues (Agrawal and Gibson 1999; Hulme and Murphree 2001b).

Monitoring and Evaluation

Securing effective biodiversity conservation is one of the weakest aspects of many CBC and ICDP interventions. Strengthening linkages between benefits received and biodiversity conservation is important, as is incorporating appropriate systems to monitor and evaluate the impacts of different initiatives on fauna, flora, and the community. This information can then contribute to informed management decisions. Encouraging community participation in the process of monitoring and interpretation of the results would help foster a sense of ownership locally and increase transparency, especially important where data are used to set extraction rates or hunting quotas for local consumption of resources.

Time Scale

Sufficient trust and rapport between the various stakeholders need to be established and maintained for community-based initiatives to succeed. This may be further hampered in situations where previously communities have been in conflict with wildlife agencies or other relevant institutions. Considerable sensitivity to local cultural systems and structures is required. Consequently, developing and implementing participatory conservation management programs is a lengthy and multifaceted process that extends beyond the period of time that most funding agencies are willing or able to support interventions. Setting up such programs includes the initial development and implementation of the project, and the incorporation of monitoring and evaluation systems to oversee progress and inform further modifications where appropriate. This may take ten years or more (Polansky 2003), yet projects are often expected to achieve long-term success in less than half this time. Many donor agencies work on three- to five-year funding cycles and expect tangible outputs during that period, which can provide a further barrier to positive outcomes to community-based initiatives and programs.

Conclusion

Despite the great enthusiasm for CBC and ICDP strategies to involve local communities in achieving conservation during the latter part of the twentieth century, their capacity to deliver reliable community development and biodiversity conservation has not met expectations. While some conservationists, and more recently funding agencies, have become disillusioned with this apparent lack of success, it is clear that community participation in conservation initiatives and the delivery of even quite small development opportunities generally promotes a much more positive regard for wildlife, wildlife agencies, and protected areas. The challenge remains, however, how best to develop the necessary strategies and institutional structures to secure a more reliable future for wildlife and local communities.

Literature Cited

Abbot, J. I. O., D. H. L. Thomas, A. Gardner, S. E. Neba, and M. W. Khen. 2001. Understanding the links between conservation and development in the Bamenda Highlands, Cameroon. *World Development* 29(7):1115–36.

Adams, W. M., and D. Hulme. 2001. If community conservation is the answer in Africa, what is the question? *Oryx* 35(3):193–200.

Agrawal, A., and C. C. Gibson. 1999. Environment and disenchantment: The role of community in natural resource management. *World Development* 27:629–49.

Alexander, S. E. 2000. Resident attitudes towards conservation and black howler monkeys in Belize: The Community Baboon Sanctuary. *Environmental Conservation* 27(4):341–50.

Alpert, P. 1996. Integrated conservation and development projects. *BioScience* 46 (11):845–55.

Arjunan, M., C. Holmes, J.-P. Puyrarand, and P. Davidar. 2006. Do developmental initiatives influence local attitudes towards conservation? A case study from the Kalakad-Mundanthurai Tiger Reserve, India. *Journal of Environmental Management* 79: 188-97.

Bajracharya, S. B., P. A. Furley, and A. C. Newton. 2005. Effectiveness of community involvement in delivering conservation benefits to the Annapurna Conservation Area, Nepal. *Environmental Conservation I* 32(3):239–47.

Barrett, C. B., and P. Arcese. 1995. Are integrated conservation-development projects (ICDPs) sustainable? On the conservation of large mammals in sub-Saharan Africa. *World Development* 23(7):1073–84.

Bell, R. H. V. 1987. Conservation with a human face: Conflict and reconciliation in African land use planning. In *Conservation in Africa: People, policies and practice*, ed. D. Anderson and R. Grove, 79–101. Cambridge: Cambridge University Press.

Blaikie, P., and S. Jeanrenaud. 1997. Biodiversity and human welfare. In *Social change and conservation*, ed. K. Ghimire and M. Pimbert, 46–70. London: Earthscan Publications.

Brockington, D. 2002. *Fortress conservation: The preservation of the Mkomazi Game Reserve, Tanzania*. Oxford: James Currey.

———. 2004. Community conservation inequality and injustice: Myths of power in protected area management. *Conservation and Society* 2(2):411–32.

Caro, T. M., N. Pelkey, M. Borner, K. L. I. Campbell, B. L. Woodworth, B. P. Farm, J. L. Kuwai, S. A. Hiuish, and E. L. M. Severre. 1998. Consequences of different forms of conservation for large mammals in Tanzania: Preliminary analyses. *African Journal of Ecology* 36:303–20.

Dzingirai, V. 2003. CAMPFIRE is not for Ndebele migrants: The impact of excluding outsiders from CAMPFIRE in the Zambezi Valley, Zimbabwe. *Journal of Southern African Studies* 29(2):445–59.

Emerton, L. 2001. The nature of benefits and the benefits of nature: Why wildlife conservation has not economically benefited communities in Africa. In *African wildlife and livelihoods: The promise and performance of community conservation*, ed. D. Hulme and M. Murphree, 208–26. Oxford: James Currey.

Gray, G. G. 1993. *Wildlife and people: The human dimensions of wildlife ecology*. Urbana and Chicago: University of Illinois Press.

Hackel, J. D. 1999. Community conservation and the future of Africa's wildlife. *Conservation Biology* 13(4):726–34.

Hill, C. M. 2002. Primate conservation and local communities: Ethical issues and debates. *American Anthropologist* 104(4):1184–94.

Hulme, D., and M. Murphree. 2001a. Community Conservation in Africa: An introduction. In *African wildlife and livelihoods: The promise and performance of community conservation*, ed. D. Hulme and M. Murphree, 1–8. Oxford: James Currey.

———. 2001b. Community conservation as policy: Promise and performance. In *African wildlife and livelihoods: The promise and performance of community conservation*, ed. D. Hulme and M. Murphree, 280–97. Oxford: James Currey.

Infield, M., and A. Namara. 2001. Community attitudes and behaviour towards conservation: An assessment of a community conservation programme around Lake Mburu National Park, Uganda.*Oryx* 35(1):48–60.

Kangwana, K. 2001. Can community conservation strategies meet the conservation agenda? In *African wildlife and livelihoods: The promise and performance of community conservation*, ed. D. Hulme and M. Murphree, 256–66. Oxford: James Currey.

Kellert, S. R., J. N. Mehta, S. A. Ebbin, and L. L. Lichtenfeld. 2000. Community natural resource management: Promise, rhetoric, and reality. *Society and Natural Resources* 13:705–15.

King, B. H. 2007. Conservation and community in the new South Africa: A case study of the Mahushe Shongwe Game Reserve. *Geoforum* 38:207–19.

Leach, M., R. Mearns, and I. Scoones. 1999. Environmental entitlements: Dynamics and institutions in community-based natural resource management. *World Development* 27:225–47.

Leader-Williams, N., and S. Albon. 1988. Allocation of resources for conservation. *Nature* 336:353.

Lepp, A., and S. Holland. 2006. A comparison of attitudes toward state-led conservation and community-based conservation in the village of Bigodi, Uganda. *Society and Natural Resources* 19:609–23.

MacKenzie, J. M. 1988. *The empire of nature: Hunting, conservation and British imperialism*. Manchester, UK, and New York: Manchester University Press.

Masozera, M. K., J. R. R. Alavalapati, S. K. Jacobson, and R. K. Shrestha. 2006. Assessing the suitability of community-based management for the Nyungwe Forest Reserve, Rwanda. *Forest Policy and Economics* 8:206–16.

Mehta, J. N., and J. T. Heinen. 2001. Does community-based conservation shape favourable attitudes among locals? An empirical study from Nepal. *Environmental Management* 28:165–77.

Moran, E. F. 2000. *Human adaptability: An introduction to ecological anthropology*. Boulder, CO: Westview Press.

Neumann, R. P. 1997. Primitive ideas: protected area buffer zones and the politics of land in Africa. *Development and Change* 28:559–82.

Newmark, W., and J. Hough. 2000. Conserving wildlife in Africa: Integrated conservation and development projects and beyond. *BioScience* 50:585–92.

Norton-Griffiths, M., and C. Southey. 1995. The opportunity costs of biodiversity conservation in Kenya, *Ecological Economics* 12:125–39.

Oates, J. F. 1995. The dangers of conservation by rural development: A case-study from the forests of Nigeria. *Oryx* 2 (2):115–22.

———. 1999. *Myth and reality in the rain forest*. Berkeley, Los Angeles, London: University of California Press.

Polansky, C. 2003. Participatory forest management in Africa: Lessons not learned. *International Journal of Sustainable Development and World Ecology* 10:109–18.

Scholte, P., W. T. De Groot, Z. Mayna, and Talla. 2006. Protected area managers' perceptions of community conservation training in West and Central Africa. *Environmental Conservation* 32(4):349–55.

Sharpe, B. 1998. "First the forest": Conservation, "community" and "participation" in South-West Cameroon. *Africa* 68(1):25–45.

Songorwa, A. N. 1999. Community-based wildlife management (CWM) in Tanzania: Are the communities interested? *World Development* 27(12):2061–79.

Spiteri, A., and S. K. Nepal. 2006. Incentive-based conservation programs in developing countries: A review of some key issues and suggestions for improvement. *Environmental Management* 37(1):1–14.

Walpole, M. J., and H. Goodwin. 2000. Local economic impacts of dragon tourism in Indonesia. *Environmental Conservation* 28:160–66.

Weladji, R. B., S. R. Moe, and P. Vedeld. 2003. Stakeholder attitudes towards wildlife policy and the Bénoué Wildlife Conservation Area, North Cameroon. *Environmental Conservation* 30(4):334–43.

Wild, R. G., and J. Mutebi.1997. Bwindi Impenetrable Forest, Uganda: Conservation through collaborative management. *Nature and Resources* 33(3–4):33–51.

Zimmerman, B., C. A. Peres, J. R. Malcolm, and T. Turner. 2001. Conservation and development alliances with the Kayapo of south-eastern Amazonia, a tropical forest indigenous people. *Environmental Conservation* 28(1):10–22.

CHAPTER 10

Humans and Wildlife as Ecosystem Components in Integrated Assessments

Kathleen A. Galvin, Randall B. Boone, Shauna B. BurnSilver, and Philip K. Thornton

Historically, humans have been considered external to ecosystems and seen as perturbations on natural systems. Their land use was seen as disturbing ecological systems otherwise in equilibrium. This notion has changed in part due to the realization that there are few if any ecosystems that have been untouched by human land use. Further, many ecosystems, such as the savannas of Africa, which still hold the greatest numbers of wildlife, may have coevolved with human land use, especially pastoral land use (Galvin et al. 2002; Reid, Galvin, and Kruska 2008). However, today, for example, loss of wildlife habitat is the leading threat to biodiversity, but treating it as a single sector problem has proved futile (e.g., Brooks et al. 2002; Naeem 2002). To understand the interactions between humans, particularly their land use, and ecosystem components such as wildlife requires a systems approach. This is particularly useful when several forces simultaneously affect humans and their environments such as climate change, high human population growth rates, land tenure and land use changes, among others (e.g., Galvin et al. 2008; Reynolds et al. 2007). Such a comprehensive framework aims to create a better understanding of humans and ecosystems

Our thanks to Richard Solonga Supeet, Leonard Onetu, and participating Maasai. These analyses were supported by the Belgian-supported Reto-o-Reto *project to the International Livestock Research Institute, Nairobi, Kenya (Reid, Principal Investigator), and by the U.S. National Science Foundation Biocomplexity program under grant DEB-0119618 to N. T. Hobbs et al.*

by investigating interactions of the linked systems and by acknowledging that socioecological systems are complex adaptive systems (Davidson-Hunt and Berkes 2003; Galvin et al. 2006).

Why take such an approach? It is currently acknowledged that we cannot separate humans from the environment when discussing either human development or ecosystem sustainability. For reasons elucidated earlier, they are linked and processes of global change have made it abundantly clear that humans have impact on ecological processes and vice versa (National Research Council 1999; Adger et al. 2007; Christensen et al. 2007).

This general framework is called the resilience framework. It is presented here in some detail and describes concepts of resilience, adaptation, adaptive capacity, and ecosystem services that are useful when addressing research and management problems that link humans to their environments. Use of this framework may enable us to transition toward sustainability in ways that meet human needs and conserve the life support systems better than if each were addressed alone.

Resilience Framework

Resilience refers to the capacity of a social and ecological system to withstand disturbances and absorb change (e.g., from climate, economic shocks, policy flips) and continue to maintain itself and develop. It assumes that change and unpredictability is a natural state of a human-ecological system and that this is very different from the paradigm that assumes stability with a mechanistic view of nature (Berkes, Colding, and Folke 2003). Loss of resilience can cause loss of valuable ecosystem services such as climate regulation, fresh water and clean air, production of plants and animals, food and wood, and fiber (Millennium Ecosystem Assessment 2005) and thus can limit sustainability. Many terrestrial and marine systems have, as a result of human impacts, shifted into less productive states in their capacity to generate ecosystem services to society. Yet all societies rely on ecosystem services, and when those services degrade, it affects not only the ecosystem but human well-being as well.

One way of measuring resilience is to understand the adaptive capacity of the socioecological system, which is the set of mechanisms or preconditions that a society has that allows responses to changes (Nelson, Adger, and Brown 2007). Adaptive capacity is represented by the set of available cultural/societal resources both public and private. These resources include technology and infrastructure, economic capital, governance institutions, information, and social learning, for example.

People adapt through activities that help them to cope with changes. These might include public actions such as using crop insurance or humanitarian relief and private actions such as household livelihood diversification and intensification, selling assets, or community monitoring of the change. These management strategies are adaptive if they emphasize learning by doing and take the view that resource management policies can be treated as experiments from which managers can learn. By doing this, systems are managed for flexibility rather than for maintaining stability. If the system is flexible, then it is considered adapted; however, system adaptedness changes as the context changes.

As populations increase and needs and expectations rise, one of the changes that is occurring in many societies but particularly in pastoral systems is that land use is intensifying (Reid, Galvin, and Kruska 2008; Little et al. 2001). Pastoral land use or ranching is the raising of domestic livestock for direct consumption and for market production. Both subsistence-based livestock production and commercial production are undergoing multiple changes. Some changes are external forces such as immigration into better-watered pastoral lands where agriculture is possible, and others are policies that promote land tenure changes such as protected-area development. However, many forces internal to pastoral systems are forcing changes in production strategies. These forces include population growth, rising expectations, and land tenure changes from communal property rights to private property (BurnSilver, Worden, and Boone 2008). As a result of these forces, and where herders have sufficient capital, herders have intensified the production of livestock by developing water, fencing lands to control grazing, and investing in greater veterinary care and changing livestock breeds (Blench 2001; BurnSilver, Worden, and Boone 2008; Stokes et al. 2008).

The integrated assessment case study presented here is from Kajiado District, Kenya, a place where many of the forces of change mentioned above are being played out. Diversification of livelihoods and intensification of livestock production are emerging strategies in this economy, as households struggle to increase outputs under conditions of declining mobility due to increased sedentarization. This has been triggered by the ongoing process of fragmenting the land into group and individual ranches. The result is the increase of private parcels of land with limited or no seasonal mobility. Maasai pastoralists who live here have begun to invest in water development, the subject of the case study.

Integrated Assessment

Land use intensification may be an inevitable, and in some cases desirable, process in pastoral landscapes. However, there are many pathways to intensified use. Pathways will have deleterious effects on some ecosystem traits or some households and positive effects on others. The myriad compensatory changes systems exhibited when land use is intensified are impossible for humans to fully grasp. We use an approach called *integrated assessment* as one means of forming views about how intensification may affect at least some aspects of ecosystems and households (Rotmans and van Asselt 1996; Galvin et al. 2006). Integrated assessment is best suited for local contexts where land change is predominately a local issue. Computer models that capture the important ecological processes and rules of interaction between people form the foundation of our methods. Integrated assessment involves far more than computer modeling. Ecological and anthropological fieldwork, policy analyses, literature review, and the creation of management scenarios are some components of an integrated assessment. That said, the tools that integrate the information remain the models and are the focus of the work described here.

Ecosystem and Household Modeling

We use an integrative ecosystem model called SAVANNA in our work, tightly joined with a model called PHEWS that simulates pastoral households and decision making. Coughenour began developing SAVANNA in the Turkana region of Kenya more than twenty years ago, and it has been improved continually and applied around the world (e.g., Coughenour 1992; Thornton, Galvin, and Boone 2003; Boone et al. 2005). SAVANNA is a spatially explicit ecosystem model that divides landscapes into a grid of square cells. Spatial data are used to characterize the cells as to elevation, slope, aspect, and soil and land cover type. The model uses weather data from stations to create estimates of rainfall and temperature. During simulations, plants represented by functional groups compete for water, nutrients, light, and space. Herbivores are represented as functional groups as well but are often species, such as wildebeest (*Connochaetes taurinus*), cattle, and sheep. Animals feed on specified plant functional groups, gain energy, and use energy for basal metabolism, gestation, lactation, and travel. Surplus energy goes to weight gain, reflected in reported condition indices. Birth rates decrease and mortality increases as condition indices decline, one of many potential feedbacks within the model.

Thornton, Galvin, and others developed PHEWS, the Pastoral Household Economic Welfare Simulator. PHEWS is a rule-based model that represents decision making by pastoralists (Thornton et al. 2006). In PHEWS, people consume milk and homegrown grain and vegetables, sugar in tea, and some meat. Their energy intake is compared with their needs, and if inadequate and they have funds, they will purchase grain for consumption. If funds are in surplus, they may purchase livestock. If the pastoralists cannot afford to purchase food, it is assumed that relatives and friends or agencies contribute it.

We assess each SAVANNA/PHEWS application by various means. Then in scenario analyses, we represent the most important interactions in the ecosystem as it exists currently, in baseline or control simulations. We then alter select attributes of the simulations, and only those attributes, to address land use or policy questions that are pending. We share simulation results with local stakeholders to ensure that our findings are plausible and useful.

Adding Water Sources in Imbirikani Group Ranch, Kajiado, Kenya

For much of the year, water is a rarity in semiarid and arid systems. For many wild and domestic ungulates, their need to drink regularly and the energetic costs of travel limit their grazing areas to points around water sources (Western 1975; Redfern et al. 2003). In Imbirikani Group Ranch, Kajiado, Kenya, wells, boreholes, and small reservoirs augment a series of natural water sources used by livestock and wildlife. Wildlife migrate from the swamps of Amboseli Basin they use in dry seasons into the surrounding landscape during wet seasons. An important additional series of water sources are from a pipeline that extends from the Tanzanian border and slopes of Mount Kilimanjaro and draws from Nolturesh River (fig. 10.1).

An appreciation for grazing resources is shared by all Maasai, and they know that unlimited access to all areas would risk having no forage reserved for dry periods. Instead, group ranch elders implement what BurnSilver (2007) calls "staged grazing." Maasai maintain perma-

FIGURE 10.1 **Southern Kajiado District, Kenya.**

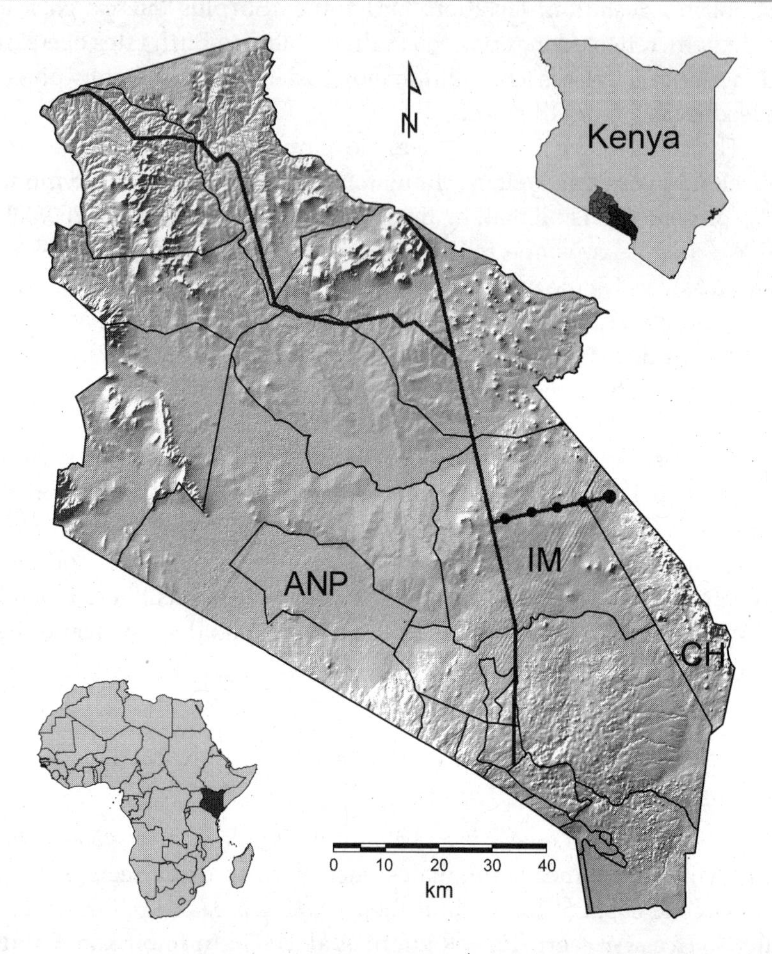

Areas labeled include Imbirikani Group Ranch (IM), the Chyulu Hills (CH), and Amboseli National Park (ANP). The dark lines show the Nolturesh Pipeline moving water northward from the slopes of Mount Kilimanjaro, and the new pipeline spur extending from the existing pipeline into the Chyulu Hills. Water points at the end of the spur and at 5 km intervals are shown as dots. District boundaries are shown in light black lines, topography in shaded gray, and the location of the area in inserts.

nent households near reliable water sources. During the wet season, areas near the permanent households are grazed, while areas far from water are kept as grazing reserves. As the area dries and forage near the households is depleted, Maasai elders open a stage farther from permanent water. In northern Imbirikani Group Ranch, permanent households are clustered around the Nolturesh Pipeline (fig. 10.1), and stages used in grazing run parallel to that. The Chyulu Hills and areas far west of the pipeline compose the final grazing stage in Imbirikani; at the end of the dry season, cattle are grazed in the Chyulu Hills grazing reserves. When the rains return, herders collapse back into the permanent zones of settlement.

One means of alleviating constraints of water shortages is to add water sources to areas far from existing sources. In 2004, the Imbirikani Group Ranch Committee received permission to construct a spur extending east-northeast from the Nolturesh Pipeline in the center of the group ranch, adding a water source to the Chyulu Hills (fig. 10.1). Stakeholders and researchers alike are cautious about adding a water source to a grazing reserve. If managed well, in the dry season cattle could reduce their energy use by avoiding the long walk back to the Nolturesh Pipeline. If managed poorly, cattle will feed in the grazing reserve when not necessary and leave no reserves for livestock or wildlife, for use when forage shortages occur.

The Nolturesh Pipeline has been pierced at intervals along its length, both legally and illegally, to provide water for residents, and damage or leaks can occur. Some of the existing water sources along the Nolturesh Pipeline are available only to livestock (and people), whereas others (e.g., from leaks) are available to livestock and wildlife. We model some effects of adding the water tank at the terminus of the Chyulu pipeline spur. We also model the repercussions of adding water sources at five-kilometer intervals along the pipeline. In each case we ask what effects might be on Maasai households and ecosystem services if livestock and wildlife only have access to the new water sources. We asked what the effects from the new water sources would be if they were freely available, and available only after particularly dry periods.

Model Adaptation

Boone and colleagues (2005, 2006) provide a detailed description of the SAVANNA application, a brief review of which follows. Imbirikani Group Ranch was represented by cells at 500 by 500 meter resolution. Seven plant functional groups and nine animal functional groups were modeled, including three livestock groups (cattle, goats, and sheep). Livestock were only allowed to use the Chyulu Hills the driest four months of the year, emulating the grazing reserve. Distance-to-water maps within SAVANNA were modified to represent the new terminal water source and water sources every five kilometers along the new pipeline. Sets of maps for livestock and wildlife were edited, allowing water sources to be used only by livestock or livestock and wildlife.

Methods of Analyses

Our results must be interpreted in light of two modeling approaches we use, one with the PHEWS model disabled, so that livestock sales and purchases do not occur, and one with PHEWS enabled. When PHEWS is disabled, the ungulate populations approach the capacity of the system. When PHEWS is enabled, Maasai who are food insecure sell cattle to purchase maize, other foods, and goats or sheep at that time, as in reality (BurnSilver 2007). These livestock sales often decrease the number of animals supported in the group ranch.

Results and Interpretation

Figure 10.2a shows the changes in ungulates reported when livestock sales (PHEWS) were disabled, and figure 10.2b shows changes in ungulates with sales enabled, for the scenarios described in the figure legend. In all simulations, the retention of the Chyulu Hills as a grazing reserve (i.e., grazed four months out of the year) continued to be in effect. Adding a water source at the end of the Chyulu pipeline had a small effect on ungulates. Adding sources every five kilometers had a larger effect, causing a decline in the overall biomass of livestock and wildlife supported (fig. 10.2a). More continual livestock grazing in areas treated as reserves (for the terminal water source) and in areas used in staged grazing (for the five-kilometer sources) decreased the numbers of animals that could be supported overall. When the new terminal water source was allowed to be used only during the driest periods (i.e., when the previous three months had less than 75 millimeters precipitation, which occurred eighty-one times during the 288 months simulated), livestock populations were much higher than in current conditions (fig. 10.2a). Wildlife biomass was higher in the simulation as well. When livestock sales (PHEWS) were enabled, livestock populations declined when herders had unlimited access to the new water source in the grazing reserve. Animals foraged in the reserve more than they otherwise would have, and populations declined when grasses were unavailable during drought. Livestock sales compounded declines, and families made up for these large deficits in monetary or energy needs by selling livestock. For example, using standardized tropical livestock units (TLUs) and human adult equivalents (AE) for

FIGURE 10.2 **Changes in livestock and wildlife populations with new water sources.**

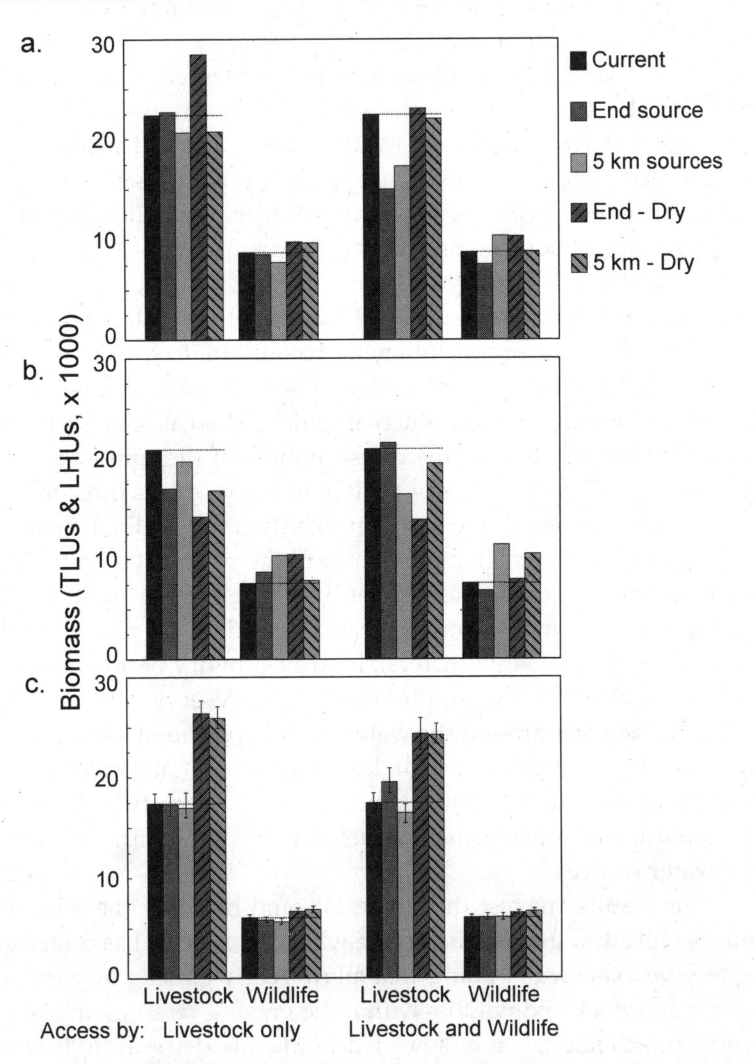

Changes in livestock (TLUs) and wildlife (LHUs) under current water conditions (Current), with an end source available (End source), with sources every 5 km along the new pipeline spur (5 km sources), and when the new water sources were used when the prior three months were dry (End–Dry; 5 km–Dry). Results are shown with (a) household modeling disabled, (b) household modeling enabled, and (c) repeated simulations with household modeling disabled. Groups of bars for livestock and wildlife are grouped into two sets, one where livestock only had access to new water sources, and one where both livestock and wildlife had access. TLUs (Tropical Livestock Units) and LHUs (Large Herbivore Units) are functionally equivalent, representing 250 kg of biomass of livestock and wildlife, respectively.

reference, adding the new water source reduced livestock from 5.27 TLUs/AE to 4.37 TLUs /AE.

If livestock and wildlife have access to the new water sources (fig. 10.2a), the pattern is in some ways opposite to that when livestock only have access. Livestock are prevented from using the Chyulu Hills for eight months of the year, but wildlife are not restricted in that way. Adding a water source allowed wildlife to use the area more often. However, use of the grazing reserve ultimately led to a decline in livestock as well as wildlife. Last, allowing animals to use the water sources only when they are dry yielded relatively high ungulate biomass (fig. 10.2a).

To reinforce these results, we ran twenty simulations for each type of access at one square kilometer resolution (to speed the simulations), using randomized weather, and with livestock sales disabled. The results were striking. When ungulates had access to the new water sources only during the driest months of the simulated period (i.e., less than 75 millimeters of rainfall in the previous three months), the number of livestock increased markedly, and wildlife increased as well (fig. 10.2c). The region surrounding the new water sources continued to act as a grazing reserve for livestock in most months (i.e., 72 percent of the 288 months modeled had rainfall in the preceding three months exceeding 75 millimeters). However, in dry periods when forage was in the shortest supply and energy reserves of the animals were low, the areas around the water sources provided forage without the need and energetic cost of traveling to distant water sources. Presumably wildlife benefited somewhat by the redistribution of livestock, reducing interspecific competition in places farther from the new water sources.

Our results suggest that there is some risk that the new water sources will allow grazers to overuse what to this point has been a grazing reserve. New water points that allow yearly grazing by either livestock or livestock and wildlife within the grazing reserve can leave the reserve unsuitable when it is needed in the late dry season. If herders and their livestock were allowed to use the new sources only when the previous three months had less than 75 millimeters of rainfall, an additional 7,000 TLUs were supported in simulations.

During dissemination meetings in June 2006 at Imbirikani Group Ranch, these results were greeted with the response, "Yes, this is what we were thinking, that the new tank could not be open all the time." Integrated assessment confirmed and quantified Maasai suspicions.

Conclusion

In general, the value of our results was not so much in the specifics, but in the discussion of directional trends and trade-offs associated with the different options for management of the new water sources, which had initially come from community members themselves. However, use of integrated assessment as a tool of analysis and management options is only as good as the data that are used in the model. In addition, the science of integrated assessment is still developing, and advancements are needed in many areas. Nevertheless, assuming the data used are accurate and appropriate, integrated assessment provides a fairly unbiased appraisal. It can explore the effects of management options on ecosystem attributes as well as on human well-being independently and together. It can address the effects of management decisions into the future and thus has implications for the long-term viability of the coupled system. It allows for active adaptive management by providing a spatial and temporal dimension to various scenario outcomes. This often allows all stakeholders to readily understand the results. Further, this type of analysis is particularly salient for those coupled human-environmental systems where people depend directly on their environment for their livelihood security, such as is the case for most pastoralists around the world. Sustainability science mandates that human-environment problems be handled together (Clark 2007; Turner et al. 2003). Species loss, water and air quality, and human needs such as food, energy, water, and shelter are linked. They are best studied together as an integrated system to maintain the adaptive capacity for those surprises that are bound to occur in the future (Nelson, Adger, and Brown 2007). Integrated assessment is a useful tool for doing just that.

Literature Cited

Adger, W. N., S. Agrawala, M. M. Q. Mirza, C. Conde, K. O'Brien, J. Pulhin, R. Pulwarty, B. Smit, and K. Takahashi. 2007. Assessment of adaptation practices, options, constraints and capacity. In *Climate change 2007: Impacts, adaptation and vulnerability*. Contribution of Working Group II to the Fourth Assessment Report of the Intergovernmental Panel on Climate Change, ed. M. L. Parry, O. F. Canziani, J. P. Palutikof, P. J. van der Linden, and C. E. Hanson, 717–43. Cambridge: Cambridge University Press.

Berkes, F., J. Colding, and C. Folke. 2003. Introduction. In *Navigating social-ecological systems: Building resilience for complexity and change*, ed. F. Berkes, J. Colding, and C. Folke, 1–29. Cambridge:: Cambridge University Press.

Blench, R. 2001. *"You can't go home again": Pastoralism in the new millennium.* London: Overseas Development Institute; Rome: the Food and Agriculture Organisation of the United Nations.

Boone, R. B., S. B. BurnSilver, and P. K. Thornton. 2006. *Optimizing aspects of land use intensification in southern Kajiado District, Kenya.* Report to the International Livestock Research Institute (ILRI), Nairobi, Kenya: ILRI.

Boone, R. B., S. B. BurnSilver, P. K. Thornton, J. S. Worden, and K. A. Galvin. 2005. Quantifying declines in livestock due to land subdivision. *Rangeland Ecology and Management* 58:523–32.

Brooks, T. M., R. A. Mittermeier, C. G. Mittermeier, G. A. B. da Fonseca, A. B. Rylands, W. R. Konstant, and P. Flick, et al. 2002. Habitat loss and extinction in the hotspots of biodiversity. *Conservation Biology* 16(4):909–23.

BurnSilver, S. B. 2007. Economic strategies of diversification and intensification among Maasai pastoralists: Changes in landscape use and movement patterns in Kajiado District, Kenya. PhD diss. Colorado State University, Fort Collins.

BurnSilver, S. B., J. Worden, and R. B. Boone. 2008. Processes of fragmentation in the Amboseli ecosystem, Southern Kajiado District, Kenya. *Fragmentation in semi-arid and arid landscapes: Consequences for human and natural systems,* ed. K. A. Galvin, R. S. Reid, R. H. Behnke Jr., and N. T. Hobbs, 225–53. Dordrecht, Netherlands: Springer Verlag.

Christensen, J. H., B. Hewitson, A. Busuioc, A. Chen, X. Gao, I. Held, and R. Jones, et al. 2007. Regional climate projections. In *Climate change 2007: The physical science basis.* Contribution of Working Group I to the Fourth Assessment Report of the Intergovernmental Panel on Climate Change, ed. S. Solomon, D. Qin, M. Manning, Z. Chen, M. Marquis, K. B. Averyt, M. Tignor, and H. L. Miller. Cambridge and New York: Cambridge University Press.

Clark, W. C. 2007. Sustainability science: A room of its own. *Proceedings of the National Academy of Sciences* 104:1737–38.

Coughenour, M. B. 1992. Spatial modelling and landscape characterization of an African pastoral ecosystem: A prototype model and its potential use for monitoring drought. *Ecological indicators,* Vol. 1, ed. D. H. McKenzie, D. E. Hyatt, and V. J. McDonald, 787–810. New York: Elsevier.

Davidson-Hunt, I. J., and F. Berkes. 2003. Nature and society through the lens of resilience: Toward a human-in-ecosystem perspective. In *Navigating social-ecological systems: Building resilience for complexity and change,* ed. F. Berkes, J. Colding, and C. Folke, 53–82. Cambridge: Cambridge University Press.

Galvin, K. A., J. Ellis, R. B. Boone, A. L. Magennis, N. M. Smith, S. J. Lynn, and P. Thornton. 2002. A test case using integrated assessment in the

Ngorongoro Conservation Area, Tanzania. In *Conservation and mobile indigenous people: Displacement, forced settlement, and sustainable development*, ed. D. Chatty and M. Colchester, 36–60. *Studies in Forced Migration* 10. Oxford: Berghahn Books.

Galvin, K. A., R. S. Reid, R. H. Behnke Jr., and N. T. Hobbs, eds. 2008. *Fragmentation in semi-arid and arid landscapes: Consequences for human and natural systems*. Dordrecht, Netherlands: Springer.

Galvin, K. A., P. K. Thornton, J. R. de Pinho, J. Sunderland, and R. B. Boone. 2006. Integrated modeling and its potential for resolving conflicts between conservation and people in the rangelands of East Africa. *Human Ecology* 34:155–83.

Little, P. D., K. Smith, B. A. Cellarius, D. L. Coppock, and C. Barrett. 2001. Avoiding disaster: Diversification and risk management among East African herders. *Development and Change* 32(3):401–33.

Millennium Ecosystem Assessment. *2005 Ecosystems and Human Well-Being: Synthesis*. Washington, DC: Island Press.

Naeem, S. 2002. Ecosystem consequences of biodiversity loss: The evolution of a paradigm. *Ecology* 83(6):1537–52.

National Research Council (NRC). 1999. *Our common journey: A transition toward sustainability*. Washington, DC: National Academy Press.

Nelson, D. R., W. N. Adger, and K. Brown. 2007. Adaptation to environmental change: Contributions of a resilience framework. *Annual Review of Environment and Resources* 32:11.1–11.25.

Redfern, J. V., R. Grant, H. Biggs, and W. M. Getz. 2003. Surface-water constraints on herbivore foraging in the Kruger National Park, South Africa. *Ecology* 84:2093–2107.

Reid, R. S., K. A. Galvin, and R. S. Kruska. 2008. Global significance of extensive grazing lands and pastoral societies: An introduction. *Fragmentation in semi-arid and arid landscapes: Consequences for human and natural systems*, ed. K. A. Galvin, R. S. Reid, R. H. Behnke Jr., and N. T. Hobbs, 1–24. Dordrecht, Netherlands: Springer.

Reynolds, J. F., D. M. Stafford Smith, E. F. Lambin, B. L. Turner II, M. Mortimore, S. P. J. Batterbury, and T. E. Downing, et al. 2007. Global desertification: Building a science for dryland development. *Science* 316:847–51.

Rotmans, J., and M. van Asselt. 1996. Integrated assessment: A growing child on its way to maturity. *Climatic Change* 34:327–36.

Stokes, C. J., R. R. J. McAllister, A. J. Ash, and J. E. Gross. 2008. Changing patterns of land use and tenure in the Dalrymple Shire, Australia. In *Fragmentation in semi-arid and arid landscapes: Consequences for human and natural systems*, ed. K. A. Galvin, R. S. Reid, R. H. Behnke Jr., and N. T. Hobbs, 93–112. Dordrecht, Netherlands: Springer Verlag.

Thornton, P. K., S. B. BurnSilver, R. B. Boone, and K. A. Galvin. 2006. Modelling the impacts of group ranch subdivision on agro-pastoral households in Kajiado, Kenya. *Agricultural Systems* 87:331–56.

Thornton, P., K. Galvin, and R. Boone. 2003. An agro-pastoral household model for the rangelands of East Africa. *Agricultural Systems* 76:601–22.

Turner, B. L. II , R. E. Kasperson, P. A. Matson, J. J. McCarthy, R. W. Corell, L. Christensen, and N. Eckley, et al. 2003. A framework for vulnerability analysis in sustainability science. *Proceedings of the National Academy of Sciences* 100:8074–79.

Western, D. 1975. Water availability and its influence on the structure and dynamics of a savannah large mammal community. *East African Wildlife Journal* 13:265–86.

PART III

Dealing with Legal and Institutional Factors of Fish and Wildlife Management

Exploding human populations around the globe have intensified human-wildlife interaction and have highlighted the need for new wildlife management strategies. Emerging international environmental problems such as global warming and biodiversity loss have clarified the need for policy, funding, and infrastructure capable of focusing on long-term management needs and objectives. Sweeping legal and institutional changes have already occurred in the first few years of the twenty-first century. The chapters in Part III provide an analysis of the changing legal and institutional landscape of wildlife management in the early twenty-first century.

Laws define the structure that society uses to manage the interface of humans with fish and wildlife. Chapter 11 overviews current legal trends in fish and wildlife policy and highlights the influence of political power in transforming wildlife management policy. Examples of political influence on wildlife management and the role of wildlife law in defining the future of wildlife management are discussed and clarified.

Wildlife law in the United States has been built on the Public Trust Doctrine. From this perspective, wildlife are ownerless property managed in trust by the government for the greatest common good. The history, conception, and threats to this Public Trust Doctrine are detailed in chapter 12. This chapter also explores institutionalization and privatization of wildlife, game ranching, unsustainable land use practices, and other issues pertaining to the Public Trust Doctrine and the future of wildlife management.

Given the uncertain future of wildlife management, the final two chapters in Part III identify creative ways to address institutional and funding problems. Developing funding sources capable of supporting long-term projects will require a creative collaboration and restructuring as recommended in chapters 13 and 14.

CHAPTER 11

Legal Trends in Fish and Wildlife Policy

Ruth S. Musgrave

The first years of the twenty-first century have proven to be an interesting and unique period for fish and wildlife policy. This chapter provides a limited overview of a few emerging and continuing legal trends in the first eight years of the twenty-first century, reviewed mostly in the context of court decisions.[1] Some trends discussed include changes in federal conservation of threatened and endangered species, political influence over science, management of species determined to be recovered and delisted under the Endangered Species Act, balancing management of scarce water and wildlife resources with pressures of growth and industry, the concept of the "built" environment, state and federal cooperation in fish and wildlife management, access to public lands, private property interests, international impacts of fish and wildlife management, and climate change.

Laws provide the structure that society utilizes to manage the interface of humans with fish and wildlife. Legal trends in fish and wildlife policy can be observed through new or changed federal, state, or local statutes, regulations, or policies. These trends are also vividly illustrated when judicial review is sought as a direct result of active, unresolved clashes between interest groups and others over fish and wildlife management and protection and proposed or existing actions that affect fish and wildlife. Since the rise of environmental activism in the 1970s and increasingly in the new century, courts have become the final arbiter of human interests that want to enforce, influence, change, or ignore fish and wildlife policy. Thus case law provides a bird's-eye view of the legal trends in fish and wildlife policy that will continue and expand as the twenty-first century unfolds.

This nation's future actions regarding climate change and other issues affecting wildlife, including decisions by its courts, will have enormous impact on the management and even the availability and survival of fish and wildlife resources all over the world. It may be acceptance of the reality of climate change, and the resulting call to action, that motivate a fundamental shift in cooperation and planning for management of valuable and dwindling fish and wildlife resources.

Species Conservation and Protection: The Endangered Species Act

The most obvious human dimension affecting wildlife is current political power that can literally transform wildlife management policy overnight. On the national level, the George W. Bush administration consistently produced policy and regulations that tended to disfavor wildlife conservation, especially endangered species, in favor of commercial stakeholder interests. The rise of skillful litigation by nonprofit membership groups that support wildlife protection kept some of the federal executive's actions or refusals to act in check. Conversely, industry and other stakeholders were also emboldened by the policies of the administration to sue the government to challenge Endangered Species Act (ESA) agency actions and decisions. Both groups' suits experienced mixed success in the courts.

For example, environmental groups increasingly and repeatedly sued the U.S. Fish and Wildlife Service for failure to act on petitions to list species under the ESA. Some courts held, for example, that new policies or claimed budgetary constraints cannot be used to avoid compliance with the listing requirements of the ESA.[2] Other courts held that the U.S. Fish and Wildlife Service's decision not to list is not considered "final agency action" that is subject to judicial review under the Administrative Procedure Act.[3] The U.S. Fish and Wildlife Service was ordered by courts to explain why species were listed as threatened (likely to become endangered) rather than endangered (in danger of extinction throughout all or a significant portion of its range), and in some instances why species were not ESA-listed despite overwhelming scientific evidence of a species' decline toward extinction.[4]

Courts also ordered the federal government to designate critical habitat for ESA-listed species, in the face of a new administration policy that designation of critical habitat is disfavored, and even threatened to hold the government in contempt of court for ignoring court orders.[5] The government also was found by courts to have issued faulty "biological opinions" issued under Section 7 of the ESA, which biological opinions concluded that a federal agency action will cause "no jeopardy" to the continued existence of an ESA-listed species.[6] Courts also held that certain ESA regulations, such as the definition of "destruction or modification of critical habitat," violate the letter of the law and thus are invalid.[7] In the meantime, developers and other industry interests jumped on the litigation bandwagon to challenge ESA listings, critical habitat designations, and related decisions.[8]

Since the 1990s, legislation in the form of riders attached to congressional bills has been used to override judicial decisions unfavorable to litigants, especially industry stakeholders. In those instances, courts must generally hold that a pending lawsuit has been rendered moot because the law that was under judicial consideration has been changed altogether.[9] Political will continued to drive federal management of wildlife in the early 2000s, to the intense frustration of some judges [10] and to the point that certain ESA-listing or critical habitat decisions were re-reviewed by the U.S. Fish and Wildlife Service because of questions about the integrity of the science and legal standards applied.[11]

In 2007 the ESA's broad reach was reined in by the U.S. Supreme Court in *National Association of Home Builders v. Defenders of Wildlife*, 127 S.Ct. 2578 (U.S., June 26, 2007). By a five-to-four majority, the Supreme Court held that the Environmental Protection Agency's granting of water discharge–permitting authority to a state is not subject to the Endangered Species Act. The Court found that the transfer of Clean Water Act (CWA) permitting authority to a state is mandatory, if the state meets nine required criteria. The majority opined that the CWA is an older statute than the ESA and that the ESA did not amend or repeal the CWA, so ESA agency consultation on impacts to listed species is not required. The overall impact of this ruling is not yet clear.

Wolves: The Next Phase of the ESA

The ESA is over thirty-five years old, and despite its broad goals and requirements for protection of listed species, and despite efforts to amend or dilute it, the law remains relatively intact, in part because of popular support. Under its protections, populations of a few listed species have been deemed recovered to the point that they are being considered for delisting or are actually delisted. As a result of delisting efforts, the ESA is entering a new phase in which fish and wildlife managers must negotiate new and complex management decisions and walk a tightrope between outspoken stakeholder opinions and interests. The reintroduction, recovery, management, and delisting of wolves illustrate the human dimensions of wildlife management in all its complexity and controversy. Wolves awaken three interests in particular: ranching, hunting, and the populist notion that generally no longer fears wolves and favors returning the charismatic predator to its natural state. Challenges to wolf management at the state, local, and federal levels are fierce, even when wildlife managers attempt to give stakeholders a voice in the final management decisions.

Wolves were nearly extirpated from most areas of the United States, but from the late 1980s to the late 1990s were reintroduced into the South, the northern Rocky Mountains, and the Southwest, and at every site legal conflicts have been intense. For example, ranchers and others who strongly opposed reintroduction of gray wolves in the Yellowstone area sued the federal government, claiming a "taking" of private property as a result of wolf reintroduction.[12] And when the gray wolf was downlisted in 2003 from endangered to threatened, wildlife groups sued, and a court found that the government's delisting policy for gray wolves was overbroad.[13] As certain wolf populations recover, states become direct stakeholders when they are requested to submit plans for taking over management of the wolf from the federal government, and may even sue the federal government if the U.S. Fish and Wildlife Service rejects their plan.[14] The state of Wyoming, incensed at having its wolf management plan rejected, went so far as to attempt to criminally prosecute federal wolf recovery officials for trespass and litter.[15]

As wolf populations are delisted under the ESA, state fish and wildlife managers for the first time are also starting to reclassify formerly protected wolves as game animals, allowing licensed hunting of once-protected wolves. This is a very new development in management of a species previously extinct in the wild, then ESA-listed, reintroduced, federally protected, and now "legally" recovered under the ESA. Hunting of formerly protected species may be an emerging trend as states have more voice in the management of wolves as well as other recovering charismatic species such as grizzly bears and bison. Meanwhile, wildlife protection interests will undoubtedly resist these changes and in particular will litigate the delisting of western gray wolf populations and Yellowstone grizzlies. Management of recovered species will have to include development of a creative and flexible multi-stakeholder framework as more species are recovered and delisted under the ESA.

The state of Alaska, though unique, may provide some insight into future trends and conflicts in state management of wolves. Wolf populations in Alaska are not listed as threatened or endangered under the ESA, and the state has a very active predator control policy that includes aerial hunting of wolves. Hunting interests, pro-wildlife groups, wildlife managers, and state citizenry clash over the aerial chasing and killing of wolves in particular. The current fish and wildlife policy of Alaska strongly favors hunting interests and pushes the envelope of, and may at times even ignore, legal requirements such as state laws, citizen voter initiatives, and court orders.[16] Other states such as Idaho and Wyoming may look to Alaska as a model for wolf management.

Allocation of Resources and the "Built" Environment

The allocation of increasingly scarce water supplies among not only aquatic and other wildlife species, but also communities and industry presents challenges for fish and wildlife and other agencies to find ways to protect fish and wildlife resources. The ESA and other laws require federal agencies to manage water supplies so that species are not placed in jeopardy. This is no easy task when at the same time federal water contracts require the U.S. Army Corps of Engineers to supply water to farmers and other commercial water users. Managing water for protection of fish and wildlife now has an added artificial dimension of the "human-built" environment, as dams and levees now affect the flow regime of almost all rivers in the United States. In addition, released hatchery fish share the same habitat as wild fish. The Bush administration argued that the altered environment should become the new "environmental baseline" for analyzing impacts to species. Courts, however, thus far disagree.[17]

These issues are at the forefront in areas such as the Columbia and Snake river basins, as courts hold time and again that the federal government must protect listed salmon and steelhead and cannot sacrifice species protection for energy production or irrigation.[18] One judge ruled against the federal government's analysis of impacts to ESA-listed salmon multiple times, and some stakeholder litigants want to consider ordering breaching of dams on the Snake River if the government cannot find a way to provide for the needs of the fish.[19] As the potential for breaching older dams becomes a reality around the country, managers will be challenged to consider the notion of removal, renewal, or even creation of the "built" environment to ensure survival of protected fish and wildlife species.

In other places such as the Missouri and Klamath river basins, fish and wildlife resources were again at the heart of goliath tug-of-wars over uses of water in the built environment, as cases were filed in multiple courts on a number of issues by multiple stakeholders, sometimes including states and local municipalities as well as Native American tribes.[20] These complex and enormous lawsuits illustrate a growing trend of legal conflicts over scarce water resources, between various and growing human needs and the need to protect and recover ESA-listed species and fish and aquatic resources.[21] One example that may provide a model for resolution of other fish and wildlife/water use issues is the eventual settlement by all parties of the conflict over allocation of water in the Rio Grande watershed, a settlement that attempts to ensure the survival of the critically endangered Rio Grande silvery minnow.[22]

Federal/State and Interstate Cooperation

In spite of conflicts over wildlife, water, and endangered species, the early years of the twenty-first century witnessed new and compelling instances of federal and state cooperation in wildlife management. States historically have been considered to be the owners of the wildlife within their borders in trust for the citizens, and as such, states shoulder the lion's share of management of game and nongame fish and wildlife.[23] In 2000 Congress approved new programs to provide additional federal assistance to the states, such as the State Wildlife Action Grants Program and the Wildlife Conservation and Restoration Program.[24] Under these programs, every state has successfully completed State Wildlife Action Plans for conservation and protection of fish and wildlife, including and especially nongame wildlife.[25]

State fish and wildlife agencies, often through the work of committees of the Association of Fish and Wildlife Agencies, are also cooperating with each other in new legal efforts as diverse as restricting the spread of exotic species and wildlife-borne diseases, developing State Wildlife Action Plans, outlawing a high-tech and unethical form of hunting using Internet cameras ("cyberhunting"), and even mitigating climate change impacts.[26] The Interstate Wildlife Violator Compact, developed in the late 1980s and continually gaining state members, also represents an example of effective cooperation among the states.[27] The compact is an interstate agreement for reciprocal enforcement of the hunting, fishing, and other wildlife laws of participating states. As an example, upon receiving a report of a hunting license suspension from a member state, the licensing authority of the home state will enter the conviction as though it occurred in the home state for the purposes of suspending hunting license privileges. More than half of the states are now compact members, and courts are upholding the compact against legal challenges, even, for example, when a neighboring state's statutory language regarding the nature of a wildlife law violation is somewhat different from a partner state's statute.[28]

Access to Wildlife and Public Lands

Growing demand for physical, recreational, and legal access to fish and wildlife as well as to public lands is a human dimension that is affecting fish and wildlife policy in a number of ways. For example, "right-to-hunt" state constitutional amendments and other pieces of legislation are being proposed or have passed in a number of states since the late 1990s.[29] However, these provisions are not necessarily beneficial for fish and wildlife management. They are generally not supported by the state fish and wildlife agencies, in part because of the higher legal burden of proof required for prosecuting wildlife law violations, and the uncertainty of an amendment's impact on existing fish and wildlife management laws.[30]

Regarding access to federal public lands for hunting opportunities, the Bush administration attempted to provide more access for hunters on public lands such as National Wildlife Refuges (NWRs). Wildlife protection advocates, however, have resisted this effort. One such organization sued and a court enjoined plans to allow hunting on thirty-seven NWRs, ordering the U.S. Fish and Wildlife Service to provide an analysis of the cumulative impacts of a plan for increased hunting.[31] But another court refused to enjoin a black bear hunt on a single NWR, when the government showed that the hunt would have a nominal impact.[32]

And in a sweeping show of support for access to public lands for hunting opportunities, in August 2007 President George W. Bush issued an executive order that directs federal agencies to promote expansion and enhancement of hunting opportunities on federal lands and to manage wildlife and wildlife habitat to enhance hunting.[33] It is unclear what impact this order will have on public lands that are historically restricted for preservation of wildlife species.

The exponential growth of the use of off-road vehicles, or ORVs, has created a huge new demand for access to public lands in the early years of this century. Fish and wildlife and other managers—and the courts—are increasingly being asked to decide ORV access issues when such use is often at cross-purposes with the protection of fish and wildlife and habitat. Public land managers, who must also manage to conserve wildlife and habitat, are caught in the middle. Agencies have been ordered to allow some ORV use while protecting the habitat of critically endangered species such as the woodland mountain caribou,[34] and in one instance the U.S. Supreme Court found that a federal agency has some discretion to allow ORV use under federal land management laws that do not explicitly exclude ORVs from protected areas.[35]

Courts have even issued directly conflicting decisions over the ORV access issue. For instance, one federal court enjoined a "politically driven" National Park Service plan for allowing a large number of snowmobiles in Yellowstone National Park, but another court held that the first court's injunction was not mandatory. The first court then issued an order to show cause why the secretary of the interior and others should not be held in contempt of its injunction order.[36] The issue of snowmobile access in Yellowstone remains politically charged and as yet unresolved.

In the meantime, the age-old conflict between resident and nonresident access to hunting and fishing opportunities in the various states has been actively litigated. Some states' restrictions on nonresident hunting or fish hauling have been held to be unconstitutional restrictions on commerce and/or a violation of the Privileges and Immunities Clause of the U.S. Constitution, which grants the citizens of each state all privileges and immunities of citizens in other states.[37] But other courts held that the Commerce Clause, which gives Congress authority to regulate commerce between the states, and the Privileges and Immunities Clause do not protect recreational hunting.[38] The issue came to a head in 2005 during an appeal of a suit by the state of Minnesota against North Dakota over North Dakota's nonresident waterfowl hunting restrictions, when a rider was attached to a congressional appropriations bill with a provision stating that it is the policy of Congress that states should regulate fish and wildlife in the public interest, including differentiating between residents and nonresidents.[39]

Although it remains to be seen, this congressional statement of policy may finally settle the issue of whether states can legally discriminate against nonresidents who seek to hunt and fish in other states.

Private Property Rights

Individuals and others increasingly challenge fish and wildlife managers with claims that private property interests have been "taken" by government for wildlife conservation purposes without due compensation, in violation of the Fifth Amendment to the U.S. Constitution. Lawsuits by grazing, logging, and farming interests, landowners, and even commercial fishing licensees asserting that property was taken without just compensation by governmental entities for protection of wildlife are almost universally unsuccessful. Nevertheless, fish and wildlife managers find themselves devoting time, money, and effort in defending against these claims. Further, huge damages are sometimes awarded at the trial court level, only to be eventually overturned by a higher court.

Courts generally conclude, for example, that restrictions on private property imposed by fish and wildlife managers to protect species do not take all economic uses of the land or are temporary in nature and thus are not a taking.[40] Courts of late have also held that commercial licenses or permits to take fish or wildlife bestow a revocable license, not a Fifth Amendment property right.[41] In one instance a court found that restricting the right of access to a private waterfront is subordinate to public trust obligations such as a local town's plan to protect sea turtle nesting habitat.[42] And both a state court and a federal court found that a state fish and wildlife commission's ordering a property owner to destroy illegal captive wildlife is not a taking.[43]

Conversely, Central Valley water users were awarded millions of dollars for loss of contract water as a result of restrictions imposed to protect ESA-listed fish. The Ninth Circuit Court of Appeals, however, overturned the award and the U.S. Supreme Court affirmed, holding that sovereign immunity bars the irrigators' water contract violation and takings claims.[44] The issue of whether the government is "taking" property when it enforces restrictions to protect wildlife continues to evolve, however, as in 2002 a jury awarded several million dollars to a lumber company that was restricted from logging its property by a state natural resources department because of the presence of a breeding pair of protected northern spotted owls.[45]

Climate Change and Wildlife

Scientists now generally agree that climate change is caused in large part by human emissions of greenhouse gases. As such, it should be considered an "unintended" human dimension that will nonetheless have an enormous impact on management of fish and wildlife. The courts, including the U.S. Supreme Court, are reviewing a number of cases and petitions on the impacts of climate change on the environment in general and on fish and wildlife in particular. State and federal agencies are also being forced to deal with the issue. For example, citizen petitions to list the polar bear and twelve species of penguins under the ESA were filed in 2005 and 2006, based on the accelerating loss of habitat and species populations caused by climate change. After no action was taken on the polar bear petition, suit was filed in federal court, and a proposed rule to list the polar bear was then issued.[46] The U.S. Fish and Wildlife Service also issued a ninety-day finding that ten of the twelve species of penguins under petition may also be listed under the ESA.[47] And for the first time ever, a state, California, received a petition to list a species because of impacts from climate change.[48]

Even the U.S. Supreme Court in 2007 embraced the paradigm shift regarding legal recognition of climate change impacts and government responsibility to take action to mitigate impacts, albeit not in the context of fish and wildlife. In *Massachusetts v. EPA*, 127 S.Ct. 1438 (U.S., April 2, 2007), the Supreme Court held that the plaintiffs had standing to sue the government to force action to regulate greenhouse gases, in this case, carbon emissions from new vehicles. The Court found the harms associated with climate change are serious and well recognized. It held that the Environmental Protection Agency's failure to dispute the causal connection between greenhouse gas emissions and climate change, makes its refusal to regulate a contributor to plaintiff Massachusetts' injuries.

In addition, a federal court in 2007 ordered the Bush administration to comply with the mandatory climate change–reporting requirements of the Global Climate Change Research Act of 1990, including those relating to biological diversity and human health.[49] Even international bodies are being petitioned with claims of violations of human rights caused by failure to mitigate climate change when those rights, including aboriginal hunting and subsistence rights, are threatened by the effects of global warming.[50] Petitions, lawsuits, and new laws that require a response to climate change are going to present inevitable, and massive, new challenges for fish and wildlife managers.[51]

International Impacts of Fish and Wildlife Policy

Early twenty-first century court rulings, policies, and laws of the United States regarding the management of wildlife, especially nongame wildlife, are closely observed by the rest of the world. In international arenas such as the Conference of the Parties of the Convention on International Trade in Endangered Species of Wild Fauna and Flora (CITES) and the meetings of the International Whaling Convention, the United States has an enormous influence on the outcome of the issues discussed. The Endangered Species Act is the United States' enabling statute for CITES, and many of the species listed under CITES and the ESA are found outside U.S. borders. For example, the polar bear and a number of species of penguins being considered for ESA protection are found only partly, or not at all, on U.S. soil. Actions taken by the United States to protect those species by restricting their import, for example, will have a direct international impact.

The global impact of U.S. policy is clearly illustrated in the context of ocean fisheries. The crash of fisheries all over the world has caused the United States to consider and even begin to restrict commercial and recreational fishing of some stocks in order to rebuild those fisheries. In addition, as a result of pressure from wildlife groups, certain methods of fishing that are lethal to other species such as dolphins and sea turtles have been restricted.[52] The United States itself, however, has been influenced by international pressure to allow imports of fish that are caught by methods that may not be allowed on American vessels, such as importation of tuna caught with gear that is not "dolphin-safe."[53] The federal government's policy in the early years of the twenty-first century was to refuse to restrict imports of, for example, shrimp and endangered salmon, and it found some support in the courts.[54] U.S. fish and wildlife policies and protections are also being scrutinized by international bodies such as the World Trade Organization, a new legal development that is very likely to continue and expand.[55]

Conclusion

The condition of fish and wildlife populations is one of the most graphic indicators of the health of this planet and of humans. It may be the specter and the increasingly undeniable impact of climate change, loss of habitat, and loss of species diversity that brings stakeholders to the table with common goals that include saving habitat for both game and nongame fish and wildlife resources, while meeting demands for resources and land of an exploding human population. Above all, adapting and responding to global warming and climate change may prove to be the greatest future challenge for state, national, and global fish and wildlife management, and legal trends in the twenty-first century will undoubtedly continue to reflect this new challenge.

Notes

1. For a review of federal wildlife law trends in the twentieth century, as well as of wildlife law, see chapters 2 and 3 in Ruth S. Musgrave et al., *Federal Wildlife Laws Handbook with Related Laws* (Rockville, MD: Government Institutes, 1998). See also Michael Bean and Melanie Rowland, *The Evolution of National Wildlife Law*, 3rd ed. (Westport, CT: Praeger Publishers, 1997). See also generally Ruth Musgrave, ed., *Wildlife Law News Quarterly* and "Wildlife Law News Weekly Alerts" (Albuquerque: University of New Mexico Center for Wildlife Law, 1993–present).
2. *Center for Biological Diversity v. Norton*, 254 F.3d 833 (9th Cir. 2001); *Center for Biological Diversity v. Norton*, No.CIV 01-0258 (D.N.M. 2001). But see *Center for Biological Diversity v. Norton*, 163 F.Supp.2d 1297 (N.D.Calif. 2001).
3. *Fund for Animals v. Hogan*, 428 F.3d 1059 (D.C.Cir. 2005).
4. *Defenders of Wildlife v. Kempthorne*, No.04-1230 (D.D.C. 2006); *Defenders of Wildlife v. Kempthorne*, No.CV 05-99-M-DWM (D.Mont. 2006); *Trout Unlimited v. Lohn*, No.CV-06-1493 (D.Ore. July 13, 2007); *Western Watersheds Project v. Foss*, No.CV 04-168-MHW (D.Idaho 2005).
5. *Center for Biological. Diversity v. Norton*, 304 F.Supp.2d 1174 (D.Ariz. 2003); *Save the Manatee Club v. Ballard*, 215 F.Supp.2d 88 (D.D.C. 2002); *Center for Biological Diversity v. Norton*, No.02-1067 (D.N.M. 2001).
6. *Sierra Club v. Kempthorne*, No.CV 07-0216-WS-M (S.D.Ala., July 2007); *NRDC v. Kempthorne*, 506 F,Supp.2d 322 (E.D.Ca., May 25, 2007).
7. *Sierra Club v. U.S.*, 245 F.3d 434 (5th Cir. 2001); *Spirit of the Sage Council v. Norton*, Civ.No.98-1873 (D.D.C. 2003).
8. *National Association of Home Builders v. Norton*, No.02-15212 (9th Cir. 2003).
9. *Desarrollo v. U.S.*, 482 F.3d 1157 (9th Cir., April 6, 2007).
10. See notes 4 and 5; *Pacific Coast Federation of Fishermen's Associations v. National Marine Fisheries Svc.*, 482 F.Supp.2d 1248 (W.D.Wa., March 30, 2007); *Trout Unlimited et al. v. Lohn*, No.CV-06-1493 (D.Ore., July 13, 2007).
11. U.S. Fish and Wildlife press release, July 20, 2007, www.fws.gov.
12. *Gordon v. Norton*, 322 F.3d 1213 (10th Cir. 2003).

13. *Defenders of Wildlife v. U.S. Fish and Wildlife Service*, 354 F.Supp.2d 1156 (D.Ore. 2005).
14. *State of Wyoming v. U.S. Dept. Interior*, 360 F.Supp.2d 1214 (D.Wyo. 2005), *aff'd*, 442 F.2d 1262 (10th Cir. 2006).
15. *State of Wyoming v. Livingston*, 443 F.3d 1211 (10th Cir. 2006).
16. For example, *Friends of Animals v. Alaska*, No.3AN-03-13489 (Alaska Sup.Ct. 2006); 2007 Alaska Op.Atty.Gen. 1; *Friends of Animals v. State of Alaska*, Nos. 3AN-06-10956-CI, 3AN-06-13087-CI (Alaska Sup.Ct., Mar. 30, 2007).
17. The Office of the Solicitor at the Department of the Interior on March 16, 2007, issued an opinion regarding the meaning of the phrase in the ESA: "endangered throughout a significant portion of its [a species'] range." The office concluded that the phrase means the range where a species currently exists, not its historical range. Department of the Interior Solicitor General, www.doi.gov/solicitor/M37013.pdf. But see *National Wildlife Federation v. National Marine Fisheries Service*, No. CV01-640-RE (D.Ore. 2005); *Alsea Valley Alliance v. Lautenbacher*, No.06-6093-HO (D.Ore., Aug. 14, 2007).
18. *National Wildlife Federation v. National Marine Fisheries Service*, 254 F.Supp.2d 1196 (D.Ore. 2003); *National Wildlife Federation v. National Marine Fisheries Service*, 422 F.2d 782 (9th Cir.2005); *Id.*, 481 F.3d 1224 (9th Cir., April 9, 2007); American Rivers v. NOAA Fisheries, No.CV-04-0061-RE (D.Ore. 2006).
19. See note 20; Northwest Energy Coalition, "Going With the Flow," http://nwenergy.org/publications/reports/miscellaneous-reports-and-studies/going-with-the-flow/; "Revenue Stream," http.nwenergy.org/publications/reports/revenue-stream/.
20. *In re: Operation of the Missouri River System Litigation*, 421 F.3d 618 (8th Cir. 2005); *Pacific Coast Federation of Fishermen's Associations v. Bureau of Reclamation*, 138 F.Supp.2d 1228 (N.D.Calif. 2001), *aff'd*, 426 F.3d 1082 (9th Cir. 2005), *injunction reaff'd*, No.06-16296 (9th Cir. Mar. 22, 2007); *Kandra v. US*, 145 F.Supp.2d 1192 (D.Ore. 2001); *U.S. v. Adair*, 187 F.Supp.2d 1273 (D.Ore. 2002).
21. The influence of industry stakeholders in the Klamath water conflict allegedly goes all the way to the top. Congress attempted to investigate whether Vice President Dick Cheney improperly overrode, and ordered the rewriting of, government scientific documents so that water would be released to irrigators in 2006. Cheney refused to appear before Congress. For whatever reason, the water was released in 2006, resulting in the death of over seventy thousand salmon returning to spawn.
22. The conflict came to a head when the Tenth Circuit held that the Bureau of Reclamation has discretion to reduce contracted-for water deliveries in order to comply with the ESA and save the minnow. *Rio Grande Silvery*

Minnow v. Keys, 333 F.3d 1110 (10th Cir. 2003). Convening the ESA "God Squad" was considered, as was an expedited appeal to the U.S. Supreme Court. Then a rider attached to the FY04 Energy and Water Development Appropriations Act, Pub. L. No. 108-137, §208(a) (2004) forbade the government from failing to make water deliveries under federal contracts. The suit was eventually settled by the parties who all agreed to contribute to a water-banking system and a water-leasing program that will save the minnow and meet contractual needs.

23. *Geer v. Connecticut*, 161 U.S. 519 (1896). See discussions of public trust doctrine in other chapters of this book. See also chapter 10 in Clifford Rechtschaffen and Denise Antolini, eds., *Creative Common Law Strategies for Protecting the Environment* (Washington, DC: ELI Press, 2007).

24. Title IX of the Commerce, Justice, State Appropriations Act of 2000 contained a Wildlife Conservation and Restoration Account, and Title VIII of the Interior Appropriations Act (Land Conservation, Preservation and Infrastructure Improvement). See 66 FR 7657 (January 24, 2001). See also "CARA-Lite," 16 U.S.C. 669(b), §3(2)(C)(c)(1)(2000).

25. Association of Fish and Wildlife Agencies, State Wildlife Action Plans, www.fishwildlife.org/wildlife_action_plans.html; Teaming With Wildlife, State Wildlife Grants, www.teaming.com/state_wildlife_grants.htm.

26. Almost one-half of the states outlawed cyberhunting within two years after introduction of the practice in Texas. And in February 2007 Arizona, California, New Mexico, Oregon, and Washington signed an agreement to work on climate change issues, including identification of measures to adapt to impacts of climate change. Western Climate Initiative, www.westernclimateinitiative.org/.

27. See, for example,, Wildlife Violator Compact of New Mexico, N.M.S.A. §§11-16-1 through 12 (1978).

28. *Stapley v. Arizona*, 966 P.2d 1031 (Ariz.Ct.App. 1998); *Gray v. North Dakota Game and Fish Department*, 706 N.W.2d 61 (N.D. 2005).

29. Twelve states have right to hunt amendments or other provisions, though only six specifically use the term "right": Alabama, California (right to fish only), Rhode Island (right to fish), Virginia, West Virginia, and Wisconsin.

30. See, for example, *NEB.OP.A.G.* No.04003 (2004).

31. *Fund for Animals v. Williams*, 391 F.Supp.2d 132 (D.D.C. 2005).

32. *Moore v. Kempthorne*, 464 F.Supp.2d 519 (E.D.Va. 2006).

33. Executive Order No. 13443, Facilitation of Hunting Heritage and Wildlife Conservation, Aug. 16, 2007.

34. *Defenders of Wildlife v. Martin*, No.CV-05-248-RHW (E.D.Wa., *injunctions*

entered Dec. 20, 2005; Sept. 22, 2006, *order entered* Feb. 26, 2007).

35. *Norton v. Southern Utah Wilderness Alliance*, 542 U.S. 917 (U.S. 2004).
36. *Fund for Animals v. Norton*, 294 F.Supp.2d 92 (D.D.C. 2003); *Inernational Snowmobile Manufacturers Association v. Norton*, 304 F.Supp.2d 1278 (D.Wyo. 2004); *Wyoming Rest. and Lodging Association v. U.S.*, 398 F.Supp.2d 1197 (D.Wyo. 2005).
37. *Conservation Force, Inc. v. Manning*, 301 F.3d 985 (9th Cir., 2002) *cert. denied*, 537 U.S. 1112 (2003); *State of Minnesota v. Kolla*, 672 N.W.2d 1 (Ct.App.Minn. 2003); *State of Connecticut v. Crotty*, 346 F. 3d 84 (2nd Cir. 2003).
38. *Taulman v. Hayden*, No.05-1118 (D.Kan. 2006).
39. Rider to the Emergency Supplemental Appropriations Act for Defense, the Global War on Terror, and Tsunami Relief, 2005, Pub.Law No.109-13 (May 11, 2005), Section 6063. Appeal dismissed as moot, *Hatch v. Hoeven*, 456 F.3d 826 (8th Cir., 2006).
40. *Coast Range Conifers v. Board of Forestry*, 117 P.3d 990 (Ore. 2005); *Seiber v. U.S.*, 52 Fed.Cl. 570 (U.S.Ct.Fed.Claims 2002), *aff'd*, 364 F.3d 1356 (Fed.Cir. 2004).
41. *Conti v. U.S.*, 291 F.3d 1334 (Fed.Cir. 2002); *Bensen v. State of South Dakota*, 710 NW2d 131 (S.D. 2006).
42. *Slavin v. Town of Oak Island*, 584 S.E.2d 100 (Ct.App. N.C. 2003).
43. *Delancey v. State of Arkansas*, No.CR 03-615 (Ark. 2004).
44. *Tulare Lake Basin Water Storage District v. U.S.*,, 59 Fed.Cl. 246 (Ct.Fed.Claims 2003); *Orff v. U.S.*, 358 F.3d 1137 (9th Cir. 2004), *aff'd* 125 S.Ct. 2606 (U.S. 2005).
45. *SDS Lumber Co. v. Washington Dept. of Natural Resources*, No.93-2-00003-6 (Wa., *settled* 2002); but see *Avenal v. State of Louisiana and Dept. of Natural Resources*, No.03-C-3521 (La. 2004).
46. 72 FR 1063 (January 9, 2007).
47. 72 FR 37695 (July 11, 2007).
48. Petition to List American Pika, www.biologicaldiversity.org/swcbd /species/pika.
49. *Center for Biological Diversity v. Brennan*, No.C06-7062 (N.D.Calif., August 21, 2007).
50. Earthjustice, 2005 Petition to the Inter-American Commission on Human Rights, www.earthjustice.org/library/legal_docs/petition-to -the inter-american-commission-on-human-rights-on-behalf-of-the -inuit-circumpolar-conference.pdf. A 2004 Arctic Climate Impact Assessment found that the "Inuit face major threats to their food

security and hunting cultures." Arctic Climate Impact Assessment, www.acia.uaf.edu.

51. For example, in February 2007 conservation organizations petitioned seven Bush administration cabinet secretaries to establish binding rules on global warming and the growing potential of significant wildlife extinctions this century. The petition is at www.biologicaldiversity.org/swcbd/programs/bdes/gw-es/index.html. See also Bluewater Network Petitions, www.bluewaternetwork.org/campaign_gw.wildlife.shtml.
52. For example, International Dolphin Conservation Program Act, Pub.L.No.105-42 (Aug. 15, 1997).
53. *Earth Island v. Evans*, 256 F.Supp.2d 1064 (N.D.Calif., 2004) ("This court has never, in its 24 years, reviewed a record of agency action that contained such a compelling portrait of political meddling."); *Earth Island Institute v. Hogarth*, 484 F.3d 1123 (9th Cir., April 27, 2007), *amended and superceded*, 494 F.3d 757 (July 13, 2007) (agency ignored its own statistical methodology, relied on inconclusive data, and was influenced by international political rather than scientific concerns).
54. *Turtle Island Restoration Network v. Evans*, 284 F.3d 282 (Fed.Cir. 2002); *Salmon Spawning and Recovery Alliance v. Basham*, No. 06-00191 (U.S. CIT, Mar. 6, 2007).
55. U.S. embargo of Malaysian shrimp imports upheld by World Trade Organization: WT/DS58/17 (October 2, 2001).

CHAPTER 12

Reviving the Public Trust Doctrine as a Foundation for Wildlife Management in North America

John F. Organ and Gordon R. Batcheller

Wildlife conservation in North America is based on the principle that wildlife resources are owned by no one and are held in trust by government for the benefit of present and future generations (Geist, Mahoney, and Organ 2001; Geist and Organ 2004). Many have hailed the North American experience as the greatest example of wildlife conservation worldwide (Prukop and Regan 2005). With its legacy spanning nearly 150 years of history, one would think the conservation model is secure. However, as the model reaches the new millennium, its basic foundation—the Public Trust Doctrine—is under siege. We revisit the Public Trust Doctrine in light of current threats and assess its role as a foundation for wildlife management in the future.

The Public Trust Doctrine: Historical Background

The Public Trust Doctrine holds that wildlife are property owned by no one and are held in trust by government for the benefit of present and future generations of citizens. The fundamental concept of natural resources being owned by no one, and treated as public property, was first written for posterity by the Romans. The written codes of Justinian (AD 529) were based upon the second-century Institutes and Journal of Gaius, who codified the natural law of Greek philosophers (Slade, Kehoe, and Stahl 1997). What the Romans recorded in part was:

> By the law of nature these things are common to all mankind—the air, running water, the sea, and consequently

> the shore of the sea. No one, therefore, is forbidden to approach the seashore, provided that he respects habitations, monuments, and the buildings, which are not, like the sea, subject only to the law of nations. (Slade, Kehoe, and Stahl 1997)

The Magna Carta (AD 1215) drew upon Roman law (Adams 1993) in limiting the king's power to own or grant to others wild resources. A U.S. Supreme Court ruling in 1842 that denied a landowner's claim to exclude all others from taking oysters from certain mudflats in New Jersey (*Martin v. Waddell* [Bean 1983]) was based upon Chief Justice Roger Taney's interpretation of the Magna Carta. The ruling has become known as the Public Trust Doctrine.

Joseph Sax, the preeminent scholar of the Public Trust Doctrine, traces its roots so that we may better understand the modern context (Sax 1999). The Romans had an elaborate property system that recognized different kinds of property serving different functions. Each kind of property had a special status and had to be treated in a certain way. For example, some property could not be bought and sold. Another kind of property was common property (*res communis*), which (1) could not be privately owned and (2) was for common use by everyone. Roman law included wildlife (*ferae naturae*) within the law of things owned by no one—*res nullius*. These categories were probably for what the Romans perceived as the nature of things that were abundant and not appropriate for private possession and sale (Horner 2000). Ownership of a wild animal only occurred when it was physically possessed, most typically when killed for food.

The English adopted Roman civil law in substance after the Magna Carta (Slade, Kehoe, and Stahl 1997). English common law also recognized that there are special kinds of property but provided its own interpretation. English common law disliked "ownerless things," so the ownership of public resources was placed in the king (Horner 2000). The king owned these properties, but not for his private use. The king was a trustee, owning certain properties for someone else, which became a special responsibility (Sax 1999).

English law applied in the American colonies, yet after independence and the formation of the United States, there was no king to be the trustee. It was not until 1842 and the Supreme Court decision in *Martin v. Waddell* that trustee status was ascribed to the states. Subsequent court rulings (e.g., *Hughes v. Oklahoma* [Bean 1983]) have challenged the principle of state ownership of wildlife but have held wildlife in public ownership (*Geer v. Connecticut* [Horner 2000]).

In Canada, wildlife became a public resource in part by default because the Crown was the ward of huge tracts of land not claimed for settlement and was thus the de facto owner of the wildlife it contained. Moreover, as wildlife fed native populations, Canada's government had little choice but to safeguard that food supply (Hewitt 1921; Threlfall 1995).

To understand how the ancient concept of public trust and the more recent Public Trust Doctrine, neither one specific to wildlife, have formed a pillar of wildlife conservation, we must look at their legal basis.

Public Trust as Law

Sax (1999) identifies four fundamental concepts of public trust:

> *Public trust is common law.* There is no legal code specific to the Public Trust Doctrine because it has never been officially enacted. It is "judge-made law" that is interpreted and evolves through court decisions. For the last century or so, most laws in the United States have been statutory coded laws, but for most of the development of the Anglo-American legal system, common law prevailed.
>
> *Public trust is state law.* As such, there is no single law but many; yet each embodies a unifying principle of the fundamental rights of all citizens.
>
> *Public trust is property law.* One of the great strengths of the Public Trust Doctrine is that in asserting it, the state is asserting its own property rights—property rights that belong to the public—so the issue of "taking" becomes moot as one cannot be taking a property right from another while asserting such right.
>
> *Public trust is a public right.* Trust property is owned by the public and held in trust for the benefit of the public. You do not have to have special status to make a claim; you just have to be a member of the public.

Since the Public Trust Doctrine is common law, and judge-made, a legislature can never repeal it. The traditional applications of public rights under the Public Trust Doctrine were for navigation, fishing, and commerce. The New England states of Massachusetts, Maine, and

New Hampshire added fowling as a right. It was not until 1896 that wildlife became firmly established in law as a public trust resource of the states. *Geer v. Connecticut* became judge-made law that is the "heart and soul of the modern day public trust in wildlife" (Horner 2000,21). While transforming this principle into modern American law, and making the concept of wildlife as public trust resources distinctly American, the court stated:

> Whilst the fundamental principles upon which the common property in game rests have undergone no change, the development of free institutions has led to the recognition of the fact that the power or control lodged in the State, resulting from the common ownership, is to be exercised, like all other powers of government, as a trust for the benefit of all people, and not as a prerogative for the advantage of the government, as distinct from the people, or for the benefit of private individuals as distinguished from the public. (161 U.S. 519, 1896)

The trustee status of states in regard to wildlife is transferred to the federal government in the United States when wildlife falls within parameters of the United States Constitution: the Supremacy Clause (federal treaty-making power), the Commerce Clause, and the Property Clause. Chief Justice Taney, in articulating the Public Trust Doctrine in *Martin v. Waddell* in 1842, acknowledged this when he wrote that the powers assumed by the states were "subject only to the rights since surrendered by the Constitution to the general government" (41 U.S. 367, 1842).

The Public Trust Foundation of the North American Model of Wildlife Conservation

Case law on the Public Trust Doctrine is quite extensive, and while most pertains to water resources, the basic principles expounded by the courts in upholding the doctrine apply to wildlife as well, given its legally entrenched status as a public trust resource. Sax (1970) has nicely summarized case law on this topic. Of particular note in relation to the North American model is the treatment in case law of public trust resources as property. Fundamental responsibilities of trustees with regard to such property are that it must be held available for use by the general public, it cannot be sold, even for a fair cash equivalent, and it must be maintained for particular types of uses. The types of uses that resources must be maintained for have been expressed in two ways: traditional uses such as recreation or fishery and natural uses peculiar to that resource. An example of the latter is using a body of water for boating or swimming, as opposed to filling it in for a parking lot. The extension of harvest (i.e., angling, hunting, trapping) as a traditional and natural use of wildlife requires no stretch of the imagination. Sax (1970) maintains that the greatest historical standing of the trust is that certain interests are so intrinsically important to every citizen that their free availability tends to mark the society as one of citizens rather than serfs.

Fundamental components of North American wildlife conservation draw extensively from these principles. The elimination of markets for game, allocation of wildlife by law, and equal opportunity to hunt, for example, are all premised upon wildlife being owned by no one (Geist, Mahoney, and Organ 2001). While the foundation of North American wildlife conservation rests on the concept of wildlife as public trust resources, the ability of government trustees to uphold this principle is being undermined by a number of factors that may be a product of changing societal attitudes and values and opportunism in the private sector.

Erosion of Wildlife as Public Trust Resources

The need for wildlife to be held in public trust originated as "a fundamental nineteenth-century conception of the purpose of wildlife law, the preservation of a food supply" (Bean 1983,16). The architects of North American wildlife conservation believed that wildlife were no longer essential as a food supply and that they had greater value for cultural and spiritual purposes (Organ and Fritzell 2000; Reiger 1975; Trefethen 1972). Hunting as a cultural pursuit (coined "sport hunting" to distinguish it from "market" and "pot" hunting) became the driving force in development of the North American Model of Wildlife Conservation. The Roosevelt Doctrine, calling for scientific management to sustain wildlife for the benefit of present and future generations so as to achieve the greatest good for the greatest number of people (Reiger 1975) is firmly rooted in the Public Trust Doctrine. The reason that governments have agencies to manage wildlife and that state and provincial universities have programs to train scientists to manage wildlife is trustee status. Common ownership lacking a trustee would have spelled the demise of these resources (Hardin 1968). Today, the public trust in wildlife is threatened by forces that restrict or remove public access to wildlife resources and by the unwillingness of courts to apply the public trust beyond what is codified in law.

Privatization of Wildlife

There is an increasing trend throughout North America by private interests to control wildlife for personal profit. Typically, access is controlled through landownership (featuring "high fences" in many cases) and restriction of users through leasing of rights or pay-per-use. Ultimately, competition fosters efforts to control the number and quality of wild animals inhabiting the land. Consequences of such demands include the elimination of predators, less biological diversity, loss of "democracy of sport" (Leopold, quoted in Meine 1988, 169), and the erosion of the wildlife profession (Geist 1988, 1995). Science as a tool to discharge wildlife policy is a key component of the North American Model of Wildlife Conservation. A notable achievement of North Americans was the development of the wildlife management profession to institute scientific stewardship. The use of science in wildlife management and policy is predicated upon the public valuing the services of wildlife biologists to ensure the public trust is maintained. In private hands, science, when applied, is focused on profit. Some trust resources may become expendable to maximize others.

Game Ranching

Closely related to the privatization of wildlife is the growth of game farming since the 1980s, an industry devoted to raising wildlife for the sale of its parts in an open market. This industry stands in opposition to every major policy of wildlife conservation in North America (Geist 1985, 1995). Game ranching can compromise the legislative framework that has been effective in conserving wildlife—elimination of markets, allocation by law, democracy of hunting. It does this by creating a market for dead wildlife, allocating wildlife based on market forces rather than sustainable use principles, and restricting access through imposition of fees. It is most dangerous in the disease implications it presents to wildlife and humans. Game ranching represents an enormous disease bridge between wildlife and livestock and people. In addition, it has potential to destroy the genetic integrity of wildlife through assured escapes and the genetic manipulation of captive wildlife.

Unsustainable Land-Use Practices

The United States human population is projected to increase to nearly 400 million by 2050 from its 2000 census figure of about 281 million (Trauger et al. 2002). This exceeds an estimate reported a few years ago by about 50 million, suggesting an accelerated growth rate. Americans make up less than 5 percent of the world's population but consume 30 percent of its resources. The current political agenda favors economic growth, which exacerbates the effects of population and consumption on wildlife resources (Czech 2000). The land base available to and suitable for wildlife is disappearing at an alarming rate. Our current trends in human impacts on the land pose the greatest long-term threats to wildlife. We will see increased fragmentation and isolation of wildlife populations and increased conversion of wildlands to support the human economy. Moreover, the trends toward privatization of wildlife and the concomitant relegation of wildlife uses to the wealthy class suggest that a smaller number of stakeholders will be invested in the benefits of open spaces, thereby reducing the political and economic support to conserve our remaining wild spaces. Unless a major change in social values and corresponding political ideology occurs, our conservation triumphs on behalf of our trust resources will dwindle away. The impact of human population growth and associated landscape effects on the public trust in wildlife is that it is becoming more difficult for trustees to ensure sustainability of all wildlife for present and future generations. Demand for land to support humans will likely result in trade-offs over wildlife habitat. These trade-offs can result in reduced "shares" of the trust.

Solidifying the Public Trust

Smith (1980) identifies three criteria that need to be met in order for the Public Trust Doctrine to be an effective tool: (1) it must contain some concept of a legal right in the general public, (2) it must be enforceable against the government, and (3) it must be capable of an interpretation consistent with contemporary concerns. Simply stated from a wildlife conservation perspective, people must understand that wildlife, regardless of whose property they are on, belong to them. The government as trustee must be able to be held accountable so as to prevent the squandering of the trust. Finally, the doctrine must be in broad enough terms to allow inclusion of resources currently considered important, even though they might not have been considered by the architects of the public trust. For example, Roman law established the precedent for the modern view that wildlife are owned by no one, but the Romans could not have conceived of modern concerns over species extinctions and needs for management of wildlife (Horner 2000).

Sax (1970) has described the failings of the courts in upholding the Public Trust Doctrine. This stems from the inability of many courts to distinguish between the government's general obligation to act for the public benefit and the greater obligation it has as a trustee of certain public resources. For example, a court, in upholding its obligation to act for the public benefit, may consider only current conditions and not factor in its decision the special obligation as a trustee to perpetuate these resources. This narrower view may result in trade-offs that affect long-term sustainability of wildlife. The question arises whether the Public Trust Doctrine has any judicially enforceable right that restrains government entities beyond the general restraints already applicable. A recent decision in Wisconsin has gone even further in determining that the Public Trust Doctrine does not confer the right to challenge "any government action that arguably impacts any natural resources in Wisconsin." The doctrine has not been applied in Wisconsin "in a context beyond the direct infringement of the public's rights in navigable waters" (*Kramer v. Clark*, No.2005AP2970; Wis.Ct.App., Dec. 21, 2006).

The most immediate need in solidifying the public trust is to revisit the statutory charters of state and provincial fish and wildlife agencies. These codes that govern the disposition of fish and wildlife should be explicit in defining these resources as property of the jurisdiction and in mandating the trust responsibility to provide these resources to all for the benefit of present and future generations. Musgrave and Stein (1993) list all state charters for fish and wildlife agencies. Tremendous variability is found, but the underlying tenets of the public trust are evident. One should not have to reach far for interpretation, though. Where there is doubt, revisions should be executed for purposes of clarity.

Reviving and Applying the Public Trust

Assertion of trusteeship over wildlife as public resources occurred in North America during a time when the stakeholder base was narrower than it is today. Primary stakeholders were consumptive users and agricultural interests. Contemporary society has a base of stakeholders with more diverse interests, ranging from people whose interests are tangential and appreciative of the existence of wildlife to those who want to avoid interactions with wildlife altogether. Acceptance capacity for wildlife (Carpenter, Decker, and Lipscomb 2000) can vary within the same locale at the same time depending on the stakeholders. The challenge to contemporary wildlife managers is to balance competing needs and interests in decision making over allocation and management of wildlife resources.

Most of the affected public and many wildlife professionals have little understanding of and appreciation for the public trust foundation of wildlife conservation. Heightening the awareness of public trust principles among stakeholders and practitioners can help in defining the limits of management alternatives and jurisdictional responsibilities (e.g., federal vs. state). Once people understand the limits legal management authorities work within, and the origins of these mandates, working toward acceptable outcomes within those parameters may become more attainable. Biological science can define the limits of sustainability while social science defines the limits of acceptance. Integration of the two within the broader limits of the public trust can define the decision matrix. As noted earlier, in order for the public trust to be functional, people must recognize their rights under it, be able to hold the government accountable for it, and must find relevance within it for their interests and concerns. Reviving the Public Trust Doctrine as a foundation for wildlife management must begin with ensuring these factors become reality.

Literature Cited

Adams, D. A. 1993. *Renewable resource policy.* Washington, DC: Island Press.

Bean, M. J. 1983. *The evolution of national wildlife law.* New York: Praeger Publishers.

Carpenter, L. H., D. J. Decker, and J. F. Lipscomb. 2000. Stakeholder acceptance capacity in wildlife management. *Human Dimensions of Wildlife* 5:5–19.

Czech, B. 2000. Economic growth as a limiting factor for wildlife conservation. *Wildlife Society Bulletin* 28:4–15.

Geist, V. 1985. Game ranching: Threat to wildlife conservation in North America. *Wildlife Society Bulletin* 13:594–98.

———. 1988. How markets in wildlife meat and parts, and the sale of hunting privileges, jeopardize wildlife conservation. *Conservation Biology* 2:1–12.

———. 1995. North American policies of wildlife conservation. In *Wildlife conservation policy*, ed. V. Geist and I. McTaggart-Cowan, 75–129. Calgary: Detselig Enterprises.

Geist, V., S. P. Mahoney, and J. F. Organ. 2001. Why hunting has defined the North American model of wildlife conservation. *Transcripts of the North American Wildlife and Natural Resources Conference* 66:175–85.

Geist, V., and J. F. Organ. 2004. The public trust foundation of the North American model of wildlife conservation. *Northeast Wildlife* 58:49–56.

Hardin, G. 1968. The tragedy of the commons. *Science* 162:1243–48.

Hewitt, C. G. 1921. *The conservation of the wildlife of Canada*. New York: Charles Scribner's Sons.

Horner, S. M. 2000. Embryo, not fossil: Breathing life into the public trust in wildlife. *University of Wyoming College of Law, Land and Water Law Review*. 35:1–66.

Meine, C. 1988. *Aldo Leopold: His life and work*. Madison: University of Wisconsin Press.

Musgrave, R. S., and M. A. Stein. 1993. *State wildlife laws handbook*. Rockville, MD: Government Institutes.

Organ, J. F., and E. K. Fritzell. 2000. Trends in consumptive recreation and the wildlife profession. *Wildlife Society Bulletin*. 28:780–87.

Prukop, J., and R. J. Regan. 2005. The value of the North American model of wildlife conservation: An IAFWA position. *Wildlife Society Bulletin*. 33:374–77.

Reiger, J. F. 1975. *American sportsmen and the origins of conservation*. New York: Winchester Press.

Sax, J. L. 1970. The public trust doctrine in natural resource law: Effective judicial intervention. *Michigan Law Review*. 68:471–566.

———. 1999. Introduction to the public trust doctrine. In *The public trust doctrine and its application to protecting instream flows*, ed. G. E. Smith and A. R. Hoar, 5–12. Hadley, MA: U.S. Fish Wildlife Service Instream Flow Progress Assessment.

Slade, D. C., R. K. Kehoe, and J. K. Stahl. 1997. *Putting the public trust doctrine to work: The application of the public trust doctrine to the management of lands, waters, and living resources of the coastal states*. Washington, DC: Coastal States Organization.

Smith, F. E. 1980. *The public trust doctrine, instream flows and resources*. Sacramento, CA: U.S. Fish and Wildlife Service.

Threlfall, W. 1995. Conservation and wildlife management in Britain. In

Wildlife conservation policy, ed. V. Geist and I. McTaggart-Cowan, 227–74. Calgary: Detselig Enterprises.

Trauger, D. L., B. M. Czech, J. D. Erickson, P. R. Garretson, B. J. Kernohan, and C. A. Miller. 2002. The relationship of economic growth to wildlife conservation. *Wildlife Society Technology Technical Review* 02-1. Bethesda, MD: Wildlife Society.

Trefethen, J. B. 1972. *An American crusade for wildlife.* New York: Winchester Press.

CHAPTER 13

A "Wicked" Problem: Institutional Structures and Wildlife Management Success

Susan J. Buck

Wildlife management problems are classic examples of a "wicked" problem (Rittel and Webber 1973, 160–67; Wise 2002, 133). Wicked problems are "ill-defined; and they rely upon elusive political judgement for resolution" (Rittel and Webber 1973, 160). They may have fixes, but they are too complex and unstable to have solutions. They are like rivers: we may get them under control temporarily, but they inevitably burst their banks. State wildlife policies are especially wicked because they vary so widely: the wildlife problems of each state are peculiar to that state's ecology, history, culture, politics, and economics. Regional differences are sufficiently dramatic that prescribing a nationwide template for state activity is impractical. The state-specific and wicked nature of wildlife management problems means that, although agency staff may borrow useful ideas from innovative states, they must craft individual solutions for their own agencies.

The wildlife management literature is rife with articles about the need for institutional change. Over seventy-five years ago, Aldo Leopold wrote that "preoccupation with [the] form of organization pervades popular thought on federal as well as state administration of conservation affairs" (Leopold 1986 [1933], 408).

The most recent upheaval has many causes. First, state wildlife agencies are the most visible bureaucratic venue that addresses wildlife concerns, so they become the "go-to" place for new wildlife issues, especially problems with the human-wildlife interface. Second, public attitudes toward wildlife management in general and hunting in particular are shifting away from consumptive uses (Gill 1996; Klay and McElveen

1991; Nie 2004; Organ and Fritzell 2000); the total number of hunters and anglers in the United States is declining while the number of people engaged in nonhunting wildlife recreation is increasing (U.S. Fish and Wildlife Service 2007, 7). Third, wildlife management now faces a wide range of new demands such as wildlife tourism (Shackley 1996), regulating nuisance wildlife practices (Barnes 1997; Hadidian et al. 2001), wildlife rehabilitation (Dubois and Fraser 2003a, 2003b), game farms (Robbins and Luginbuhl 2005), and urban wildlife (Adams 2005; Knuth et al. 2001). This problem is not just a matter of expanding mandates, although that would be problematic in itself. There are also other drivers of conflict: natural resource scarcity, conflicting values, scientific uncertainty, and electoral politics (Nie 2003, 312–33). Finally, rising distrust of wildlife professionals (Minnis 1998) challenges part of the fundamental culture of wildlife management (Jacobson and Decker 2006; Riley et al. 2002). All of these concerns create new stakeholders and new policy networks that strain established alliances among the old stakeholders (Anderson and Loomis 2006; Beck 1998; Decker and Brown 2001; Manfredo, Teel, and Bright 2003; Minnis 1998; Nie 2004).

The question is not whether wildlife agencies should change; it is how they will change. This chapter addresses one aspect of that change: the institutional structure of wildlife agencies. Proposals for new structures tend to fall somewhere between two alternatives: expand the mandate of existing agencies and provide them with the necessary resources without significantly changing their organizations, or fold existing agencies into either state natural resources or environmental protection agencies where the costs of incorporating new stakeholders can be shared. The middle ground is to leave the formal wildlife agency structure essentially unchanged and to create new formal and informal institutional networks among all the agencies.

This chapter applies a public administration perspective to institutional design in wildlife agencies. The first section uses the policy process framework (Ripley and Franklin 1991) to examine problems that occur when wildlife agencies become involved with regulatory activities such as protecting environmental quality or licensing businesses and professional groups. The second section draws on the emerging literature on the creation of the Department of Homeland Security to examine potential risks and opportunities that come from folding existing wildlife agencies into larger umbrella organizations. The final section discusses permeable administrative boundaries (Kettl 2006) and clarifies the challenges of creating new institutional designs for wildlife agencies.

Expanding Wildlife Agency Mandates

Wildlife agencies have assumed some auxiliary responsibilities such as hunter safety programs and law enforcement. Because wildlife and their habitats are affected by air and water quality, toxic and hazardous waste, and land management issues such as erosion, an untutored observer might expect wildlife agencies to take on environmental protection programs. However, the political and practical reality is quite different, in part because the kinds of activities in which wildlife agencies usually engage require a different set of managerial competencies than regulatory actions. The policy process framework (Ripley and Franklin 1991) captures an institutional dynamic that suggests wildlife agencies should be extremely careful when taking on tasks proposed by new stakeholders. Agencies that cope with overlapping policy types face especially difficult administrative problems because the two policy types involve different policy actors, different legislative committees, different legal issues, different funding sources, and new interest groups that are schooled in confrontational and litigious approaches to policy making (Ripley and Franklin 1991, 18–19). The challenge is to find the best way to assimilate all the demands on state agencies while retaining efficient and effective policy outcomes.

Most wildlife agencies administer *distributive policies*: government activities that support and monitor private activities beneficial to society as a whole that would not usually be undertaken by the private sector (Ripley and Franklin 1991, 17, 20). Wildlife agency policies are classified as distributive because agencies provide habitat and monitor populations for sustainable yields, provide access to licensed hunters, and monitor hunting practices; the private sector alone is unlikely to provide these services. Nonconsumptive wildlife policies are also distributive, but because they have different goals, implementation requires adjustments in administrative routines. For example, to provide recreational experiences such as bird-watching, wildlife photography, or mountain biking, agency personnel need new expertise, funding must come from different sources than the usual federal aid and licence revenues, and new interest groups and new legislators must come to the bargaining table.

The actors involved in stable distributive policy maintain generally cordial relations, and unless some unexpected event triggers media interest, the decisions governing this sort of policy are usually made by *subgovernments* (stable networks of policy actors with similar interests and goals). In consumptive wildlife policy, the subgovernment consists of hunters and the businesses that serve them, the wildlife agency, and the commissioners or state legislators who are most directly involved in making wildlife policy. When controversy or conflict cause subgovernments to fall apart, *issue networks* (Heclo 1978) may become strong factors in policy decisions. Issue networks are fluid as participants move in and out without clear leadership. Adding new interests destabilizes the existing subgovernments, and new issue networks are more difficult to manage.

Some new responsibilities proposed for current wildlife agencies are *regulatory policies*: they protect the public good either by regulating private activities (agriculture, mining, toxic or hazardous waste disposal) or by licensing or certifying service providers. Expectations that state wildlife agencies will regulate wildlife nuisance businesses or game farms or monitor environmental quality in wildlife habitats force agencies into protective regulatory policy. Policy outcomes demanded by stakeholders in regulatory policy are not the same as they are in distributive policy because the needs of the target groups differ. Regulated businesses generally want stable regulations; they want to minimize compliance costs and to maximize profits. Such businesses are already dealing with federal and other state regulators; the last thing they want is one more agency watching them. In contrast, service providers such as wildlife nuisance control operators and wildlife rehabilitators may welcome some regulation because it provides legitimacy and quality control, both of which are good for business for legitimate operators (Dubois and Fraser 2003a, 20).

Another problem for wildlife agencies with regulatory responsibilities comes from a new level of legislative involvement. Regulatory policy is initially set by legislators who delegate varying levels of discretion to each agency. If the new tasks given to the wildlife agency involve regulation, stakeholders who object to agency decisions are likely to go straight to the agency's political superiors. In fact, they often go to the legislators even before the agencies have begun to formulate regulations. A second problem is economic: because the economic interests of those being regulated often affect political decisions, legal issues in protective regulatory policy differ from those in traditional wildlife policy. Partly to safeguard those interests, under the federal Administrative Procedure Act and state equivalents, regulated actors have protected rights to "notice and hearing" when regulations are promulgated, and in most cases, they have access to the courts to resolve disputes (Buck 2006, 75–82). Litigation is a resource sink that agencies try to avoid; one avoidance strategy is to craft regulations that minimize the risk of either legislative corrections or costly and time-consuming litigation. This strategy may lead agencies to make decisions that do not reflect their best, expert opinion. For example, in one southern state, the statutory definition of wildlife does not include reptiles or amphibians. When several reptile species began to fail, state wildlife biologists considered recommending that the statutory definition be changed to include all large-scale animals. However, because this would open the door to lobbyists advocating wholesale changes in the statutory definition, they instead recommended a narrowly focused bill to add the specific species to their commission's jurisdiction. Such piecemeal tinkering with legislative language may be expedient, but it is not the best way to address legislative change.

A third problem is that federal regulators also influence and sometimes dictate policies in environmental regulatory areas such as air and water quality, toxic and hazardous waste disposal, and wetlands regulation. This further constrains state legislative and agency options. In contrast, distributive policies such as game management are usually resolved at the state level, although the federal government may intervene in areas that affect federally protected species or habitats. Unlike many distributive programs that provide federal benefits for participating state agencies, there is no direct benefit to wildlife agencies that become involved in federal regulatory programs. A final problem with assigning regulatory policies to state wildlife agencies is that state legislatures often have separate legislative structures for dealing with environmental protection and wildlife management. In both environmental protection and wildlife management, lobby interests diverge more than they converge, and it could be counterproductive to place state wildlife commissions and agencies in the sights of manufacturing lobbyists, industrialists, and trade unions.

Folding Wildlife Agencies into Larger Agencies

Rather than ask wildlife agencies to assume new responsibilities in isolation, a second option is to move wildlife agencies into an existing umbrella agency that might already cover some of the new demands. By 2005, seventeen states had wildlife agencies folded into larger departments of natural resources; three agencies were with environmental protection departments while five were in departments that seem to combine both natural resources and environmental protections (National Wildlife Federation 2005). Cannamela and Warren (1999) favor combining state wildlife management and environmental protection because the program goals are complementary; for example, adequate habitat depends on air and water quality and the absence of dangerous waste. They suggest that combining programs would reduce duplication of effort, improve efficiency, and increase public support for both programs. According to Nie (2004), embedding state wildlife departments in larger umbrella agencies (either environmental or natural resources) would broaden constituencies, increase environmental management responsibilities, and increase funding sources. These new constituencies might be more accepting of wildlife agency decisions (Nie 2004, 228).

Moving wildlife agencies into umbrella organizations is more likely to succeed if the umbrella agency is natural resources rather than environmental protection because natural resource programs are generally distributive, and many of the problems with adding regulatory policies could be avoided. Although the range of stakeholders for natural resources is wider than just wildlife interests, folding wildlife agencies into departments of natural resources may ease the accommodations for new stakeholders because the agency staff can use the reorganization to justify policy changes. If the wildlife agencies are already committed to nonconsumptive activities, the transition may be even easier.

Wildlife agencies might find that their resources are more constrained by being embedded in a larger organization. Administrators of these combined programs should expect competition for resources (e.g., operation budgets, line and staff personnel, space, technology, and equipment) as well as more paperwork for clearances, permissions, reports, and analyses. Funding conflicts will still exist; wildlife agencies bring their protected federal funding and license revenues, but the resources of the wider agencies are still subject to the vagaries of state appropriation processes. The larger organization may be justifiably reluctant to expend its own scarce resources for the new addition (Donley and Pollard 2002, 141). Without control over wildlife agency budgets, department directors have diminished authority over the agencies; this violates basic bureaucratic norms of statutory line authority and control (Newmann 2002, 131).

In a blended organization, developing both formal (within the official hierarchy) and informal communication paths that are effective is risky business. Agencies that have substantive expertise and effective functions and capacities may work well on their own, but they may not be able to do their best work if they are forced to integrate into a larger organization. This is as much a concern for the larger umbrella agency as it is for the wildlife agency because the larger agency will face challenges of its own. The larger agency must be able to recognize the differences between its old mandates and the new goals and objectives as well as the policy costs of incorporating new goals, and then it must decide how to find resources to fill the gap between them (Donley and Pollard 2002, 140).

A third approach that is already occurring in some states is to develop more regular linkages among existing agencies without changing their formal administrative structures. Cannamela and Warren (1999, 1063) suggest that rather than going through the bother of a formal reorganization, these connections may be made more simply by adding liaison positions to existing agencies to facilitate communications, holding regular interagency meetings, or just housing the agencies in the same office areas. One indication that these linkages are developing is that there have been no significant changes in state agency institutional structures since 1995 (National Wildlife Federation 1995, 2005) despite recent pressures on wildlife agencies to respond to new stakeholder demands. If wildlife agencies are addressing new demands, presumably they are forming cooperative links with other state agencies.

Wicked Problems and Administrative Boundaries

In modern administration, "wicked problems, virtually by definition, challenge existing organizational and political boundaries" (Kettl 2006, 13). The five critical administrative boundaries are mission, resources, capacity, responsibility, and accountability (Kettl 2006, 14). Across American public administration, the struggle to address new, complex policy issues and to include increasingly insistent stakeholders finds agencies redrawing their old institutional boundaries (Kettl 2006, 11). This is precisely the task before wildlife agencies today: those boundaries have become porous, and working at their margins requires wildlife administrators to collaborate with other stakeholders.

Mission defines the purpose of an agency as well as its limits. For example, in 2005 the mission of the Idaho Department of Fish and Game was "to preserve, protect, perpetuate, and manage all wildlife within the state of Idaho, to make and declare such rules and regulations, and to employ personnel necessary to administer and enforce the harvest of wildlife" (National Wildlife Federation 2005, 120). Contrast this consumption-oriented statement with the mission of the Florida Fish and Wildlife Conservation Commission: "Managing fish and wildlife resources for their long-term well-being and for the benefit of the people" (National Wildlife Federation 2005, 116–17). These two statements provide a clear contrast in what the states intend to do and, by omission, what they do *not* intend to do. Mission statements may be mere window dressing, but public agencies often use them to justify decisions. However, as new stakeholders gain legitimacy and exert pressure on wildlife agencies, agency missions may no longer reflect the reality of public expectations.

Resources indicates the level of central government commitment to the agency mission. The level and stability of funding is generally a good indicator of legislative support for an agency, but using funding levels to assess support for wildlife agencies is complicated by federal aid programs and reserved license revenues. These have given some level of independence to the agencies and established a unique relationship between the agencies and the sportsmen. Combining agencies may create new wildlife agency funds, but it might also make existing agency funding vulnerable to creative diversions within the umbrella agency.

Capacity is the expertise and structure of an agency that, combined with its resources, enables it to meet its mission. This is the boundary most at risk when new stakeholders and their new policy issues are added to the wildlife agencies' missions. One unavoidable source of conflict between wildlife professionals and other stakeholders is the justifiable view of wildlife professionals that, because of their training and experience, they have better and more scientific information than other stakeholders to make final decisions on wildlife matters (Decker and Chase 2001, 135; Sparrowe 1995). The notion of professional expertise as the final word in management decisions has a great deal of administrative law to support it. Bureaucrats are trained in the substantive fields in which they work, and they apply their own experiences and institutional memories to decisions. Few legislators have technical expertise in wildlife issues, which is one reason that wildlife commissions are created to act as legislative surrogates.

Some agencies have a great deal of discretion conferred by their enabling statutes. Legislation sets the outline of agency responsibilities and the tools available to meet their responsibilities. The cumbersome legislative process cannot specify agency rules and regulation; if it did, the entire lawmaking process would bog down. The agency rule-making process is more streamlined and more flexible, allowing agencies to respond to new circumstances and scientific or technological advances. All public agency rule making requires public notice and an opportunity for comment. This process provides all stakeholders—even those with small stakes—with an opportunity to affect outcomes by providing input on the language of administrative rules and the strategies for enforcing them. Because rule-making decisions are important to those being affected, debates over rules can become lengthy, expensive, and extremely adversarial. Although providing comments on proposed rules may not be good practice for civil discourse, it does create a vehicle for debate over administrative decisions.

Responsibility defines the responsibilities of each individual for achieving the agency mission. When interagency connections are multiplied, opportunities for increased effectiveness multiply as well. However, as oversight also becomes more complex, individuals are able to shirk their duties, to pass blame on to others, and to build personal networks that increase their own status at the expense of the agency missions (Kettl 2006, 16).

Accountability is the reality of political oversight and, in our democratic system, ultimate responsibility to the citizens who elect the officials. This is another area in which boundaries are becoming flexible. Failure to maintain this chain of accountability may lead to citizens bypassing the legislative process in favor of the courts or other options such as citizen initiatives (Beck 1998; Burkhardt and Ponds 2006; Nie 2004). This behavior indicates a significant change in the old norms of representative government.

Two areas implicit in any discussion of agency reorganization are rarely addressed explicitly: administrative ethics and administrative law. The first provides internal norms to regulate the behavior of government bureaucrats, and the second provides an external force that not only imposes restrictions on bureaucratic behavior, but also protects the agencies when their decisions are challenged. Both are a species of *rule*; administrative ethics require bureaucrats to consider constitutional values when making decisions and to balance social requirements against resource availability, legislative mandates, professional training, and organizational loyalty (Rohr 1988), while administrative law frames the "possible" for agencies. The scope of the agencies' administrative authority and the intent of the legislature in giving them that authority are important parameters. Unless the legislative branch has given so much discretion to an agency that it has essentially abdicated its legislative function, agency officials are expected to use their discretion to meet legislative expectations as effectively as possible, not to cater to public preferences that have not been filtered through a legislatively approved process.

Wildlife agencies have always been immersed in institutional change. Wise administrators will embrace change early to maximize their opportunities for successful transitions to the next phase of wildlife management.

Literature Cited

Adams, L. 2005. Urban wildlife ecology and conservation: A brief history of the discipline. *Urban Ecosystems* 8:139–56.

Anderson, L., and D. Loomis. 2006. Balancing stakeholders with an imbalanced budget: How continued inequities in wildlife funding maintains [sic] old management styles. *Human Dimensions of Wildlife* 11(6):455–58.

Barnes, T. 1997. State agency oversight of the nuisance wildlife control industry. *Wildlife Society Bulletin* 25(1):185–88.

Beck, T. 1998. Citizen ballot initiatives: A failure of the wildlife management profession. *Human Dimensions of Wildlife* 3(2):21–28.

Buck, S. 2006. *Understanding environmental administration and law*, 3rd ed. Washington, DC: Island Press.

Burkhardt, N., and P. Ponds. 2006. Using role analysis to plan for stakeholder involvement: A Wyoming case study. *Wildlife Society Bulletin* 35(5):1306–13.

Cannamela, B., and R. Warren. 1999. Should state wildlife management and environmental protection programs be combined? *Wildlife Society Bulletin* 27(4):1059–63.

Decker, D. J., and T. L. Brown. 2001. Understanding your stakeholders. In *Human dimensions of wildlife management*, ed. D. J. Decker, T. L. Brown, and W. F. Siemer, 109–32. Bethesda, MD: Wildlife Society.

Decker, D. J., and L. C. Chase. 2001. Stakeholder involvement: Seeking solutions in changing times. In *Human dimensions of wildlife management*, ed. D. J. Decker, T. L. Brown, and W. F. Siemer, 133–52. Bethesda, MD: Wildlife Society.

Donley, M., and N. Pollard. 2002. Homeland security: The difference between a vision and a wish. *Public Administration Review* 62 (September, special issue):138–44.

Dubois, S., and D. Fraser. 2003a. Conversations with stakeholders, part I: Goals, impediments, and relationships in wildlife rehabilitation. *Journal of Wildlife Rehabilitation* 26(1):14–22.

———. 2003b. Conversations with stakeholders, part II: Contentious issues in wildlife rehabilitation. *Journal of Wildlife Rehabilitation* 26(2):8–14.

Gill, R. B. 1996. The wildlife professional subculture: The case of the crazy aunt. *Human Dimensions of Wildlife* 1(1):60–69.

Hadidian, J., M. Childs, R. Schmidt, L. Simon, and A. Church. 2001. Nuisance-wildlife control practices, policies, and procedures in the United States. In *Wildlife, land, and people: Priorities for the 21st century*, ed. R. Field, R. Warren, H. Okarma, and P. Sievert, 165–68. Bethesda, MD: Wildlife Society.

Heclo, H. 1978. Issue networks and the executive establishment. In *The new American political system*, ed. A. King, 87–124. Washington, DC: American Enterprise Institute.

Jacobson, C., and D. Decker. 2006. Ensuring the future of state wildlife management: Understanding challenges for institutional change. *Wildlife Society Bulletin* 34(2):531–36.

Kettl, D. 2006. Managing boundaries in American administration: The collaboration imperative. *Public Administration Review 66* (December, special issue):10–19.

Klay, W., and J. McElveen. 1991. Planning as a vehicle for policy formulations and accommodation in an evolving subgovernment. *Policy Studies Journal* 19(3–4): 527–33.

Knuth, B. A., W. F. Siemer, M. D. Duda, S. J. Bissell, and D. J. Decker. 2001. Wildlife management in urban environments. In *Human dimensions of wildlife management*, ed. D. J. Decker, T. L. Brown, and W. F. Siemer, 195–217. Bethesda, MD: Wildlife Society.

Leopold, A. 1986 (1933). *Game management.* Madison: University of Wisconsin Press.

Manfredo, M., T. Teel, and A. Bright. 2003. Why are public values toward wildlife changing? *Human Dimensions of Wildlife* 8:287–306.

Minnis, D. 1998. Wildlife policy-making by the electorate: An overview of citizen-sponsored ballot measures on hunting and trapping. *Wildlife Society Bulletin* 26(1):75–83.

National Wildlife Federation. 1995. *1995 conservation directory*, 40th ed. Washington, DC: Island Press.

———. 2005. *Conservation directory 2005–2006*, 50th ed. Washington, DC: Island Press.

Newmann, W. 2002. Reorganizing for national security and homeland security. *Public Administration Review* 62 (September, special issue):126–37.

Nie, M. 2003. Drivers of natural resource-based political conflict. *Policy Sciences* 36: 307–41.

———. 2004. State wildlife policy and management: The scope and bias of political conflict. *Public Administration Review* 64(2):221–33.

Organ, J., and E. Fritzell. 2000. Trends in consumptive recreation and the wildlife profession. *Wildlife Society Bulletin* 28(4):780–87.

Riley, S., D. Decker, L. Carpenter, J. Organ, W. Siemer, G. Mattfield, and G. Parsons. 2002. The essence of wildlife management. *Wildlife Society Bulletin* 30(2):585–93.

Ripley, R., and G. Franklin. 1991. *Congress, the bureaucracy, and public policy*, 5th ed. Belmont, CA: Wadsworth.

Rittel, H., and M. Webber. 1973. Dilemmas in a general theory of planning. *Policy Sciences* 4: 155–69.

Robbins, P., and A. Luginbuhl. 2005. The last enclosure: Resisting privatization. *Capitalism, Nature, Socialism* 16(1):45–61.

Rohr, J. A. 1988. *Ethics for bureaucrats*, 2nd ed. New York: Marcel Dekker.

Shackley, M. 1996. *Wildlife tourism.* Boston: International Thomson Business Press.

Sparrowe, R. 1995. Wildlife managers: Don't forget to dance with the one that brung you. *Wildlife Society Bulletin* 23(4):556–63.

U.S. Fish and Wildlife Service. 2007. *2006 National survey of fishing, hunting, and wildlife associated recreation: National overview.* Washington, DC: U.S. Fish and Wildlife Service.

Wise, C. 2002. Organizing for Homeland Security. *Public Administration Review* 62(2):131–44.

CHAPTER 14

Fueling the Conservation Engine: Where Will the Money Come from to Drive Fish and Wildlife Management and Conservation?

Michael Hutchins, Heather E. Eves, and Cristina Goettsch Mittermeier

Management and conservation of fish and wildlife resources, including endangered species recovery, requires a constant stream of revenue to pursue its core goals. Effective nonprofit organizations, academic institutions, government agencies, and individual experts who support biodiversity and habitat conservation must be sustained, meaning salaries must be paid and related management, research, and educational projects supported. Such efforts have contributed significantly toward slowing threats facing wildlife around the globe (Meyer 2006).

In this chapter we review briefly the major sources of funding available to those who work in fish, wildlife, and habitat management and conservation. We concentrate on sources of funding for nonprofit organizations, academicians, and other experts engaged in relevant activities. Our review is not exhaustive but rather provides examples of the kinds of support currently available to those working in our field. We also make some suggestions for the future of fish, wildlife, and habitat funding.

Private and Corporate Foundations

Foundations are major sources of support for fish and wildlife conservation and management. Their influence has grown as wealthy individu-

---

Thanks are due to John Organ (U.S. Fish and Wildlife Service), Dan Decker (Cornell University), and Laura Bies (the Wildlife Society) for reading and commenting on earlier versions of this manuscript.

als, families, and companies have increasingly given priority to wildlife and habitat conservation. According to Jankowski Associates (2006), more than one-third of all U.S.-based private grant-making foundations have been created since 1996. Of the five thousand newest foundations, approximately 20 percent supported environmental or animal-related causes. However, this listing does not include many major corporate foundations that also give regularly to environmental, wildlife, or related activities. For example, Disney's Wildlife Conservation Fund now provides over $1 million in support annually for conservation projects worldwide (Walt Disney World Conservation Initiatives 2005).

The Foundation Center's *Grants for Environmental Protection and Animal Welfare* lists 10,259 grant opportunities of $10,000 or more made by 819 foundations, primary in 2004 and 2005 (Foundation Center 2006). Many other compilations of grant-giving organizations exist, both in print and online, both nonprofit and commercial. Researching the range and scope of potential donor foundations is the first step in formulating a successful fund-raising plan.

Working with private or corporate foundations has become more challenging in recent years because of trends in both the donor and recipient communities. First, competition for limited foundation dollars has increased. Not only have the overall needs increased, but organizations, agencies, and experts competing for funds have proliferated. Second, as the conservation field has matured, so has the expectation for accountability for how foundation money is spent. Third, many foundations have sought to clarify and narrow their missions or geographical range to improve impact. Consequently, proposed projects must clearly fit within the stated mission and/or geographical range of a given foundation, and projected costs must be both reasonable and within the donor's pre-established limits. This requires entities seeking foundation support to demonstrate the highest level of project planning and implementation, including (1) developing an appropriate conceptual model with clear management or conservation targets, (2) identifying qualified personnel responsible for completing the work, and (3) accurately estimating financial and logistical requirements. Details are important and careful planning is essential, especially when making the case for support (Schaff and Schaff 1999). It is advisable to study a particular foundation's history of gift giving to see if similar projects have been funded in the past.

Fortunately, there are many publications that can assist in successful fund-raising such as Schaff and Schaff (1999), Weinstein (2002),

Lansdowne (2005), and Mutz and Murray (2006). Topics covered in these volumes include planning and prospect analysis, budgeting, development of presentation materials and proposals, capital campaigns, planned giving programs, working with consultants, donor recognition, and how to maintain appropriate records. Because marketing and branding your organization's mission and work are critical components of successful fund-raising (Mutz and Murray 2006), it is advisable that organizational leadership also strives to understand the basic principles underlying these activities (see Hiam 2004).

Measurement of management or conservation impact is another important trend (Ferraro and Pattanayak 2006; Christensen 2003). Most contemporary donors insist that some measures of success be built into project administration and that regular progress reports be submitted. Empirical evaluation needs to be an integral aspect of wildlife conservation projects, including those focused on policy.

Granting organizations need to ensure that their funds are used efficiently and for purposes stated in the proposal to protect their credibility. Therefore, it is essential that organizations, agencies, or individuals seeking support are beyond reproach and that recipients have the proper checks and balances in place (e.g., appropriate ethical governance and financial management policies). It is also essential to ensure that unethical behavior is unlikely, and if it does occur, that it can be easily detected. In the United States, this means compliance with the Sarbanes-Oxley Act (nonprofit organizations are subject to similar oversight as for-profit companies) (Ostrower and Bobowick 2006). Several "watchdog" groups, such as Charity Navigator (www.charitynavigator.org/) and the American Institute of Philanthropy (www.charitywatch.org/toprated.html), evaluate the financial policies and practices of nonprofit organizations and inform potential donors about the credibility, viability, and efficiency of potential recipients of charitable giving. Organizations that limit "overhead" (administrative) spending and direct more resources toward on-the-ground action are usually considered preferable (see Conclusions, below).

Government Funding

Government funding for conservation activities became a necessity in the United States around the beginning of the twentieth century (Trefethen 1975). This shift enabled the emergence of a North American Model of Wildlife Conservation (Geist 2006). This model includes (1) public ownership of wildlife (the Public Trust Doctrine), (2) planning for recovery of wildlife across expansive landscapes, (3) a user-pay system to support conservation and associated management activities and enabling the emergence of a strong wildlife profession, (4) a wildlife-based industry that is focused on recreational and subsistence hunting and fishing and the closure of commercial wildlife markets, and (5) appropriate legislation to support enforcement (Organ and Mahoney 2007).

One hundred years later, as nations in the twenty-first century set their agendas, government funding for regional and global wildlife conservation and associated management and restoration activities is one of the most important sources of support available. Not only do governments have access to significant financial resources to contribute directly to fish- and wildlife-related activities, they are also linked to important national and international legislative, diplomatic, and political processes. Assuring the future of ecological processes on which all nations, their citizens, and wildlife depend necessitates a strong commitment and significant, long-term support through government funding mechanisms.

There are numerous sources of government funding available with significantly different systems and mechanisms of operation. In the United States, conservation and related management activities are supported by a range of government programs to meet the estimated $5 to $8 billion annual need for a nationwide system of conservation lands (Lerner, Mackey, and Casey 2007). Included among these is the Farm Bill that subsidizes millions of farmland hectares for habitat and fish and wildlife conservation (Haufler 2007). The most recently authorized bill (2002) provided $17 billion for conservation on private lands over a five-year period (Gray and Teels 2006).

An extremely important mechanism for federal funding is linked with the Association of Fish and Wildlife Agencies (AFWA). In addition to providing a collective process for addressing U.S. wildlife and conservation priorities at the state level, AFWA has led an important initiative, called Teaming with Wildlife, to secure long-term funding for state-based wildlife conservation efforts. The State Wildlife Grants Program, established by Congress in 2000 and administered by the U.S. Fish and Wildlife Service, provides approximately $70 million per year to states (Brooke 2006).

The National Fish and Wildlife Foundation (NFWF) was established in 1984 by an act of Congress. NFWF works with federal funds and partners to leverage additional funding to support conservation both nationally and internationally. Over the period 1984–2006 it leveraged nearly $400 million in federal funds to provide over $1.2 billion toward conservation efforts (National Fish and Wildlife Foundation 2006).

An additional source of government-linked funding is open-space ballot measures that enable local land conservation efforts. Between 1996 and 2004, U.S. voters allocated over $27 billion to help support state and local land conservation initiatives (Szabo 2007). Even with long-term state funding, and federal funding that typically supports shorter-term efforts, there is a funding deficit in the United States to support a nationwide network of lands for fish and wildlife conservation (Lerner, Mackey, and Casey 2007).

In developing nations around the globe, the funding shortfall is similar. Focusing on protected areas alone, researchers have estimated the cost for effectively managing a global protected-areas system at approximately $2.1 billion annually. Unfortunately, the data suggest that actual expenditures fall far below this need at $0.8 billion annually (Bruner, Gullison, and Balmford 2004).

In short, funds exist but priorities often do not include fish and wildlife management and conservation. If this pattern is to shift in the twenty-first century, then the perspective of the average person must be fundamentally transformed. While each individual on the planet is certainly a potential agent for change, both positive (through monetary donations, volunteerism, recycling, and reduced carbon "footprints") and negative (through waste, pollution, and uncontrolled consumerism), there is a global imbalance among citizens in terms of their potential levels of impact. The residents of developed nations that put greater demands on global resources and have significantly more financial assets are viewed as having greater responsibility to help address these problems (Balmford and Whitten 2003). Such mechanisms are beginning to emerge in carbon-trading systems, in which nations that create higher carbon costs financially support conservation. This has potential to provide much-needed revenue to poorer nations that have the ability to maintain globally important carbon resources (e.g., tropical forests) over the long term (Laurance 2007).

Several mechanisms for government-funded international conservation have emerged in recent decades. The World Bank's Global Environment Facility (GEF) is a significant source of support for biodiversity conservation, for example, through its funding of the global Convention on Biological Diversity (CBD). International government-funding mechanisms, including the European Commission, the European Development Fund, GEF, the United Kingdom, Germany, the

Netherlands, Japan, the U.S. Agency for International Development (Biodiversity), and others, contribute approximately $1 billion annually toward conservation efforts (Dublin and Volonte 2004). Major nongovernmental organizations such as Conservation International, the Audubon Society, the Wildlife Conservation Society, the World Wildlife Fund, the World Resources Institute, IUCN-The World Conservation Union, and others contribute approximately $0.7 billion annually (Dublin and Volonte 2004).

Although there have been great strides in increasing the global focus on fish and wildlife and habitat conservation issues, governments still provide relatively minute levels of funding that are directly applied to conservation activities. Many projects from these "biodiversity" funds are strongly linked to human economic development and not to fish and wildlife conservation per se (Eves 2006). As an example, the U.S. Fish and Wildlife Service's Multinational Species Conservation Funds that support conservation activities for African and Asian elephants, great apes, tigers, rhinos, and other species are allocated a relatively small budget (e.g., $5.8 million in fiscal year 2005) as compared with the $165 million allocated to the U.S. Agency for International Development's Biodiversity Program (International Conservation Partnership 2005). For improved global conservation results in the twenty-first century, significant increases are needed urgently in government funding for direct conservation activities, coupled with improved monitoring and evaluation of projects and programs.

Individual Donors

As stated, funding for charitable causes comes from many sources, including governments, multilateral and bilateral agencies, and foundations. Donations by individuals, however, are the largest single source of charitable funds and the best prospects for fueling the engine of fish and wildlife management and conservation. The good news is that charitable projections are encouraging. In 2006, individual giving for all charitable causes rose by 4.4 percent (1.2 percent adjusted for inflation), reaching an estimated $222.89 billion per annum. This was equivalent to 75.6 percent (out of $295.02 billion) that was raised from all sources that year. However, only a small fraction of individual gifts go to environmental causes, and an even smaller percentage goes to studying, managing, and conserving fish and wildlife resources (Giving USA 2007).

The United States is a nation with an unmatched philanthropic tradition. Almost 80 percent of Americans contribute annually to at least one charity, and many of them are loyal donors (Giving USA 2007). A recent survey commissioned by SunTrust Bank found that respondents were most likely to support causes relating to their church or other religious organizations (53%) and organizations that combat hunger and poverty (50%) or disaster relief from natural catastrophes (48%). Unfortunately, the poll also found that the nonprofit organizations least likely to receive donations were those supporting animal causes (32%), environmental issues (25%), or the arts and culture (21%) (www.suntrust.com\mycause). Charitable contributions for environmental purposes have always been, and to this day remain, a marginal part of philanthropy. Furthermore, fish and wildlife conservation is just a small part of the "environmental charity mosaic" (Ames 1981).

Part of the problem is that when it comes to giving to the "environment," there has always been tremendous donor confusion. The lines that distinguish broader environmental issues, such as pollution, from animal rights and welfare, pets, and endangered species and habitat, have always been blurry in the minds of many Americans. For some, all of these issues are mistakenly perceived as one and the same (Hutchins 2001, 2007). As a result, individual giving tends to be skewed toward immediate and highly emotional or scary issues (e.g., those that affect pets or human health) and tends to be lacking when it comes to longer-term scientific research, social change, and policy-related projects. Ironically, it is often easier to raise funds for radical animal rights groups than it is to raise money for fish and wildlife or habitat conservation. Yet an investment in the long-term health of ecosystems and fish and wildlife conservation would do more, overall, to improve animal welfare than all other efforts combined (Hutchins 2001).

Although only a small fraction of individual gifts goes to conservation and the environment, a handful of American billionaires, such as Ted Turner and Gordon Moore, have consistently supported environmental causes. These individuals not only understand the importance of addressing environmental challenges, they also are personally involved in many of the projects they fund, which, in turn, helps ensure their continued support (Di Mento and Lewis 2007).

Most of these mega-gifts, however, are not specifically allocated to fish and wildlife management or conservation but to alleviation of environmental problems in general. Desegregating these various causes under the "environmental umbrella" will go a long way toward increasing individual giving to fish and wildlife management and conservation issues. Also important is the funding of basic and applied scientific research to understand the underpinnings of biodiversity conservation and the consequences of its loss (see Moore Foundation at www.moore.org).

Conservation organizations are becoming more innovative in their methods to attract wealthy donors. For example, the Monaco-Asia Society and Conservation International, under the patronage of Monaco's Prince Albert II, recently auctioned off the naming rights to newly discovered species to the highest bidder (Eilperin 2007).

Luckily, it is not only multimillionaires who are footing the bill for a better environment. Individuals of all income levels are the most consistent supporters of nonprofit conservation organizations. The Nature Conservancy's overall support, for example, reached an all-time high in fiscal year 2006, topping the $1 billion mark. Looking at the source of all donations to the Nature Conservancy, one can see that the amount donated by individuals represented 66 percent of the total, followed by 26 percent from foundations and 5 percent from corporations (Nature Conservancy 2006).

Similarly, in fiscal year 2005 the World Wildlife Fund (WWF) raised a total of $32.4 million from individuals, of which $13.6 million was raised from wealthy donors and the remaining from the general membership. For comparison purposes, government awards to WWF totaled $28.1 million, and an additional $13.8 million came from foundations, $12.5 million from WWF network organizations, and $3.3 million from corporations (World Wildlife Fund 2006). Results of a recent study on the direct links between conservation activity and the U.S. economy, however, indicate reason to be concerned about the future of small membership donations. The study found a correlation between large drops in the stock market and precipitous declines in NGO revenues (Pergams et al. 2004).

Individual giving for conservation and the environment is often encouraged by direct-mail appeals, face-to-face solicitation, and fund-raising events of all sizes. Donations range from a few dollars to several million dollars, and fund-raising is one of the core activities of all scientific, professional, and conservation organizations. The four largest international conservation organizations, the World Wildlife Fund, the Nature Conservancy, Conservation International, and the Wildlife Conservation Society, all rely on the cultivation of individual donors for their funding needs. Smaller organizations, such as the Wildlife Society and the American Fisheries Society, also rely on the generosity and commitment of a small proportion of interested individuals to support their programs, particularly dedicated organizational members. Competition is intense, but the good news is that never before has this country seen so many millionaires and billionaires and that never before has philanthropy been so popular.

Reliable analyses of what percentage of total annual contributions to charity by individuals goes to environmental and conservation causes today are not available, but if we use the estimate of less than 1 percent of the total as proposed by Ames (1981), it is clear that if we are to succeed in fish and wildlife management and conservation, we must work to earn the attention and trust of individual donors at all levels of giving.

Conclusion

We have attempted to summarize some of the current sources of funding available to support fish, wildlife, and associated habitat management and conservation. However, numerous related concerns are beginning to emerge. First, support for fish and wildlife management and conservation has tended to be focused on relatively short-term rather than long-term projects, yet most research, management, and conservation needs are long term. Thus, for effective management and/or conservation to occur, funding cannot be intermittent or inconsistent. It can take many years, sometimes even decades, to understand complex ecosystems, evaluate the reasons for species endangerment, and develop the necessary relationships and trust for real conservation impacts (and associated social norms or policies) to result.

We believe that the donor community must eventually shift its practice away from numerous, relatively small annual project cycles toward larger, longer-term investments. In addition, as the importance of interdisciplinary collaboration when seeking solutions to complex problems has been recognized, the need for collaboration among fish and wildlife scientists, managers, veterinarians, and human dimensions specialists is especially acute. Donor organizations could greatly facilitate collaboration by giving preference to projects that feature multidisciplinary teams of scientists and practitioners. Such a shift in priorities would help ensure that the appropriate expertise is available and that limited funding is used most efficiently.

Second, while support for fish and wildlife management and conservation in the United States and in other countries has traditionally come from state or federal government sources, this appears to be changing. In fact, government is cutting back on its support of both government agencies and nongovernmental organizations that support wildlife research, management, and conservation (Unger 2007a). It is therefore imperative that alternative and reliable sources of funding be established for the future, and established quickly. Time is of the essence because the opportunities we have to preserve natural landscapes and native fish and wildlife decline with each passing year and, once lost, cannot be retrieved.

Third, we also believe that increased donor attention must be focused on organizations that support and help develop fish and wildlife professionals. In the United States alone, it is estimated that more than 70 percent of leading fish and wildlife professionals will be retiring in the coming decade (McMullin 2004; Unger 2007b). Effective management and conservation simply cannot occur in the absence of highly skilled professionals to do the job. Thus, it is imperative that a new generation of fish and wildlife scientists, managers, and conservationists be nurtured and made ready to take on these important responsibilities. Organizations that represent, support, help train, and certify fish and wildlife professionals, such as the Wildlife Society, the American Fisheries Society, and their international equivalents, will therefore become increasingly important.

Fourth, it is notoriously difficult to obtain overhead expenses for various projects, yet planning and administration are essential aspects of any fish or wildlife management or conservation program. One way to address this issue would be for more corporate or private foundations to assist with the development of endowments for relevant NGOs and academic institutions. Endowments can provide long-term and consistent support for necessary administrative costs, such as salaries and benefits, planning, and communication. However, most current grant givers shy away from giving to endowments, preferring instead to have their money spent on activities that will directly or immediately affect resources on the ground. While the bottom line must necessarily be conservation of the fish, wildlife, and habitat resources in question, we must also find ways to support and sustain the organizations, institutions, and agencies that perform and facilitate this important work.

Fifth, much of the work that needs to be accomplished is going to require unprecedented levels of cooperation among government agencies, nongovernmental organizations, academia, and industry

(Gindrich and Maple 2007). Donors would do well to consider funding conservation-oriented consortiums that seek to find collaborative solutions to complex conservation challenges and to take advantage of the considerable development in information technology and management tools. Such networks can effectively link often remote, field-based professionals with important policy makers and urban-based conservation professionals. Many such collaborative efforts exist, including the Bushmeat Crisis Task Force (www.bushmeat.org), the Amphibian Survival Alliance (www.amphibians.org./asa.php), Turtle Survival Alliance (www.turtlesurvival.org/), Bird Conservation Alliance (www.birdconservationalliance.org/), and the Human-Wildlife Conflict Collaborative (www.humanwildlifeconflict.org). Such programs, defined by a multiorganizational and multidisciplinary approach, have been effective in marshaling limited human and financial resources, information sharing, collaborative political action, and awareness building, but they also have been difficult to sustain. Reasons for this vary but include donor burnout, infighting among collaborating organizations, and breakdowns in communication.

Last, new and innovative sources of government and private funding must be found to ameliorate the effects of current societal trends. Of particular concern is the increasing urbanization of the American public, which is resulting in a disconnection between children and nature (Louv 2005), declining visitation in natural parks (American Trails 2007), and significant reductions in the number of recreational fishers and hunters (Unger 2007a; Dute 2007). The U.S. Fish and Wildlife Service reported that the number of hunters dropped from 14 million in 1996 to 12.5 million in 2006, with an associated drop in licensing and recreational equipment sales. This, in turn, could potentially result in a significant drop in revenue for fish and wildlife management and conservation, particularly at the state level (Phillips 2007; Unger 2007a).

Sufficient funding is perhaps the most important "fuel" for the future of fish and wildlife in the twenty-first century. To help ensure that adequate resources are available, nonprofit organizations, agencies, academic institutions, and individual experts must become more business-like in their approach, using their limited human and financial resources as efficiently and economically as possible. They must also become more adept at marketing and fund-raising. Similarly, donor organizations need to address the evolving needs of the fish and wildlife management and conservation community, by thinking outside the current grant-giving box.

Literature Cited

American Trails. 2007. *National park visitation continues downward trend.* Redding, CA: American Trails. www.americantrails.org/resources/fedland/npsvisit07.html.

Ames, E. 1981. Philanthropy and the environmental movement in the United States. *Environmentalist* 1:9–14.

Balmford, A., and T. Whitten. 2003. Who should pay for tropical conservation, and how could the costs be met? *Oryx* 37(2):238–50.

Brooke, R. 2006. *State wildlife grants five-year accomplishment report: Cost effective conservation to prevent wildlife from becoming endangered.* Washington, DC: Association of Fish and Wildlife Agencies; Arlington, VA: U.S. Fish and Wildlife Service. www.teaming.com/pdf/swg_report.pdf.

Bruner, A. G., R. E. Gullison, and A. Balmford. 2004. Financial costs and shortfalls of managing and expanding protected area systems in developing countries. *BioScience* 54(12): 1119–26.

Christensen, J. 2003. Auditing conservation in an age of accountability. *Conservation in Practice* 4:12–19.

Di Mento, M., and N. Lewis, 2007. Record-breaking giving. *The Chronicle of Philanthropy.* www.philanthropy.com/free/articles/v19/i09/09000601.htm.

Dublin, H. T., and C. Volonte. 2004. *GEF Biodiversity Program Study 2004.* Washington, DC: Global Environment Facility Office of Monitoring and Evaluation, World Bank.

Dute, J. 2007. Pittman-Robertson Act: 70 years of conservation dollars. www.al.com/sports/mobileregister/index.ssf?/base/sports/1190139336232800.xml&coll=3.

Eilperin, J. 2007. New species owe names to the highest bidder. *Washington Post Friday,* September 14, A1, A8.

Eves, H. E. 2006. The bushmeat crisis in Central Africa: Resolving a common pool resource problem in the common interest. PhD diss., School of Forestry and Environmental Studies, Yale University.

Ferraro, P. J., and S. K. Pattanayak. 2006. Money for nothing? A call for empirical evaluation of biodiversity conservation investments. *PLoS Biology* 4(4):482–88.

Foundation Center. 2006. *Grant guidelines #4: Grants for environmental protection and animal welfare.* New York: Foundation Center.

Geist, V. 2006. The North American Model of Wildlife Conservation: A means of creating wealth and protecting public health while generating biodiversity. In *Gaining ground: In pursuit of ecological sustainability,* ed. D.

M. Lavigne, 285–93. Guelph, ON: International Fund for Animal Welfare; Limerick: University of Limerick.

Gindrich, N., and T. L. Maple. 2007. *Contract with the earth.* Baltimore, MD: Johns Hopkins University Press.

Giving USA. 2007. *The annual report on philanthropy for the year 2006.* Glenview, IL: Giving Institute. http://sforce.benevon.com/images/GivingUSA2007.htm.

Gray, R. L., and B. M. Teels. 2006. Wildlife and fish conservation through the Farm Bill. *Wildlife Society Bulletin* 34(3):906–13.

Haufler, J. B., ed. 2007. *Fish and wildlife responses to Farm Bill conservation practices.* Bethesda, MD: Wildlife Society.

Hiam, A. 2004. *Marketing kit for dummies.* Hoboken, NJ: Wiley Publishing.

Hutchins, M. 2001. Rattling the cage: Toward legal rights for animals. *Animal Behaviour* 61(4):855–58.

——-2007. The limits of compassion. *Wildlife Professional* 1(2):42–44.

International Conservation Partnership (ICP). 2005. *The international conservation budget 2005: Building on America's historic commitment to conservation.* Washington, DC: International Conservation Partnership (CI, TNC, WCS, WWF).

Jankowski Associates, Inc. 2006. *The leading 500 new foundations funding conservation, wildlife and the environment.* Frederick, MD: Jankowski Associates, Inc.

Lansdowne, D. 2005. *The relentlessly practical guide to raising serious money: Proven strategies for non-profit organizations.* Medfield, MA: Emerson and Church Publishers.

Laurance, W. F. 2007. A new initiative to use carbon trading for tropical forest conservation. *Biotropica* 39(1):20–24.

Lerner, J., J. Mackey, and F. Casey. 2007. What's in Noah's wallet? Land conservation spending in the United States. *BioScience* 57(5):419–23.

Louv, R. 2005. *Last child in the woods: Saving our children from nature deficit disorder.* Chapel Hill, NC: Algonquin Books of Chapel Hill.

McMullin, S. L. 2004. *Demographics of retirement and professional development needs of state fisheries and wildlife agency employees.* Prepared for U.S. Fish & Wildlife Service, National Conservation Training Center and The International Association of Fish and Wildlife Agencies.

Meyer, S. M. 2006. *The end of the wild.* Somerville, MA: Boston Review; London: MIT Press.

Mutz, J., and K. Murray. 2006. *Fundraising for dummies.* Hoboken, NJ: Wiley Publishing.

Nature Conservancy. 2006. *The Nature Conservancy annual report financial report*

2006. Arlington, VA: Nature Conservancy. www.nature.org/aboutus /annualreport/.

National Fish and Wildlife Foundation (NFWF). 2006. *National Fish and Wildlife Foundation annual report 2006*. Washington, DC: National Fish and Wildlife Foundation. www.nfwf.org/AM/Template.cfm?Section=Annual _Report&Template=/CM/ContentDisplay.cfm&ContentID=5195].

Organ, J., and S. Mahoney. 2007. The future of public trust. *The Wildlife Professional* 1(2):18–22.

Ostrower, F., and M. J. Bobowick. 2006. *Nonprofit governance and the Sarbanes-Oxley Act*. Washington, DC: The Urban Institute, Center on Nonprofits and Philanthropy.

Pergams, R. W., B. Czech, J. C. Haney, and D. Nuberg 2004. Linkage of conservation activity to trends in the U.S. economy. *Conservation Biology* 18(6):1617–23.

Phillips, A. 2007. Hunters are going the way of the dinosaur. *Washington Post Sunday*, September 9:D4.

Schaff, T., and D. Schaff. 1999. *The fundraising planner*. San Francisco: Jossey-Bass Publishers.

Szabo, P. S. 2007. Noah at the ballot box: Status and challenges. *BioScience* 57(5):424–27.

Trefethen, J. 1975. *An American crusade for wildlife*. New York: Winchester Press and Boone and Crockett Club.

Unger, K. 2007a. Slash and burn: Threadbare budgets weaken the fabric of wildlife management. *The Wildlife Professional* 1(2):23–27.

———. 2007b. The graying of the green generation. *The Wildlife Professional* 1(1):18–22.

Walt Disney World Conservation Initiatives 2005. *Disney's commitment to conservation*. Walt Disney World Conservation Initiatives, Lake Buena Vista, FL.

Weinstein, S. 2002. *The complete guide to fundraising management*. New York: John Wiley and Sons.

World Wildlife Fund. 2006. *Annual report (Income and expenditure)*. www.panda.org/news_facts/publications/key_publications/index.cfm.

PART IV

Social Perspectives on Contemporary Fish and Wildlife Management Issues

The first three parts of this book (1) provided a theoretical and historical context for human dimensions (HD) of fish and wildlife management, (2) presented an overview of the changing culture of fish and wildlife management, and (3) examined institutional policy and funding changes in wildlife agencies and nonprofit organizations. Chapters in this final part investigate contemporary social science issues in fish and wildlife management.

Given increasing urbanization, urban wildlife are the only wildlife that many city dwellers may ever encounter in person. Chapter 15 draws attention to this shift in human demographics, explains the implications for wildlife management, and expresses concern for agency neglect of this growing urban population of both people and animals.

Increases in human mobility and population pressure have also increased human-wildlife conflicts. Chapter 16 details the struggles between small rural communities and global populations that often result in political clashes over protected-area management and wildlife policy. This chapter suggests that integrating the economic needs of people living near protected areas into the planning process is essential for successful protected-area and wildlife management. Understanding and applying human dimensions theory (e.g., wildlife values, attitudes) is essential for public acceptance of community-based conservation or comanagement approaches.

Chapter 17 focuses specifically on contemporary

issues facing anglers. Rapid demographic changes occurring throughout the world are affecting the future of recreational fishing. This chapter discusses the pros and cons of a market approach to recreational fishing to address these concerns. Although primarily focused on Western postindustrialized societies, the chapter provides commentary on similar issues in other parts of the world.

Human-wildlife interaction can increase the risk of disease transmission between people and wildlife. Although there are numerous studies on the pathology, transmission, and epidemiology of wildlife diseases, HD research on critical zoonoses is limited. Chapter 18 (1) highlights the range of wildlife diseases that can affect humans, as well as have negative impact on wildlife, (2) suggests that most human dimensions studies on wildlife diseases do not follow a systematic paradigm of research, and (3) provides an illustrated approach to studying the HD of wildlife diseases using chronic wasting disease as an example. Similar to biological research, a systematic program of HD inquiry is necessary to understand and prepare for the next wildlife disease crisis.

The historical utilitarian relationships between people and wildlife are giving way to more nonconsumptive uses like wildlife viewing. Chapter 19 applies a systems thinking approach to exploring major trends affecting wildlife management including the rise in wildlife viewing as a recreation activity, expanding policy to use nature-based tourism as an economic development tool, and deepening human concern about wildlife. The chapter presents innovative ideas arising at the intersection of marketing and management.

Hunter access to wildlife is a classic HD research topic that is still relevant today as issues of access continue to have impact on hunter participation. Increased development, reduced access to private land, and increased privatization of public lands are a few of the topics discussed in chapter 20. Case studies are used to provide insight into recent trends in hunter access.

The challenges of managing hunting in tropical forests are often more complex than in other parts of the world. Chapter 21 introduces the essential elements of effective hunting management systems in tropical forests through a series of successful examples and guidelines. Public and private sectors, local communities, conservation organizations, and governments are all players that bring both problems and skills to the table. This chapter provides realistic guidelines for successful cooperation.

New research indicates that people around the world are concerned about environmental degradation, but channeling this concern into support for wildlife conservation has proved difficult. Low environmental literacy and cultural diversity contribute to an increased need for effective environmental communication. Chapter 22 describes the communication process, explains communication tools, and presents strategies for communication about wildlife issues in a diverse world.

Overall, the chapters in Part 4 provide examples of how HD science is making it possible for fish and wildlife managers to respond to contemporary issues. The growth of HD science is a proactive response to the complex and rapidly changing relationship between society and wildlife in the twenty-first century.

CHAPTER 15

The Socioecology of Urban Wildlife Management

John Hadidian

In 1915 slightly more Americans came to live in cities than not. Today urbanites, those of us who live in cities or towns with a population of fifty thousand or more, compose more than 80 percent of the American population. Sometime early in 2008 there were finally more people living in cities worldwide than outside them, as humans crossed an urban threshold reached in less than 1 percent of the time we have been identifiable as a species. For those who subscribe to the idea that connection to the natural world improves the human lot, looking into this future raises a host of questions and concerns.

If it were only a matter of considering the immediate occupancy of space, urbanization might not qualify as one of the most significant environmental issues of our time. After all, cities occupy barely a fraction of the land area committed to agriculture and livestock production. But those commitments are themselves simply part of the urban "footprint" (Rees 1992), the land area each city actually requires to meet its basic subsistence needs. Beyond their physical presence, cities have obvious influence on what can be called the human social environment. Their demographic dominance makes them de facto centers of political power and control. Their neighborhoods, schools, and cultural centers create the experiential environment within which the attitudes, beliefs, and values of the resident population are formed. These translate readily into policy and law, not to mention more fundamental cultural mores. Urban problems and conflicts dominate local politics, while urban markets set economic standards and influence social values far beyond any city boundaries.

Urban policy rests heavily on the political, economic, and social theory that traditionally focuses on such problems as transport, poverty, class representation, housing, and other commonly recognized societal concerns. Far less consideration is given to any "natural" systems context within which the ebb and flow of human and nonhuman life goes on. To many, cities remain "artificial" environments, apart from nature and natural processes. To a growing number of others, they are simply a different sort of ecosystem, amenable to many of the same ecological forces that regulate process and function elsewhere (Platt, Rowntree, and Muick 1994). To a few, they are integrated ecological and social communities where moral consideration is due to both human and nonhuman members (Wolch 1998; Lynn 1998).

This chapter addresses the socioecology[1] of urban wildlife, a minor crossroad where one aspect of urban ecology intersects with urban society. Wild animals do not play as significant a role in the ecology of a city as do its soil, water, or plant communities. But as objects of interest and concern to people they can come to represent the ecological community in ways those others cannot. Because of this, urban wildlife will increasingly become a principal forcing factor in determining the future of the average American's relationship to the nonhuman world. Our wildlife institutions and agencies have not yet recognized this in a meaningful way. If a theory and, more important, a praxis for urban wildlife cannot be found, then we ought to look with concern to our future relationship with wild animals and the values they represent.

Urban Wildlife: A Newly Emerging Bridging Subdiscipline

The field of urban wildlife is only a few decades old and, understandably, lacks much of the theoretical rigor other aspects of wildlife science and management can claim. Adams (2005) discusses the origins of urban wildlife as deriving from the principles inherent in the theory and practice of game management, suggesting urban wildlife as a branch or subdiscipline within that broader tradition. For all practical purposes, the formal, professional pursuit of urban wildlife in North America began with a technical session on the subject held at the Thirty-second North American Fish and Wildlife Conference (Scheffey 1967).

---

[1] I use this term rather than "social ecology" because of the fairly strong and somewhat confusing association the latter has with social theory (Bookchin 1993), including spillover into the general "ecological" school in sociological research (Berry and Kasarda 1977).

This was almost immediately followed by the first national conference (U.S. Department of the Interior 1968) and a subsequent blossoming of other conferences and urban-themed activities supporting growth through about the mid-1980s (Adams 2005).

Despite its early involvement, federal support for urban wildlife has not been sustained. Babbitt (1999) assured that urban ecology was being "rediscovered" at high levels in American government, but beyond a U.S. Fish and Wildlife Service initiative to create partnerships with cities under an "Urban Bird Treaty," there has been little evidence that this rediscovery has had anything to do with wild animals. More critically, the resources that state agencies have devoted to urban wildlife issues have long been cited as not being equal to the need or demand of urban residents (San Julien 1987; Lindsey 2003). In the first survey of its kind, Lyons and Leedy (1984) found only six state agencies claiming urban wildlife programs, a number that is little changed today. C. Adams (2003) recently resurveyed those states and found that fewer than 1 percent of all agency biologists (46 of 5, 409) identified themselves as working on urban wildlife issues. Yet more than 80 percent of the agencies acknowledged that urban wildlife was a growing management concern, and more than half claimed all responsibility for urban wildlife management. Regarding university involvement, an early survey (Adams, Leedy, and McComb 1985) found that 92 percent of responding academic institutions did not have a recognized urban wildlife program, while another survey a decade and a half later found that only 2 percent (7 of 545) of the faculty polled were teaching urban wildlife (Adams 2003).

Some focus on urban wildlife appears to have recently developed within nontraditional interests, particularly those engaged with broader ecological and biodiversity conservation concerns. Special technical sessions that in part dealt with urban wildlife have been held at the annual meetings of the Ecological Society of America, and the annual conference of the Society for Conservation Biology was almost entirely devoted to an urban theme in 2004. Among nonprofit animal protection and wildlife conservation organizations, the National Wildlife Federation has a long tenure with its backyard habitat certification program, a highly successful initiative now emulated by almost thirty state natural resource agencies. The Humane Society of the United States has had an urban wildlife program since the mid-1980s (Hodge 1988) and People for the Ethical Treatment of Animals, the Animal Protection Institute, and local groups such as Portland Audubon Society have program focus in the area as well, variously supported and maintained. These involvements, together with others coming from emerging fields in more traditional wildlife areas, such as human-wildlife dimensions research, suggest that urban wildlife will be addressed in the future through a plurality of different academic and institutional foci. As such it could come to represent a "bridging subdiscipline" (Carpenter 1969) connecting traditional and emerging interests in wildlife science, policy, and management.

The Ecological Context for Urban Wildlife Is Dynamic

Cities are highly dynamic environments characterized by landscape heterogeneity and rapid land use change as two dominating environmental variables. Human actions create rapid transformation cycles that destroy, create, or modify habitats capable of supporting wildlife communities. This, and the fact that the study of urban wildlife remains a nascent field primarily focused on individual species or species-groups (e.g., birds) rather than communities or ecological associations, militates against a more general understanding of urban wildlife ecology and the factors that might influence the abundance, distribution, and behavior of wild animals in urban environments. Add to this the apparent fact that many of the niches that exist in urban environments have yet to be colonized by wild animals, and it may become clearer why human-wildlife relationships often seem to be dynamically in flux in cities. Not long ago, white-tailed deer and Canada geese were real rarities in urban areas; now they are common and, some say, pests.

It is fair to say that most, if not all, species of urban wildlife are synanthropes, tolerant of living in proximity to humans but likely as well to be cryptic, often engaging in nocturnal activity patterns that do not put them into much direct contact with humans. Most are dietary and habitat generalists, occurring at population densities that exceed levels achieved in nonurban habitats. Whether this has to do with the greater and more consistent availability of resources or greater freedom from human exploitation, or both, remains to be determined. These elevated populations can be declared "overabundant" at a point where the conflicts they have with humans exceed a threshold that is often called the cultural carrying or wildlife acceptance capacity (Decker, Lauber, and Siemer 2002). Where the species is not particularly valued to begin with, this may trigger control actions that would not be accepted if directed at other animals. For example, it is common for rock pigeons (*Columba livia*) to be poisoned when they are declared as "pests," while to do so to mourning doves (*Zenaida macroura*) would be a violation of federal law, not to mention common mores widely held among different interest groups.

The Social Context for Urban Wildlife Is Dynamic

Stephen Kellert and his colleagues (Kellert 1996) measured American attitudes, knowledge, and perception of wildlife in a series of pioneering studies that produced a typology of value categorizations to help explain how people related to the natural world. The polar axes in this typology distinguish "utilitarian" and "protectionist" sentiments. Utilitarian beliefs include the feelings that animals can, and should, be used by humans for human benefit, while protectionist sentiments include values that might even stretch to according wild animals some of the same rights as felt due to humans, including freedom from exploitation. There is considerable interest in this dichotomy among both wildlife scientists and agency professionals, owing in part to a widespread belief that American society is moving away from being predominantly dominated by utilitarian sentiments to protectionist ones (Langeneau 1987; Manfredo, Teel, and Bright 2003).

That movement toward protectionist sentiments has been tied largely to the growth of an urban populace (Kellert 1984). Manfredo and colleagues (2003) found a strong inverse correlation between the presence of "traditionalists" and factors such as urbanization, income, and education, while a positive correlation existed with residential stability. Butler and colleagues (2003), however, called for a reevaluation of the "trend-toward-protectionist" concept, citing longitudinal data that suggested declining problem tolerance over time, which they suggest may represent a shift back toward greater utilitarian values.

The sentiments urbanites hold toward wild animals are almost certainly based on multiple determinants (Zinn and Miller 2003) open to rapid change as people's experiences with either individuals or groups of wild animals vary (Decker and Gavin 1987; Coluccy et al. 2001). The apparent urgency over issues such as "too many" Canada geese (Ankney 1996) undoubtedly shapes public attitudes, at least in the short term. Further, situation-specific experiences may be quite powerful in shaping individual attitudes (Zinn and Miller 2003) and, perhaps, broader value and belief systems. Lynn (1998) argues that the site and situation-specific aspects of conflicts are a constitutive element of all ethical problems involving wildlife, contributing to a much broader moral background than would be apparent upon consideration of individual interests only.

Urbanites, of course, are no more assignable to a single class of attitudes and values than any other segment of the population. Indeed, fairly strong "negativistic" feelings about certain types of wildlife, such as snakes, prevail among this group (Kellert 1984), despite whatever protectionist sentiments they may be said to hold. Urbanites are often said to be less knowledgeable about wild animals than their rural counterparts (Langeneau 1987; Dahlgren et al. 1977; Adams 2003). If this is true, and if the finding that childhood affiliation with nature among urbanities is declining holds equally true (Kahn 2002), it is probable that valuing wild animals from any reference point—utilitarian or protectionist or other—is likely to trend downward in succeeding generations.

Still, for the present, urbanites express considerable empathy for wildlife (Mankin, Warner, and Anderson 1999; Miller, Campbell, and Yeagle 2001), although much of this seems to be selective in favoring specific groups such as songbirds (Dagg 1974; Brown, Dawson, and Miller 1979). Indeed, the number of people identifying themselves as bird-watchers, as well as those engaged in bird feeding, dominates all other groups of Americans with nameable interests in wildlife-related activities (U.S. Fish and Wildlife Service 2007) and may have held that status for some time. People value and often cherish contact with other living things, as the theory surrounding the concept of biophilia suggests (Kellert and Wilson 1993).

Human-wildlife interactions in urban environments can also be negative, of course. Conflict events can broadly be said to fall into three general classes: those involving one or a few animals and proprietary to individual homeowners, those involving groups of animals and proprietary to more corporate (managerial) entities, and those involving entire populations and proprietary to the state itself. The individual homeowner may be confronted with a problem when a raccoon takes up residence in her chimney, the manager of a municipal park may have complaints about a large number of pigeons frequenting his site, and the governor's office may hear from many different stakeholders that the "deer problem" has gotten out of hand and needs to be dealt with. All require different forms of response, are likely to involve different types of participants in those responses, and raise different questions concerning the ethical basis for responses generated.

Are Our Social Responses to Urban Wildlife Lacking?

The attitudes, values, and beliefs urbanites hold about wild animals help shape and determine institutional responses, although to what extent they play a determinative role in setting policy or practice is not well understood. Interest in and responsibility for urban wildlife is widely divided among a variety of agencies, organizations, businesses, and other entities, and the bulk of regulatory authority is vested in state wildlife agencies, less in federal agencies, and even less in the municipalities. But the average urban resident is far more likely to need and demand services for the control of "nuisance" wildlife than for any other wildlife concern, and the state agencies have traditionally demonstrated little involvement in this area of concern (Barnes 1997; Hadidian et al. 2001). Brocke (1977) argued that wildlife management had no "urban game plan," a sentiment echoed nearly thirty years later in C. Adam's (2003) comment that state agencies and universities had been "caught off guard" with respect to urban wildlife issues. That thirty years would pass without the apparent indication of much, if any, change in agency perspective suggests a fundamental and inherent resistance to any change at all, and raises concerns that the state agencies have been subject to some form of bureaucratic "capture" by special interests (Langaneau 1982) for whom urban wildlife holds no meaning.

Whatever the cause, much of the demand for public assistance with wildlife problems (a highly tangible concern), as well as for educational and heuristic resources (a much less tangible concern), is currently falling on others. Municipal animal shelters and animal control agencies, as well as law enforcement agencies, typically do not have a mandate to deal with wildlife issues but become involved in handling significant numbers of wild animals (Kirkwood 1998). Private wildlife control businesses fill in other gaps. Private consulting groups have as yet to be used as has become common in environmental management (Dorney 1989), but may be one real possibility for the future.

Meanwhile, nontraditional, alternative ways of looking at human-wildlife relationships in cities are emerging through other disciplinary orientations. The "ecological city" concept (Platt, Rowntree, and Muick 1994) raises consideration of wildlife as but one community among others whose treatment occurs at a systems rather than individual species level. Alternate views of the urban human-animal relationship arise from combinations of ecological and social theory (Wolch 1998) as well as anthropological viewpoints (Sabloff

2001). Lynn's (1998) call to place contextual emphasis on geographical being and community through the practice of geoethics opens another dialogue entirely, to which might be included even broader efforts to embrace the ethical concerns surrounding wildlife management (Eggleston, Rixecker, and Hickling 2003; Littin, Mellor, and Eason 2004).

Conclusion

Addressing the human dimensions aspects of urban wildlife is an important and increasingly obvious need, both for the practitioners of urban wildlife management and for the broader public. A great deal more needs to be known about the basic attitudes, values, and beliefs of the urban populace before an understanding can be reached about how much it might influence the future of management, not to mention other urban wildlife conservation needs. The urban public seems to be a wild card in which sentiments may be moving more toward protectionism, or reverting to a form of utilitarian acceptance of removal and destruction of wild animals because of their "nuisance" or "pest" status, or, paradoxically, in both directions. It is hard to tell as well who the key interest groups might be and what interests they would seek to most protect. For example, there may be wholly unanticipated agreement between hunting and animal protection interests, traditional antagonists, over the ethics of mass killing of urban Canada geese (Hadidian 2002).

Much of what has been said here has been about the institutional neglect of urban wildlife. This cannot be blamed solely on agency disregard. The rapid growth of urban centers, the dynamically changing context within which conflicts with wild animals arise, and the open-ended nature of colonization that finds new species continuing to probe and explore urban habitats combine to create change at a pace that would challenge any bureaucracy. The future of urban wildlife rests on the potential for it to comprise a bridge between the science that can inform decision makers and the diverse public opinions that create the rest of the social context within which decision making must take place. Our social institutions must rise to the challenges urban wildlife presents. Long ago predicted to be "one of the most difficult and important problems confronting wildlife managers" (Kellert and Berry 1980, 89), urban wildlife remains so today and, in all likelihood, will remain so into the foreseeable future.

Literature Cited

Adams, C. 2003. The infrastructure for conducting urban wildlife management is missing. *Transactions of the 68th North American Wildlife and Natural Resources Conference*, 252–65.

Adams, L. 2005. Urban wildlife ecology and conservation: A brief history of the discipline. *Urban Ecosystems* 8:139–56.

Adams, L., D. Leedy, and W. McComb. 1985. Urban wildlife research and education in North American colleges and universities. *Wildlife Society Bulletin* 15:591–95.

Ankney, C. D. 1996. An embarrassment of riches: Too many geese. *Journal of Wildlife Management* 60:217–23.

Babbitt, B. 1999. Noah's mandate and the birth of urban bioplanning. *Conservation Biology* 13:677–78.

Barnes, T. 1997. State agency oversight of the nuisance wildlife control industry. *Wildlife Society Bulletin* 25:185–88.

Berry, B., and J. Kasarda. 1977. *Contemporary urban ecology.* New York: Macmillan.

Bookchin, M. 1993. What is social ecology? In *Environmental philosophy: From animal rights to radical ecology*, ed. M. E. Zimmerman. Englewood Cliffs, NJ: Prentice-Hall.

Brocke, R. 1977. What future for wildlife management in an urbanizing society? *Transactions of the Northeast Fish and Wildlife Conference*, 71–79.

Brown, T., C. Dawson, and R. Miller. 1979. Interests and attitudes of metropolitan New York residents about wildlife. *Transactions of the 44th North American Wildlife and Natural Resources Conference*, 289–97.

Butler, J., J. Shanahan, and D. Decker. 2003. Public attitudes toward wildlife are changing: A trend analysis of New York residents. *Wildlife Society Bulletin* 31:1027–36.

Carpenter, C. R. 1969. Approaches to studies of the naturalistic communicative behavior in nonhuman primates. In *Approaches to Animal Communication*, ed. T. Sebeok and A. Ramsey, 40–70. The Hague: Mouton.

Coluccy, J., R. Drobney, D. Graber, S. Sheriff, and D. Witter. 2001. Attitudes of central Missouri residents toward local giant Canada geese and management alternatives. *Wildlife Society Bulletin* 29:116–23.

Dagg, A. 1974. Reactions of people to urban wildlife. In *Wildlife in an urbanizing environment*, ed. J. Noyes and D. Progulski, Planning and Resource Development Series, no. 28, 163–65. Amherst: University of Massachusetts.

Dahlgren, R., A. Wywialowski, T. Bubolz, and V. Wright. 1977. Influence of knowledge of wildlife management principles on behavior and attitudes toward resource issues. *Transactions of the North American Wildlife and Natural Resources Conference* 42:146–55.

Decker, D., and T. Gavin. 1987. Public attitudes toward a suburban deer herd. *Wildlife Society Bulletin* 15:173–80.

Decker, D., T. B. Lauber, and W. Siemer. 2002. *Human-wildlife conflict management*. Ithaca, NY: Northeast Wildlife Damage Management Research and Outreach Cooperative.

Dorney, R. 1989. *The professional practice of environmental management*. New York: Springer Verlag.

Eggleston, J., S. Rixecker, and G. Hickling. 2003. The role of ethics in the management of New Zealand's wild mammals. *New Zealand Journal of Zoology* 30:361–76.

Hadidian, J. 2002. Resolving conflicts between people and Canada geese: The need for comprehensive management approaches. *Proceedings of the 20th Vertebrate Pest Conference*, ed. R. Timm and R. Schmidt, 175–79. Davis: University of California, Davis.

Hadidian, J., M. Childs, R, Schmidt, L. Simon, and A. Church. 2001. Nuisance wildlife control practices, policies and procedures in the United States. In *Wildlife, land and people: Priorities for the 21st century*, Proceedings of the Second International Wildlife Management Congress, ed. R. Field, R. Warren, H. Okarma, and P. Sievert, 165–68. Valko, Hungary: Wildlife Society.

Hodge, G. 1988. The plight of urban animals. *The Animal's Agenda* (April):12–19, 57.

Kahn, P. 2002. Children's affiliations with nature: Structure, development, and the problem of environmental generational amnesia. In *Children and nature*, ed. P. Kahn and S. Kellert, 93–116. Cambridge, MA: MIT Press.

Kellert, S. 1984. Urban American perceptions of animals and their natural environment. *Urban Ecology* 8:209–28.

———. 1996. *The value of life*.Washington, DC: Island Press.

Kellert, S., and J. Berry. 1980. Phase III: Knowledge, affection and basic attitudes toward animals in American society. United States Fish and Wildlife Service Report.

Kellert, S., and E. O. Wilson, ed. 1993. *The biophilia hypothesis*. Washington, DC: Island Press.

Kirkwood, S. 1998. Answering the call of the wild. *Animal Sheltering* 21:4–11.

Langeneau, E. 1982. Bureaucracy and wildlife: A historical overview. *International Journal for the Study of Animal Problems* 3:140–57.

———. 1987. Anticipating wildlife values of tomorrow. In *Valuing wildlife: Economic and social perspectives*, ed. Daniel Decker and Gary Goff, 309–17. Boulder, CO: Westview Press.

Lindsey, K. 2003. A national assessment of wildlife information transfer to the public. Master's thesis, Texas A&M University.

Littin, K. E., D. J. Mellor, and C. T. Eason. 2004. Animal welfare and ethical issues relevant to the humane control of vertebrate pests. *New Zealand Veterinary Journal* 52:1–10.

Lynn, W. 1998. Animals, ethics, and geography. In *Animal geographies*, ed. J. Wolch and J. Emel. London: Verso, 280–97.

Lyons, J., and D. Leedy. 1984. The status of urban wildlife programs. *Transactions of the 49th North American Wildlife and Natural Resources Conference*, 233–51.

Manfredo, M., T. Teel, and A. Bright. 2003. Why are public values toward wildlife changing? *Human Dimensions of Wildlife* 8:287–306.

Mankin, P., R. Warner, and W. Anderson. 1999. Wildlife and the Illinois public: A benchmark study of attitudes and perceptions. *Wildlife Society Bulletin* 27:465–72.

Miller, C., L. Campbell, and J. Yeagle. 2001. *Attitudes of homeowners in the greater Chicago metropolitan region toward nuisance wildlife*, Program Report SR-00-02. Champaign: Illinois Natural History Survey.

Platt, R., R. Rowntree, and P. Muick. 1994. *The ecological city.* Amherst: University of Massachusetts Press.

Rees, W. 1992. Ecological footprints and appropriated carrying capacity: What urban economics leaves out. *Environment and Urbanization* 4:121–30.

Sabloff, A. 2001. *Reordering the natural world: Humans and animals in the city.* Toronto: University of Toronto Press.

San Julien, G. 1987. The future of wildlife damage control in an urban environment. *Proceedings of the 3rd Eastern Wildlife Damage Control Conference*, ed. Nicholas R. Holler, 229–33. Auburn, AL: Auburn University.

Scheffey, A. 1967. Farm and urban resources: Remarks of the chairman. *Transactions of the North American Fish and Wildlife Conference* 32:49–50.

U.S. Department of the Interior. 1968. *Man and nature in the city.* Washington, DC: Bureau of Sport Fisheries and Wildlife.

U.S. Fish and Wildlife Service. 2007. *2006 National Survey of Fishing, Hunting, and Wildlife-Associated Recreation: National Overview.* Washington, DC: U.S. Government Printing Office.

Wolch, J. 1998. Zoopolis. In *Animal geographies: Place, politics, and identity in the nature-culture borderlands*, ed. J. Wolch and J. Emel, 19–38. London: Verso.

Zinn, H., and C. Miller. 2003. Public values and urban wildlife: A love-hate relationship or too much of a good thing? *Transactions of the 68th North American Wildlife and Natural Resources Conference*, 178–96.

CHAPTER 16

The Human Dimensions of Conflicts with Wildlife around Protected Areas

Adrian Treves

Protected areas are credited with saving a number of wildlife populations from regional or rangewide extinction, and they remain a cornerstone of conservation (Terborgh et al. 2002; Woodroffe and Ginsburg 1998). They have also faced substantial criticism for undemocratic imposition of a societal goal on local peoples (Cernea and Schmidt-Soltau 2006; West and Brockington 2006). Allegations of social inequity often intensify when wildlife populations recover near to human ones. In particular, individual, far-ranging, large-bodied wild animals will eventually leave protected areas and resume an ancient competition with people for the necessities of life. This competition consists of wildlife eating crops, livestock, and other resources we claim, or occasionally attacking people. This human-wildlife conflict (HWC) can further undermine political support for protected areas and can revive calls for eradication of the problematic wildlife (Feral 1995; Okwemba 2004). HWC occurs worldwide and its annual frequency and severity has been rising for three reasons: (i) human uses of wildlife habitat are expanding in many regions, (ii) a few wildlife populations are recovering and expanding into areas with people and property; and (iii) environmental changes such as climate change are driving some sensitive species into areas with more people and property (Gompper 2002; Treves et al. 2002; Raik et al. 2005; Breitenmoser 1998; Hunter et al. 2007; Cope, Vickery, and Rowcliffe 2005; Knight 2003; Naughton-Treves et al. 2003; Linnell and Broseth 2003; Regehr et al. 2007).

Because a traditional and widespread response of affected human communities is to kill problem wildlife and clear wild habitat (Treves and Naughton-Treves 2005), natural resource managers and wildlife protectionist groups become involved. Political conflicts ripple outward from there. Thus, HWC is more than simple competition for space, food, and life; it pits different nature values against one another and demands attention from economic, legal, social, and environmental policy makers (Knight 2000a).

Academics and lay audiences have paid more attention to HWC in the last fifteen years. Between 1992 and 1999, Google Scholar returned 3,140 hits for "human AND wildlife AND conflict OR depredation OR damage" compared with 8,060 hits between 2000 and 2007. Public attention has also increased. Searching all Web pages in 2007, Google returned 2,010,000 hits for the same search terms, similar to 2,060,000 hits for "wildlife AND disease" or 1,980,000 hits for "wildlife AND ('climate change' OR 'global warming')." The growing attention and energetic research efforts have advanced understanding and made clear how HWC can undermine wildlife protections and reverse conservation gains.

This chapter examines peoples' responses to HWC, especially those of wildlife managers and individuals who live and work in and around protected areas. Protected areas reveal the fundamental dilemma posed by global and national concerns for biodiversity conservation on the one hand and individual and economic motivations to safeguard human life and livelihood on the other hand. Thus, the chapter pays particular attention to political clashes because these are likely to affect wildlife policy and protected-area management.

Background, Definitions, and Assumptions

HWC is defined here as wildlife threats to property, recreation, and human safety. This chapter examines HWC involving larger animals (greater than two or three kilograms) with particular attention to predation on livestock by mammals. Although smaller animals cause far greater damage in aggregate, this focus is justifiable on several grounds. First, large carnivores and other megafauna (e.g., elephants) have special ecological importance and are often icons of protected areas and wildlife conservation groups. Second, carnivores and megafauna are particularly sensitive to human causes of mortality, according to Woodroffe and Ginsburg (1998). Indeed, these authors concluded that humans were the foremost threat to carnivore populations globally. The risk of extirpation of carnivore populations was most severe around small, protected areas, presumably because their far-ranging habits and resultant encounters and competition with people placed them in harm's way. Efforts to separate large wildlife from people (the core strategy of protected areas) may have reduced the geographic extent of some HWC (Riley, Nesslage, and Maurer 2004), but it has also magnified the consequences at the boundaries (Naughton-Treves 1997). Widespread efforts to "soften" park boundaries and integrate people's economic needs will have a profound effect on HWC rates and distribution in the future, as will climatic changes that further fragment wild habitat or shift it in altitude and latitude.

HWC takes various forms according to the animal, its behavior, or the human community involved (Sillero-Zubiri, Sukumar, and Treves 2007). But patterns repeat. Fishermen may resent sharks for "stealing the catch" just as game hunters resent wolves for taking "their" elk; and bear damage to timber in Japan resembles moose damage in Sweden. In addition, local communities appear to respond in a limited number of ways to HWC, whereupon wildlife managers typically counterreact in a limited number of ways.

In interpreting human responses to HWC, one should keep in mind well-established features of human dimensions theory. First, wildlife values are believed to take shape early in life and change slowly (Bright and Manfredo 1996; Manfredo, Teel, and Bright 2003; Bruskotter, Schmidt, and Teel 2007)—thus, recent experiences rarely change basic values or beliefs (Heberlein and Ericsson 2005; Manfredo and Dayer 2004). In contrast, recent experiences and reports from associates may shape attitudes toward management as well as tolerance for HWC (Karlsson and Sjostrom 2007; Naughton-Treves, Grossberg and Treves 2003; Treves and Naughton-Treves 2005). Second, a complex mix of individual, social, and environmental factors correlate with perceptions of environmental hazards and their management (Manfredo and Dayer 2004). For example, lack of control or predictability of hazards may intensify perceived risk (Starr 1969), and HWC is not easy to predict or mitigate (Treves et al. 2004, 2006; Wydeven et al. 2004; Backeryd 2007). Third, we should expect incongruence between perceptions of HWC and scientific measures of wildlife damage (Treves et al. 2006). Perceptions and attitudes are influenced by testimonials and entertaining stories that may reflect (a) extreme events and imagination, (b) long memories and a history of human-animal interactions, and (c) experiences from a broad region. By contrast, systematic field data on HWC events and losses tend to emphasize variation around averages and shorter time periods in smaller regions. For example, the costliest and most frequent crop raider around Kibale National Park, Uganda, was the baboon, but most respondents reported a stronger dislike of elephants (Naughton-Treves 1997). Similarly, wolves have caused less damage to property and attacked fewer people in North America than have bears, yet people report higher fear of and anger about wolves (Kellert 1985; Montag, Patterson, and Sutton 2003). Rather than conclude that people are irrational about wildlife or controlled entirely by social tradition and symbolism, human dimensions researchers assume a multivariate role of intrinsic (individual experience and evolutionary history) and extrinsic (economic, social, and cultural) factors in shaping perceptions and attitudes.

Evidence for perceptions of HWC comes from a variety of social scientific studies and is typically measured by interview, self-administered questionnaire, or focus group. Measuring people's behavior is difficult when reactions are influenced by social norms or behavior is illicit ("shoot, shovel, and shut up"). Therefore, the data are dominated by self-reported perceptions and emotions or researchers' inferences of these, with all the weaknesses this can entail.

Perceptions of HWC and Attitudes toward Its Management

When threats derive from large, wild animals, affected people often report fear, anger, or hopelessness. Women and children tend to report higher levels of fear than men (Kaltenborn, Bjerke, and Nyahongo 2006; Kellert 1980). Fear is understandable given an evolutionary history of attacks by large, dangerous wildlife and current, widespread reporting of conflicts, despite their absolute and relative rarity (Beier 1991; Linnell and Bjerke 2002; Treves and Palmqvist 2007). More often than emotional responses, researchers measure perceptions of wildlife in relation to economic losses, risk. and vulnerability. Table 16.1 summarizes some common predictors of tolerance for different wildlife.

There is also a long tradition in the United States of measuring attitudes toward management of HWC (Kellert 1980, 1985; Manfredo et al. 1998; Williams, Ericsson, and Heberlein 2002). Such studies often expose sharp contrasts between those who hold protectionist wildlife values and those who hold more utilitarian values, such as rural residents with low residential mobility, those having less formal education, older people, men, those with lower incomes, and those with more direct experience with wildlife damage. Similar results are beginning to emerge from other countries (Ericsson and Heberlein 2003; Hill 1998; Knight 2003, 2000b; Kuriyan 2002).

TABLE 16.1 **Predictors of Tolerance for Conflict-causing Wildlife**

	HIGHER TOLERANCE	LOWER TOLERANCE
Socioeconomic predictors		
Land availability	Abundant	Scarce
Labor availability	Abundant, inexpensive	Rare, expensive
Coping strategies	Varied, collective	Narrow, individualized
Social unit absorbing loss	Communal, group	Individual, household
Value of wildlife	High (game, tourism, etc.)	Low (pest, vermin)
Value of property	Low	High
Type of damage	Subsistence	Cash or emergency reserve
Alternate income	Various	None
Ownership of wildlife	God, self, community	Government, elite
Ecological predictors		
Wildlife body size	Small, non-threatening	Large, dangerous
Wildlife group size	Solitary	Large
Damage pattern	Cryptic	Obvious
Timing of damage	Early crop or young livestock	Late crop or adult livestock
Circadian timing of damage	Diurnal	Nocturnal
Damage per incident	One or few	Surplus or many
Frequency of raiding	Rare	Chronic

Source: Treves and Naughton-Treves 2005

Different values, perceptions, and attitudes toward HWC based on urban-rural divisions or differences in reliance on natural resources can easily generate political clashes over HWC because people often disregard or discount the views of those with different values. As Gill (1996) noted, if wildlife managers are drawn from rural backgrounds rather than urban areas, then one tends to see greater conflict with protectionists than with the communities threatened by wildlife. For example, the U.S. Department of Agriculture wildlife control agency staffed by individuals with rural or user group backgrounds (Gill 1996) has faced decades of criticism from protectionists (Robinson 2005). By contrast, in many poorer countries, urban elites most often benefit from university training and are more likely to join the civil service as natural resource managers than would rural agriculturalists. Hence, political clashes over HWC tend to pit the affected communities against the state in poorer countries (Hazzah and Dolrenry 2007; Hill 2004; Karanth and Madhusudan 2002).

Behavioral Responses to HWC

Following threats from wildlife, people typically act, and their behavioral responses can be classified simply (table 16.2). Direct retaliation against wildlife is clearly most directly opposed to wildlife protections. Human retaliation can "drain" protected areas because humans can enter and carnivores can exit. In Laikipia, Kenya, one commercial livestock producer's intolerance of lions produced a population sink for a wide region (Woodroffe and Frank 2005). In an example of rapid decimation, villagers destroyed eleven leopards while trying to eliminate one "man-eater" in India (Karanth and Madhusudan 2002).

Killing many wild animals to control a few is sure to draw the attention of wildlife managers and protectionist interests, setting the stage for more political clashes over mitigation of HWC and over the purpose and future of protected areas. In some cases, interventions may cause indirect problems (table 16.2). For example, guard animals such as free-running dogs may spread disease or injure wildlife (Bowers 1953). Building barriers may constrain wildlife movements; in the case of elephants in southern Kenya, the result was drastic changes in vegetation within the fenced area (Kahumbu 2002). Some deterrents using chemicals, lights, sounds, or fires may have unintended consequences for nontarget wildlife.

TABLE 16.2 **Common Interventions to Mitigate Human-wildlife Conflicts**

CLASS OF INTERVENTION AND SUBTYPES	POTENTIAL, SIGNIFICANT NEGATIVE IMPACTS ON WILDLIFE IN PROTECTED AREAS	POTENTIAL, SIGNIFICANT NEGATIVE IMPACTS ON PEOPLE AFFECTED BY WILDLIFE
Direct interventions reduce the severity or frequency of interactions with wild animals:		
Barriers	Barriers may block wildlife movement paths.	Some barriers may impede use of resources from the protected area or impose property regimes on communally owned resources.
Deterrents and Repellents	Use of chemicals, fires, lights, or sound may disrupt non-target wildlife. Target wildlife may be displaced to other locations, disrupting established social networks.	Some repellents and deterrents may pose health hazards or safety risks. Dispersed wildlife may damage proviously unaffected properties.
Guards (animals or human)	Some domestic animals introduce health hazards or safety risks.	Some domestic animals introduce health hazards or safety risks.
Change in human behavior or husbandry	This will have variable effects.	This will have variable effects. It may intensify political and economic inequity.
Manipulation of wildlife (lethal control, relocation, sterilization, etc.)	Manipulations may harm individuals, disrupt social networks, or relocate the problems.	Manipulations may exacerbate or relocate the problems.

CONTRASTS BETWEEN WEALTHY AND POOR NATIONS

In some areas of Europe and North America, changing societal values toward nature have spurred protectionist policies. Enforcement of these policies has facilitated wildlife recovery in some regions or promoted reintroduction efforts in others (Breitenmoser 1998; Gompper 2002; Hunter et al. 2007; Mech 1995). By contrast, in many poor agrarian nations, the range of large carnivores has contracted, even within protected areas (Plumptre et al. 2007; Rajpurohit and Krausman 2000). Poor

and Their Potential, Significant Impacts on Wildlife and People

CLASS OF INTERVENTION AND SUBTYPES	POTENTIAL, SIGNIFICANT NEGATIVE IMPACTS ON WILDLIFE IN PROTECTED AREAS	POTENTIAL, SIGNIFICANT NEGATIVE IMPACTS ON PEOPLE AFFECTED BY WILDLIFE
Indirect interventions raise tolerance for wildlife threats:		
Annulment of wildlife protections	Unsustainable uses of wildlife and protected areas may follow.	If unsustainable uses ensue, ecosystem services from the protected area may degrade.
Compensation	Fewer resources may be left for protected area management.	This may create dependence on donors or intensify political and economic inequity.
Incentives	Fewer resources may be left for protected area management.	This may create dependence on volatile market forces or external inputs. it may intensify political and economic inequity.
Environmental Education and Research	Misinterpreted or misguided research can lead to unsustainable management.	This may intensify political and economic inequity.
Participation and Co-management	Unsustainable uses of wildlife and protected areas may follow.	This may intensify political and economic inequity.

countries rarely have adequate resources to enforce wildlife protection policies, so they have attempted an alternative conservation approach variously called community-based conservation, participatory comanagement, and so on. A key aim of this alternative is to channel benefits to local communities by sharing revenue from consumptive or nonconsumptive use of wildlife (Archabald and Naughton-Treves 2001; Brandon and Margoluis 1996; Frost and Bond 2006; Loveridge, Reynolds, and Milner-Gulland 2007). Wildlife managers in wealthier nations are increasingly turning to similar methods (Carr and Halvorsen 2001; Raik et al. 2005; Wiedenhoeft, Boles, and Wydeven 2003). Collaborative wildlife management is a key area for future research on HWC. Some predict involvement of affected households in comanagement would raise tolerance for wildlife damages by itself (Treves et al. 2006).

A further difference between wealthy and poor nations is the populace surrounding protected areas. In many developing countries, politically marginalized peoples inhabit protected areas or their margins, often in poverty (Hazzah and Dolrenry 2007; Karanth 2005; Karanth and Madhusudan 2002; Naughton-Treves et al. 2003a; Mishra et al. 2003). By contrast, wealthy countries have seen an increase in recreational use of protected areas along with an increasing number of jobs created by protected areas or wildlife industries (Duffield and Neher 1996; Hunter et al. 2007). Also, wealthy nations build more houses and more expensive ones adjacent to wildlife habitat (Torres et al. 1996; Tucker and Pletscher 1989). As a result, populations fringing protected areas are often neither poor nor politically marginalized. We found that wealthier, better-educated landowners with larger holdings and herds were more likely to seek and win compensation for wolf damage in Wisconsin (Naughton-Treves, et al. 2003b). In addition, influential or wealthy landowners may have more direct access to policy makers or litigate more effectively.

Conclusion

HWC stands out among challenges faced by wildlife managers as a situation that has often escalated into political clashes. Contrasting wildlife values between affected households, wildlife managers, and wildlife protection interests are the most common cause of political clashes. When the various actors drawn into HWC incidents respond differently to data than to testimonials, one may find political clashes arising earlier and more perniciously than in areas where the primary actors are swayed by the same sources of evidence and modes of communicating them. Anger arising from economic losses, fear of wildlife, or distrust of government also precipitates more intense political clashes. Confronting angry people can put wildlife managers or protectionists on the defensive. Defensive responses may lead listeners to minimize wildlife threats by referring to their relative rarity or perceived low value of the losses (e.g., Valentino 1998). Wealthy nations' protected areas are often surrounded by wealthy people who will demand accountability from wildlife managers, whereas poorer nations' protected areas are often fringed by the poor and politically marginal, to whose defense champions of economic development and poverty alleviation will leap (Karanth 2005). Political clashes, in turn, have sometimes undermined political support for protected areas and wildlife managers, at many levels. Protected areas have been annulled or their boundaries changed, and wildlife policy has been altered dramatically (Feral 1995; Okwemba 2004). Wildlife managers have lost authority and flexibility to manage wildlife that damage property, after their chosen management interventions did not satisfy a litigious or populous interest group (Gill 1996; Torres et al. 1996).

Because the stakes can be high in HWC situations, theoreticians and field researchers should study the politics and measure the sociopolitical acceptance of proposed management *before* it is implemented and then disseminate the results and lessons efficiently to many audiences, particularly policy makers. Human dimensions researchers are challenged to move beyond description and understand causality of perceptions and attitudes, as well as to guide the selection, design, and monitoring of creative interventions.

Literature Cited

Archabald, K., and L. Naughton-Treves. 2001. Tourism revenue sharing around national parks in western Uganda: Early efforts to identify and reward local communities. *Environmental Conservation* 23:135–49.

Backeryd, J. 2007. *Wolf attacks on dogs in Scandinavia 1995–2005.* Ecology Institute, Swedish University of Agricultural Sciences, Grimso.

Beier, P. 1991. Cougar attacks on humans in the United States and Canada. *Wildlife Society Bulletin* 19:403–12.

Bowers, R. R. 1953. The free-running dog menace. *Virginia Wildlife*14:5–7.

Brandon, K. B., and R. Margoluis. 1996. Structuring ecotourism success: Framework for analysis. In *The ecotourism equation: Measuring the impact,* ed. E. Malek-Zadeh, 28–38. New Haven, CT: Yale School of Forestry and Environmental Studies.

Breitenmoser, U. 1998. Large predators in the Alps: The fall and rise of man's competitors. *Biological Conservation,* 83: 279–89.

Bright, A. D., and M. J. Manfredo.1996. A conceptual model of attitudes toward natural resource issues: A case study of wolf reintroduction. *Human Dimensions of Wildlife* 1(1):1–21.

Bruskotter, J. T., R. H. Schmidt, and T. L. Teel. 2007. Are attitudes toward wolves changing? A case study in Utah. *Biological Conservation* 139:211–18.

Carr, D. S., and K. E. Halvorsen. 2001. An evaluation of three democratic, community-based approaches to citizen participation: Surveys, conversations with community groups, and community dinners. *Society and Natural Resources* 14:107–26.

Cernea, M., and K. Schmidt-Soltau. 2006. Poverty risks and national parks: Policy issues in conservation and resettlement. *World Development* 34:1808–30.

Cope, D., J. Vickery, and M. Rowcliffe. 2005. From conflict to coexistence: a case study of geese and agriculture in Scotland. In *People and Wildlife, Conflict or Coexistence?* edited by R. W. S. Thirgood and A. Rabinowitz. Cambridge, UK: Cambridge University Press.

Duffield, J. W., and C. J. Neher. 1996. Economics of wolf recovery in Yellowstone National Park. *Transactions of the North American Wildlife and Natural Resources Conference* 61:285–92.

Ericsson, G., and T. A. Heberlein. 2003. Attitudes of hunters, locals, and the general public in Sweden now that the wolves are back. *Biological Conservation* 111:149–59.

Feral, C. 1995. Kenya rethinks wildlife policy. *African Wildlife News* 30(5):1–4.

Frost, P., and I. Bond. 2006. *CAMPFIRE and payments for environmental services.* London: Marketing Environmental Services Publication Series, IIED.

Gill, R. B. 1996. The wildlife professional subculture: The case of the crazy aunt. *Human Dimensions of Wildlife* 1(1):60–69.

Gompper, M. E. 2002. Top carnivores in the suburbs? Ecological and conservation issues raised by colonization of North-eastern North America by coyotes. *BioScience* 52(2):185–90.

Hazzah, L., and S. Dolrenry. 2007. Coexisting with predators. *Seminar* 577:1–12.

Heberlein, T. A., and G. Ericsson. 2005. Ties to the countryside: Accounting for urbanites attitudes toward hunting, wolves, and wildlife. *Human Dimensions of Wildlife* 10:213–27.

Hill, C. M. 1998. Conflicting attitudes towards elephants around the Budongo Forest Reserve, Uganda. *Environmental Conservation* 25(3):244–50.

———. 2004. Farmers' perspectives of conflict at the wildlife–agriculture boundary: Some lessons learned from African subsistence farmers. *Human Dimensions of Wildlife* 9:279–86.

Hunter, L. T. B., K. Pretorius, L. C. Carlisle, M. Rickelton, C. Walker, R. Slotow, and J. D. Skinner. 2007. Restoring lions *Panthera leo* to northern KwaZulu-Natal, South Africa: Short-term biological and technical success but equivocal long-term conservation. *Oryx* 41(2):1–11.

Kahumbu, P. 2002. Forest lephant ecology at Shimba Hills. PhD diss., Princeton University.

Kaltenborn, B. P., T. Bjerke, and J. Nyahongo. 2006. Living with problem animals: Self-reported fear of potentially dangerous species in the Serengeti region, Tanzania. *Human Dimensions of Wildlife* 11(6):397–409.

Karanth, K. K. 2005. Addressing relocation and livelihood concerns: Bhadra Wildlife Sanctuary. *Economic and Political Weekly* 40(46):4809-4811.

Karanth, K. U., and Madhusudan, M. D. 2002. Mitigating human-wildlife conflicts in southern Asia. In *Making parks work: Identifying key factors to implementing parks in the tropics*, ed. J. Terborgh, C. P. Van Schaik, M. Rao, and L. C. Davenport, 250–64. Washington, DC: Island Press.

Karlsson, K., and M. Sjostrom. 2007. Human attitudes towards wolves, a matter of distance. *Biological Conservation* 137(4):610–16.

Kellert, S. R. 1980. Contemporary values of wildlife in American society. In *Wildlife values*, ed. W. W. Shaw and E. H. Zube, 31–60. Fort Collins, CO: U.S. Forest Service, Rocky Mt. Forest and Range Experiment Station.

———. 1985. Public perceptions of predators, particularly the wolf and coyote. *Biological Conservation* 31:167–89.

Knight, J. 2000a. Introduction. In *Natural enemies: People-wildlife conflicts in anthropological perspective*, ed. J. Knight, 1–35. London: Routledge.

———, ed. 2000b. *Natural enemies: People-wildlife conflicts in anthropological perspective*. London: Routledge.

———. 2003. *Waiting for wolves in Japan*. Oxford: Oxford University Press.

Kuriyan, R. 2002. Linking local perceptions of elephants and conservation: Samburu pastoralists in northern Kenya. *Society and Natural Resources*, 15:949–57.

Linnell, J. D. C., and T. Bjerke. 2002. Frykten for ulven. En tverrfaglig utredning (Fear of wolves: An interdisciplinary study). *NINA oppdragsmelding*, 722:1–110.

Linnell, J. D. C., and H. Broseth. 2003. Compensation for large carnivore depredation of domestic sheep. *Carnivore Damage Prevention News* 6:11–13.

Loveridge, A. J., J. C. Reynolds, and E. J. Milner-Gulland. 2007. Does sport hunting benefit conservation? In *Key topics in conservation biology*, ed. D. W. Macdonald, 224–41. Oxford: Oxford University Press.

Manfredo, M. J., and A. A. Dayer. 2004. Concepts for exploring the social aspects of human–wildlife conflict in a global context. *Human Dimensions of Wildlife* 9:317–28.

Manfredo, M. J., T. L. Teel, and A. D. Bright. 2003. Why are public values toward wildlife changing? *Human Dimensions of Wildlife* 8:287–306.

Manfredo, M. J., H. C. Zinn, L. Sikorowski, and J. Jones. 1998. Public acceptance of mountain lion management: A case study of Denver, Colorado, and nearby foothill areas. *Wildlife Society Bulletin* 26:964–70.

Mech, L. D. 1995. The challenge and opportunity of recovering wolf populations. *Conservation Biology* 9:270–78.

Mishra, C., P. Allen, T. McCarthy, M. D. Madhusudan, A. Bayarjargal, and H. H. T. Prins. 2003. The role of incentive schemes in conserving the snow leopard, *Uncia uncia*. *Conservation Biology* 17:1512–20.

Montag, J., M. E. Patterson, and B. Sutton. 2003. *Political and social viability of predator compensation programs in the West*. Missoula: School of Forestry, University of Montana.

Naughton-Treves, L. 1997. Farming the forest edge: Vulnerable places and people around Kibale National Park. *Geographical Review* 87:27–46.

Naughton-Treves, L., R. Grossberg, and A. Treves. 2003a. Paying for tolerance: The impact of livestock depredation and compensation payments on rural citizens' attitudes toward wolves. *Conservation Biology* 17:1500–11.

Naughton-Treves, L., J. L. Mena, A. Treves, N. Alvarez, and V. C. Radeloff. 2003b. Wildlife survival beyond park boundaries: The impact of swidden agriculture and hunting on mammals in Tambopata, Peru. *Conservation Biology*. 17:1106–17.

Okwemba, A. 2004. Proposals to reduce sizes of national parks. *The Nation*. March 18th, 2004.

Plumptre, A. J., D. Kujirakwinja, A. Treves, I. Owiunji, and H. Rainer. 2007. Transboundary conservation in the Greater Virunga landscape. *Biological Conservation* 134:279–87.

Raik, D. B., T. B. Lauber, D. J. Decker, and T. L. Brown. 2005. Managing community controversy in suburban wildlife management: Adopting practices that address value differences. *Human Dimensions of Wildlife* 10:109–22.

Rajpurohit, R. S., and P. R. Krausman. 2000. Human-sloth-bear conflicts in Madhya Pradesh, India. *Wildlife Society Bulletin* 28:393–99.

Regehr, E. V., N. J. Lunn, S. C. Amstrup, and I. Stirling. 2007. Effects of earlier sea ice breakup on survival and population size of polar bears in Western Hudson Bay. *Journal of Wildlife Management* 71 (8):2673–83.

Riley, S. J., G. M. Nesslage, and B. A. Maurer. 2004. Dynamics of early wolf and cougar eradication efforts in Montana: Implications for conservation. *Biological Conservation* 119(4):575–79.

Robinson, M. 2005. *Predatory Bureaucracy*. Boulder: University of Colorado Press.

Sillero-Zubiri, C., R. Sukumar, and A. Treves. 2007. Living with wildlife: The roots of conflict and the solutions. In *Key topics in conservation biology*, eds. D. MacDonald and K. Service, 266–72. Oxford: Oxford University Press.

Starr, C. 1969. Social benefit versus technological risk. *Science* 165:1232–38.

Terborgh, J., C. P. Van Schaik, M. Rao, and L. C. Davenport, ed. 2002. *Making parks work: Identifying key factors to implementing parks in the tropics.* Washington, DC: Island Press.

Torres, S. G., T. M. Mansfield, J. E. Foley, T. Lupo, and A. Brinkhaus. 1996. Mountain lion and human activity in California: Testing speculations. *Wildlife Society Bulletin* 24:457–60.

Treves, A., and L. Naughton-Treves. 2005. Evaluating lethal control in the management of human-wildlife conflict. In *People and wildlife, conflict or coexistence?*, ed. R. Woodroffe, S. Thirgood, and A. Rabinowitz, 86–106. Cambridge: Cambridge University Press.

Treves, A., R. R. Jurewicz, L. Naughton-Treves, R. A. Rose, R. C. Willging, and A. P. Wydeven. 2002. Wolf depredation on domestic animals: control and compensation in Wisconsin, 1976–2000. *Wildlife Society Bulletin* 30:231–41.

Treves, A., L. Naughton-Treves, E. L. Harper, D. J. Mladenoff, R. A. Rose, T. A. Sickley, and A. P. Wydeven. 2004. Predicting human-carnivore conflict: A spatial model based on 25 years of wolf predation on livestock. *Conservation Biology* 18:114–25.

Treves, A., and P. Palmqvist. 2007. Reconstructing hominin interactions with mammalian carnivores (6.0 - 1.8 Ma). In *Primates and their predators*, ed. K. A. I. Nekaris and S. L. Gursky. New York: Springer.

Treves, A., R. B. Wallace, L. Naughton-Treves, and A. Morales. 2006. Co-managing human-wildlife conflicts: A review. *Human Dimensions of Wildlife* 11(6):1–14.

Tucker, P., and D. H. Pletscher. 1989. Attitudes of hunters and residents toward wolves in northwestern Montana. *Wildlife Society Bulletin* 17(4):509–14.

Valentino, P. C. 1998. Of wolves, cows and humans. In *Proceedings of the Defenders of Wildlife Restoring the Wolf Conference*, ed. N. Fascione, 47–53. Washington, DC: Defenders of Wildlife.

West, P., and D. Brockington. 2006. An anthropological perspective on some unexpected consequences of protected areas. *Conservation Biology* 20:609–16.

Wiedenhoeft, J. E., S. R. Boles, and A. P. Wydeven. 2003. Counting wolves—integrating data from volunteers. Paper presented at the World Wolf Congress 2003: Bridging Science and Community, Banff, AB.

Williams, C. K., G. Ericsson, and T. A. Heberlein. 2002. A quantitative summary of attitudes toward wolves and their reintroduction (1972–2000). *Wildlife Society Bulletin* 30(2):575–84.

Woodroffe, R., and L. G. Frank. 2005. Lethal control of African lions (*Panthera leo*): Local and regional population impacts. *Animal Conservation*. 8:91–98.

Woodroffe, R., and J. R. Ginsburg. 1998. Edge effects and the extinction of populations inside protected areas. *Science* 280:2126–28.

Wydeven, A. P., A. Treves, B. Brost, and J. E. Wiedenhoeft. 2004. Characteristics of wolf packs in Wisconsin: Identification of traits influencing depredation. In *People and predators: From conflict to coexistence*, ed. N. Fascione, A. Delach, and M. E. Smith, 28–50. Washington, DC: Island Press.

CHAPTER 17

New Markets for Recreational Fishing

Øystein Aas and Robert Arlinghaus

Everyone working with recreational fishing, whether as managers, representatives of nongovernmental organizations (NGOs), or commercial actors in the tackle, travel, accommodations, or service provider industries, is concerned about the future of this leisure activity and the characteristics and preferences of current and future anglers. Questions of relevance include the following: Is the absolute *number* of recreational anglers increasing or decreasing or is it stable? Is the *rate* of participation among the public increasing or decreasing or is it unchanged? What are the *characteristics* of these anglers, what preferences and behaviors do they display now, and what changes are likely in the future? Do those who are involved in recreational angling, for example, become *more or less active over time*? Do their *preferences* for the fish species and type of fishing experience they are pursuing change and are they willing to purchase goods and services if specifically developed to meet this demand?

These and a number of other similar questions are asked for a variety of reasons. Fishery managers, for example, may ask these questions because they want to find out the audience they are serving and how to best align the maximization of total angler benefits or angler satisfaction with biocentric objectives such as preserving biodiversity or social objectives such as minimizing user conflicts (Arlinghaus 2005). The number and types of anglers might affect issues such as the social, economic, and ecological costs and benefits associated with recreational fishing (see Weithman 1999; Arlinghaus, Mehner, and Cowx 2002; Pitcher and Hollingworth 2002). Increased numbers of anglers or increased frequency of fishing may increase revenues and resources for management and angler-dependent industries, but they may also result in overfishing, crowding, and intensified user or management conflicts (Arlinghaus 2005). NGO representatives are interested in trends in recreational fishing because they want to find out about the political influence of the recreational fishing sector in public policy decision making or implementation of relevant legislation. Commercial actors want to know about their customers in order to increase revenue generated through angling and thus the profitability of their businesses. Interestingly, despite the importance of these questions about the angler market, there have been few incentives to invest in appropriate research to answer them, and many stakeholders think that such important information comes at no or little cost.

Relevance of a Market Approach

The term *market* is not often applied to studies of the human dimensions of recreational fishing (Ditton 1999). A range of definitions and understandings exist for the term. We use it to mean a group of individuals or organizations interested in a product, willing and able to purchase it and to do so legally (Seaton and Bennett 1996). Another meaning refers to the place where products, goods, and services are sold by some and purchased by others.

These definitions introduce another term—*product*. A product can be a tangible good as well as an intangible service. As early as the 1970s, Driver and colleagues were using the term to mean a recreational fishing opportunity or a recreational fishing experience (see Driver 1985 for a summary). Their use of the term seemed to be motivated by the need for managers to be more proactive about what fishing possibilities to provide to the public in general and to anglers more specifically. They assumed that anglers are users of fisheries and that managers are in the position of delivering a product that the angling public demands. However, it should be noted that such a perspective arose mainly in North America and in other jurisdictions where angling is a public good and where the public hand therefore has the responsibility to manage fisheries based on funds provided by license sales. The product approach has been less prevalent in Europe, where fishing rights are private. In fact, many representatives of European angling NGOs rejected this approach because it conflicted with the idea that angling is a more private affair, disconnected from work and business. Clearly, this is a narrow viewpoint since every angling activity creates economic effects in regional and local economies.

Nevertheless, the "private-affair," noncommercial understanding of recreational fishing has probably hindered a market approach to providing fishing in many places. Despite the long-lasting existence of a significant market for recreational fishing tackle and for fishing holidays, many, especially in public management agencies and in angling NGOs, have resisted or opposed applying a market approach in recreational fishing provision, probably because they feel it could add to commercialization of angling and maybe reduce the dominating "public service" approach of angling as being "everybody's right."

However, we would argue that a market approach is highly relevant for a public service as well as for a private fishing rights approach to recreational fishing. The following are arguments in favor of a market approach to public and private recreational fishing in both public and private fishing rights regimes:

- The market approach takes into account that the recreational fishing market must be segmented into submarkets in order to better satisfy the different needs that the highly diverse angling public expresses.
- The market approach underscores that managers, outfitters, tackle tradespeople, and, in some countries, commercial fishing enterprises and charter operators must behave actively and not passively toward the market (or the public), despite whether they are in the "business" for commercial or public service reasons.
- The market approach acknowledges that fishing is just one of many activities in the leisure market; this poses a challenge to retain, recruit, and enhance angling interest among the public.
- The market approach has the potential to maximize the potential benefits associated with recreational fisheries by trading off angling interest with more commercial interests of local and regional industries.

Fishing participation is declining in several countries, is stable in some, and is increasing in others, but data availability on these trends is generally poor except for some countries such as the United States (Ditton et al. 2008). If managers and businesses depending on recreational fishing are to halt the decline of or increase overall participation, we believe that a market approach in recreational fisheries management is relevant and needed, and in-depth understanding of new markets for recreational fishing is a key to success.

The purpose of this chapter is to identify and discuss new markets for recreational fishing. The chapter primarily focuses on Western, postindustrial societies because we are from the West, but we also comment on other regions of the world.

Overall Determinants of Participation

The stereotypical angler in Western countries is a white, middle-aged man living in rural areas, relatively near fishing opportunities (Aas 1996; Arlinghaus 2006; Murdock et al. 1992, 1996). Several studies in at least three Western countries—Germany, Norway, and the United States—show many similarities in identifying overall factors determining whether a person is an angler or not. A common finding of these studies was that men were more likely to participate in angling than women, worked full time (and had the monetary resources to participate), and lived in rural areas close to a body of water (Aas 1996; Arlinghaus 2006). Some papers found that age had a negative influence on the probability of participating in angling (Walsh et al. 1989), whereas others did not find it a significant influence (Arlinghaus 2006). What is known, however, is that participation rates usually drop considerably for elderly angler populations (Arlinghaus 2006). The process of aging reflects lifestyle changes that influence angling behavior. For example, young people starting a job in their midtwenties will likely go fishing less frequently because of new commitments in life. For older anglers, physical disabilities and health problems may limit angling participation (Walsh et al. 1989). Education and its influence on angling participation are less clear. Some studies report a positive relation between education and angling (Walsh et al. 1989), but German anglers at higher educational levels seemed less likely to fish (Arlinghaus 2006).

An important and relatively new area of research is investigating the differences in meanings, behaviors, and participation rates among different ethnic groups. This work has been mainly conducted in the United States (e.g., Hunt and Ditton 2002). Findings have suggested that minority ethnic population growth may account for the net growth in angler numbers in the United States (Murdock et al. 1992, 1996). In western and central Europe, increasing numbers of immigrants from eastern European countries are changing the culture of recreational fishing, resulting in new groups of anglers, but also in conflicts because of the different meanings these immigrants attached to several aspects of recreational fishing (e.g., as regards consumptive orientation).

Given the known negative relation between urbanization and recreational fishing participation, it is understandable that differences between urban and rural anglers have been the focus of some research in North America (Manfredo, Harris, and Brown 1984) and Europe (Arlinghaus, Mehner, and Cowx 2002). A common finding of these studies is that both angler groups differed little in motivations. However, urban anglers in general were found to be somewhat younger and less educated, more consumptive, and more avid fishers. Despite their lower overall participation rates, urbanites offer a great opportunity for recruiting and retaining anglers since it is important to socialize into the hobby early in life.

Changing Demand Factors

How angling participation will develop is essentially the result of the interplay between demand and supply factors. In previous studies, most of the focus was on demand factors. A range of texts assess trends in recreation and leisure, but none explicitly address recreational fishing (e.g., Cordell 1999; Jackson and Burton 1999; Gartner and Lime 2000). Many of the factors that apply to leisure and outdoor recreation are highly relevant for this analysis. All of these books, however, suffer from a lack of empirical, longitudinal data to support their conclusions, though they present data on demographic and economic changes.

Although some NGOs and many journalists in some countries are optimistic that recreational fishing will increase in importance in the future, research suggests that growth is less likely in many industrialized societies owing to demographic changes that are counterproductive to angling participation (Murdock et al. 1996; Arlinghaus 2006). Many of the changes, however, have the potential to work in different directions. Some of the factors working to reduce angler numbers are:

- a more urban population (geographically as well as culturally)
- an aging population
- decreasing incomes and increased level of unemployment in some countries
- changing family patterns, including more single-parent families, which likely provide a less optimal basis for recruitment
- young people's increased reliance on computer games and other leisure activities that do not involve nature, preventing socialization into fishing

Factors that might positively affect angler participation globally are:

- continued economic growth, especially in countries in eastern Europe and Asia
- more leisure time and increased travel, especially in countries with rapid economic growth
- increased desire of part of the population to relax outside and "escape from it all"

Determining how the following several important social changes will affect angling participation and new markets for recreational fishing is difficult:

- globalization and cultural exchange between different ethnic groups
- better education
- climate change and changes in the productivity of ecosystems

Limitations of the Forecast Approach: Can Effective Supply Efforts Make a Difference?

The approach to understanding future markets based only on forecasts of demographic change has severe restrictions if it is the only one used to identify interesting new markets for recreational fishing. First, the studies that have tried to project or forecast future angling participation based on overall societal and demographic change in general only explain a small percentage of why people do or do not fish (10–40 percent [see Arlinghaus 2006]). These studies implicitly create the impression that the future is fixed and determined, something that stakeholders must accept. This is opposite to the approach that fishery managers as well as business actors principally take. They expect that their efforts and mitigating actions, such as establishing a new fishing site, improving fishing quality in a lake, publishing a brochure about urban fishing sites, or running a big marketing campaign for new tackle or fishing destinations, to potentially affect people's behavior, at least regarding where and how they fish and maybe if they fish or not (Wightman et al. 2008). Indeed, a range of factors influence current and future angling participation and behavior, not demographic change alone. Specifically, factors such as a person's social background, culture, and tradition as well as personality and accessibility to fisheries and fishing gear and techniques will most likely play important roles. A range of aspects related to the fishing opportunities at hand such as "quality," distance/travel time, costs, and so on will affect the likelihood of an individual participating in fishing or not and if they are likely to to demand specific fishing products or opportunities. These "supply" factors are amenable to directed and targeted change by angling clubs, managers, and businesses and are an important component of a market approach to recreational fishing. However, the knowledge about how supply factors affect the angling market is even less than the knowledge about how demographic change might affect demand for recreational fishing.

Changing Face of Angling?

Questions about how many anglers there will be in the future and what characteristics they will possess are as interesting. However, it is also important to investigate how the active angling segment will develop and change. A broader body of research literature sheds light on what characterizes anglers, including how they can be separated into subgroups. A range of factors have been used to describe and group anglers, including demographic, behavioral, psychological, and social (Arlinghaus 2004; Ditton 2004). For example, major topics of investigation have been motivations, satisfaction, attitudes toward fishery management in general and harvest regulations more particularly, and degree of consumptiveness. Unfortunately, we are not familiar with any studies in this tradition that explicitly have focused on changes in angling behavior and preferences over time, as almost every study has been cross sectional, not comparing angler characteristics in terms of behavior, attitudes, or preferences over time.

The mantra of this body of research is that the "average angler does not exist" (Aas and Ditton 1998). Every study identifies major differences within any angler population, sometimes significant polarization in behavior and preferences, sometimes preparing ground for conflicts, or at least indicating that zoning (i.e., manage for diversity) approaches are preferable over "one-policy-fits-all" approaches when managing recreational fisheries (Arlinghaus 2004; Ditton 2004).

Early on in the tradition of human dimensions research in recreational fishing, scholars suggested several explanations for the diversity among anglers. By far the most investigated and discussed approach is Bryan's (1977) concept of specialization. Bryan studied trout anglers and defined specialization as "a continuum of behaviour from the general to the particular reflected by equipment and skills used in the sport and activity setting preferences" (Bryan 1977). He identified four main types of anglers along this continuum, from the occasional angler and the generalist angler to the technique specialist and the technique-and-setting specialist. Bryan further suggested that these groups reflected differences in terms of participation level, commitment, setting and technique preferences, motivations including importance of catch, social groups they fish with, and management preferences. Bryan's work has triggered and influenced abundant research in human dimensions of recreational fishing, and the concept has also been applied and proved its relevance to a range of other outdoor recreation activities, for example, bird-watching, hunting, and water sports (see Scott and Schafer 2001 for review and critique). The generic nature of the specialization concept, and its popularity and application in management as well as in businesses based on recreational fishing, make it an excellent basis for discussing changes among active recreational fishers across the world.

This variation and dynamic nature also suggest that it is possible that angler characteristics, such as behavior and management preferences, change over time. As stated, we were unable to identify studies that document eventual changes in any given angler population or in the use of a fishing destination over time. However, there is clear evidence that fishing practices such as voluntary catch-and-release angling and specialized techniques such as fly- and big-game fishing are growing and making up a larger proportion within several types of recreational fishing (Policansky et al. 2008; Aas, unpublished data 2006). For example, voluntary catch-and-release angling has become more practiced in a range of recreational fisheries in marine as well as in freshwater fisheries over the last few decades (Policansky et al. 2008).

Researchers have argued that recreational benefits and outcomes related to identity formation and self-realization are becoming increasingly important (Jenkins 1996). While there are no studies confirming this for recreational fishing, we suggest that anglers who are less consumptive and more involved and specialized will make up a relatively larger proportion of the angling clientele in the coming years as these create status and identity among their peers. This might affect what types of fishing experiences that people want to spend their leisure time on and be very relevant for a market approach to recreational fisheries management and development.

Fishing providers, private or public, should ask themselves what segment they will target, because there will be significant diversity of angler subgroups despite major trends toward increasing specialization. We need studies that more explicitly assess whether anglers change in behavior, including if the hypothesis we propose holds some truth.

Fishing Tourism

Recreational fishing has always been closely linked to tourism, and recreational fishing away from home varies on a continuum from independent, self- organized fishing trips with few purchases, if any, to a full fishing package offered by travel groups or agents, including fishing licences, transportation, food and lodging and guiding, sometimes of high standard and cost. We predict that more recreational fishing in the future will be done in a commercial tourist context. Commodification, the process by which objects and activities are evaluated primarily in terms of their exchange value in the context of trade (Cohen 1988), obviously is going on in the field of recreational fishing as in other forms of outdoor recreation (Veal 1999). Many active anglers have a medium-high income but often lack time. This sparks the commodification process, leading to more organized fishing opportunities available in the market. Given the close link between recreational fishing and tourism, it is surprising that rather few studies have looked at fishing from a tourism perspective (Borch, Policansky, and Aas 2008). If we are to successfully identify future markets for recreational fishing, we need a better understanding of recreational fishing as tourism.

Fish and fisheries constitute several types of tourist attractions. Fish can be the object of viewing experiences, especially where they migrate or gather to spawn. Several places in many countries have established facilities such as visitor or information centers to enhance and utilize such phenomena. Also, commercial and recreational fisheries are attractions in specific locations, particularly if rare, exceptional specimens are targeted in the fishery. However, it is mostly as an activity that fishing plays a part in tourism. Recreational fishing is an activity for several types of tourists and travels. It can be just one of many activities on a single-destination or round-trip holiday. And it can be the major or only activity on such holidays.This type of holiday has been the subject of the few scientific studies that have been conducted (Zwirn, Pinsky, and Rahr 2006; Stoeckl, Greiner, and Mayocchi 2006). Fishing can also be a part of what is called corporate tourism when fishing is part of a meeting or seminar or used as an incentive for employees or customers. The specialized fishing tourism industry is mostly targeting involved and active anglers with a medium-high income offering experiences where fishing is the main activity, from a base located in wilderness or exotic environments (Borch, Policansky, and Aas 2008).

Tourism is becoming increasingly diversified in terms of both market segments and products. Terms such as ecotourism, nature-based tourism, and wildlife tourism are used to characterize types of tourism with some common features. Fishing tourism has many commonalities with these forms of tourism, and the development in fishing tourism probably follows closely some of the major trends in related tourism sectors, such as ecotourism and adventure tourism. Driving forces in tourism push the industry many different directions, and the paradoxes embedded in tourism grow bigger every day.

For fishing tourism, some of the more relevant trends (Veal 1999; Borch, Policansky, and Aas 2008) are the following:

- more demand for shorter holidays and more people taking several shorter holidays instead of or in addition to one long holiday
- more senior tourists
- more demand for experiences and products that include active rather than passive experiences and learning
- more demand for "authentic tourism" products
- more demand for environmentally friendly holidays
- more demand for the rare, exceptional holiday

Major New Markets for Recreational Fishing

Recreational anglers today exhibit a wide variety of behaviors and attitudes, and the participation in and the role of recreational fishing in different regions and countries worldwide vary even more. Overall, trends make it safe to assume that angler diversity will increase even more in the coming years. The middle-aged white male, living in rural areas will be supplemented with recreational anglers that have differing backgrounds. Demand-determining factors, especially demographic changes, will work against future growth in recreational fishing participation in Western, postindustrial countries. In other regions, such as eastern Europe and Asia, economic, social, and political factors are likely to increase numbers of recreational anglers. In Western countries it is likely that for public as well as private fishing providers, a growing economy and increasing purchases per angler might make up for a reduced number of participants in terms of consumption of products. However, stakeholders should be aware that in a period when a reduced number of people have some orientation toward fishing, a more active supply side will be important in order to uphold and maybe increase the general interest for angling. Quality matters to retain interest in the face of competing leisure activities and changing cultures within countries.

Despite the lack of good studies aimed at identifying future markets, we end this chapter by pointing out what we believe are key future markets. We stress that these markets should be subject to modification and clarification in the future and that more research should be conducted.

Senior anglers

The safest conclusion to be drawn from current demographic changes is that there will be more active anglers in the older age brackets, from fifty to eighty years of age. While future senior anglers likely will have better health than elderly fishers of the past, it is still advisable for fishery managers and businesses to tailor products and opportunities for this clientele. Elderly have time and often money to follow up their interests, and this segment is growing strongly in many forms of tourism and outdoor recreation.

Urban Youth

Urban fishing opportunities have been in focus for several decades (Manfredo et al. 1984). Traditionally, people become anglers in their youth, introduced to the sport by male family members at lakes, rivers, or the sea near where they live. As more people live in areas with fewer or no angling opportunities, and with changing family structures in which more children grow up in single-parent families, programs and efforts aiming at providing fishing and ensuring recruitment among urban youth will be important for the future of angling. In addition to the interest in targeting urban youth to ensure future participation in recreational fishing, recreational fishing probably holds qualities that make urban youth a group to whom recreational fishing has something to offer (Wightman et al. 2008).

Middle- and Upper-Class Segments in Regions with a Growing Economy

Several regions of the world have strong economic growth, an increased standard of living, and thus, often better-regulated holidays and leisure time. In addition, changing political regimes are opening up some regions for more travel. Some of these regions already have a strong tradition of recreational fishing, such as eastern Europe and China. This established culture, together with economic, social, and political changes, make for strong growth in recreational fishing, such as that seen, for instance, in China, Lithuania, and Malaysia (Ditton et al. 2008). This will lead to increased demand for recreational fishing opportunities, not only in domestic and in nearby regions, but also in more exotic and distant fishing destinations. Anglers from Western countries will meet more anglers from these regions in angling destinations across the world.

Growing Numbers of Fishing Tourists

As the urban population grows all over the world, more and more recreational fishing will be enjoyed as tourism. Therefore, a better understanding of fishing as tourism is needed. There is currently a growth in exotic fishing tourism, often in developing countries. We believe that this development will continue and that the clientele visiting these destinations will become more diverse, though they mainly originate from urban areas. While some of the growth in fishing tourism seems to take place in the less-consumptive, ecotourism-inspired tourism segment (Zwirn et al. 2005), there are also major forms of fishing tourism that are less "exotic" and far more consumptive, such as the Norwegian marine recreational fishing tourism targeting the European market (Borch 2004), and major parts of the domestic Australian fishing tourism (Stoeckl, Greiner, and Mayocchi 2006). Few fishing tourism businesses today specifically target the large market for fishing as part of multiple-activity holidays, a segment that likely will grow.

Conclusion

In this chapter we have tried to analyze and discuss market trends in recreational fishing. As stated, appropriate studies analyzing changes in the recreational fishing market is largely lacking. We especially recommend conducting studies in which business representatives and scientists working in recreational fishing come together and apply methods such as Delphi techniques, Scenario writing, and time series analysis (Veal 1999). The future of recreational fishing is not fixed but is made up of a complex interplay in which the many stakeholders within the recreational fishing sector can make a difference.

Literature Cited

Aas, Ø. 1996. Recreational fishing in Norway from 1970 to 1993: Trends and geographical variation. *Fisheries Management and Ecology* 3: 107–18.

———. 2008. Global challenges in recreational fisheries. Oxford: Blackwell Publishing.

Aas, Ø., and R. B. Ditton 1998. Human dimensions perspectives on recreational fisheries management: Implications for Europe. In *Recreational fisheries, social economic and management aspects*, ed. P. Hickley and H. Tompkins, 153–64. Oxford: FAO/Fishing News Books.

Arlinghaus, R. 2004. *A human dimensions approach towards sustainable recreational fisheries management*. London: Turnshare.

———. 2005. A conceptual framework to identify and understand conflicts in recreational fisheries systems, with implications for sustainable management. *Aquatic Resources, Culture and Development* 1:145–74.

———. 2006. Understanding recreational angling participation in Germany: Preparing for demographic change. *Human Dimensions of Wildlife* 11:229–40.

Arlinghaus, R., and T. Mehner, 2004. A management-orientated comparative analysis of urban and rural anglers living in a metropolis (Berlin, Germany). *Environmental Management* 33, 331–44.

Arlinghaus, R., T. Mehner, and I. G. Cowx. 2002. Reconciling traditional inland fisheries management and sustainability in industrialized countries, with emphasis on Europe. *Fish and Fisheries* 3:261–316.

Borch, T. 2004. Sustainable management of marine fishing tourism: Some lessons from Norway. *Tourism in Marine Environments* 1:49–57.

Borch, T., D. Policansky, and Ø. Aas. 2008. International fishing tourism. In *Global challenges in recreational fisheries*, ed. Ø. Aas, 268–91. Oxford: Blackwell Publishing.

Bryan, H. 1977. Leisure value systems and recreation specialization: The case of trout fishermen. *Journal of Leisure Research* 9:174–87.

Cohen, E. 1988. Authenticity and commodification in tourism. *Annals of Tourism Research* 15:371–86.

Cordell, K. 1999. Outdoor recreation in American life: A national assessment of demand and supply trends. Champaign, IL: Sagamore Publishing.

Ditton, R. B. 1999. Human dimensions in fisheries. In *Natural resource management: The human dimension*, ed. A. Ewert, 73–90. Boulder, CO: Westview Press.

———. 2004. Human dimensions of fisheries. In *Society and natural resources: A summary of knowledge prepared for the 10th International Symposium on Society and Resource Management*, ed. M. J. Manfredo, J. J. Vaske, B. L. Bruyere, D. R. Field, and P. J. Brown, 199–208. Jefferson, MI: Modern Litho.

Ditton, R. B., T. Aarts, R. Arlinghaus, A. Domarkas, T. Eriksson, A. Lofthus, E. Radaityte, et al. 2008. An international perspective on recreational fishing. In *Global challenges in recreational fisheries*, ed. Ø. Aas, 5–55. Oxford: Blackwell Publishing.

Driver, B. L. 1985. Specifying what is produced by management of wildlife by public agencies. *Leisure Sciences* 7:281–94.

Gartner, W. C., and D. W. Lime. 2000. *Trends in outdoor recreation, leisure and tourism*. Wallingford, CT: CABI Publishing.

Hunt, K. M., and R. B. Ditton. 2002. Freshwater fishing participation patterns of racial and ethnic groups in Texas. *North American Journal of Fisheries Management* 22: 52–65.

Jackson, E. L., and T. L. Burton. 1999. *Leisure studies: Prospects for the twenty-first century*. State College, PA: Venture Publishing.

Jenkins, R. 1996. *Social identity*. London: Routledge.

Manfredo, M. J., C. C. Harris, and P. J. Brown. 1984. The social values of an urban recreational fishing experience. In *Urban fishing symposium proceedings*, ed. L. J. Allen, 156–64. Bethesda, MD: American Fisheries Society.

Murdock, S. H., K. Backman, R. B. Ditton, M. Nazrul Hoque, and D. Ellis. 1992. Demographic change in the United States in the 1990s and the twenty-first century: Implications for fisheries management. *Fisheries* 17(2):6–13.

Murdock, S. H., D. K. Loomis, R. B. Ditton, and M. Nazrul Hoque. 1996. The implications of demographic change for recreational fisheries management in the United States. *Human Dimensions of Wildlife* 1:14–37.

Pitcher, T. J., and C. Hollingworth. 2002. *Recreational fisheries: Ecological, economic and social evaluation*. Oxford: Blackwell Publishing.

Policansky, D., R. Arlinghaus, R. Lukacovic, G. Mawle, T. F. Næsje, J. Schratwieser, E. Thorstad, and J. H. Uphoff Jr. 2008. Trends and development in catch and release. In *Global challenges in recreational fisheries*, ed. Ø. Aas, 202–236. Oxford: Blackwell Publishing.

Scott, D., and C. S. Schafer. 2001. Recreational specialization: A critical look at the construct. *Journal of Leisure Research* 33:319–43.

Seaton, A. V., and M. M. Bennett. 1996. *Marketing tourism products: Concepts, issues, cases*. London: International Thompson Business Press.

Stoeckl, N., R. Greiner, and C. Mayocchi. 2006. The community impacts of different types of visitors: An empirical investigation of tourism in North-west Queensland. *Tourism Management* 27:97–112.

Veal, A. J. 1999. Forecasting leisure and recreation. In *Leisure studies: Prospects for the twenty-first century*, ed. E. L. Jackson and T. L. Burton, 385–98. State College, PA: Venture Publishing.

Walsh, R. G., K. H. John, J. R. McKean, and J. G. Hof. 1989. Comparing long-run forecasts of demand for fish and wildlife recreation. *Leisure Sciences* 11:337–51.

Weithman, A. S. 1999. Socioeconomic benefits of fisheries. In *Inland fisheries management in North America*, 2nd ed., ed. C. C. Kohler and W. A. Hubert, 193–213. Bethesda, MD: American Fisheries Society.

Wightman, R., S. Sutton, K. Gillis, B. Matthews, J. Colman, and J. R. Samuelsen. 2008. Recruiting new anglers: Driving forces, constraints and examples of success. In *Global challenges in recreational fisheries*, ed. Ø. Aas, 303–23. Oxford: Blackwell Publishing.

Zwirn, M., M. Pinsky, and G. Rahr. 2005. Angling ecotourism: Issues, guidelines, and experiences from Kamchatka. *Journal of Ecotourism* 4:16–31.

CHAPTER 18

Preparing for the Next Disease: The Human-Wildlife Connection

Jerry J. Vaske, Lori B. Shelby, and Mark D. Needham

Human dimensions (HD) research is essential for managing wildlife and understanding the societal consequences of wildlife diseases (Decker et al. 2006; Otupiri et al. 2000). Although there have been numerous studies on the pathology, transmission, and epidemiology of wildlife diseases, HD research on wildlife diseases is limited. Managers reluctant to make decisions without biological and ecological information should be equally hesitant without information about the general public and other interest groups. Disease risks can be mitigated by understanding and educating relevant stakeholders and implementing policies that incorporate public opinion. Simonetti (1995), for example, noted that understanding landowner attitudes was helpful for Chilean park managers to address foot-and-mouth disease in deer. HD research provides important information to managers by attempting to describe, predict, and affect human thought and action toward wildlife.

This chapter has three objectives: (1) highlight the range of wildlife diseases that can affect humans, as well as negatively affect wildlife, (2) suggest that human dimensions research for most diseases is sparse and does not follow a systematic paradigm of research, and (3) provide an illustrated approach to studying the human dimensions of wildlife diseases using chronic wasting disease as an example. Similar to biological research, a systematic program of HD inquiry is necessary to understand and prepare for the next wildlife disease crisis.

An Overview of the Human-Wildlife Disease Connection

Diseases transmitted between animals and humans (i.e., zoonoses) caused more than two-thirds of emerging diseases in the last decade (Friend 2006). These diseases can be transmitted by direct or indirect contact with wildlife or domestic animals. Direct contact may occur through bites or contact with infectious fluids or tissues. Individuals also encounter diseases through direct contact as an occupational hazard (e.g., wildlife scientists, fish and wildlife law enforcement personnel, butchers). Consumptive recreationists (e.g., hunters, anglers, trappers) can be exposed to infected wildlife and game meat, and nonconsumptive recreationists are also at risk (e.g., hikers contracting Lyme disease, campers contracting hantavirus [Friend 2006]). Feeding wildlife, for example, increases contact with humans and encourages animals to unnaturally congregate, potentially spreading disease. People can be exposed to zoonoses from wildlife being kept as pets (e.g., some amphibians, reptiles, birds), domesticated pets (e.g., dogs, cats), and other animals (e.g., sheep, cattle). Domesticated animals can encounter zoonotic pathogens and transmit them to humans either directly or indirectly (e.g., transferring carriers such as ticks). Humans contract zoonoses indirectly by coming into contact with contaminated water or soil, or inhaling airborne pathogens (e.g., bat guano can be inhaled in caves once it is disturbed).

Three primary trends have made zoonoses a critical issue. First, human population growth has increased fragmentation of wildlife habitats and proximity of wildlife to humans, which increase the potential for humans to contract diseases from wildlife and for wildlife to contract diseases from humans. Second, globalization of travel and trade has led to increasing the rates of disease transmission and the spread of diseases. Severe acute respiratory syndrome (SARS), for example, caused economic losses in tourism owing to fear of rapid disease transmission. As global trade intensifies, the potential for spreading diseases increases (e.g., contaminated food supplies or transporting diseased wildlife). Third, increased participation in some outdoor recreation activities is increasing the proximity of wildlife to humans. The popularity of ecotourism and adventure tourism, for example, has increased exposure of wildlife and humans to diseases not common in their respective home environments (e.g., transmission of human tuberculosis to African wildlife, or whitewater rafters contracting leptospirosis in Costa Rica [Friend 2006]).

Understanding the *scope, biology,* and *human impacts* of wildlife disease is essential for developing a systematic paradigm of HD

Continued on p. 248

TABLE 18.1 **Wildlife Diseases by Wildlife Type and Their Impacts on Humans**

WILDLIFE TYPE	DISEASE	SOME HUMAN IMPACTS AND CHARACTERISTICS
Amphibians and reptiles	Salmonellosis	Handling of pets (e.g., lizards, turtles) has been a major source in humans Found worldwide in animals such as mammals, birds, reptiles, amphibians, and crustaceans Transmission to humans also through food, occupational, and recreational exposure
Birds	Avian influenza	Worldwide zoonosis transmitted through contact exposure Noted for transmission to poultry, humans, cats, and swine in Asia Concern that this virus could evolve and be spread by humans
	West Nile fever (West Nile virus)	Transmission to mammals (e.g., humans, horses) and birds through mosquito bites Transmission also through blood transfusion, tissue transplant, and rarely milk Found throughout the world, but spread particularly fast in U.S. horses with 25 known cases in 1999 rising to 15,000 in 2007
Freshwater fish	Whirling disease	Decimates fish populations, leading to economic consequences (e.g., fish hatcheries, commercial and noncommercial anglers) Introduced to the United Kingdom through translocation of rainbow trout from the United States
Marine mammals	Brucellosis, tuberculosis, leptospirosis, influenza	Transmission to humans through direct handling of animals
Terrestrial mammals	Bovine spongiform encephalopathy (BSE, mad cow)	Economic impacts due to loss of cattle Eating infected beef linked to cases of Creutzfeldt-Jakob disease in humans primarily in the United Kingdom, Europe, and Canada
	Bovine tuberculosis	Worldwide zoonosis primarily in cattle, swine, monkeys, bison, deer, elk, and other animals Has been associated with feeding deer and elk Transmissions to humans through ingestion of meat, inhalation, and occupational exposure

Modified from Friend (2006) and Kahn, Line, and Aiello (2006).

Disease examples may be applicable to other types of wildlife and have other human impacts not listed

TABLE 18.1 (CONTINUED)

WILDLIFE TYPE	DISEASE	SOME HUMAN IMPACTS AND CHARACTERISTICS
Terrestrial mammals	Brucellosis	Strains found in cattle, bison, elk, caribou, goats, sheep, camels, wild pigs, dogs, and coyotes Transmission to humans from occupational exposure, recreational exposure, and milk Brucellosis in elk associated with feeding of elk Transmission from wildlife to farm animals a concern
	Foot-and-mouth disease	Found in cattle, swine, and other cloven-hoofed animals in Asia, Africa, and South America Economic impacts such as loss of livestock and farmer compensation in the United Kingdom
	Hantavirus	Worldwide transmission to humans by contact with urine, feces, or saliva of deer mice or other rodents (e.g., through bites, inhalation, or contaminated soil)
	Human immuno-deficiency viruses (HIV)	Primate harvesting and meat processing believed to be origin of HIV and AIDS in humans
	Johne's disease	Widespread disease of ruminants (e.g., deer, bison, goats) Associated with Crohn's disease in humans and economic impacts on farmers
	Leptospirosis	Worldwide zoonotic disease with hosts ranging from rodents to large mammals Transmission to humans by contaminated recreational waters and occupational means
	Lyme disease	Found in deer and rodents worldwide and transmits to humans through ticks
	Rabies	Found primarily in carnivores (e.g., skunks, raccoons, foxes, coyotes) and bats Translocation of raccoons to northern United States resulted in rabies as a zoonosis in multiple states Transmission through bites of diseased animals and inhalation in enclosed areas (e.g., caves)
	Severe acute respiratory syndrome (SARS)	Zoonosis in China and Southeast Asia transmitted by direct contact Likely originated in civet cats Caused severe economic impacts due to decreased tourism

research. Only a limited number of diseases have been studied from a human dimensions perspective, yet wildlife diseases span a variety of species and environments (e.g., rodents to large mammals; marine mammals to freshwater fish). Table 18.1 illustrates a sample of these wildlife diseases and their associated human impacts for different types of wildlife (see Childs, Mackenzie, and Richt 2007; Friend 2006; Kahn, Line, and Aiello 2006; Williams and Barker 2000; Wobeser 2007 for reviews). Understanding the biology of wildlife diseases facilitates HD research by defining the range of the problem and the issues involved (e.g., Is the disease transmittable to humans? Can education decrease the transmission of the disease? What wildlife species are involved?). Human impacts of wildlife disease shown in table 18.1 include economic, social and recreational, and human health. Human dimensions of wildlife disease research needs to consider each of these potential consequences, as well as human impacts on wildlife.

Human Dimensions of Wildlife Diseases

Compared with research on the epidemiology and transmission of wildlife diseases, few studies have examined the HD of these diseases (see table 18.2 for examples). Diseases such as bovine tuberculosis (Brook and McLachlan 2006; Dorn and Mertig 2005; Stronen et al. 2007), foot-and-mouth (Poortinga et al. 2004), fowl pest (i.e., Newcastle disease [Brunet and Houbaert 2007]), Johne's disease (Daniels et al. 2002), Lyme disease (Deblinger et al. 1993; Kilpatrick and LaBonte 2003), and rabies (Gibbons et al. 2002; Sexton and Stewart 2007; Schopler, Hall, and Cowen 2005) have received some attention in the HD literature. Although the specific studies listed in table 18.2 have contributed to our knowledge, most HD research on wildlife diseases, with the exception of chronic wasting disease (CWD), can be characterized as one-shot cross-sectional studies that are applied in focus. A systematic and theory-based program of HD wildlife disease research is needed to address the range of potential human and wildlife impacts. Theoretical concepts (e.g., knowledge, risk perceptions, beliefs, attitudes, behavioral responses) drawn from a variety of disciplines (e.g., social psychology, economics, communication) used by HD researchers can facilitate understanding of the human component of wildlife diseases and broaden the generalizability, reliability, and validity of the findings. Human dimensions research on chronic wasting disease illustrates this recommended systematic approach.

Human Dimensions of Chronic Wasting Disease

Unlike other diseases discussed in this chapter, there is a body of HD research on CWD. In the past five years, at least twenty-three HD journal articles on CWD have appeared (see table 18.3). This section briefly describes CWD and synthesizes the results from current HD studies on CWD. This body of work directly incorporated concepts found in social psychological, economic, and communication theory to understand the beliefs, attitudes, and behaviors of multiple stakeholders (e.g., hunters, nonhunters, guide outfitters) across multiple states in the United States, often using identical surveys instruments. Although different wildlife diseases (e.g., tables 18.1 and 18.2) pose specific human dimensions questions (e.g., relevant stakeholders), the general approach utilized by HD research on CWD can be applied in each case.

CWD is a neurological disease of deer, elk, and moose that is similar to scrapie in sheep, bovine spongiform encephalopathy in cattle (i.e., mad cow), and Creutzfeldt-Jakob disease in humans. CWD was identified in captive deer and elk in the 1960s and 1970s and free-ranging herds in the 1980s and 1990s in Colorado and Wyoming. The disease is currently known to exist in free-ranging herds in eleven states (Colorado, Illinois, Kansas, Nebraska, New Mexico, New York, South Dakota, Utah, West Virginia, Wisconsin, Wyoming) and two Canadian provinces (Alberta, Saskatchewan). CWD exists in captive herds in additional states (e.g., Minnesota, Montana, Oklahoma) and countries (e.g., South Korea). In all infected animals, CWD causes emaciation, abnormal behavior, and death. There is no evidence that CWD poses a human health risk, but transmission to humans cannot be dismissed (see Williams et al. 2002 for a review).

One of the primary stakeholder groups affected by CWD is hunters. As a result, most HD research on CWD has examined hunters': (a) participation in response to the disease, (b) perceptions of potential human health risks associated with CWD, and (c) concerns about impacts of the disease on wildlife (Brown et al. 2006; Gigliotti 2004; Miller 2003, 2004; Needham et al. 2007; Needham, Vaske, and Manfredo 2004, 2006; Stafford et al. 2007; Vaske et al. 2004, 2006a, 2006b). Studies have also measured hunters' knowledge of CWD, acceptance of management (e.g., testing, herd reduction), and trust in agencies to address the disease (Brown et al. 2006; Miller 2003; Needham and Vaske 2008; Vaske et al. 2006b). Research has compared subgroups of hunters (e.g., deer/elk, residents/nonresidents [Needham, Vaske, and Manfredo

Continued on p. 254

TABLE 18.2 **Human Dimensions Research on Wildlife Disease**

DISEASE	FOCAL SPECIES	SAMPLE*
Bovine tuberculosis	Deer	Stakeholders in MI
Bovine tuberculosis	Elk, cattle	Farmers near Riding Mountain National Park, Manitoba, Canada
Bovine tuberculosis	Wolves	Farmers near Riding Mountain National Park, Manitoba, Canada
Foot-and-mouth disease	Livestock	Two communities (Norwich, Bude) in the United Kingdom
Fowl pest (Newcastle disease)	Birds	Multiple stakeholders
Johne's disease	Multiple	Farmers in east Scotland
Lyme disease	Deer	Hunters on Richard T. Crane, Jr. Memorial Reservation and Cornelius and Miné Crane Wildlife Refuge in MA
Lyme disease	Deer	Residential community in Groton, CT
Multiple	Multiple	Public and wildlife agency personnel in MI
Multiple	Multiple	Residents in CO
Rabies	Bats	National Speleological Society convention attendees
Rabies	Bats	Residents in Fort Collins, CO
Rabies	Bats	Residents in MN
Rabies	Multiple	Wildlife rehabilitators in NC
Zoonoses	Multiple	Laypersons and expert perceptions within food sector
Zoonoses	Multiple	Teton County, ID
Zoonoses	African wildlife	17 rural Central African villages
Zoonoses	Cattle	Slaughterhouse butchers in Ghana

* Two-letter postal codes are used for U.S. states.
There have also been numerous studies on chronic wasting disease (see table 18.3).

CONCEPTS	CITATIONS
Attitudes, knowledge, communication	Dorn and Mertig 2005
Risk perception, acceptability of management actions	Brook and McLachlan 2006
Attitudes	Stronen et al. 2007
Attitudes, risk perception, trust	Poortinga et al. 2004
Risk perception, communication	Brunet and Houbaert 2007
Risk perception, beliefs, behavior	Daniels et al. 2002
Beliefs, concerns	Deblinger et al. 1993
Public perceptions, expectations	Kilpatrick and LaBonte 2003
Attitudes toward lethal management to control wildlife diseases	Koval and Mertig 2004
Cognitive hierarchy, acceptability of trapping to control wildlife diseases	Manfredo et al. 1999
Knowledge, risk perception	Gibbons et al. 2002
Familiarity, knowledge, risk perception, cognitive hierarchy, communication	Sexton and Stewart 2007
Knowledge	Liesener et al. 2006
Knowledge, policy	Schopler, Hall, and Cowen 2005
Risk perception, communication, values, morals	Jensen et al. 2005
Attitudes	Peterson, Mertig, and Liu 2006
Risk perception, hunting patterns	LeBreton et al. 2006
Knowledge, attitudes, beliefs, behaviors	Otupiri et al. 2000

TABLE 18.3 **Human Dimensions Research on Chronic Wasting Disease**

CONCEPTS*	SAMPLE†	CITATIONS
Social psychology		
Values, trust, knowledge, risk perception	Big-game guides and outfitters in CO and WY	Anderies 2006
Behavioral intentions, satisfaction, information, communication, trust, knowledge	General public and deer hunters in NY	Brown et al. 2006
Concerns, behavior	Deer hunters in Black Hills, SD	Gigliotti 2004
Attitudes, behavior	Hunters in WI	Holsman and Petchenik 2006
Behavior, risk perception, information	Seven counties in northern IL	Miller 2003
Beliefs, behavior	Deer hunters in IL	Miller 2004
Behavior, acceptability, risk perception	Deer hunters in 8 states (AZ, CO NE, ND, SD, UT, WI, WY); elk hunters in 3 states (CO, UT, WY)	Needham, Vaske, and Manfredo 2004
Behavior, risk perception, recreation specialization	Deer hunters in 8 states; elk hunters in 3 states	Needham et al. 2007
Attitudes, behavior, knowledge	Landowners residing in WI's southwest CWD eradication zone	Petchenik 2006
Beliefs	Hunters and nonhunters residing in WI's southwest CWD eradication zone	Stafford et al. 2007
Attitudes, behavior, acceptability	Deer hunters in WI	Vaske et al. 2006a
Behavior, risk, trust, similarity	Deer hunters in WI	Needham and Vaske 2008 Vaske et al. 2004

TABLE 18.3 (CONTINUED)

CONCEPTS*	SAMPLE†	CITATIONS
Demographic groups		
Beliefs across states, years, and interest groups	Deer hunters in 8 states; elk hunters in 3 states Hunters and nonhunters residing in WI's southwest CWD eradication zone	Needham and Vaske 2006
Risk behavior across state and residency differences	Deer hunters in 8 states; elk hunters in 3 states	Needham, Vaske, and Manfredo 2006
Communication		
Communication, information	State wildlife agency Web sites	Eschenfelder 2006; Eschenfelder and Miller 2007
Information sources, knowledge	Hunters in CO and WI	Vaske et al. 2006b
Economics		
Economic impacts	Existing data	Bishop 2004
Economic impacts	Existing data and public information sources	Seidl and Koontz 2004
Other		
Policy	Existing data in WI	Heberlein 2004
Organizational capacity	24 state wildlife and agricultural agencies in 12 states	Burroughs, Riley, and Taylor 2006
Managerial frameworks	Existing information	Decker et al. 2006

*Many studies listed here cover multiple concepts and types of information, including economic, communication, and social psychology.

†Two-letter postal codes are used for U.S. states.

2004, 2006]) and perceptions of other stakeholder groups (e.g., landowners [Stafford et al. 2007] and guide outfitters [Anderies 2006]). Some studies have addressed the capacity of agencies to manage CWD and the extent to which they use various channels such as the Internet to disseminate information about the disease (Eschenfelder 2006; Heberlein 2004). Research has also estimated economic impacts of CWD on hunting, wildlife viewing, tourism, and the captive deer and elk industry (Bishop 2004; Seidl and Koontz 2004). Similar to the CWD research, HD research needs to identify and analyze the stakeholder groups for each wildlife disease of interest.

Behavioral Intentions

Studies conducted soon after discovery of CWD in some states showed that few hunters (less than 10 percent) would change their hunting frequency or location (e.g., Gigliotti 2004; Miller 2003, 2004). At current CWD prevalence levels, hunters were likely to watch for abnormal behavior in animals, test animals, and/or not eat meat from harvested animals (Brown et al. 2006; Gigliotti 2004; Miller 2003, 2004; Vaske et al. 2004). If prevalence increases dramatically, however, substantial changes in participation are more probable.

In a series of articles (Needham, Vaske, and Manfredo 2004, 2006; Needham et al. 2007), hunters in eight states responded to hypothetical scenarios of increasing CWD prevalence levels and human health risks (i.e., death). If 50 percent of the deer or elk across the state were infected, 38 percent of residents and 52 percent of nonresidents would stop hunting deer or elk in their state. In scenarios where hunters died from CWD at this prevalence level, 53 percent of residents and 64 percent of nonresidents would quit. Arizona and North Dakota hunters were most likely to change behavior. Given that CWD is not in these states, it may pose a new risk. In Wisconsin, where hunting is a strong tradition, hunters were least likely to change behavior. Across scenarios and states (a) hunters were more likely to quit hunting deer or elk rather than switch states to hunt these species, (b) residents were more likely to quit hunting and nonresidents were more likely to hunt in other states, and (c) novice hunters or those new to hunting were more likely to quit and veteran hunters would switch states. These findings are important because hunting declines attributable to CWD can impact wildlife agency revenues (e.g., license sales) and programs, erode support of these agencies, and constrain cultural traditions and the socioeconomic stability of communities dependent on hunting.

Concerns and Perceptions of Risk

Studies have examined hunters' concerns and perceptions of risk associated with CWD. Needham and Vaske (2006, 2008), for example, found that the majority of hunters in eight states agreed that CWD poses a risk to humans, should be eliminated, and may cause disease in humans and that they and their families were concerned about eating deer or elk. Hunters disagreed that the threat of CWD has been exaggerated.

Gigliotti (2004) reported that two-thirds of South Dakota hunters were worried about CWD. In Illinois, many hunters were concerned about effects of CWD on deer and believed that the disease could infect humans (Miller 2004). The majority of New York hunters were concerned about effects of CWD on hunting, human health, and deer health (Brown et al. 2006). Following discovery of CWD in Wisconsin, hunters who did not hunt because of CWD were sixteen times more likely than hunters to perceive risks associated with the disease (Vaske et al. 2004). Research such as this facilitates an understanding of the concerns and perceptions of risk in the general public and stakeholder groups for a wildlife disease, which is essential for determining the necessity and potential effectiveness of management techniques and information campaigns.

Information Sources and Knowledge

Vaske et al. (2006b) examined hunters' information sources and knowledge about CWD. In response to several true-false questions about CWD, 32 percent of Wisconsin hunters and 44 percent of Colorado hunters failed to answer at least half of the questions correctly, suggesting that many hunters in the states are not highly knowledgeable about CWD despite agency efforts to provide information about the disease. Effective sources for improving hunters' CWD knowledge were newspapers, wildlife agency Web sites, and hunting regulations brochures.

Miller (2003) found that most hunters in northern Illinois were aware of CWD and knew where the disease was located in Illinois and other states. Most hunters received CWD information from newspapers, friends or relatives, television reports, and magazines. In New York, most hunters knew that CWD was in the state, were familiar with CWD, and heard or read about the disease mostly from newspapers and the television news (Brown et al. 2006). Understanding relationships among knowledge and commonly used and effective sources of information on a disease may allow agencies to improve information and education about the disease.

Trust in Wildlife Agencies

The majority of hunters trust wildlife agencies to manage CWD to the best of their abilities. Hunters in eight states, on average, trusted their respective state agency to inform the public about CWD and disease management (Needham and Vaske 2008). Despite controversial actions taken to address CWD in Wisconsin (e.g., dramatic herd reduction to eradicate CWD), hunters still trusted the Wisconsin Department of Natural Resources (Stafford et al. 2007). Similarly, the majority of hunters in Illinois and New York were satisfied with agency efforts to address CWD and inform the public about the disease (Brown et al. 2006; Miller 2003).

Needham and Vaske (2008) examined the extent to which hunters perceived personal health risks associated with CWD and the influence of trust in state wildlife agencies to manage the disease as a determinant of this risk. Hunters who trusted the agencies perceived less risk associated with CWD, but trust only explained up to 8 percent of the variance in risk. Hunters trusted the agencies but still perceived personal health risks associated with CWD. It is important to understand public trust in agencies tasked to manage wildlife diseases because lack of trust can increase perceptions of risk, which may cause people to change behavior (e.g., quit hunting). Efforts to maintain agency trust can foster positive relationships with constituents and increase support for management actions.

Acceptance of Management

A number of studies have examined hunters' attitudes toward current and potential strategies for managing CWD (e.g., Needham, Vaske, and Manfredo 2004, 2006; Petchenik 2006; Vaske et al. 2006a). Among hunters in most states and studies, (a) testing harvested animals for CWD and using hunters to reduce herds in CWD areas were *acceptable* strategies, (b) agencies taking no action and allowing CWD to take its natural course were considered *unacceptable,* and (c) using agency staff to reduce herds in CWD areas was *controversial*. Hunters also generally supported efforts to minimize spread of CWD and eliminate the disease from animal herds. Incentives such as longer hunting seasons and free licenses and tags were supported by most hunters, whereas monetary incentives for harvesting infected animals were less preferred (Petchenik 2006). HD research that considers the acceptability of management actions provides information that encourages incorporating public opinion. Such research may also illuminate public education or communication needs. Having public and stakeholder support facilitates the success of wildlife disease management.

Other Stakeholders

A few CWD studies have focused on groups other than hunters. Stafford and colleagues (2007), for example, found that nonhunting landowners in Wisconsin trusted the state wildlife agency to manage CWD, agreed that the disease should be managed, and were concerned about deer health and safety of venison. Compared with hunters, nonhunters were less concerned about hunting. Brown et al. (2006) reported that compared with hunters, the general public in New York was: (a) less familiar with and knowledgeable about CWD and how officials were informing the public about the disease and (b) equally concerned about potential effects of CWD on wildlife and humans. In the only study to examine guide outfitters' responses to CWD, Anderies (2006) found that most outfitters were knowledgeable about CWD, trusted agencies to manage the disease, and were concerned about impacts of CWD on their company and industry. In general, HD of wildlife disease research should incorporate multiple constituency groups. Different stakeholders may have different beliefs regarding acceptable strategies for controlling wildlife disease.

Economic Impacts

Potential economic effects of CWD include (a) hunting declines and impacts on revenue sources such as license sales and tourism, (b) reduced wildlife viewing, (c) trade restrictions and perceptions of meat safety affecting the captive industry, (d) federal indemnity payments for herd reduction and depopulation, and (e) funding for research and testing (Seidl and Koontz 2004). In Wisconsin, for example, the largest single-year decline in hunting license sales (11 percent) occurred in 2002, the year following discovery of CWD in the state (Heberlein 2004). Economic consequences of this decline approached $55 million in 2002 and were estimated at $33 million in 2003 (Bishop 2004). Six million dollars was lost per year in nonresident license sales and more than $15 million was spent combating the disease in the state (Bishop 2004). HD research can provide information about the public and other interest groups that is useful for predicting and preparing for potential economic impacts of wildlife diseases.

Conclusion

This chapter summarized the human-wildlife disease connection. Diseases transmitted between animals and humans are responsible for more than two-thirds of emerging diseases. These diseases have social, economic, recreational, and environmental ramifications. Although the pathology and the epidemiology of wildlife diseases have received substantial attention, HD studies on this topic are limited. This chapter reviewed some of the sporadic HD research on most wildlife diseases. However, a systematic program of research on multiple HD aspects of wildlife diseases is needed. Recent research on CWD offers a starting point in this direction and highlights the types of HD information necessary to prepare for the next wildlife disease.

Literature Cited

Anderies, A. J. 2006. *The impact of shared values, trust, and knowledge on big game outfitters' risk perceptions associated with chronic wasting disease.* Master's thesis, Colorado State University.

Bishop, R. C. 2004. The economic impacts of chronic wasting disease (CWD) in Wisconsin. *Human Dimensions of Wildlife* 9:181–92.

Brook, R. K., and S. M. McLachlan. 2006. Factors influencing farmers' concerns regarding bovine tuberculosis in wildlife and livestock around Riding Mountain National Park. *Journal of Environmental Management* 80:156–66.

Brown, T. L., D. J. Decker, J. T. Major, P. D. Curtis, J. E. Shanahan, and W. F. Siemer. 2006. Hunters' and other citizens' reactions to discovery of CWD in central New York. *Human Dimensions of Wildlife* 11:203–14.

Brunet, S., and P. Houbaert. 2007. Involving stakeholders: The Belgian fowl pest crisis. *Journal of Risk Research* 10:643–60.

Burroughs, J. P., S. J. Riley, and W. W. Taylor. 2006. Preparedness and capacity of agencies to manage chronic wasting disease. *Human Dimensions of Wildlife* 11:227–28.

Childs, J. E., J. S. Mackenzie, and J. A. Richt. 2007. *Wildlife and emerging zoonotic diseases: The biology, circumstances and consequences of cross-species transmission.* Oxford: Springer.

Daniels, M. J., M. R. Hutchings, D. J. Allcroft, I. J. McKendrick, and A. Greig. 2002. Risk factors for Johne's disease in Scotland: The results of a survey of farmers. *Veterinary Record* 150:135–39.

Deblinger, R. D., D. W. Rimmer, J. J. Vaske, G. M. Vecellio, and M. P. Donnelly. 1993. Ecological benefits and hunter acceptance of a controlled deer hunt in coastal Massachusetts. *Northeast Wildlife* 50:11–20.

Decker, D. J., M. A. Wild, S. J. Riley, W. F. Siemer, M. M. Miller, K. M. Leong, J. G. Powers, and J. C. Rhyan. 2006. Wildlife disease management: A manager's model. *Human Dimensions of Wildlife* 11:151–58.

Dorn, M. L., and A. G. Mertig. 2005. Bovine tuberculosis in Michigan: Stakeholder attitudes and implications for eradication efforts. *Wildlife Society Bulletin* 33:539–52.

Eschenfelder, K. R. 2006. What information should state wildlife agencies provide on their CWD websites? *Human Dimensions of Wildlife* 11:221–23.

Eschenfelder, K. R., and C. A. Miller. 2007. Examining the role of website information in facilitating different citizen-government relationships: A case study of state chronic wasting disease websites. *Government Information Quarterly* 24:64–88.

Friend, M. 2006. *Disease emergence and resurgence: The wildlife-human connection.* (circular 1285). Reston, VA: U.S. Geological Survey.

Gibbons, R. V., R. C. Holman, S. R. Mosberg, and C. E. Rupprecht. 2002. Knowledge of bat rabies and human exposure among United States cavers. *Emerging Infectious Diseases* 8:532–34.

Gigliotti, L. M. 2004. Hunters' concern about chronic wasting disease in South Dakota. *Human Dimensions of Wildlife* 9:233–35.

Heberlein, T. A. 2004. Fire in the Sistine Chapel: How Wisconsin responded to chronic wasting disease. *Human Dimensions of Wildlife* 9:165–79.

Holsman, R. H., and J. Petchenik. 2006. Predicting deer hunter harvest behavior in Wisconsin's chronic wasting disease eradication zone. *Human Dimensions of Wildlife* 11:177–89.

Jensen, K. K., J. Lassen, P. Robinson, and P. Sandoe. 2005. Lay and expert perceptions of zoonotic risks: Understanding conflicting perspectives in the light of moral theory. *International Journal of Food Microbiology* 99:245–55.

Kahn, C. M., S. Line, and S. E. Aiello, eds. 2006. *Merck Veterinary Manual*, 9th ed. Whitehouse Station, NJ: Merck. www.merckvetmanual.com/mvm /index.jsp (accessed December 13, 2007).

Kilpatrick, H. J., and A. M. LaBonte. 2003. Deer hunting in a residential community: The community's perspective. *Wildlife Society Bulletin* 31:340–48.

Koval, J. H., and A. G. Mertig. 2004. Attitudes of the Michigan public and wildlife agency personnel toward lethal wildlife management. *Wildlife Society Bulletin* 32:232–43.

LeBreton, M., A. T. Prosser, U. Tamoufe, W. Sateren, E. Mpoudi-Ngole, J. L. D. Diffo, D. S. Burke, and N. D. Wolfe. 2006. Patterns of bushmeat hunting and perceptions of disease risk among central African communities. *Animal Conservation* 9:357–63.

Liesener, A. L., K. E. Smith, R. D. Davis, J. B. Bender, R. N. Danila, D. F. Neitzel, G. E. Nordquist, S. R. Forsman, and J. M. Scheftel. 2006. Circumstances of bat encounters and knowledge of rabies among

Minnesota residents submitting bats for rabies testing. *Vector-Borne and Zoonotic Diseases* 6:208–15.

Manfredo, M. J., C. L. Pierce, D. Fulton, J. Pate, and B. R. Gill. 1999. Public acceptance of wildlife trapping in Colorado. *Wildlife Society Bulletin* 27:499–508.

Miller, C. A. 2003. Hunter perceptions and behaviors related to chronic wasting disease in Northern Illinois. *Human Dimensions of Wildlife* 8:229–30.

———. 2004. Deer hunter participation and chronic wasting disease in Illinois: An assessment at time zero. *Human Dimensions of Wildlife* 9:237–39.

Needham, M. D., and J. J. Vaske. 2006. Beliefs about chronic wasting disease risks across multiple states, years, and interest groups. *Human Dimensions of Wildlife* 11:215–20.

———. 2008. Hunter perceptions of similarity and trust in wildlife agencies and personal risk associated with chronic wasting disease. *Society and Natural Resources* 21:197–214.

Needham, M. D., J. J. Vaske, and M. J. Manfredo. 2004. Hunters' behavior and acceptance of management actions related to chronic wasting disease in eight states. *Human Dimensions of Wildlife* 9:211–31.

———. 2006. State and residency differences in hunters' responses to chronic wasting disease. *Human Dimensions of Wildlife* 11:159–76.

Needham, M. D., J. J. Vaske, M. P. Donnelly, and M. J. Manfredo. 2007. Hunting specialization and its relationship to participation in response to chronic wasting disease. *Journal of Leisure Research* 39:413–37.

Otupiri, E., M. Adam, E. Laing, and D. B. Akanmori. 2000. Detection and management of zoonotic diseases at the Kumasi slaughterhouse in Ghana. *Acta Tropica* 76:15–19.

Petchenik, J. 2006. Landowner responses to harvest incentives in Wisconsin's southwest chronic wasting disease eradication zone. *Human Dimensions of Wildlife* 11:225–26.

Peterson, M. N., A. G. Mertig, and J. G. Liu. 2006. Effects of zoonotic disease attributes on public attitudes towards wildlife management. *Journal of Wildlife Management* 70:1746–53.

Poortinga, W., K. Bickerstaff, I. Langford, J. Niewohner, and N. Pidgeon. 2004. The British 2001 foot and mouth crisis: A comparative study of public risk perceptions, trust and beliefs about government policy in two communities. *Journal of Risk Research* 7:73–90.

Schopler, R. L., A. J. Hall, and P. Cowen. 2005. Public veterinary medicine: Public health survey of wildlife rehabilitators regarding rabies vector species. *JAVMA—Journal of the American Veterinary Medical Association* 227:1568–72.

Seidl, A. F., and S. R. Koontz. 2004. Potential economic impacts of chronic wasting disease in Colorado. *Human Dimensions of Wildlife* 9:241–45.

Sexton, N. R., and S. C. Stewart. 2007. *Understanding knowledge and perceptions of bats among residents of Fort Collins, Colorado.* (open-file report 2007-1245). U.S. Geological Survey, Biological Resources Division.

Simonetti, J. A. 1995. Wildlife conservation outside parks is a disease-mediated task. *Conservation Biology* 9:454–56.

Stafford, N. T., M. D. Needham, J. J. Vaske, and J. Petchenik. 2007. Hunter and nonhunter beliefs about chronic wasting disease in Wisconsin. *Journal of Wildlife Management* 71:1739–44.

Stronen, A. V., R. K. Brook, P. C. Paquet, and S. McLachlan. 2007. Farmer attitudes toward wolves: Implications for the role of predators in managing disease. *Biological Conservation* 135:1–10.

Vaske, J. J., M. D. Needham, P. Newman, M. J. Manfredo, and J. Petchenik. 2006a. Potential for conflict index: Hunters' responses to chronic wasting disease. *Wildlife Society Bulletin* 34:44–50.

Vaske, J. J., M. D. Needham, N. T. Stafford, K. Green, and J. Petchenik. 2006b. Information sources and knowledge about chronic wasting disease in Colorado and Wisconsin. *Human Dimensions of Wildlife* 11:191–202.

Vaske, J. J., N. R. Timmons, J. Beaman, and J. Petchenik. 2004. Chronic wasting disease in Wisconsin: Hunter behavior, perceived risk, and agency trust. *Human Dimensions of Wildlife* 9:193–209.

Williams, E. S., and I. K. Barker. 2000. *Infectious diseases of wild mammals.* Malden, MA: Blackwell.

Williams, E. S., M. W. Miller, T. J. Kreeger, R. H. Kahn, and E. T. Thorne. 2002. Chronic wasting disease of deer and elk: A review with recommendations for management. *Journal of Wildlife Management* 66:551–63.

Wobeser, G. A. 2007. *Disease in wild animals: Investigation and management.* Oxford: Springer.

CHAPTER 19

Challenges and Opportunities at the Interface of Wildlife-Viewing Marketing and Management in the Twenty-first Century

Stephen F. McCool

The convergence of three significant trends in the twenty-first century is providing wildlife managers, protected-area stewards, and community developers new opportunities for conserving biodiversity, enhancing local livelihoods, and increasing the quality of life for many. And while these trends provide interesting and productive prospects, they also pose extraordinary challenges at the intersection of wildlife-viewing marketing and management. Given the importance of healthy wildlife populations to the quality of life for many, understanding and responding to these challenges and opportunities is an important policy arena.

At the center of these trends is the rising interest in wildlife viewing as a recreational activity; about one-fourth of all U.S. households report participating in wildlife viewing—in their yards or on a special trip (U.S. Fish and Wildlife Service 2007). The number of Americans engaged in wildlife viewing is increasing over time, and they spend over a billion dollars on the activity—certainly a symbol of the meaning of the activity to their lives. Of the millions of international tourist arrivals for 2005, the World Tourism Organization estimates that about 7 percent involve nature-based tourism, which includes activities such as hiking, viewing nature, and wildlife viewing. Whether it is bird viewing in one's backyard, watching polar bears just outside Churchill, Canada, cage diving for great white sharks off the coast of South Africa, or a close-up view of mountain gorillas in Rwanda, wildlife viewing is a growing activity.

A second trend is the expanding policy to use tourism as an economic development tool. This interest is important in many third-world regions, such as Africa, where receipts from tourism form a significant source of foreign exchange and visitor expenditures not only provide employment for local residents, but also help fund conservation of wildlife and biodiversity. For example, in sub-Saharan Africa, about 300 million people (over 40 percent of the population) live in extreme poverty (earning US$1 or less per day). Given the rich biodiversity that exists in many very poor places, tourism development (and the revenues it produces) based not on the standard sun, sea, and sand model but on wildlife and associated biodiversity can have major impacts on the quality of people's lives. Finally, in North America, many rural communities are interested in tapping into their wildlife resources as a basis for developing or expanding a nature-based tourism industry.

A third trend is a deepening concern about the environment, often contemporaneously articulated through discussions about global climate change, biodiversity protection, and clean water. Significant changes in people's values and beliefs have occurred since the 1980s about the dependency of human life on its environment and, consequently, about the need to think and act in ways to reduce the negative consequences of human activity. Wildlife viewing is often a convenient and effective vehicle for conservation agencies and nongovernmental organizations to communicate the consequences of these environmental impacts.

The junction of these three trends in the twenty-first century not only places new demands on wildlife managers, but also provides the seeds for innovative opportunities for conserving biodiversity and improving the condition of human life. As these trends converge, and as people begin to appreciate this confluence, there is a growing understanding of connectedness of biodiversity protection and the quality of human life. In particular, as local communities seek out the economic benefits of wildlife viewing and as wildlife managers search for methods of enhancing wildlife habitat and populations, there is a need to better understand the intersection of both marketing and management.

The demands and opportunities posed by this convergence can only be addressed through a framework that considers marketing and management as two intersecting systems. This chapter briefly explores the nature of this intersection and explicates the resulting challenges and opportunities by applying systems thinking to the question of wildlife viewing. The focus is on structured, intentionally designed nature-dominated wildlife-viewing settings. This chapter is deliberately impressionistic and is not intended to be a systematic review of relevant literature. Instead, it is based on my understanding and experience in engaging wildlife managers in discussions about management and marketing.

The Interface of Marketing and Management

Wildlife-viewing opportunities, to be meaningful and to have positive impacts, just don't happen; they must be thought out, worked through, and carefully implemented. Not only must the biological side of things be carefully examined, but the sociological side must be cautiously studied as well. Creating opportunities for a wildlife-viewing experience requires sensitive integration of both biology and sociology.

In this sense, then, our traditional notions of management and marketing may have to be revised. Management here is defined not only as the on-the-ground production and conservation of wildlife habitats and populations, but also as an activity that facilitates access to wildlife-viewing opportunities through the necessary facilities, interpretive programs, and information about wildlife habitats and behavior.

Marketing is an activity designed to ensure that connections are made between the experiences people seek and the opportunities that are offered by management. More traditional definitions of marketing view it as the combination of price, promotion, place, and product that meets a certain demand (Heath and Wall 1991). Marketing also deals with access, but access in the sense of information, knowledge, and awareness. Both definitions of marketing are consistent, but the important point is that marketing is more than the promotional activity often associated with tourism development.

Application of systems thinking (Senge 1990) can greatly assist in understanding how marketing and management themselves converge. A system is a group of related events connected by relationships that compose a whole and is itself complex. Systems have a purpose and are situated within larger systems. Finally, systems contain loops that serve as feedback. Management and marketing can be viewed as subsystems of a larger societal system that deals with economic development and environmental protection. Figure 19.1 represents a simplified display of each subsystem and shows that they intersect at the wildlife-viewing setting. Each of the subsystems consists of a set of elements, relationships, and delays between causes and effects. As a result, the experiences visitors construct is a function of other actions and policies, which may collide with or reinforce each other. For example, a destination marketing organization (DMO) may promote a particular park or protected area as an ideal location for viewing bald eagles. The local management agency may or may not be aware of this promotional activity, and thus may not be prepared for the number of guests arriving, and as a result may become overwhelmed with visitors and the need for asso-

FIGURE 19.1 **Wildlife Viewing Settings**

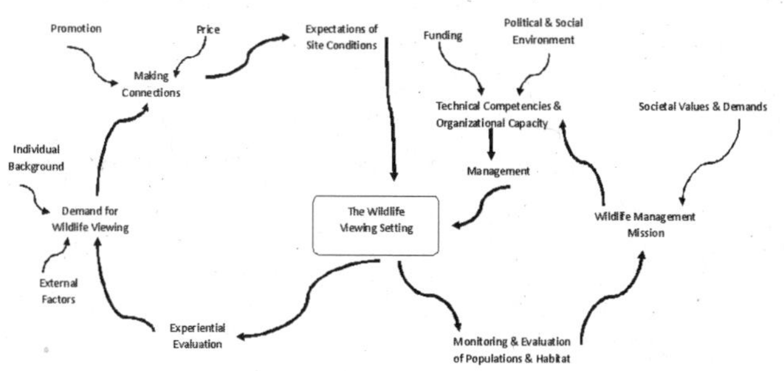

Wildlife viewing settings occur as a result of two subsystems of human activity as represented here. The subsystems intersect at the setting, and thus construction of high quality viewing opportunities requires each subsystem to coordinate and cooperate with the other.

ciated supporting facilities, such as parking, restrooms, water, and trails. The managing agency may respond to this level of visitation by implementing a set of rules to reduce the potential for disruption of the eagles' natural habits, and these rules may restrict viewing opportunities as well as have negative impact on the visitor's experience—an experience anticipated as a result of the DMO's promotional media.

The interests of the three entities involved in this situation (the DMO, the managing agency, and the visitor) are somewhat competing and overlapping. Destination marketing organizations are normally charged with the mission of enhancing tourism visits in order to increase expenditures that have positive impact on the local economy. The managing agency normally holds a mission of protecting (and enhancing) wildlife populations and habitats. At the setting, wildlife managers are concerned about controlling and informing visitor behavior to minimize impacts on wildlife. The visitor is seeking the opportunity to view and appreciate various species of wildlife. These interests are somewhat competitive, but also overlapping in the sense that the DMO cannot be successful if visitors unacceptably disturb wildlife to the extent that it is difficult to view them; the managing agency needs public support to fund its wildlife enhancement programs; too much restriction on visitor behavior results in people not appreciating wildlife; and the visitor expects to view wildlife in its natural habitats.

The setting is the key place in each subsystem where beliefs, expectations, policies, and actions intersect. While biologists may describe the setting in terms of vegetation type, ecological relationships, and disturbance processes, the recreation and tourism specialists would describe the same place in terms of its social, biological, and managerial character—the basis of the Recreation Opportunity Spectrum (Driver and Brown 1978). The setting provides the opportunities for visitors to achieve certain experiences, such as appreciating and learning about nature, adventure, excitement, escape, and family cohesiveness (Driver, Tinsley, and Manfredo 1991). How this setting is managed is the result of integration (deliberate or accidental) of the various beliefs and policies of the DMOs and wildlife-managing agencies.

Prior events in both systems influence what happens at the setting and what outcomes result. The wildlife manager manipulates vegetation, water, cover, and species populations, which, after a delay, result in a certain density of wildlife (or a probability of viewing) at the setting. The DMO (or individual private firms, sometimes the management agency) builds expectations of what experiential dimensions are afforded at the setting through dissemination of information and promotional material; however, these expectations may also be influenced by interpersonal interaction with other viewers who may have visited the site. How the setting is managed may hinder or facilitate achievement of those desired experiences.

The intersection of marketing and management is most prominent for the generally large iconic species of various places, popularly termed *charismatic megafauna*: the bison, wolves, grizzly bears, and polar bears of North America; the "Big Five" (elephant, rhinoceros, Cape buffalo, lion, and leopard) in southern Africa; the sharks, dolphins, and whales of the oceans; large marsupials in Australia; the panda in Asia; the mountain gorilla of eastern Africa; and the eagles and other raptors of the skies. Not only do large numbers of people desire to view these animals in their natural habitats, but many have become the poster icons at the basis of appeals for conservation (and funding for conservation) of many nongovernmental conservation groups. In a sense, the wildlife-viewing setting is the engine of both conservation and economic growth.

Some Opportunities and Challenges

A fundamental barrier to recovery and management of wildlife populations has been the impact of human activity and development on habitats and populations. These barriers have traditionally been focused on activities such as habitat destruction, harvesting or culling of animals, and human-induced disturbance. Wildlife viewing tends to be "softer" in its impacts, if properly managed. For example, Litchfield (2001) discusses the steps taken to reduce impacts of humans engaged in viewing on the great apes in Uganda. Human behavior is highly regulated in this setting, but people are allowed to get very close to the apes. Likewise, Newsome and colleagues (2005) describe the rules and guidelines for observing whales in Australian waters. A combination of rules, interpretation, and supervision ensures that people do not unacceptably disturb these animals but yet provides them with the viewing opportunity. People will accept very restrictive rules for wildlife viewing under certain conditions (Frost and McCool 1988).

While the conditions under which wildlife are viewed vary, depending upon the species, setting objectives and conditions, and visitor background and anticipations, the effects of such viewing are clearly not well established for most species. While the question of what effects result from wildlife viewing is fundamental, equally significant is the question of how much and what types of consequences are *unacceptable.* For example, in many places in the United States, it is quite common to encounter white-tailed deer during a suburban walk. An encounter may result in the deer running off, and thus certain physiological and behavioral effects on the animal occur. But at what level do these effects become unacceptable?

The acceptability of impacts is not a biological concept but one that is highly value laden and a function of the situational context (including setting objectives), institutional factors, individual beliefs about consequences, and willingness to make certain trade-offs (Kakoyannis, Shindler, and Stankey 2001; Stankey and Shindler 2006) and can only be resolved through deliberation and negotiation. Identifying acceptable or unacceptable levels of impact requires an understanding of the trade-offs involved. For example, do the benefits accruing to people (in terms of a high-quality experience, greater employment and incomes) outweigh the costs (in terms of possible disturbance) to the animals? The question of acceptability is also involved in other dimensions of the viewing setting, such as the acceptability of conditions that might affect desired experiences. These conditions might include the density and visibility of wildlife species, number of other people present, rules restricting visitor behavior, and interpretation programs.

Not every viewing site or area contains the charismatic megafauna at the heart of many current wildlife-viewing opportunities. A popular myth in Africa is that the Big Five are needed for an economically viable wildlife-viewing opportunity. This is not necessarily true. Game reserves containing the Big Five are costly to develop and maintain: they must be fenced and strictly managed and visitors closely regulated to prevent injury and possible death. There are many modest game reserves, farms, and bed-and-breakfast businesses that have developed viewing opportunities, but without the Big Five present. For example, these businesses may have a small reserve containing several species of antelope, zebra, wildebeest, and giraffe that provide a value-added benefit for visitors. This benefit may allow the business to be more profitable.

In the United States, private game reserves that emphasize wildlife viewing are relatively rare. While many large ranches in the West provide opportunities for hunting big game, such as deer, elk, and bear, few specialize in wildlife viewing using the southern Africa model of an upscale game lodge. Game lodges that cater to private hunting are also found around the country, depending upon state laws allowing hunting of game. Within Alaska, many lodges do combine wildlife viewing (particularly for Alaska brown bears) with fishing. However, lodges on private lands focusing on wildlife viewing represent an opportunity currently "untapped" for the U.S. market.

Many large ranches (say, ten thousand acres and more) in the West contain the potential of reestablishing herds of bison and elk along with other animals, even including wolves and bear with careful management. Following models of conservation employed in southern Africa, groups of ranchers could join together in a conservancy (an organization of private landowners with conservation and wildlife viewing as major objectives), drop intervening fences, and establish even larger areas for wildlife to roam and be viewed. Managing habitat differently than for cattle may also mean a return of native bird and waterfowl populations, thus providing additional opportunities. Implementing such a project would not be easy, but it can be done as dozens of conservancies in southern Africa have demonstrated (e.g., see Weaver and Skyer 2003).

In traditional marketing terms, attending to the product is an essential element of a successful campaign to increase sales, just as promotion is critical to building awareness and pricing is important to the product's competitiveness. To be successful, all components must be well integrated into a cohesive strategy. Because wildlife, and the lands that support wildlife, are usually publicly administered in the United States, management of the product (wildlife-viewing opportunities) tends to be distinct and separate from promotion activities, which are inclined to be administered by DMOs and local tourism-oriented businesses. This compartmentalization is more than simply two different groups conducting two activities without a lot of coordination. These activities are performed by individuals who come from very different intellectual cultures—one business, the other biology—that hold beliefs that are often opposed (e.g., profit vs. service, utilization vs. protection). The two cultures use different languages, with terms that may sound the same but often have very different meanings, making the communication needed for a system to function difficult.

Compartmentalization of functions in a system is a typical way of dealing with complexity: bureaucracies reduce the complexity to a set of components around which specialties can be developed to deal with each component. While Figure 19.1 displays two such systems, they may be viewed as related, interacting subsystems when the objective of the system becomes economic development. So while compartmentalization may function effectively for one subsystem or the other alone, it does not work well when the two systems are put together with the goal of optimizing the functioning of the entire system.

While simply watching wildlife may lead to a satisfactory viewing experience, appreciation and understanding often underlie management goals for public support of wildlife protection. Interpretation thus serves a key role in achieving larger goals. Interpretation involves more than relaying biological facts about a species to the viewer, which is often an emphasis in many viewing settings today. While it may be interesting to know the gestation period of an elephant or the number of calories a grizzly bear requires in the fall just before it goes into a deep sleep, interpretation involves building awareness and understanding of connectedness. While actually observing an animal is a key component of an experience, creating understanding of "connectedness" (say, linkages between wildlife, habitat, and people) adds tremendous experiential value to a wildlife-viewing experience.

The opportunity to build understanding of the concept of connectedness, a key component underlying any notion of ecological literacy, would not only enhance the experience of visitors seeking appreciation of nature, but eventually would result in better-informed decisions about choices back home. Here, the goals of the two systems overlap, for satisfactory wildlife-viewing experiences will likely lead to increased demand and to more citizen activism in protecting habitat.

In a very real way, employees at wildlife-viewing settings integrate habitat, populations, facilities, and information to create the opportunity for a "memorable experience" (Jager et al. 2006). Such experiences begin with understanding visitors—their backgrounds, "life stories," and expectations—and continue as interpreters make the wildlife-viewing setting relevant to the visitor. This is not an easy task and will require more coordination between wildlife managers and wildlife-viewing marketing staffs.

Unfortunately, if there is one area of the connection between management and marketing that is least understood, it is ensuring that the visitors are connected to the settings that provide opportunities for the experiences they seek. Internationally, conservation has recently emphasized biodiversity conservation funded by revenues developed in the private sector. Wildlife-based tourism is frequently mentioned not only as an economic development tool, but also as the source of revenues through which conservation will be funded (e.g., Bushell and McCool 2007).

The key component of this strategy involves providing opportunities for high-quality wildlife-viewing experiences. There seems to be an underlying assumption that if wildlife exists, then the quality of the viewing experience will be high and thus it will be memorable. The presence of animals to view could be considered a necessary but not sufficient condition for these experiences. The viewing setting (Driver and Brown 1978; Clark and Stankey 1979) consists of a biophysical component (animals, habitat, human-induced modifications), a social component (number and type of other people present), and a managerial component (presence of uniformed personnel, interpretation, rules). How these setting components are linked to the experiences visitors construct remains a substantial research challenge (McCool 2006).

Understanding how the wildlife-viewing market is segmented is critical. Viewers have varying preferences, expectations, and behaviors. Even if the probability of sighting an animal is low, many people will spend hours waiting for that opportunity (Montag, Patterson, and Freimund 2005), suggesting there is an enthusiast segment as opposed to a casual, opportunistic segment. Some will even be "happy" if they encounter spoor or other evidence of wildlife being present. Each segment would differ in terms of the setting conditions desired, such as type of access, probability of viewing an animal, type of interpretation, and even spending amounts and patterns (e.g., see Loker and Perdue 1992). While there are a variety of methods to segment a recreation market, the lesson is that a better understanding of market segments is critical to provision of high-quality wildlife-viewing opportunities.

A final challenge concerns the technical capacity of wildlife management agencies to provide viewing opportunities. Such agencies generally have a high degree of professionalism and technical capacity in the biophysical aspects of wildlife—disease, habitat, predator-prey relationships, nutrition, and so on—but generally lack the capacity for understanding wildlife viewers, their motivations, expectations, behaviors, and spending patterns. Construction of a wildlife-viewing opportunity is the result of skills in both areas, and the ability to make effective connections (marketing) is a result of integration of sociology and biology (of course, both fields contain a number of important subdisciplines relevant to this discussion). However, wildlife professionals have a tightly knit professional culture, as Kennedy (1985) argues:

> Wildlife managers world-wide seem to share a mission and knowledge that bind them together in noble purpose. This bond is an asset, for without such dedication and esprit de corps protecting rhinoceros (*Ceratotherium simus*) and whooping crane (*Grus americana*) populations, managing waterfowl habitat, implementing antlerless deer harvests, or regulating DDT use would probably have been less successful.

This sharing of values and a mission has led to much success in the recovery of wildlife populations, however, as Riley and colleagues (2002) note that integration of varying disciplines is needed for twenty-first-century wildlife management:

> The value of biological knowledge for wildlife management is not in question. However, we argue that such knowledge is not a sufficient stand-alone basis for the practice of wildlife management.

While cultural and organizational beliefs help individuals cope and respond to difficult situations, and therefore create success, those same beliefs can lead to failures as future situations such as the technological, social, and climate changes that create uncertainty and also characterize the twenty-first century unfold. When managing wildlife has as an important objective the provision of wildlife-viewing opportunities, then this statement is even more salient. Integration remains one of the most critical challenges confronting both wildlife managers and marketing professionals.

Conclusion

The market for wildlife viewing is growing and diversifying, from casual, sometimes accidental viewing opportunities to those that are highly structured and regulated with visitors seeking to view specific animals, birds, fish, and even insects. This growth and diversification in demand presents numerous opportunities for wildlife managers to create better understanding of the natural world and how humans are connected to it. At the same time, wildlife viewing presents excellent prospects for enhancing the quality of life for people living adjacent to the managed settings where wildlife occur. However, exploiting these opportunities, for both learning and economic development, requires close consideration of wildlife viewing as a system, composed of marketing and management subsystems.

Marketing and management are inextricably linked because of their connection to the setting. The intersection of both subsystems at the setting requires on the one hand managers to understand wildlife-viewing visitors and their needs, motivations, and desires, and on the other hand marketers to recognize the nuances of wildlife management. Both must understand that the product being produced (the experience) is more than simply the biophysical setting. Use of concepts such as the Recreation Opportunity Setting can help both professions focus on creating high-quality viewing opportunities.

The convergence of increased and diversifying demand for wildlife viewing, the use of nature-based tourism as an economic development tool, and a deepening concern for the environment and how it is expressed through climate change represents a unique opportunity that cannot be bypassed. Such convergence not only can provide better viewing opportunities, but also can increase awareness and the potential for action to address global environmental issues.

Literature Cited

Bushell, R., and S. F. McCool. 2007. Tourism as a tool for conservation and support of protected areas: Setting the agenda. In *Tourism and protected areas: Benefits beyond boundaries*, ed. R. Bushell and P. F. J. Eagles, 12–26. Oxfordshire, UK: CAB International.

Clark, R. N., and G. H. Stankey. 1979. *The recreation opportunity spectrum: A framework for planning, management and research*. PNW-98. Portland, OR: U.S. Department of Agriculture Forest Service, Pacific Northwest Forest and Range Experiment Station.

Driver, B. L., and P. J. Brown. 1978. The recreation opportunity concept and behavior information in outdoor recreation resource supply inventories. In *Integrated inventories of renewable natural resources: Proceedings of the work-*

shop, 24–31. Vol. Gen. Tech. Rep. RM-55. Fort Collins, CO: U.S. Department of Agriculture Forest Service Rocky Mountain Forest and Range Experiment Station.

Driver, B. L., H. E. A. Tinsley, and M. J. Manfredo. 1991. The paragraphs about leisure and recreation experience preference scales: Results from two inventories designed to assess the breadth of perceived psychological benefits of leisure. *Benefits of Leisure*. B. L. Driver, P. J. Brown, and G. L. Peterson (eds.), 263–86. State College, PA: Venture Publishing.

Frost, J. E., and S. F. McCool. 1988. Can visitor regulations enhance recreational experiences? *Environmental Management* 12(1):5–9.

Heath, E., and G. Wall. 1991. *Marketing tourism destinations: A strategic planning approach*. New York: John Wiley and Sons.

Jager, E., C. Sheedy, F. Gertsch, T. Phillips, and G. Danchuk. 2006. Managing visitor experiences in Canada's national heritage places. *Parks* 16(2):18–24.

Kakoyannis, C., B. Shindler, and G. H. Stankey. 2001. *Understanding the social acceptability of natural resource decisionmaking processes by using a knowledge base modeling approach*. GTR-PNW-518. Portland, OR: U.S. Department of Agriculture Forest Service, Pacific Northwest Research Station.

Kennedy, J. J. 1985. Viewing wildlife managers as a unique professional culture. *Wildlife Society Bulletin* 13(4):571–79.

Litchfield, C. 2001. Responsible Tourism with Great Apes in Uganda. Tourism, Recreation and Sustainability: Linking Culture and the Environment, S. F. McCool, and R. N. Moisey (eds), 105–32. Oxxon, UK: CABI Publishing.

Loker, L. E., and R. R. Perdue. 1992. A benefit-based segmentation of a non-resident summer travel market. *Journal of Travel Research* 31(1):30–35.

McCool, S. F. 2006. Managing for visitor experiences: Promising opportunities and fundamental challenges. *Parks* 16(2):3–9.

Montag, J., M. E. Patterson, and W. A. Freimund. 2005. The wolf viewing experience in the Lamar Valley of Yellowstone National Park. *Human Dimensions of Wildlife* 10(4):273–84.

Newsome, D. R., Dowling, and S. Moore. 2005. *Wildlife tourism*. Aspects of Tourism. Clevedon, UK: Channel View Publications.

Riley, S. J., D. J. Decker, L. H. Carpenter, J. F. Organ, W. F. Siemer, G. F. Mattfeld, and G. Parsons. 2002. The essence of wildlife management. *Wildlife Society Bulletin* 30(2):585–93.

Senge, P. M. 1990. *The fifth discipline: The art and practice of the learning organization*. New York: Doubleday/Currency.

Stankey, G. H., and B. Shindler. 2006. Formation of social acceptability judgments and their implications for management of rare and little-known species. *Conservation Biology* 20(1):28–37.

U.S. Fish and Wildlife Service. 2007. *2006 National survey of fishing, hunting and wildlife associated recreation: National overview.* Washington, DC: U.S. Fish and Wildlife Service, Department of the Interior.

Weaver, C. L., and P. Skyer. 2003. Conservancies: Integrating wildlife land-use options into the livelihood, development, and conservation strategies of Namibian communities. Paper presented at the Fifth World Parks Congress, WWF-LIFE Program, Durban, South Africa.

CHAPTER 20

Trends in Access and Wildlife Privatization

Tommy L. Brown and Terry A. Messmer

Access to fish and wildlife resources has been a management concern historically and is also one of the oldest topics of human dimensions inquiry. Both long-term and newer trends indicate issues and concerns regarding access to public fish and wildlife resources will only intensify. Increased development and changes in landownership will continue to restrict access to thousands of acres that were once open. Owners of private lands are less willing today to allow hunting except for friends and family members. In addition, a global economy is encouraging privatization of recreational access through fees and leases, thus further reducing alternatives for those of limited means who seek places to hunt. Collectively, these forces are changing the very nature of traditional hunting experiences.

After providing a historical overview, this chapter examines recent trends in hunting and the provision of access, particularly to private lands. The chapter explores selected access issues, especially landowner liability, and recent efforts in several states to provide broader liability coverage to landowners who allow access for hunting and other activities. The effects of privatization on access, and efforts of government and other organizations to maintain adequate access into the future, in the face of these trends, are also examined. Special consideration of the likely impacts of these trends on wildlife management is also noted.

Overview

The need for public access to lakes and streams was expressed as early as Fanselow (1952). A decade later, the Sportfishing Institute and Outdoor Boating Club of America (1962) began an annual conference on access to recreational waters in 1961. State agencies have focused on access to fish and wildlife because a majority of these resources in the United States inhabit private lands (Brown et al. 2001). Concomitantly, most states have had decades-long programs to acquire easements to lakes and streams for fishing access and to maintain hunting access on private lands. Studies of posting practices of rural landowners date at least from Larson (1959) and became more widespread in the 1960s and 1970s.

Concerns of state wildlife agencies about access to private lands for hunting relate to achieving population objectives for some species and maintaining hunting opportunity, critical to sustaining an active hunter population and the revenue streams hunters provide for funding management activities. Agencies also are concerned about keeping wildlife damage to crops and landscape plantings at acceptable levels and providing beneficial uses of wildlife that are culturally and economically important to local communities.

While free access to private lands for hunting has been common in many parts of the United States, some forms of fee hunting have existed for many decades. For example, over 440 New Jersey farmers (primarily) purchased permits to raise pheasants and other game for monetary return in 1938 (Leopold et al. 1939). Reports of the Texas leasing system occurred as early as Leopold et al. (1939). Waterfowl-hunting leases or other fee hunting arrangements have been used in a number of states for several decades (e.g., Uhlig 1961). Thus, fee-based hunting, whether via permits, user fees, or leases, has been in practice in the United States for over a half-century. Fee hunting was in common use by large timber companies in the South (Shelton 1987) and more recently has come into use in other parts of the United States. Internet sites now advertise properties that may be leased for hunting.

Outside Texas, where leasing has existed for perhaps seventy years, fee hunting has grown less rapidly. Only 4 percent of landowners in Illinois who allow hunting charged a fee in 1999 (Miller et al. 2002). Only 6 percent of New York owners received gifts, services, or payments for access privileges in 1991–92 (Siemer and Brown 1993). Twelve percent of owners of large ranches in Montana had fee hunting or leasing operations in 1994 (Swensson and Knight 2001).

Hunting Participation, Access, and Economic Consequences

Over 12.5 million Americans sixteen years old and older hunted in 2006 (U.S. Fish and Wildlife Service (2007, 6) and upward of 44 million Americans have hunted at some time in their lives (Aiken 2005). Hunting, in addition to being a traditional recreational activity, provides a strong economic force. It produces nearly $3 billion annually in federal income taxes and nearly $25 billion in retail sales, and it generates almost 600,000 jobs in the United States (Southwick 2001). These figures do not include what hunters may contribute to various conservation efforts.

Data collected since 1980 indicate a general decline in the number of hunting participants (U.S. Department of the Interior, Fish and Wildlife Service, and the U.S. Department of Commerce, Bureau of the Census, 1994,, B-7; Aiken 2005, 6–9). More recently, hunting participation decreased from 14 million hunters in 1991 to 12.5 million hunters in 2006 (Aiken 2005, 28; U.S. Fish and Wildlife Service 2007, 6). Accompanying the decrease in the hunting population was a shift in hunting activity from public land to private land hunting between 1980 and 2001, particularly for big-game hunting (Aiken 2005, 31).

Declining hunting participation affects the budgets of many state fish and wildlife agencies because most of their income comes from the sale of hunting and fishing licenses and because federal-aid dollars are tied to participant numbers and related equipment expenditures. In addition, many businesses depend on hunting-related expenditures. Rural economies may be disproportionately affected because many rural economies depend on hunting-related expenditures as a significant source of revenue (Duda et al. 2004, 9).

Lack of access and poor quality of the hunts on public land are common reasons given by hunters with decreasing participation (Duda et al. 1998, 576–85). However, a major factor determining individual use of public and private land for hunting continues to be availability. Although hunters who lived in the eight western states dominated by federal lands hunted public lands primarily in 2001, a majority of hunters in the other forty-two states hunted on private land (Aiken 2005).

A major access-related change over the past half-century has been the amount of private land, both farm and nonfarm, that is posted against hunting. In New York, the posting rate increased from 26 percent in 1963 (Waldbauer 1966) to over 60 percent in 1991 (Siemer and Brown 1993). More recently, 69 percent of Pennsylvania owners posted their lands in 2003 (Jagnow et al. 2006). Substantial amounts of hunting occur on posted lands (Siemer and Brown 1993), but simultaneous to the increase in posted land in more recent years, the number of owners who allow hunting by permission to people other than friends, neighbors, or relatives has decreased. Only 14 percent of New York owners permitted people they did not know to hunt on their lands in 1991 (Siemer and Brown 1993). In Illinois, 32 percent of the owners surveyed in 2000 allowed strangers who asked permission to hunt on their lands (Miller et al. 2002). However, for hunters without connections to landowners (i.e., new hunters, hunters who have moved to a new region, hunters seeking new habitat for a species they wish to hunt for the first time), access to private lands is a critical problem.

Some of the earliest posting studies (Larson 1959; Waldbauer 1966) indicated that bad experiences with hunters such as leaving a gate open, shooting in an unsafe manner, and leaving refuse behind constituted an important reason for posting. In a recent study, many Pennsylvania owners posted for similar reasons (Jagnow et al. 2006). Some posting is also done to give the owner and/or selected others exclusive hunting privileges, and some owners deem hunting to be incompatible with other uses of the property. Liability concern also has been cited as an important reason for limiting access. It was the leading reason by a margin of two to one given by Illinois owners who do not grant hunting access (Miller et al. 2002), and it was an important reason for posting by New York owners (Siemer and Brown 1993).

All fifty states now have limited liability recreation statutes that offer landowners substantial protection against liability to hunters and other recreationists in situations where owners are not charging a fee or receiving some other consideration. Studies in Illinois (Miller et al. 2002) and New York (Siemer and Brown 1993) have found that most owners are not aware of or do not understand these statutes.

Recent Trends in Limited Liability Statutes

The limited liability recreation statutes date from the 1950s, when they were first enacted in Michigan and New York (Brown 2006). Many other states passed statutes in the 1960s and 1970s, and by the late 1980s nearly all states had such statutes. Most states have modified their statutes to some extent since original passage; changes that have occurred since 1990 in several states to provide additional liability protection to landowners are of particular interest.

Changes in the statutes of states that have updated them fall primarily into two categories: (1) providing protection for additional groups of users, and thereby closing loopholes in existing statutes that became apparent through court cases and (2) expanding the coverage of the statutes to include landowners who receive some compensation or services from hunters and other users. The following are examples of the expansion of the statutes in each of these areas.

Expansion of Activities and Situations Covered

Before 1990, the statutes of many states included a list of specified recreation activities, and owners were protected only for those activities. Hunting, fishing, and trapping were specified activities in virtually all states from the time the statutes were enacted. However, activities such as bird-watching and wildlife photography were less frequently covered. Even in hunting and fishing situations, if hunters or anglers had an accident on the property enroute to or from the hunting or fishing site, plaintiffs would sometimes argue that the recreationists were not actually hunting or fishing at the time of the accident, and therefore the statute did not apply. Moreover, owners often were not covered if anglers or hunters were injured while assisting owners in constructing or maintaining trails that facilitated access for hunting, hiking, bird-watching, or other activities.

Over half of the states now include all recreation activities in their statutes, and sixteen states have added noncommercial uses, such as for educational purposes. For example, coverage under the current Massachusetts statute applies to "any person having an interest in land including the structures, buildings, and equipment attached to the land, including without limitation, wetlands, rivers, streams, ponds, lakes, and other bodies of water, who lawfully permits the public to use such land for recreational, conservation, scientific, educational, environmental, ecological, research, religious, or charitable purposes without imposing a charge or fee" (Annotated Laws of Massachusetts, Chapter 21, § 17C [a]).

Coverage When the Landowner Receives a Gift, Service, or Payment

Previous versions of these state statutes typically did not apply if the owner received a cash payment, gift, or in some cases, any consideration from the recreationist. These limitations now have been broadened in some states. For example:

- Allowing the users to share fish, game, or other products from the land with the owner (Arkansas—Arkansas Code, Title 18-11-302[1])

- Allowing a fee of unstated amount if the property is not used primarily for commercial purposes (Maine, which further requires that the payment is not for exclusive use—Maine Revised Statutes, Title 14, § 159-A)
- Allowing the owner to collect specified dollar amounts, sometimes tied to the amount of property taxes (North Dakota—North Dakota Century Code, Title 53, §53-08-05)

The limited liability statutes of many states allow a governmental payment to a landowner, but often the governmental entity is at a particular level, such as the state.

Incentives to Landowners

Many state fish and wildlife agencies have worked for decades with farmers and other rural landowners to encourage them to allow access for hunting and fishing. Under these cooperative programs, landowners were rarely offered cash incentives, but rather, other agency services. Typical examples were the posting of areas around residences, increased law enforcement protection, a free subscription to the state conservation magazine, and free tree and shrub seedlings (Waldbauer 1966). In some situations these agreements are still in place, while in others the agreements have been terminated for various reasons on the part of both landowners (e.g., change in ownership) and agencies (e.g., staff cuts limited the services that could be provided in some cases).

Privatization and Commercialization of Wildlife in North America

Privatization has been defined as "the ability of private groups of individuals to dictate or control access and/or utilization of public and private land, waters, and/or fish and wildlife resources, and subsequent to this control the state is obligated to transfer its trust responsibilities over public wildlife resources to private parties or groups" (South Dakota Chapter of the Wildlife Society [SDCTWS] 1989). The SDCTWS further defined commercialization of wildlife as "the sale, barter, exchange of access to free ranging, public fish and wildlife resources by private groups or individuals." Thus, by these definitions any activity that supplants a state's ability to manage free-ranging wildlife for public use in favor of private enterprise economics is privatization of wildlife.

Recent litigation over fees and regulations that apply to nonresident hunters has renewed concerns regarding the impact of economics on wildlife management and conservation. Economics has consistently been an integral component of modern wildlife management. Most of the revenue used to support state wildlife management programs originates from market-based economic activities involving the sale of state-issued hunting licenses and permits to private individuals. However, it is the other market-based wildlife management programs that are being implemented on private lands (i.e., landowners collecting simple "trespass fees" to state legislatively enacted "game or wildlife ranching" enterprises) that are becoming major focal points in the debate over the impact of privatization and commercialization on the future of wildlife conservation (Duda 1998, 361–76; Butler et al. 2005, 381–82). Some view this increased interest in and emphasis on generating private profits from wildlife as undermining the public trust doctrine (Hawley 1993, 2–3).

Public Wildlife and Private Land: The Wildlife Manager's Dilemma

The basic tenet of wildlife management in North America, that is, the North American Model of Wildlife Conservation, derives from the public trust doctrine (Wildlife Society 2007). This doctrine, which dates from an 1842 Supreme Court decision (Matthews 1986, 460), maintains that government holds wildlife in trust for its citizens. Although not legally binding, the public trust doctrine remains a well-accepted concept because most people agree that government should be entrusted with managing wildlife for the public good.

In accordance with the public trust doctrine, wildlife managers have sought to maintain or increase desirable wildlife species to meet human food and recreational needs by directly manipulating their habitats (indirect management) or the populations (direct management) themselves (Messmer and Rohwer 1996, 25–26). Indirect management approaches are implemented to improve habitat conditions that result in gradual increases in the size of desirable populations by raising birthrates or survival rates. Direct management approaches include those activities (e.g., regulation of harvest, predation management) that immediately affect population birth- or death rates.

However, because most wildlife are highly mobile, the success of these traditional wildlife management strategies largely depend on managers having access to the land wildlife inhabits and control over its uses. Given that over 60 percent of the land (over 1.4 billion acres) is privately owned and 28 percent (635 million acres mostly in the West) is owned by the federal government (U.S. Department of Agriculture, Economic Research Service 2002, 35–36), state management of wildlife for the "public good" has become an intricate balancing act.

Although many assume the states have "exclusive" control over wildlife (Matthews 1986, 460), constitutional limits in areas regarding commerce, discrimination (U.S. Constitution Article IV, Section 2, Clause 1), and conflicting state laws under the federal law supremacy clause (U.S. Constitution Article VI, Section 2) may supersede state authority. Other federal legislation and treaties have given the federal government and tribes additional authority on some lands for certain purposes. Some examples of these include the Endangered Species Act, the Migratory Bird Treaty of 1916, and the Lacey Act.

Private landowners are increasingly recognizing that selling hunting rights or trespass access to their lands is a new source of income (Benson, Shelton, and Steinbeck 1999). In addition, many state wildlife agencies have implemented public access programs, and several now include financial incentives for landowners to maintain or improve wildlife habitat and open their lands to hunters (Duda et al. 1998, 360–65; Aiken 2005, 5). Some western states have implemented more formalized fee-access hunting programs (see Case Study: Utah's Cooperative Wildlife Management Unit Program—Revisited) that include substantial economic and operation incentives for landowners to manage for wildlife and increased public access to private lands (Leal and Grewell 1999, 18). Critics of these programs argue that they may constitute nothing more than a state endorsement of wildlife privatization (Eliason 2000, 264).

Recent trends suggest that hunters will place greater effort on obtaining opportunities on private land. These efforts will include both leasing hunting rights and purchasing properties (Aiken 2005, 31). The money spent by hunters to lease land doubled from 1989 to 2000 to $625 million, a trend that likely will continue. In 2001, 982,000 hunters spent an average of $635 each on leases. Another 919,000 hunters spent an average of $403 for daily or seasonal access to private land (Aiken 2005, 28).

Although the practice of leasing land for hunting has been common practice for several decades, it will remain controversial (Benson, Shelton, and Steinbeck 1999). For landowners, farmers, and ranchers, hunting leases are a means by which to generate additional income from wildlife resources that the landowners sustain through their crops and habitat maintenance. For the hunter, the increasing number and prevalence of lease arrangements are an indication of diminishing public access opportunities. While some see these trends as a way to increase private landowner involvement in conservation (Benson 1998), others view these programs as an erosion of professional wildlife management and principles espoused under the North American Model of Wildlife Conservation (Giest 2006).

Multistate and National Initiatives

State fish and wildlife agency administrators report that access to private land for hunting is important to achieving their agency's legal mandates (Benson 2001, 354). In response to decreased access opportunities on private land and increased leasing of private lands for hunting, twenty-one states, largely in the West, have implemented programs that have opened 27 million acres of private land to hunting and fishing access (Theodore Roosevelt Conservation Partnership 2007a). The "walk-in" access programs typically offer rural landowners small per-acre payments to voluntarily open their land to hunters and improve habitat. The ultimate goal of the programs is to expand access to private lands, thus potentially offsetting the effects of leasing and privatization on hunting participation.

Perhaps the clearest evidence of the growing concern over improved access is the attention given the issue in recent years at the federal level. Starting in 2003, significant attempts have occurred in the U.S. Congress to provide state fish and wildlife agencies a new source of funds to bolster current and establish new hunter access programs (Theodore Roosevelt Conservation Partnership 2007b). Other efforts at the federal level have included proposed amendments to the Farm Bill to provide payments to landowners who allow recreational access. Such funding could help state fish and wildlife agencies to address landowner liability concerns, enhance rural economies, and promote wildlife management by tailoring programs to fit their state's respective needs.

Case Study: Utah's Cooperative Wildlife Management Unit Program—Revisited

Utah's Cooperative Wildlife Management Unit (CWMU) Program began as a pilot program in 1990 and was codified by the Utah Legislature in 1994. The CWMU program was established with the intent of (1) providing income for landowners, (2) creating satisfying hunting opportunities, (3) increasing wildlife habitat, (4) providing adequate trespass protection for landowners who open their lands for hunting, and (5) increasing access to private lands for hunting big game. Messmer and colleagues (1998) concluded that the program was achieving most management objectives. A survey was conducted of program participants in 2002 to assess the status of the program (McCoy 2003; McCoy, Reiter, and Briem 2003). The program continued to provide new income for both landowners and operators. Nevertheless, the primary enterprise for most landowners remained agriculture, as livestock and crops averaged 46 percent of total household income. The CWMU program also appears to have offered stability that earlier informal fee hunting programs lack. The legislative authority establishing the program provided landowners and operators economic confidence and the incentives to improve wildlife habitat ranch infrastructures. Concomitantly, many participating landowners reinvested in their CWMU enterprise to enhance wildlife habitat and operations. While landowners and operators continue to report some trespassing problems, alleviating trespass pressure is no longer the primary motivation for respondents enrolling in the program. Before enrolling in the program, many landowners (68 percent) did not allow any public hunting access to their lands. In 2003, over 1.6 million acres were enrolled in the program, providing access to both resident and nonresident hunters. The program continued to create satisfying hunting opportunities for resident and nonresident hunters and an economic boost to rural economies (McCoy, Reiter, and Briem 2003).

Conclusion

While the number of hunters has decreased in recent years, the total number of outdoor recreationists continues to increase. Thus, the value of private and public lands as recreational areas will continue to grow, as will the problems associated with increasing human use. Access to private lands has become more tightly controlled in recent years, to the point that in much of the United States, small proportions of landowners allow hunting except by family and friends. Programs implemented by public wildlife management agencies and organizations to encourage landowners and other stakeholders to manage for wildlife and/or allow public hunting and other recreational access have included a strengthening of state limited-liability recreation statutes and federal legislative attempts to provide funds to owners who provide free hunting access. To date, these programs have not been sufficient to effectively counteract the trend of continuing access restrictions to private lands. Hunting leases in Texas, and to a lesser degree in other southern and western states, may be contributing to the privatization of both wildlife and hunting.

Last, increased diversity of stakeholders creates new management dilemmas regarding the use of traditional approaches to managing wildlife. In some cases, population management techniques such as hunting, fishing, and trapping, which were once used to manage wildlife populations and provide recreational opportunities for traditional resource users, are becoming unacceptable to new constituents. Increased concerns for privacy, property damage, and safety may result in larger areas being closed to the use of traditional population management options, thus further exacerbating the conflicts. Thus, the need for research, education, outreach, and extension programs to identify, design, communicate, and evaluate alternative strategies that can be implemented to meet public demands for wildlife-related recreation will intensify. In addition, new strategies and approaches must be developed to address landowner, homeowner, and other stakeholder concerns regarding wildlife and their management.

Literature Cited

Aikin, R. 2005. *Private and public land use by hunters: Addendum to the 2001 national survey of fishing, hunting, and wildlife-association recreation.* 2001-8. Arlington, VA: U.S. Fish and Wildlife Service, Division of Federal Assistance.

Benson, D. 1998. Enfranchise landowners for land and wildlife stewardship: Examples from the western United States. *Human Dimensions of Wildlife* 3:59–68.

———. 2001. Survey of state programs for habitat, hunting, and nongame management on private lands in the United States. *Wildlife Society Bulletin* 29:354–58.

Benson, D., R. Shelton, and D. Steinbeck. 1999. *Wildlife stewardship and recreation on private lands.* College Station: Texas A&M University Press.

Brown, T. L. 2006. *Analysis of limited liability recreation use statutes in the Northern Forest states.* 06-12. Ithaca, NY: Human Dimensions Research Unit, Department of Natural Resources, Cornell University.

Brown, T. L., T. A. Messmer, and D. J. Decker. 2001. Access for hunting on agricultural and forest lands. In *Human dimensions of wildlife management in North America*, ed. D. J. Decker, T. L. Brown, and W. F. Siemer, 269–88. Bethesda, MD: The Wildlife Society.

Butler, M. J., A. P. Teaschner, W. B. Ballard, and B. K. McGee. 2005. Commentary: Wildlife ranching in North America—argument, issues and perspectives. *Wildlife Society Bulletin* 33:381–89.

Duda, M. D., B. J. Gruver, S. Jacobs, T. Mathews, A. Lanier, O. Augustus, and S. J. Bissell. 1998. *Wildlife and the American mind*. Harrisonburg, VA: Responsive Management.

Duda, M. D., P. E. De Michele, C. Zurawski, M. Jones, J. E. Yoder, W. Testerman, A. Lanier, S. J. Bissell, P. Wang, and J. B. Herrick. 2004. *Issues related to hunting and fishing access in the United States: A literature review.* Harrisonburg, VA: Responsive Management.

Eliason, S. L. 2000. Some polemical observations on Utah's Cooperative Wildlife Management Unit Program. *Wildlife Society Bulletin* 28:264–67.

Fanselow, F. G. 1952. Public access to lakes and streams in Michigan. Paper presented at the Midwest Fish and Wildlife Conference, Des Moines, December 18.

Geist, V. 2006. The North American Model of Wildlife Conservation: A means of creating wealth and protecting public health while generating public diversity. In *Gaining ground: In pursuit of ecological sustainability*, ed. D. M. Lavigne, 285–93. Guelph, Canada, and University of Limerick: International Fund for Animal Welfare.

Hawley, A. W. L. 1993. *Commercialization and wildlife management: dancing with the devil*. Malabar FL: Krieger Publishing Company.

Jagnow, C. P., R. C. Stedman, A. E. Luloff, G. J. San Julian, J. C. Finley, and J. Steele. 2006. Why landowners in Pennsylvania post their property against hunting. *Human Dimensions of Wildlife* 11:15–26.

Larson, J. S. 1959. Straight answers about posted land. *Transactions of the North American Wildlife Conference* 24:480–87.

Leal, D. R., and J. B. Grewell. 1999. *Hunting for habitat: A practical guide to state-landowner partnerships*. Bozeman, MT: Political Economy Research Center.

Leopold, A., G. W. Wood, J. H. Baker, W. P. Taylor, and L. G. MacNamara. 1939. Farmer-sportsmen, a partnership for wildlife restoration. *Transactions of the North American Wildlife Conference* 4:144–75.

Matthews, O. P. 1986. Who owns wildlife? *Wildlife Society Bulletin* 14:459–65.

McCoy, N. 2003. *A survey of Utah Cooperative Wildlife Management Unit landowners, operators, and landowner/operators.* Logan: Jack H. Berryman Institute, Utah State University.

McCoy, N., D. Reiter, and J. Briem. 2003. *Utah's Cooperative Wildlife Management Unit Program: A survey of hunters.* Logan: Jack H. Berryman Institute, Utah State University.

Messmer, T. A., C. E. Dixon, W. Shields, S. C. Barras, and S. A. Schroeder. 1998. Cooperative Wildlife Management Units: Achieving hunter, landowner, and wildlife management agency objectives. *Wildlife Society Bulletin* 26:325–32.

Messmer, T. A., and F. C. Rohwer. 1996. Issues and problems in predation management to enhance avian recruitment. *Transactions of the North American Wildlife and Natural Resource Conference* 61:25–30.

Miller, C. A., L. K. Campbell, J. A. Yeagle, and R. J. Williams. 2002. *Results of studies of Illinois hunters, landowners, and participants in Access Illinois.* SR-02-01. Champaign: Illinois Natural History Survey.

Shelton, R. 1987. Fee hunting systems and important factors in wildlife commercialization on private lands. In *Wildlife values: Economic and social perspectives*, ed. D. J. Decker and G. R. Goff, 109–16. Boulder, CO: Westview Press.

Siemer, W. F., and T. L. Brown. 1993. *Public access to private land for hunting in New York: A study of 1991 landowners*, 93-4. Ithaca, NY: Human Dimensions Research Unit, Department of Natural Resources, Cornell University.

South Dakota Chapter of the Wildlife Society. 1989. A resolution to establish SDCTWS position on privatization of wildlife in South Dakota. http://sdwildlife.org/SDTWS%20RESOLUTION%20Privatization%201989.pdf.

Southwick, R. 2001. *Economic contributions of hunting.* Washington, DC: International Association of Fish and Wildlife Agencies.

Sportfishing Institute and Outdoor Boating Club of America. 1962. Access to recreational waters. Workshop Summary. Chicago: Sportfishing Institute and Outdoor Boating Club of America.

Swensson, E. J., and J. E. Knight. 2001. Hunter management strategies used by Montana ranchers. *Wildlife Society Bulletin* 29:306–10.

Theodore Roosevelt Conservation Partnership. 2007a. States with walk-in access programs. www.trcp.org/stateprograms.aspx.

Theodore Roosevelt Conservation Partnership. 2007b. Guaranteeing public access to hunting and fishing through "Open Fields." www.trcp.org/ea_openfields.aspx.

Uhlig, H. G. 1961. Survey of leased waterfowl hunting rights in Minnesota. *Journal of Wildlife Management* 15:204.

U.S. Fish and Wildlife Service. 2007. *2006 National survey of fishing, hunting, and wildlife-associated recreation: National overview.* Washington, DC: U.S. Fish and Wildlife Service.

U.S. Department of Agriculture, Economic Research Service. 2002. Major land uses in the United States. www.ers.usda.gov/publications/EIB14/eib14j.pdf.

U.S. Department of the Interior, Fish and Wildlife Service, and the U.S. Department of Commerce, Bureau of the Census. 1994. *1991 National survey of fishing, hunting, and wildlife-associated recreation.* Washington, DC: U.S. Government Printing Office.

Waldbauer, E. C. 1966. Posting on private lands in New York State. *New York Fish and Game Journal* 13:1–78.

Wildlife Society. 2007. Final TWS position statement: The North American Model of Wildlife Conservation. www.wildlife.org/policy/positionstatements/41-NAModel%20Position%20Statementfinal.pdf.

CHAPTER 21

Social Dimensions of Managing Hunting in Tropical Forests

Elizabeth L. Bennett

Management of hunting in tropical forests is a major challenge because hunting threatens many species in such forests yet also sustains some of the world's poorest peoples (Robinson 2005; Bennett et al. 2006). The productivity for most large-bodied mammals in tropical forests is low, so hunting levels for such species must be very low to be sustainable (Robinson and Bennett 2000a, 2004). Yet wild animals are often critical to the diets of impoverished forest-dwelling peoples who often have few or no alternative sources of protein (Infield and Adams 1999). Domestic animals can be difficult to maintain in the humid tropics owing to the problems of transporting feed into remote forest areas and the high incidence of livestock disease. Moreover, livestock in many forest villages are often perceived as savings and insurance against illness or disasters, not as a daily supply of protein (Wilkie and Carpenter 1999; Milner-Gulland et al. 2003).

The problems are exacerbated by rapid changes occurring throughout much of the humid tropics. Traditional management systems and taboos are breaking down. Efficient modern hunting technologies are replacing traditional ones. A vast commercial hunt has been added to subsistence hunting, a change facilitated by almost ubiquitous access to forests through logging and other roads (Robinson, Redford,

Thanks to John Robinson, for discussions on the thinking behind this chapter, and commenting on drafts. John Fraser and David Wilkie also kindly commented on the draft.

and Bennett 1999). In addition, the wildlife trade is increasingly globalized, especially to rapidly expanding markets in East Asia, creating demand for numerous tropical forest species, from large carnivores to turtles and songbirds (Bennett 2006). New markets are developing so rapidly that resource exploitation overwhelms the ability of local management institutions to respond. Often, the result is uncontrolled hunting, local extirpations of species, and loss of the resource on which rural peoples depend (Robinson and Redford 1991; Robinson and Bennett 2000b; Robinson 2005; Bennett et al. 2006).

This chapter examines the systems for managing hunting of tropical forest wildlife, focusing on the different players involved in management, including the public and private sectors, local communities, and conservation organizations. The chapter explores the management roles and capacities that each player can bring to bear and the problems and benefits that each contributes to conservation.

Different Management Systems

Good governance systems are essential in managing hunting in tropical forests, although good governance does not necessarily mean good conservation because the primary aim of management can vary between players (Dwyer 1994) and parts of the landscape (Robinson 1993). Nevertheless, good governance is an essential prerequisite to effective conservation, including hunting management.

Management as the Responsibility of the State

In many countries, national or local governments have assumed the role of guardians and managers of the nation's wildlife and have established legal and administrative systems placing responsibility for management of hunting with government agencies. The primary advantage of this approach is that governments are uniquely positioned to consider national interests, a role often perceived to include protection of wildlife for future generations. Governments have authority to designate large tracts of land for national parks and sustainable-use areas and to regulate hunting in those lands. In many tropical forest countries, however, governments are ineffective in promoting good wildlife conservation. The capacity of their wildlife management agencies is generally low, with insufficient staff in the field, poor training, insufficient resources, and inadequate legal and management systems. Moreover, government-run management systems do not always recognize the legitimate needs and desires of local communities living in and around forests, impeding local buy-in and adherence to management regulations (see chapter 4). In the absence of strong government capacity, this inevitably results in ineffective management across large swathes of the landscape, including protected areas.

Another complication is the high level of corruption in many tropical forest governments, which reduces incentives for long-term conservation and promotes short-term exploitation of wildlife and their habitats. Tropical forest countries are mostly perceived as "highly corrupt"; only one nation with significant areas of tropical forests (Malaysia) falls in the top 50 countries of 164 assessed (Transparency International 2006). Conservation is particularly susceptible to subversion by corrupt officials because corruption reduces effective public spending; most wildlife officials are poorly paid, which encourages bribes especially when dealing with natural resources of high value; and wildlife departments usually lack political weight, making it hard to prevent abuses from high-placed politicians, officials, the military, and wealthy resource extraction companies (Smith et al. 2003; Smith and Walpole 2005). If the judiciary is also weak, as is often the case, strong regulations do little to enhance good management but merely provide more opportunities for corruption (Damania 2002).

Good governance of wildlife at tropical forest sites where authority is fully vested in the government has rarely been documented. An exception is Nagarahole National Park, India, where wildlife management is of a high standard and healthy populations of globally important species of large animals flourish (Karanth and Sunquist 1992; Madhusudan and Karanth 2000; Karanth et al. 2006). Contributors to success include (1) a close relationship with an outside partner (the Wildlife Conservation Society [WCS]), which has provided technical expertise continuously for more than ten years at the site, including staff training and long-term research and monitoring that feed results into management, (2) the legal authority to exclude outsiders from the area, and (3) sufficient well-trained staff. The 644-square-kilometer Nagarahole has about 250 government personnel. They are not distributed evenly throughout the park, but where staff density is one person per 1.9 square kilometer, staff have a jeep, walkie-talkies and arms, and daily patrols; large, spectacular animals such as elephants, tigers, and gaur are conserved, even amid high human populations (Madhusudan and Karanth 2000).

Management as the Responsibility of the Private Sector

In theory, private ownership by an individual or company of rights to harvest wildlife allows for good control—privatization clarifies ownership, thereby removing the "tragedy of the commons" (Hardin 1968), and the owner has a vested interest in protecting his own resources. In tropical forests, private management of wildlife is enabled via three avenues. One is privately owned land. Owing to government regulations in many tropical forest countries, private ownership of forest lands is rare, either because all land belongs to governments or because private ownership is only recognized after the forest has been cleared. The main exceptions are in parts of Latin America where private land ownership is common, but even there, most significant areas of forest are under government or community management. Moreover, private lands tend to be fragmented and reallocated over time (Naughton-Treves and Sanderson 1995). As a result, private lands in tropical forests contribute little to wildlife conservation.

Second is land where rights to hunt animals have been granted to private safari companies. This practice is rarer in tropical forests than in open habitats because of the relative scarcity of spectacular animals with large horns and tusks, the problems of monitoring and enforcement, high levels of corruption, and potential conflicts between the needs of safari hunters and those of subsistence hunters. No successful examples of safari hunting promoting good wildlife management in tropical forests have been documented.

The third avenue to private management of wildlife is on lands where the rights to extract natural resources (e.g., timber, minerals) have been granted to private companies. These do not include the rights to harvest wildlife, but the resource extraction companies are often the only institutional presence and, by default, the ones potentially capable of managing the wildlife (Robinson, Redford, and Bennett 1999). The companies have vested interests in establishing effective governance systems to allow efficient exploitation of their own resources, including preventing loss of resources to outsiders and ensuring social stability among their employees and their families. Such systems can provide an environment for good management of hunting, but only if that is a specified management aim. This might occur if the companies are interested in timber certification to allow them access to a wide range of markets for their products, in which case they might need to ensure that unsustainable hunting does not occur (Donovan 2001). Companies seeking certification for tropical forest operations are rare (Bennett 2004). In most cases, wildlife is either irrelevant to them or viewed as a free subsidy to feed their workers (Robinson, Redford, and Bennett 1999). Also, the needs of local subsistence hunters are frequently ignored, and major antagonisms can occur when logging-associated hunting sweeps away the wildlife on which local communities depend (Bennett and Gumal 2001; Rúmiz et al. 2001; Wilkie et al. 2001).

Good wildlife management in such lands is possible. A private company operating in logging concessions surrounding Nouabalé Ndoki National Park, northern Congo, has collaborated with the Congolese government, WCS, and local communities to manage wildlife in its concessions, especially to control unsustainable hunting and wild meat trade (Elkan and Elkan 2005; Elkan et al. 2006). The program includes creating hunting and nonhunting zones, bans on long-distance transportation of wildlife and hunting protected species, implementation through education and strict enforcement programs, development of alternative protein supplies, and an intensive monitoring program. The presence of abundant populations of large mammals throughout the concession, including gorillas, chimpanzees, forest elephants, and bongo, is testimony to the conservation success of the project. Local communities have bought in because the program supports their traditional hunting practices. They also gain employment opportunities and increased food and cultural security. The private sector benefits from the increased law enforcement through a decrease in theft of company property, improved corporate image, and, their ultimate aim, gaining internationally recognized certification of their timber. Factors contributing to success are (1) the different aims of all players being recognized and incorporated into management, including the needs of local communities, the company and its workers, and the conservation community, (2) sufficient well-trained staff, including a cadre of highly trained and well-supervised ecoguards, who use cross-checking systems between teams to ensure transparency and accountability, and (3) continuous presence of technical expertise for more than ten years, including long-term research and monitoring and results used in management (Elkan and Elkan 2005; Elkan et al. 2006).

Management as the Responsibility of Local Communities

Management vested in local communities should, in theory, promote good governance because the managers are on the ground at the site and have long-term, even multigenerational, commitments to the area. This is especially true if local communities depend strongly on wildlife for their protein. Some form of local community management of hunted wildlife species is universal among subsistence hunting societies across the humid tropics (see Robinson and Redford 1991; Robinson and Bennett 2000b). Locally managed subsistence hunting can be sustainable under some conditions, especially in areas of low human population density, and most examples of effective management are from South America, where areas of land are large and human population densities low (e.g., Hill and Padwe 2000) and where many communities have developed management techniques to enhance sustainability, such as dispersing the location and intensity of hunting (Vickers 1991; Leeuwenberg and Robinson 2000; Townsend 2000).

Such systems do not always conserve the full range of species, however. Sometimes communities and conservationists perceive the resource base and management needs very differently (Dwyer 1994). Conservation of any one species is not necessarily a high priority for local communities if other species can readily act as food substitutes. For example, in lands managed by the Huaorani in Ecuador, hunting of ungulates and large-bodied rodents is sustainable, but that of primates is not (Mena et al. 2000). In twenty-five sites across the Brazilian Amazon, the total number of mammals at sites is not affected by hunting pressure, but the species composition changes (Peres 2000).

Community-based management systems are also vulnerable to externally triggered change (Naughton-Treves and Sanderson 1995). Local communities seldom have legal authority or practical mechanisms for excluding outsiders when their communities become accessible. Community members themselves have multiple interests, and different actors within a community have differential access to resources and channels of influence (Agrawal 1997). This can become even more pronounced as interaction increases with the outside world and its correlated commercialization, leading to social stratification and reduction of community-minded decision making. When traditional systems start to break down, the incentive for individuals to conserve disappears.

Successful examples of community-based wildlife management in tropical forests in the face of change typically involve external players who work with communities to manage wildlife. Whether the initiative to conserve the wildlife comes from the community reaching out, or from outside conservationists contacting the community, multiple partners bringing different strengths aid success. In Amazonian Brazil, a collaboration of indigenous Kayapó and Conservation International protected indigenous lands from intrusion and conserved an exceptionally diverse fauna (Chernela 2005). In the Gran Chaco, Bolivia, a partnership between an organization representing the Isoceño peoples and WCS resulted in successful management of the area's wildlife while preserving the quality of life of the Isoceños (Arambiza and Painter 2006). In Amazonian Peru, a comanagement system between local communities, scientists, and extension workers resulted in sustainable hunting for subsistence and a unique example of a sustainable commercial trade in tropical forest wildlife (Bodmer and Puertas 2000). In such cases, resilience comes from the diverse strengths that the different players bring to bear (Robinson 2007).

Conclusion

Examples of effective systems for managing hunting at sites across the humid tropics are lamentably rare. Examination of the few success stories reveals essential elements:

1. *Multiple partners.* Successful wildlife management occurs only when sufficient capacity is present. This requires partnerships with collective strengths including long-term vested interests in the resource; skilled manpower with sufficient training and equipment to be effective; technical expertise in wildlife management and, if appropriate, alternative sources of livelihood; legal and enforcement skills; political influence; and funding. Other elements of success include the aims of each partner being clearly understood by all and areas of common and divergent interests specified (Robinson 2007); a clear process of communication and negotiation between partners to provide transparency, buy-in, and adequate checks and balances between the authority of the different players; and results of monitoring applied in decision-making processes (Agrawal 1997; Robinson and Queiroz, forthcoming).
2. *Long-term planning and implementation.* Given the complexities of managing resource use in tropical forests, short-term projects involving sudden infusions of outside personnel and funds are doomed to failure (Oates 1999). All examples of good management systems involve long planning horizons, well beyond the political and funding cycles common

to governments and funding agencies. At least ten years are needed to gather detailed knowledge of the resource base and socioeconomic systems, build partnerships, and implement effective management systems that run smoothly and are fully institutionalized. Planning for personnel and long-term funding to allow for this is critical.

3. *Landscape-level planning*. Appropriate allocation of land at an international, national, or other large scale is essential to ensure effective species conservation in protected areas, sustainable natural resource extraction in use areas, and more intensive land uses in agricultural and other lands, together forming a sustainable landscape (Robinson 1993; Bennett et al. 2006).
4. *Appropriate legal mechanisms.* Legal and administrative systems must support good wildlife management, with clear designation of hunting rights and mechanisms to enforce them. These must move beyond the current paradigm of often postcolonial and inappropriate legal systems that assume central government control and allow rights, decision making, and management to include local communities and other appropriate partners, while still taking into account the need for government participation where appropriate (e.g., prosecutions, judicial support).
5. *Sufficient capacity to establish and enforce regulations.* Wherever the management authority lies, sufficient manpower with high levels of training and equipment must be in place to enforce regulations and monitor wildlife populations and hunting levels. One problem in many tropical forest countries is that the governments do not have sufficient personnel and funds, and local communities and conservation organizations do not have legal authority to do enforcement. Again, some form of cooperative agreement between partners is likely to be necessary.
6. *Mechanisms to reduce corruption.* Transparency and accountability are essential. Clear and transparent reporting systems, including cross-checking between systems and people, are needed (Smith and Walpole 2005). This often is achieved when multiple agencies are involved in management; the earlier examples of "best cases" are all in countries with high corruption indices, yet they constitute good governance

because of the plethora of agencies involved in management, promoting transparency and accountability.

7. *Adaptable management systems.* The rapid rate of ecological, economic, and social change in tropical forests means that management systems must be "light on their feet." Frequent monitoring of hunting levels and wildlife populations is essential, feeding results into management. It is challenging to develop a system that can be adaptable in the face of rapid change, with strong, robust enforcement to control the corruption and organized criminal networks running much of the illegal wildlife trade today (Zimmerman 2003). Again, multiple partners with different skills are likely to be the only way to achieve such adaptability, as well as resilience in the face of change.

Management of hunting in tropical forests is complex and challenging owing to the pressures of conserving threatened species and supporting poor people's livelihoods in an intrinsically unproductive system where weak governance is the norm. Unless we think in a different way about the roles of different players involved in management, the forests will have fallen silent while we grapple with mobilizing anachronistic, cumbersome, and intrinsically flawed management systems into action.

Literature Cited

Agrawal, A. 1997. *Community in conservation: Beyond enchantment and disenchantment.* Gainesville, FL: Conservation and Development Forum.

Arambiza, E., and M. Painter. 2006. Biodiversity conservation and the quality of life of the indigenous people in the Bolivian Chaco. *Human Organization* 65:20–34.

Bennett, E. L. 2004. *Unable to see the wildlife for the trees? Timber certification and its role in conserving tropical forest wildlife.* Washington, DC: World Bank.

———. 2006. Consuming the world's wildlife. *Chinese National Geography* (November):126–35. (In Chinese.)

Bennett, E. L., E. Blencowe, K. Brandon, D. Brown, R. W. Burn, G. Cowlishaw, G. Davies, et al. 2006. Hunting for consensus: reconciling bushmeat harvest, conservation and development policy in West and Central Africa. *Conservation Biology* 21(3):884–87.

Bennett, E. L., and M. T. Gumal. 2001. The inter-relationships of commercial logging, hunting, and wildlife in Sarawak, and recommendations for forest management. In *The cutting edge: Conserving wildlife in managed tropical forests*, ed. R. A. Fimbel, A. Grajal, and J. G. Robinson, 359–74. New York: Columbia University Press.

Bodmer, R., and P. E. Puertas. 2000. Community-based comanagement of wildlife in the Peruvian Amazon. In *Hunting for sustainability in tropical forests*, ed. J. G. Robinson and E. L. Bennett, 95–409. New York: Columbia University Press.

Chernela, J. 2005. Response to "A challenge to conservationists." *World Watch* (March/April).

Damania, R. 2002. Environmental controls with corrupt bureaucrats. *Environment and Development Economics* 7:407–27.

Donovan, R. Z. 2001. Tropical forest management certification and wildlife conservation. In *The cutting edge: Conserving wildlife in logged tropical forest*, ed. R. A. Fimbel, A. Grajal, and J. G. Robinson, 601–13. New York: Columbia University Press.

Dwyer, P. D. 1994. Modern conservation and indigenous peoples: In search of wisdom. *Pacific Conservation Biology* 1:91–97.

Elkan, P. W., and S. W. Elkan. 2005. Mainstreaming wildlife conservation in multiple-use forests of the northern Republic of Congo. In *Mainstreaming biodiversity in production landscapes*, ed. C. Petersen and B. Huntley, 51–65. Washington, DC: Global Environment Facility.

Elkan, P. W., S. W. Elkan, A. Moukassa, R. Malonga, M. Gangoue, and J. L. D. Smith. 2006. Managing threats from bushmeat hunting in a logging concession in the Republic of Congo. In *Emerging Threats to Tropical Forests*, ed. L. F. Laurance and C. A. Peres. Chicago: University of Chicago Press.

Hardin, G. 1968. The tragedy of the commons. *Science* 162:1243–48.

Hill, K., and J. Padwe. 2000. Sustainability of Aché hunting in the Mbaracayu Reserve, Paraguay. In *Hunting for sustainability in tropical forests*, ed. J. G. Robinson and E. L. Bennett, 9–105. New York: Columbia University Press.

Infield, M., and W. M. Adams. 1999. Institutional sustainability and community conservation: A case study from Uganda. *Journal of International Development* 11: 305–15.

Karanth, K. U., J. D. Nichols, N. S. Kumar, and J. E. Hines. 2006. Assessing tiger population dynamics using photographic capture-recapture sampling. *Ecology* 87(11):2925–37.

Karanth, K. U., and M. E. Sunquist. 1992. Prey selection by tiger, leopard and dhole in tropical forests. *Journal of Animal Ecology* 64:439-50.

Leeuwenberg, F. E., and J. G. Robinson. 2000. Traditional management of hunting in a Xavante community in central Brazil: The search for sustainability. In *Hunting for sustainability in tropical forests,* ed. J. G. Robinson and E. L. Bennett, 375–94. New York: Columbia University Press.

Madhusudan, M. D., and K. U. Karanth. 2000. Hunting for an answer: Is local hunting compatible with large mammal conservation in India? In *Hunting for sustainability in tropical forests,* ed. J. G. Robinson and E. L. Bennett, 339–55. New York: Columbia University Press.

Mena, P. V., J. R. Stallings, J. Regalo B., and R. Cueva L. 2000. In *Hunting for sustainability in tropical forests,* ed. J. G. Robinson and E. L. Bennett, 57–78. New York: Columbia University Press.

Milner-Gulland, E. J., E. L. Bennett, and the SCB 2002 Annual Meeting Wild Meat Group. 2003. Wild meat: The bigger picture. *Trends in Ecology and Evolution (TREE)* 18(7):351–57.

Naughton-Treves, L., and S. Sanderson. 1995. Property, politics and wildlife conservation. *World Development* 23(8):1265–75.

Oates, J. F. 1999. *Myth and reality in the rain forest: How conservation strategies are failing in West Africa.* Berkeley: University of California Press.

Peres, C. A. 2000. Evaluating the impact and sustainability of subsistence hunting at multiple Amazonian forest sites. In *Hunting for sustainability in tropical forests,* ed. J. G. Robinson and E. L. Bennett, 31–56. New York: Columbia University Press.

Robinson, J. G. 1993. The limits to caring: Sustainable living and the loss of biodiversity. *Conservation Biology* 7:20–28.

———. 2005. Biting the hand that feeds you: The consumption of nature and natural resources in the tropics. In *2006 State of the wild: A global portrait of wildlife, wild lands, and oceans,* ed. S. Guynup, 153–56. Washington, DC: Island Press.

———. 2007. Recognizing differences and establishing clear-eyed partnerships: A response to Vermeulen and Sheil. *Oryx,* 41: 443–44.

Robinson, J. G., and E. L. Bennett. 2000a. Carrying capacity limits to sustainable hunting in tropical forests. In *Hunting for sustainability in tropical forests,* ed. J. G. Robinson and E. L. Bennett, 13–30. New York: Columbia University Press.

———. 2000b. *Hunting for sustainability in tropical forests.* New York: Columbia University Press.

———. 2004. Having your wildlife and eating it too: An analysis of hunting sustainability across tropical ecosystems. *Animal Conservation* 7:397–408.

Robinson, J. G., and H. Queiroz. Forthcoming. Márcio Ayres: New approaches to the conservation and management of protected areas in Amazônia. In

The Amazonian Váárzea: The decade past and the decade ahead, ed. M. Pinedo-Vasquez, M. L. Ruffino, R. R. Sears, E. S. Brondizio, and C. Padoch. New York: Springer Verlag and New York Botanical Gardens Press.

Robinson, J. G., and K. H. Redford. 1991. *Neotropical wildlife use and conservation*. Chicago: University of Chicago Press.

Robinson, J. G., K. H. Redford, and E. L. Bennett. 1999. Wildlife harvest in logged tropical forests. *Science* 284 (April 23):595–96.

Rúmiz, D. I., D. Guinart S., L. Solar R., and J. C. Herrara F. 2001. Logging and hunting in community forests and corporate concessions: Two contrasting studies in Bolivia. In *The cutting edge: Conserving wildlife in logged tropical forest*, ed. R. A. Fimbel, A. Grajal, and J. G. Robinson, 333–58. New York: Columbia University Press.

Smith, R. J., R. D. J. Muir, M. J. Walpole, A. Balmford, and N. Leader-Williams. 2003. Governance and the loss of biodiversity. *Nature* 426:67–70.

Smith, R. J., and M. J. Walpole. 2005. Should conservationists pay more attention to corruption? *Oryx* 39(3):251–56.

Townsend, W. R. 2000. The sustainability of subsistence hunting by the Sirionó Indians of Bolivia. In *Hunting for sustainability in tropical forests*, ed. J. G. Robinson and E. L. Bennett, 267–81. New York: Columbia University Press.

Transparency International. 2006. *Transparency International corruption perceptions index 2006*. www.transparency.org/policy_research/surveys_indices/cpi/2006.

Vickers, W. T. 1991. Hunting yields and game composition over ten years in an Amazon Indian territory. In *Neotropical wildlife use and conservation*, ed. J. G. Robinson and K. H. Redford, 53–82. Chicago: University of Chicago Press.

Wilkie, D. S., and J. F. Carpenter. 1999. Bushmeat hunting in the Congo Basin: An assessment of impacts and options for mitigation. *Biodiversity and Conservation* 8: 927–55.

Wilkie, D. S., J. G. Sidle, G. C. Boundzanga, P. Auzel, and S. Blake. 2001. Defaunation, not deforestation: Commercial logging and market hunting in Northern Congo. In *The cutting edge: Conserving wildlife in logged tropical forest*, ed. R. A. Fimbel, A. Grajal, and J. G. Robinson, 375–99. New York: Columbia University Press.

Zimmerman, M.E. 2003. The black market for wildlife: Combating transnational organized crime in the illegal wildlife trade. *Vanderbilt Journal of Transnational Law* 36:1657–89.

CHAPTER 22

Communication as an Effective Management Strategy in a Diverse World

Susan K. Jacobson and Mallory D. McDuff

A recent poll conducted in forty-six countries by the Pew Research Center found that people in countries ranging from China, India, Peru, and Canada rank environmental degradation as the greatest danger in the world, more than such threats as terrorism and AIDS (Page 2007). The results from one of the largest global samplings of public opinion reveal the need for wildlife managers to mobilize this public concern into informed decisions and action to protect habitats and wildlife.

The public is increasingly exposed to wildlife and environmental issues through the Internet and print and broadcast media. Yet in this age of information, public knowledge about wildlife is minimal. Public polling by Roper in 2003 estimated that just 2 percent of adults in the United States qualify as environmentally literate. Fifty-six percent say they want to help the environment but don't know how (Coyle 2005, cited in Corbett 2006). The "thumb generation" with iPhones and BlackBerries has almost unlimited access to information but often lacks access to the outdoors, as children spend less time outside to develop an interest in nature (Louv 2005).

Wildlife agencies have new constituents. In the United States, from 2001 to 2006 the total number of anglers and hunters dropped by 10 percent, while the number of wildlife-watching participants increased by 8 percent (2006 National Survey of Fishing, Hunting and Wildlife-Associated Recreation). The "public" is increasingly diverse, speaking different languages and viewing wildlife through different cultural lenses. Because of this complexity, effective communications is one of the most critical management strategies for wildlife. Wildlife management issues, from managing wildlife in the suburbs to setting sustainable harvests, involve people as part of the problem and therefore require communication as part of the solution. The goals of this chapter are threefold:

- First, we describe the communication process for identifying communication objectives, targeting audiences, selecting media and messages, and evaluating results.
- Second, we explore the impacts of communication tools on increasing public support, knowledge, and behavior toward wildlife conservation; improving management compliance; and influencing environmental policy.
- Third, we present strategies for wildlife communications in this diverse world, including using e-outreach; communicating through new partnerships; and planning communications for multicultural audiences.

What Is Communication?

We live in a world where communication is critical to our own survival and to our success in our personal relationships, our work, and communities. Communication is a process of exchanging ideas and imparting information. Communication involves making yourself understood and understanding others in return. If you send a message—verbal, visual, or written—that the intended receiver does not understand, communication has not occurred. The only way to ensure the message was received and understood is to incorporate feedback into the process. An evaluation of a communication program about boating safely with manatees (*Trichechus manatus*) revealed that the messages did not result in improved boating behaviors (Morris, Jacobson, and Flamm 2007). Collecting feedback is critical for improving programs and determining success (Jacobson 1999).

Communication involves both interpersonal and mass media approaches. Interpersonal communication uses face-to-face dialogue, group interaction, speeches, and participatory approaches such as citizen task forces. Mass media includes the Internet, newspapers, television, mail, films, publications, billboards, and satellite conferences. Selecting the appropriate communication medium based on communication goals and audience is critical.

Communication for Wildlife Management

The public affects the success or failure of wildlife management efforts. The mission statements of most wildlife organizations, from state agencies to the Wildlife Society, recognize the importance of communications with the public (Case 1989). Today, the goals of wildlife management have become more complex, as managers must consider the preferences of a variety of stakeholders, who expect greater participation and communication (Decker, Brown, and Siemer 2001).

As many wildlife managers can attest, a poorly informed public, even a vocal minority, can spell the end of an innovative management policy. Likewise, well-informed stakeholders have the potential to boost the efficiency of wildlife agencies. In Florida, researchers followed relocated bears and found that the bears either continued their nuisance behavior or died as a result of human contact. This study concluded that public education about ways to coexist with bears would be more cost-effective than spending money on translocation (Anderson 2007). In New Hampshire, a "Learn to Live with Bears" communications campaign includes a team of biologists and public relations specialists who use communications to mitigate conflicts between people and bears (Organ and Ellingwood 2000). All wildlife managers should understand the basics of communications to increase their efficacy as professionals.

Elements of the Communication Process

Many fields such as psychology, education, and sociology contribute to communication theory. An understanding of the components of the communication system—the source, message and medium, receiver, and feedback loop—can help in the design of effective communications.

Source

The source of the message is the person or organization doing the communicating. For example, a scientist explains the release of endangered California condors (*Gymnogyps californianus*) to media representatives. For environmental issues, the credibility of the source is critical and usually involves public perceptions of the source's expertise, trustworthiness, and power. The source knows how it wants the message to be received but cannot guarantee how the message is encoded by media gatekeepers or how it will be decoded by the receiver. Gatekeepers regulate the flow of information to receivers and can introduce additional changes to the communication. For example, a newspaper editor decides whether to accept or shorten a press release submitted by a wildlife agency and that affects how the receiver decodes the article. Both encoding and decoding are important parts of the communication process for all types of media, from an outreach program to a Web-based interactive site.

Message and medium

The goals and objectives of the wildlife agency or organization will guide selection of the message and medium. The goal may be to maintain game populations, conserve land, restore a forest, or protect threatened species. Broad goals often stem from problems, such as the recovery of the endangered manatee. A goal of reducing boat collisions with manatees helps wildlife managers identify objectives and messages for specific audiences, such as boat owners and marina operators. Communication objectives may target changes in the audience's knowledge, attitudes, or behaviors. An initial message may try only to increase awareness about a wildlife issue. Further objectives may focus on shifting an attitude, increasing concern, and finally promoting action. However, increasing awareness does not guarantee conservation action.

Knowing the needs of your audience can help you develop appropriate messages to influence attitudes. All people are motivated by various needs and desires. The psychologist Abraham Maslow (1954) developed a hierarchy of needs. He suggested that people first fulfill their physiological needs for food, health, safety, and security. The needs of humans then progress to drives for a sense of belonging, self-esteem, and ultimately self-fulfillment. The value of clean air and water and nontoxic food is central to basic needs for health and safety. Nonmaterial uses of natural resources address people's needs for a sense of belonging and include the value of nature for religious beliefs, educational uses, and recreation.

Once the objectives of the communication are determined, the source's ideas are encoded and transmitted in the form of a message. Simple messages are understood most easily. "A fed bear is a dead bear" is the direct message of the New Hampshire Fish and Game Department to discourage the public from feeding bears. Messages communicating complex issues are harder to transmit to the public. The issue of prescribed burning as a management tool for maintaining wildlife habitat, for example, has been challenging to translate into a simple message. In a survey of west Florida residents, only 12 percent knew that regular fires are a natural process maintaining their native pine forests (Jacobson and Marynowski 1997). The Division of Forestry's slogan, "Rx Fire: Prescription for Forest Health," seems difficult to say, much less understand. Personal experience with fire-adapted ecosystems or coverage of wildfires in the media may stimulate public interest in prescribed burning (Jacobson, Monroe, and Marynowski 2001).

Choosing your medium is just as important as choosing the message, and different channels present different advantages. Mass media may be more effective in setting a public agenda and reinforcing opinions, while interpersonal methods or more detailed publications may be needed to change knowledge or shift opinions. Adoption of new behaviors, from hunting to taking public transit, often occurs as a result of family members or colleagues introducing people to them (McKenzie-Mohr and Smith 1999). Communications can foster this type of social diffusion of your message. The use of more than one channel increases the likelihood of reaching a greater audience and reinforces the message.

Receiver

An understanding of the audience (your receiver) is key to designing messages and selecting media to produce effective communications. It helps ensure that your message is decoded as intended. Audience research involves collecting data through public surveys, focus groups, direct observation, Internet databases, case studies, and networks with organizations that serve the audience. Wildlife managers can solicit help from researchers in human dimensions to help agencies tailor messages to audience needs, using sociodemographic data, psychological profiles, consumer behaviors, and other variables. Research also provides a benchmark to evaluate the results of your wildlife communication campaign.

Researchers segmented an audience of rural landowners to help design specific messages for extension education programming (Tuttle and Kelley 1981, cited in Decker, Brown, and Siemer 2001). A survey gathered information such as attitudes, beliefs, land uses, and education levels from landowners. The study revealed that landowners who had already adopted wildlife management techniques needed practical, detailed information through small-group activities such as field trips and demonstrations. Landowners who had not adopted management techniques but were interested would benefit from introductory information in brochures and mass media. Studies of how ideas diffuse through society show groups of early, average, and late adopters of information (Brown 1981). Knowledge of the target audience is critical to promote a dialogue or elicit the intended response from your audience.

Feedback

Feedback is essential to evaluate whether you achieved your objectives to increase knowledge, shift attitudes, or change behaviors and to identify improvements to your communication campaign. Methods to evaluate your communications range from formal before-and-after surveys of audience members to direct observations of the audience or their impacts on wildlife populations or the environment. For example, to evaluate a communication campaign to conserve a rare wildlife species, you might count new members joining your organization, legislators' votes to pass protective measures, increases in public awareness after the campaign, and the status of the wildlife population after a time period. Continual monitoring allows you to modify activities based on feedback. Evaluation helps avoid common problems such as targeting the wrong audience or using an irrelevant message.

Impacts of Communications as a Management Strategy

The goal of many communication programs in wildlife management is to affect behavior, a challenging task. People often choose actions that are not sustainable, despite their own knowledge of the environmentally correct thing to do. Educators believe that environmental behavior depends on cognitive factors, such as an individual's knowledge of environmental issues and action strategies. Other factors such as the perception of an ability to affect change and commitment toward the environment also influence behavior (Hines, Hungerford, and Tomera 1986/87).

Social psychologists examine the social influences or norms influencing the new behavior, such as trusted friends or family members who may or may not promote the environmentally friendly behavior (Fishbein and Ajzen 1975). Communication programs must address knowledge about the environment but also attitudes and social norms regarding the behavior in order to influence environmentally responsible actions. Researchers from the field of social marketing believe that people choose environmentally sustainable behaviors if the benefits outweigh the costs, and barriers to choosing conservation actions are removed (Smith 1995).

Research shows that effective communications can enhance public support, knowledge, and behavior toward wildlife; improve compliance; and influence policy and decisions in wildlife management. In the Rocky Mountain National Park, Fazio (1974) conducted some of the first research that tested the effectiveness of communication tools, such as brochures, signs, audiovisual programs, and newspaper articles, on backpackers' sensitivity to low-impact camping behaviors and compliance with park rules. Since then, communications have improved public compliance with litter reduction and off-trail behavior (Manning 1999).

A number of studies have looked at the effects of communication on attitudes and support for recreation and land management practices (Manfredo 1992; Olson, Bowman, and Roth 1984). Communication programs offer an important strategy when compliance with regulations is necessary to protect wildlife in ecotourist settings. Tourists interacting with dolphins decreased inappropriate behaviors, such as touching dolphins, after exposure to a communication program (Orams, Hill 1998). Interpretive messages about fire ecology for visitors to Yellowstone National Park influenced positive attitudes and beliefs about fire management (Bright et al. 1993).

Communications can influence decision making and management policy (Decker, Brown, and Siemer 2001). New Hampshire uses four different public input and communication techniques to develop acceptable management plans for deer, moose, and bear. These include eight public forums, a questionnaire given at three different public hearings, a statewide random phone survey, and a two-day stakeholder meeting (Organ and Ellingwood 2000). In Alaska, a communications program that heightened public awareness of bears was credited with the acceptance of a strict ordinance regulating refuse storage and collection (McCarthy and Seavoy 1994). Data collected and shared electronically by local bird-watchers through the BirdSource program (www.birdsource.org), a collaborative Web site of the National Audubon Society and the Cornell Lab of Ornithology, helped identify the Montezuma Wetlands complex in New York as an Important Bird Area. This in turn enabled conservationists to obtain $2.5 million from the federal Land and Water Conservation Fund for habitat acquisition and restoration (Fitzpatrick and Gill 2002).

Communicating in a Diverse World

Many resources exist with strategies for developing communication messages and planning communications for media such as fact sheets, brochures, signage, presentations, meetings, and guided walks (e.g.,

Ham 1992; Knudson, Cable, and Beck 1995; Fazio and Gilbert 2000; Jacobson 1999; Jacobson, McDuff, and Monroe 2006). This section addresses some little-discussed issues in the wildlife management literature that center on communications in our diverse world, from using technology to planning communications for multicultural audiences.

E-outreach for Wildlife Management

The field of wildlife management has been effective at using technology to advance its goals, from radio telemetry to track carnivores to GIS to understand landscape data. To succeed in a Web-based world, we need the same skill set to communicate with our publics. Both youth and adults who influence the use of public and private lands communicate on Web-based forums such as YouTube, MySpace, and Facebook. To reach the "thumb generation," we must invest resources in staff that can help wildlife managers get their messages online in creative ways to keep communications relevant, accessible, and timely. E-outreach is a new term that includes communications using Web-based outlets. Virtual outreach has the potential to reach large numbers of people and enhance stakeholder involvement in management decisions.

The grassroots organization MoveOn.org has been a leader in e-outreach for battling climate change, a key issue for wildlife management in this century. MoveOn has 3.2 million members and hosted a virtual town hall meeting on climate change with the U.S. presidential Democratic candidates. The candidates responded online to questions from MoveOn members about how they would handle the climate crisis. As one e-mail noted, "Think about it for a second: two years ago, [climate change] wasn't even on the map for most people. But today, literally billions of people know about it, and all the presidential candidates have a plan to do something about it" (Hogue 2007). The success of MoveOn has prompted the growth of similar grassroots movements that operate through e-outreach with skeletal staff but powerful grassroots communication. In North Carolina, a grassroots conservation organization called PARC used the Internet to garner supporters who defeated a major hotel's plan to develop downtown open space that was habitat for urban wildlife.

Another important use of Web-based communications is for data collection for citizen science projects. An application of the BirdSource Web site mentioned previously had over sixty-seven thousand submissions to its Great Backyard Bird Count program conducted each

February to collect and share data about the distribution of bird populations in the perilous winter season (Fitzpatrick and Gill 2002). The citizen science project Road Watch in the Pass uses a Web-based GIS system that gives citizens an easy and accessible method to report observations of wildlife along a forty-four-kilometer stretch of highway in Alberta, Canada (Lee, Quinn, and Duke 2006). The increase in stakeholder involvement has prompted new Web-based models for citizen participation, including tools for accessing environmental information, creating customized maps, and modeling potential impacts of land use changes (Lucero and Watermelon 2006).

Communications through New Partnerships

Today's diverse world demands creative partnerships for communications as we compete for the attention of our publics. In this age when even Wal-Mart reports to be going green, we can look to corporate partnerships to expand the scope of our communications. Consumers who scanned the glossy pages of a recent Patagonia clothing catalog saw a full-page essay by Alice Waters, proprietor of Chez Panisse Restaurant in California and pioneer of the local, seasonal foods movement (Waters 2007). Her essay, "The Last Wild Food," highlights the importance of eating local, sustainably harvested fish. She promotes the guidelines to buying sustainable seafood advanced by the Monterey Bay Aquarium's Seafood Watch (www.mbayag.org). Waters is a national spokesperson for a campaign to promote habitat protection for wild Pacific salmon, spearheaded by Earthjustice, Trout Unlimited, and Save Our Wild Salmon. The creative placement of this essay reflects a partnership between wildlife conservation organizations and the outdoor company Patagonia.

Another creative partnership for communications is between wildlife managers and artists. The visual arts, from painting to photography, can stir emotions to inspire environmental conservation, leverage political will, enhance traditional instruction, and aid in fund-raising (Jacobson, McDuff, and Monroe 2007). At Oregon State University, the Forestry Extension faculty used an art show as a way to communicate with new urban audiences about forest management and wildlife resources. They developed a traveling art exhibit and selected ten issues, including wildlife habitat and forest health, to highlight through the fifty-three art pieces and accompanying text panels. More than sixty-five thousand people viewed "Seeing the Forest" in six Oregon communities. Feedback from attendees was collected on posted comment cards and a written survey, revealing that 77 percent agreed the show had increased their understanding of the complexity of forest issues (Withrow-Robinson et al. 2002).

Communications with Diverse Publics

The U.S. population is growing more ethnically and racially diverse, and nearly a quarter of the citizens identify themselves as Black, Hispanic, Asian and Pacific Islander, or American Indian (U.S. Bureau of the Census 2000). By 2050 ethnic minority groups are expected to make up almost half the population (Murdock 1995). Yet minorities are underrepresented in visitor populations at national parks or many other wildlife venues (Floyd 1999). Research indicates cultural differences in outdoor use, such as Hispanic Americans visiting parks in larger groups with extended families and an emphasis on the social benefits of outdoor recreation (Floyd 1999). Communicators can use human dimensions data to target the needs and desires of potential visitors.

Across the globe, communicating with stakeholders about wildlife management involves multiple languages and cultures. The current priority for the Florida Sea Grant program is providing bilingual educational materials for Spanish-speaking anglers, as well as hiring a bilingual fisheries communicator. The mandate for stakeholder involvement in wildlife management translates into a need for capacity building in language interpretation. Few wildlife management agencies receive training in setting up a public meeting so people of all languages have an equal voice. Interpretation is not just about language but also about honoring all cultures present and ensuring that one language does not dominate a space or meeting (Johnson and Parra-Lesso 2002).

The organization Clean Water for North Carolina saw the need for interpretation equipment at city council meetings in Asheville, North Carolina. The city council was meeting to consider a bid by a superstore to buy land in a mobile home community occupied by many Latino residents. Clean Water for North Carolina was concerned about the large-scale development on this land but also about the fate of the Spanish-speaking residents who would be displaced. Conservation staff organized the Spanish-English interpreters and interpretation equipment, including headphones for simultaneous translations, at the city council meeting. Using the equipment, the Latino residents got to voice their concerns and became allies with the conservation professionals, who were successful in defeating the superstore development.

Conclusion

The fate of wildlands and wildlife resources depends on our ability to communicate with a diverse array of stakeholders in a wide variety of places, from Webcasts to art exhibits. This chapter described the communications framework that includes identifying goals and objectives, analyzing audiences, selecting media and message strategies, and evaluating the activities to ensure communication success. In this diverse world, planning communications involves factors such as technology, creative partnerships for communications, and multicultural audiences. While our world is complex, the time is ripe to reach more people and connect wildlife to their quality of life through systematic planning for communications.

Literature Cited

Anderson, M. 2007. Relocating "nuisance bears" may not work. *Explore: Research at the University of Florida* 12(2):4–5.

Bright, A. D., M. Fishbein, M. J. Manfredo, and A. Bath. 1993. Application of the theory of reasoned action in the national park service's controlled burn policy. *Journal of Leisure Research* 25(3):263–80.

Brown, L. A. 1981. *Innovation diffusion: A new perspective.* New York: Methuen Publishers.

Case, D. J. 1989. Are we barking up the wrong trees? Illusions, delusions, and realities of communications in the natural resource management mix. *Transactions of the North American Wildlife and Natural Resource Conference* 54:630–39.

Coyle, K. 2005. *Environmental literacy in America.* Washington, DC: National Environmental Education and Training Foundation. Cited in Corbett, J. B. 2006.*Communicating nature: How we create and understand environmental messages.* Washington, DC: Island Press.

Decker, D. J., T. L. Brown, and W. F. Siemer. 2001. *Human dimensions of wildlife management in North America.* Bethesda, MD: Wildlife Society.

Fazio, J. R. 1974. A mandatory permit system and interpretation for backcountry user control in Rocky Mountain National Park: An evaluation study, PhD diss., Colorado State University, Fort Collins. Cited in Roggenbuck, J. W. 1992. Use of persuasion to reduce resource impacts and visitor conflicts. In *Influencing human behavior: Theories and applications in recreation, tourism, and natural resource management*, ed. M. J. Manfedo, 148–208. Champaign, IL: Sagamore Publishing.

Fazio, J. R., and D. L. Gilbert. 2000. *Public relations and communications for natural resource managers.* Dubuque, IA: Kendall/Hunt Publishing.

Fishbein, M., and I. Ajzen. 1975. *Belief, attitude, intention, and behavior: An introduction to theory and research.* Reading, MA: Addison-Wesley Publishing.

Fitzpatrick, J. W., and G. B. Gill. 2002. *BirdSource: Using birds, citizen science, and the Internet as tools for global monitoring.* In *Conservation in the Internet age: Threats and opportunities*, ed. J. N. Levitt. Washington, DC: Island Press.

Floyd, M. 1999. Race, ethnicity and use of the National Park Service. *Social Science Research Review* 1(2):1–24.

Ham, S. H. 1992. *Environmental interpretation: A practical guide for people with big ideas and small budgets.* Golden, CO: North American Press.

Hines, J. M., H. R. Hungerford, and A. N. Tomera. 1986/87. Analysis and synthesis of research on responsible environmental behavior: A meta-analysis. *Journal of Environmental Education* 18(2):1–8.

Hogue, I. 2007. E-mail communications to MoveOn.org members, July 8.

Jacobson, S. 1999. *Communication skills for conservation professionals.* Washington, DC: Island Press.

Jacobson, S. K., and S. B. Marynowski. 1997. Public attitudes and knowledge about ecosystem management on Department of Defense Lands in Florida. *Conservation Biology* 11(3):770–81.

Jacobson, S. K., M. McDuff, and M. Monroe. 2006. *Conservation education and outreach techniques.* Oxford: Oxford University Press.

———. 2007. Promoting conservation through the arts: Outreach for hearts and minds. *Conservation Biology* 21:7–10.

Jacobson, S. K., M. C. Monroe, and S. Marynowski. 2001. Fire at the wildlife interface: The influence of experience and mass media on public knowledge, attitudes, and behavioral intentions. *Wildlife Society Bulletin* 29: 929–37.

Johnson, A., and R. Parra-Lesso. 2002. Language power tools. *Grassroots leadership: Voices from the field.* Report by the Mary Reynolds Babcock Foundation. www.mrbf.org/resources/serve_resource.aspx?id=24&num=1 (accessed July 9, 2007).

Knudson, D. M., T. T. Cable, and L. Beck. 1995. *Interpretation of cultural and natural resources.* State College, PA: Venture Publishing, Inc.

Lee, T., M. S. Quinn, and D. Duke. 2006. Citizen science, highways, and wildlife: Using a Web-based GIS to engage citizens in collecting wildlife information. *Ecology and Society* 11(1):11. www.ecologyandsociety.org/vol11/iss1/art11/.

Louv, R. 2005. *Last child in the woods.* Chapel Hill, NC: Algonquin Press.

Lucero, D., and D. Watermelon. 2006. Internet tools to help citizens find environmental information, make maps, and predict impacts. Paper presented at the U.S. EPA Community Involvement Training Conference, June 29, 2006. www.epa.gov/superfund/action/community/ciconference/previous/2006/mainsessions.htm (accessed July 7, 2007).

Manfredo, M. 1992. *Influencing human behavior: Theory and applications in recreation, tourism, and natural resource management.* Champaign, IL: Sagamore Publishing.

Manning, R. E. 1999. *Studies in outdoor recreation: Search and research for satisfaction*, 2nd ed. Corvallis: Oregon State University Press.

Maslow, A. H. 1954. *Motivation and personality.* New York: Harper and Row.

McCarthy, M. T., and R. J. Seavoy. 1994. Reducing nonsport losses attributable to food conditioning: Human and bear behavior modification in an urban environment. *Ninth International Conference on Bear Research and Management* 9:75–84.

McKenzie-Mohr, D., and W. Smith. 1999. *Fostering sustainable behavior: An introduction to community-based social marketing.* Gabriola Island, BC: New Society Publishers.

Morris, J. K., S. K. Jacobson, and R. O. Flamm. 2007. Lessons from an evaluation of a boater outreach program for manatee protection. *Environmental Management* 40:596–602.

Murdock, S. H. 1995. *An America challenged: Population change and the future of the United States.* Boulder, CO: Westview Press.

National Survey of Fishing, Hunting and Wildlife-Associated Recreation. 2006. www.fws.gov. (accessed September 1, 2007).

Olson, E. C., M. L. Bowman, and R. E. Roth. 1984. Interpretation and nonformal education in natural resources management. *Journal of Environmental Education* 15:6–10.

Orams, M. B., and G. J. E. Hill. 1998. Controlling the ecotourist in a wild dolphin feeding program. *Journal of Environmental Education* 29(3):33–39.

Organ, J. F., and M. R. Ellingwood. 2000. Wildlife stakeholder acceptance capacity for black bears, beavers, and other beasts in the east. *Human Dimensions of Wildlife* 5:63–75.

Page, S. 2007. Many in global poll see pollution as biggest threat. *USA Today.* (June 28):10A.

Smith, W. A. 1995. Behavior, social marketing, and the environment. In *Planning education to care for the earth*, ed. J. Palmer, W. Goldstein, and A. Curnow, 9–20. Gland, Switzerland: International Union for the Conservation of Nature and Natural Resources.

Tuttle, A. J., and J. W. Kelley. 1981. Marketing analysis for wildlife extension programs. In *Wildlife management on private lands: Symposium proceedings from 3–6 May 1981*, ed. R. T. Dumke, G. V. Burger, and J. R. March, 307–13. Lacrosse, WI: La Crosse Printing. Cited in Decker, D., et al., 2001. *Human dimensions of wildlife management in North America.* Bethesda, MD: Wildlife Society.

U.S. Bureau of the Census. 2000. *Statistical abstract of the United States: 2000* Washington, DC: U.S. Government Printing Office.

Waters, A. 2007. The last wild food. *Patagonia catalog* (Late Summer).

Withrow-Robinson, B., S. Broussard, V. Simon-Brown, M. Engle, and A. Reed. 2002. Seeing the forest: Art about forests and forestry. *Journal of Forestry* (December):8–14.

CHAPTER 23

Conclusion: What Is Wildlife Management?

Daniel J. Decker, William F. Siemer, Kirsten M. Leong, Shawn J. Riley, Brent A. Rudolph, and Len H. Carpenter

Wildlife management is a special case of general management, which remains one of the least understood professions of our time (Margretta 2002). The difficulty of understanding "wildlife" management in particular is exacerbated because the label is misleading. Wildlife management systems consist of inputs, processes, outputs, and outcomes that encompass much more than just wildlife. The focus on the "wildlife" component belies the fundamentally human purposes and human-benefits orientation of the unique, complex enterprise of wildlife management (Organ et al. 2006). The science and practice of wildlife management will benefit from an overarching framework reflecting a robust and durable concept that can hold together the many essential pieces of an expanding professional enterprise for years to come.

A functional approach to wildlife management for the twenty-first century will focus on human-wildlife interactions and the effects and impacts arising from such interactions. Riley and colleagues (2002, 586) recently defined wildlife management from an impacts perspective:

> Wildlife management is the guidance of decision-making processes and implementation of practices to purposefully influence interactions among and between people, wildlife and habitats to achieve impacts valued by stakeholders.

As with more general definitions of management (i.e., regardless of purpose of management activity), the focus of this one is on production of value, defined not by what an organization does but by the stakeholders who experience and evaluate the result. The purpose of management is to turn complexity and specialization into value-producing performance (Margretta 2002). For wildlife management, this means increased value from human-wildlife interactions. These interactions can be recognized as causing effects. Effects that are considered important for management attention are impacts (Riley et al. 2002). An impacts approach attempts to increase wildlife value by integrating consideration of nature ecology and human ecology (Riley et al. 2003a). Understanding both aspects of human-wildlife interactions is required to identify adequately the myriad effects of interactions and to identify impacts warranting management attention. Insights from wildlife ecology and human dimensions inquiry are needed to understand factors that yield human-wildlife interactions and the positive and negative impacts experienced by stakeholders. From this perspective, wildlife management is fundamentally a process for providing optimum net positive impacts of human-wildlife interactions (Enck et al. 2006). This is applicable to a broad range of situations and capable of encompassing the full range of socially desirable benefits from management of direct and indirect human-wildlife interactions. Such a robust and positive framing of wildlife management will enable human-wildlife coexistence on a sustainable basis.

Human Dimensions in the Wildlife Management System

A simple yet comprehensive depiction of the wildlife management system contains the key elements: humans, wildlife, habitats, and their interactions (Giles 1978). To identify and understand the effects and impacts produced by the system, one has to comprehend both human and nonhuman components of the management system. This comprehensive perspective has not been characteristic of wildlife management, even though Aldo Leopold, perhaps best known as proponent of the biological science basis for modern wildlife management, pointed out the unrealized potential of integrating biological and human dimensions for a truly "ecological" approach to wildlife management when he wrote:

> One of the anomalies of modern ecology is the creation of two groups, each of which seems barely aware of the existence of the other. The one studies the human community, almost as if it were a separate entity, and calls its findings sociology, economics and history. The other studies the plant and animal community and comfortably relegates the

> hodge-podge of politics to the liberal arts. The inevitable fusion of these two lines of thought will, perhaps, constitute the outstanding advance of this century. (Meine 1988, 359)

The "fusion" or integration Leopold noted is occurring but needs acceleration to keep pace with growing demand for greater public input and participation in democratic deliberations about public wildlife management.

Wildlife management in the twenty-first century needs to place greater emphasis on more effective engagement of stakeholders in wildlife decision making if it is to maintain relevance to society (Decker and Chase 1997; Chase, Schusler and Decker 2000). Many scientists, managers, and policy makers in wildlife conservation and management recognize this need; stakeholder engagement has or is becoming viewed as essential for attaining socially acceptable, politically durable, and economically sustainable decisions. Perceptions of fairness in decision making (Blader and Tyler 2003), gained through participatory processes, may have greater influence on compliance with regulations and support for agencies than fear of consequences if caught violating, or whether decision outcomes are perceived as favorable (Winter and May 2001; Tyler 2003). Meeting stakeholder expectations for a fair process can increase satisfaction with management as well as enable sustained coexistence between humans and wildlife (Lauber and Knuth 1997).

Articulating management systems from the manager's perspective, following some of the tenets of soft systems methodology developed by Checkland (Checkland 1981; Checkland and Scholes 1999), illuminates the complex interdependency of the biological and human dimensions of wildlife management. Management systems models developed by practitioners (i.e., manager's concept maps of the systems in which they work [e.g., Decker et al. 2006]) help identify factors affecting management and the desired outcomes of management interventions. Such models typically articulate objectives of management in terms of impacts desired by humans, generally some combination of (a) relief from negative outcomes of living with wildlife and (b) benefits from human-wildlife interactions. The need to balance positive and negative impacts of wildlife is supported by numerous studies in which stakeholders report mixed reactions to the presence of wildlife (e.g., Chase, Siemer, and Decker 1999; Decker and Gavin 1987; Decker, Jacobson, and Brown 2006; Riley and Decker 2000). For example, Lischka and colleagues (2008) defined the influence of impacts on acceptance capacity of deer in southern Michigan, where rural stakeholders are torn between deriving benefits from viewing and hunting deer (stated reasons for living in a rural environment) and concern about risks of deer-vehicle collisions (nearly one in three people reported being involved in a recent deer-vehicle collision). Such insight about stakeholders is essential to successful, benefits-producing wildlife management.

Diversity and complexity of stakeholder perspectives points to another realm of human dimensions critical to success of wildlife management in the future—cooperation, collaboration, and coalition building to overcome jurisdictional impediments and bridge values chasms (Beierle and Cayford 2002; Wondelleck and Yaffee 2000; Yankelovich 1991a, 1991b). Coalitions and collaborative ventures are challenging from a human dimensions standpoint. Knowledge of the values and motivations of collaborators, cooperators, and partners may be a key to navigating a route to successful working relationships (Decker et al. 2005).

Stakeholder Perspective: A Core Aspect of Wildlife Management

A *stakeholder* is any person who is affected by or affects wildlife or wildlife management decisions or actions (Decker et al. 1996). These are people with various kinds of interests or stakes in wildlife, human-wildlife interactions, *and* management interventions. Sometimes stakeholders themselves may not even recognize their stakes, especially if they arise from proposed but not previously experienced management actions. Stakeholders may be well organized into formal interest groups, ad hoc situation-specific grassroots groups, or simply a set of individuals who are entirely unaffiliated yet have a similar stake in a management issue. Stakes typically take the form of recreational, cultural, social, economic, or health and safety impacts. Any particular wildlife issue may involve a range of stakeholder concerns and interests, and a variety of factors influence stakeholder expectations of management. Regardless of the extent and nature of stakeholder organization around wildlife issues, management of wildlife typically occurs because stakeholders have expressed a need or concurred with an agency's desire for intervention with respect to influencing impacts associated with wildlife. Typical impacts include recreational benefits, economic costs and benefits, or a species' contribution to biological diversity. In many cases, the situation can be expressed relative to the acceptance capacity of stakeholders (Decker and Purdy 1988; Carpenter, Decker, and Lipscomb 2000) for the effects resulting from human-wildlife interactions. Regardless of the species of interest (e.g., white-tailed deer [Lischka, Riley, and Rudolph 2008], black bear [Siemer and Decker 2006] cougar [Riley and Decker 2000]), stakeholders qualitatively weigh the trade-offs of positive and negative effects of human-wildlife interactions, and an acceptance capacity for wildlife results. Understanding the trade-offs of living with wildlife is aided by economics but grounded in human values and perceptions of risks versus benefits in the cumulative interactions experienced or anticipated (Carpenter, Decker, and Lipscomb 2000).

Fundamental and Enabling Objectives: Prerequisites to Action

Wildlife managers and stakeholders should avoid adopting a favored, "tried-and-true," or conventional action without adequately considering fundamental objectives in terms of impacts (i.e., desired conditions) and enabling objectives (i.e., management objectives that contribute to achievement of fundamental objectives) (Riley et al. 2002, 2003a). A representative scenario might involve a manager believing that stakeholders desire a reduction in deer-vehicle collisions, diagnosing the cause as an overabundance of deer, and identifying the solution as issuing more hunting permits to achieve an increase in harvest and decrease in abundance of deer. The wildlife manager may have made several poor assumptions and in this scenario. First, the pervasiveness of a concern may have been extrapolated too broadly based on incidental reports. Second, an implied and potentially false assumption is that a linear relationship exists between deer abundance and frequency of deer-vehicle collisions (Sudharsan et al. 2005). Third, the solution may fall short due to the full scale of the issue being outside the jurisdiction of wildlife managers. Other professionals, such as transportation planners or local government officials, may need to be involved. Fourth, unrealistic expectations may be held regarding hunter participation, willingness to harvest deer, and actual harvest success (Riley et al. 2003b). Finally, this approach also fails to consider alternative enabling objectives. For instance, education and information at key times of year, coupled with strategic placement of roadside fencing and signage, may do more to reduce deer-vehicle collisions than population manipulation (Sudharsan, Riley, and Winterstein 2006).

Clear articulation of fundamental objectives for wildlife management, including the human condition as well as the wildlife and habitat conditions, creates a backdrop against which all other considerations in the management process can be compared. Comparing what is known about actual condition (derived in part from thorough analysis of the concerns raised by stakeholders) with the fundamental objective to determine management need (i.e., disparity between actual and desired conditions) aids evaluation of whether further effort on an issue is warranted. If the analysis indicates need for management intervention, which may include or even be solely a communication effort, then enabling objectives can be developed, followed by identification, evaluation, and selection of actual management actions. More than one objective may be established and a suite of actions may be chosen to address various aspects of the current condition needing change. This process also may indicate that the enabling objectives are out of reach, because of scale or the limits and capacities of the management agency and its collaborators. Disappointing as this prospect may be, it is better to make this determination prior to investing time, effort, and money into a management intervention that had little to no potential for desired effect.

The Relationship between Interventions, Effects, and Stakeholders

Assuming a socially acceptable and otherwise viable intervention (i.e., a suite of actions aimed at a set of complementary enabling objectives) is identified, collateral and subsequent effects of management (referred to in Decker, Jacobson, and Brown [2006] collectively as collateral effects) should be assessed. Wildlife management approached comprehensively includes mitigation of these two types of effects, yet in practice they are seldom fully revealed or adequately addressed in management planning. The principally iterative approach typically taken in management considers these effects when they arise rather than proactively anticipating them and calculating their cost beforehand (in terms of impacts on stakeholders and cost to mitigate). *Collateral effects* are those that occur during implementation of management actions. *Subsequent effects* occur as a consequence of achieving management objectives. Particularly difficult management issues arise when collateral or subsequent effects have the potential to largely counteract efforts to achieve fundamental or enabling objectives. For example, a collateral effect of a ban on the use of bait by deer hunters could be reduced hunter participation owing to dissatisfaction with prohibition of this widely practiced technique. However, a subsequent effect of lower deer populations following establishment of liberalized hunting regulations could be poor compliance with a baiting ban, as hunters attempt to offset decreased encounter rates as deer densities decline. The Michigan Department of Natural Resources established both of these management interventions in an effort to eradicate an infection of bovine tuberculosis from white-tailed deer (O'Brien et al. 2006). Evaluating the potential of such offsetting outcomes complicated an already contentious series of management decisions (Rudolph et al. 2006) and continues to be a priority for future research and management consideration.

Implicit in the identification of collateral and subsequent effects is the creation of additional stakeholders for management. That is, people not necessarily affected by, experiencing problems with, or deriving benefits from wildlife. Instead, these "new" stakeholders are affected by management actions as they are implemented or by cascading effects from management meeting its enabling objectives. Thus, these stakeholders are *created by* management interventions, not the *original focus for* management interventions.

Impact Management

Wildlife impact management stresses decision making and actions that focus on trade-offs between positive and negative effects of interactions with wildlife (Riley et al. 2002). This approach enhances traditional management that focuses only on affecting wildlife populations and habitats. Because they are grounded in social values, many issues in wildlife management become contentious "wicked problems" (Rittel and Webber 1973); that is, value-laden problems for which there are no definitive and objective "right" answers. Continual learning is a key to working through wicked problems in complex management systems (Leong et al., 2007). Such learning supports informed adaptation of enabling objectives and management actions. This implies adaptive management in some form.

The extent to which management follows an intensive adaptive management approach (Lancia et al. 1996), with quantitative hypothesis testing using management action as the experimental treatment, followed by assessment of effects and adaptation of approach based on what is learned in the experiment, will be a matter of increasing interest and require considerable resources. Such an approach is considered active adaptive management (Meffe et al. 2002). This level of wildlife management sophistication is something of an ideal, yet warranted and possible under some circumstances.

Alternatively, a more attainable approach is passive adaptive management (Meffe et al. 2002), in which management interventions (which may involve multiple actions) are undertaken to achieve articulated enabling objectives and progress toward meeting those objectives is evaluated. The difference between active and passive adaptive management is that the former is keen to understand the *how* and *why* of action effectiveness, with precision in refining functions hypothesized as operating on the management system, whereas the latter is interested in *whether* and *to what extent* objectives are being met. Passive adaptive management is at minimum the use of analyzed experience (evaluation) to inform decisions about maintaining a course of action, modifying it, or stopping it altogether and replacing it with a better alternative. Integration of adaptive resource management and adaptive impact management (Enck et al. 2006), in which objective functions are expressed in terms of impacts instead of the condition of a stock or habitat, may move the profession a step closer to realizing Leopold's vision of wildlife management making an "outstanding advance" (Meine 1988, 359).

Issues for the Future

The transition of wildlife management from focusing on wildlife abundance and habitat area or quality to focusing on achieving positive impacts will not occur easily and is unlikely without integration of human and biological dimensions of management in a comprehensive philosophy and approach. A focus on impacts of human-wildlife interactions and creative ways to manage impacts will be the key to successful wildlife management going forward. This is a deceptively simple proposition, because major hurdles exist to widespread adoption and application of such a philosophy and approach. Among the tenacious issues that will affect the future shape of wildlife management are:

- culture of state wildlife management institutions, which dominate public wildlife management in the United States, that emphasizes population management and is resistant to change (Jacobson and Decker 2006, 2008)

- professional and stakeholder culture that uncritically assumes wildlife issues are fundamentally biological or ecological issues, ignoring in reality that public wildlife decision making and management are at best informed by science
- governance of wildlife management that resists informed participation of stakeholders and does not adopt a broad civic perspective on impact management (Jacobson and Decker 2008)
- securing alternate funding sources for the state wildlife management institution (Hamilton 1992; Jacobson, Decker, and Carpenter 2007) that represent a broad base of stakeholders

Research, Policy, and Practice Conventions Needed

Shifting to the vision of wildlife management presented in this chapter will require adoption of several research, policy, and practice conventions. Some of these have already been adopted.

Research

- research that integrates biological, ecological, and human dimensions inquiry to provide more comprehensive insights about management issues
- research that improves understanding about the root biological, ecological, psychological, and sociological causes of impacts arising from human-wildlife interactions
- research to better understand the relationship among wildlife abundance, the frequency and quality of interactions between wildlife and humans, and the influence of such interactions on perception of impacts
- research that tests managers' assumptions about the human dimensions of wildlife management
- research that builds theory that has foundations in basic social science yet offers bridging concepts that address applied needs of wildlife management
- research that addresses needs of active and passive adaptive management expectations of the wildlife management community

Policy

- policies that require (a) scientifically derived insights about stakeholders and (b) proactive stakeholder engagement in wildlife management decisions

- policies that promote sustainability of human-wildlife coexistence and avoid overemphasizing negative aspects of human-wildlife interactions (i.e., human-wildlife conflict management)

Practice conventions

- Assertions made by managers and others regarding stakeholder beliefs, attitudes, norms, and behaviors should be supported by human dimensions inquiry.
- Anecdotes and broad generalizations should be viewed as inadequate input for management decision making.
- Development of manager's models depicting how wildlife management programs operate should become standard procedure to ensure rigor and discipline in thinking and to enhance clarity of internal and external communication about a management situation and agency response to it.

Conclusion

So, what *is* wildlife management? In our view, wildlife management is the set of processes and actions necessary to enable coexistence of humans and wildlife on a sustainable basis. Wildlife management is more than conflict resolution, renewable harvest of wildlife, and preservation or restoration of wildlife. Wildlife management is about understanding and managing the impacts of direct and indirect human-wildlife interactions, some tangible and some intangible (i.e., wildlife have values other than instrumental). It is not a value-free technical process dictated by biological or social science. To a large extent, it is not exclusively about wildlife at all. The process of wildlife management is the guidance of decision making and implementation of practices to purposefully influence interactions among and between people, wildlife, and habitats to achieve impacts valued by stakeholders (Riley et al. 2002). Human dimensions insight rising from theory, empirical research, and analyzed experience is a necessary ingredient for wildlife management. Ensuring such insight is integrated seamlessly with other kinds of insight generated from biological and ecological spheres will be critical to the success of wildlife management in enabling human-wildlife coexistence in coming decades.

Literature Cited

Beierle, T. C., and J. Cayford. 2002. *Democracy in practice: Public participation in environmental decisions.* Washington, DC: Resources for the Future.

Blader, S. L., and T. R. Tyler. 2003. A four-component model of procedural justice: Defining the meaning of a "fair" process. *Personality and Social Psychology Bulletin* 29:747–58.

Carpenter, L. H., D. J. Decker, and J. F. Lipscomb. 2000. Stakeholder acceptance capacity in wildlife management. *Human Dimensions of Wildlife* 5:5–19.

Chase, L. C., T. M. Schusler, and D. J. Decker. 2000. Innovations in stakeholder involvement: What's the next step? *Wildlife Society Bulletin* 28:208–17.

Chase, L. C., W. F. Siemer, and D. J. Decker. 1999. Suburban deer management: A case study in the Village of Cayuga Heights, New York. *Human Dimensions of Wildlife* 4:59–60.

Checkland, P. B. 1981. *Systems thinking, systems practice.* New York: John Wiley and Sons.

Checkland, P. B., and J. Scholes. 1999. *Soft systems methodology in action.* New York: John Wiley and Sons.

Decker, D. J., and L. C. Chase. 1997. Human dimensions of living with wildlife—A management challenge for the 21st century. *Wildlife Society Bulletin* 25:788–95.

Decker, D. J., and T. A. Gavin. 1987. Public attitudes toward a suburban deer herd. *Wildlife Society Bulletin* 15:173–80.

Decker, D. J., C. A. Jacobson, and T. L. Brown. 2006. Situation-specific "impact dependency" as a determinant of management acceptability: Insights from wolf and grizzly bear management in Alaska. *Wildlife Society Bulletin* 34:426–32.

Decker, D. J., C. C. Krueger, R. A. Baer, Jr., B. A. Knuth, and M. E. Richmond. 1996. From clients to stakeholders: A philosophical shift for fish and wildlife management. *Human Dimensions of Wildlife* 1(1):70–82.

Decker, D. J., and K. G. Purdy. 1988. Toward a concept of wildlife acceptance capacity in wildlife management. *Wildlife Society Bulletin* 16:53–57.

Decker, D. J., D. B. Raik, L. H. Carpenter, J. F. Organ, and T. M. Schusler. 2005. Collaborations for community-based wildlife management. *Urban Ecosystems* 8:227–36.

Decker, D. J., M. A. Wild, S. J. Riley, W. F. Siemer, M. M. Miller, K. M. Leong, J. G. Powers, and J. C. Rhyan. 2006. Wildlife disease management: A manager's model. *Human Dimensions of Wildlife* 11(3):151–58.

Enck, J. W., D. J. Decker, S. J. Riley, J. F. Organ, L. H. Carpenter, and W. F.

Siemer. 2006. Integrating ecological and human dimensions in adaptive management of wildlife-related impacts. *Wildlife Society Bulletin* 34:698–705.

Giles, R. H. 1978. *Wildlife management*. San Francisco: W. H. Freeman.

Hamilton, C. 1992. Pursuing a new paradigm in funding state fish and wildlife programs. In *American fish and wildlife policy: The human dimension*, ed. W. Mangun, 119–35. Carbondale: Southern Illinois University Press.

Jacobson, C. A., and D. J. Decker. 2006. Ensuring the future of state wildlife management: Understanding challenges for institutional change. *Wildlife Society Bulletin* 34:531–36.

Jacobson, C. A., and D. J. Decker. 2008. Governance of state wildlife management: Reform and revive or resist and retrench? *Society and Natural Resources*. 21:441-48.

Jacobson, C. A., D. J. Decker, and L. Carpenter. 2007. Securing alternative funding for wildlife management: Insights from agency leaders. *Journal of Wildlife Management* 71:2106–13.

Lancia, R. A., C. E. Braun, M. W. Callopy, R. D. Dueser, J. G. Kie, C. J. Martinka, J. D. Nichols, T. D. Nudds, W. R. Porath, and N. G. Tilghman. 1996. ARM! For the future: Adaptive resource management in the wildlife profession. *Wildlife Society Bulletin* 24:436–42.

Lauber, T. B., and B. A. Knuth. 1997. Fairness in moose management decision-making: The citizen's perspective. *Wildlife Society Bulletin* 25:776–87.

Leong, K. M., D. J. Decker, J. F. Forester, P. D. Curtis, and M. A. Wild. 2007. Expanding problem frames to understand human-wildlife conflicts in urban-proximate parks. *Journal of Parks and Recreation Administration*. 25(4):62-78.

Lischka, S. A., S. J. Riley, and B. A. Rudolph. 2008. Effects of impact perception on acceptance capacity for white-tailed deer. *Journal of Wildlife Management*. 72(2):502-09.

Margretta, J. 2002. *What management is: How it works and why it's everyone's business*. New York: Free Press.

Meffe, G. K., L. A. Nielsen, R. L. Knight, and D. A. Schenborn. 2002. *Ecosystem management: Adaptive, community-based conservation*. Washington, DC: Island Press.

Meine, C. 1988. *Aldo Leopold: His life and work*. Madison: University of Wisconsin Press.

O'Brien, D. J., S. M. Schmitt, S. D. Fitzgerald, D. E. Berry, and G. J. Hickling. 2006. Managing the wildlife reservoir of *Mycobacterium bovis*: The Michigan, USA, experience. *Veterinary Microbiology* 112:313–23.

Organ, J. F., L. H. Carpenter, D. Decker, W. F. Siemer, and S. J. Riley. 2006.

Thinking like a manager: Reflections on wildlife management. Washington, DC: Wildlife Management Institute.

Riley, S. J., and D. J. Decker. 2000. Wildlife stakeholder acceptance capacity for cougars in Montana. *Wildlife Society Bulletin* 28:931–39.

Riley, S. J., D. J. Decker, L. H. Carpenter, J. F. Organ, W. F. Siemer, G. F. Mattfeld, and G. Parsons. 2002. The essence of wildlife management. *Wildlife Society Bulletin* 30: 585–93.

Riley, S. J., D. J. Decker, J. W. Enck, P. D. Curtis, T. B. Lauber, and T. L. Brown. 2003b. Deer populations up, hunter populations down: Implications of interdependence of deer and hunter population dynamics on management. *Ecoscience* 10:356–62.

Riley, S. J., W. F. Siemer, D. J. Decker, L. H. Carpenter, J. F. Organ, and L. T. Berchielli. 2003a. Adaptive impact management: An integrative approach to wildlife management. *Human Dimensions of Wildlife* 8:81–95.

Rittel, W. J., and M. M. Webber. 1973. Dilemmas in a general theory of planning. *Policy Sciences* 2:155–69.

Rudolph, B. A., S. J. Riley, G. H. Hickling, B. J. Frawley, M. S. Garner, and S. R. Winterstein. 2006. Regulating hunter baiting for white-tailed deer in Michigan: Biological and social considerations. *Wildlife Society Bulletin* 34:314–21.

Siemer, W. F., and D. J. Decker. 2006. *An assessment of black bear impacts in New York*. Human Dimensions Research Unit Series Publication 06-6. Ithaca, NY: Department of Natural Resources, Cornell University.

Sudharsan, K., S. J. Riley, B. A. Rudolph, and B. A Maurer. 2005. Deer-vehicle crash patterns across ecoregions in Michigan. *Wildlife Damage Conference* 11:246–325.

Sudharsan, K., S. J. Riley, and S. Winterstein. 2006. Relationship of fall hunting season to the frequency of deer-vehicle collisions in Michigan. *Journal of Wildlife Management* 70: 1161–64.

Tyler, T. R. 2003. Procedural justice, legitimacy, and the effective rule of law. *Crime and Justice* 30:283–57.

Winter, S. C., and P. J. May. 2001. Motivation for compliance with environmental regulations. *Journal of Policy Analysis and Management* 20:675–98.

Wondolleck, J. M., and S. L. Yaffee. 2000. *Making collaboration work: Lessons from innovation in natural resources management*. Washington, DC: Island Press.

Yankelovich, D. 1991a. *Coming to public judgment*. Syracuse, NY: Syracuse University Press.

Yankelovich, D. 1991b. *The magic of dialogue: Transforming conflict into cooperation*. New York: Simon and Schuster.

About the Contributors

ØYSTEIN AAS is a senior research scientist at the Norwegian Institute for Nature Research and a visiting professor in nature-based tourism at the Norwegian University of Life Sciences and in natural resources management at the University of Tromsø, Norway. He holds a doctorate in human dimensions research in recreational fisheries management and has published extensively in international scientific journals, books, and national research reports. He has served on several committees and acted as conference chair for the Fourth World Recreational Fishing Conference held in Trondheim, Norway, in 2005.

ROBERT ARLINGHAUS is a social-ecologist working at the interface of social and biological sciences in natural resource management. His main aim is to understand the dynamics of recreational fisheries and to solve pressing issues for recreational fisheries development, management, and conservation. Arlinghaus is junior professor at Humboldt-University of Berlin and group leader at the Leibniz-Institute of Freshwater Ecology and Inland Fisheries in Berlin, Germany.

GORDON R. BATCHELLER is a certified wildlife biologist with the New York State Division of Fish, Wildlife and Marine Resources in Albany, New York. He has worked as a professional wildlife biologist for twenty-six years. Gordon received a master's degree in wildlife ecology from Oklahoma State University. Gordon has been very active in multistate and international wildlife management issues under the auspices of the Association of Fish and Wildlife Agencies. He was also named a fellow to the inaugural session of the National Conservation Leadership Institute in 2006.

ELIZABETH L. BENNETT is director of the Wildlife Conservation Society Hunting and Wildlife Trade Program where she works with staff on projects addressing management of hunting and wildlife trade in twenty-seven countries. Before her current position, she worked in Malaysia for twenty-four years. She received her doctorate from the University of Cambridge. Her writing has appeared in more than ninety-five scientific and popular publications. She coedited a definitive book on hunting in tropical forests and wrote the World Bank policy paper on the same topic. Her services to conservation have been recognized by the following: Golden Ark award by Prince Bernhard of the Netherlands in 1994, the Pegawai Bintang Sarawak (PBS) by the Sarawak State Government in 2003, Member of the Most Excellent Order of the British Empire (MBE) by Queen Elizabeth II in 2005, and the Wings WorldQuest Leila Hadley Luce Award for Courage in 2006.

RICHARD BODMER is currently a reader in conservation ecology at the University of Kent. He received his doctorate from the Department of Zoology at the University of Cambridge His research interests focus on tropical wildlife ecology and conservation, emphasizing species important for rural people such as large mammals, game birds, and fish. Projects use field-based research and modeling of sustainable use.

RANDALL B. BOONE is a wildlife ecologist and modeler working with coupled natural and human systems in semiarid and arid areas globally and in Colorado. He focuses on the spatial occurrence and movements of wildlife and livestock. He is a research scientist within the Natural Resource Ecology Laboratory, Colorado State University, Fort Collins.

PERRY J. BROWN is dean and professor at the College of Forestry and Conservation and director of the Montana Forest and Conservation Experiment Station at the University of Montana-Missoula. A lifelong westerner, he has served on the faculties of Utah State University, Colorado State University, and Oregon State University in addition to his current assignment in Montana. He has published over one hundred scientific papers, books, and book chapters. He has been elected a fellow of both the Academy of Leisure Sciences and the Society of American Foresters.

TOMMY L. BROWN is senior research associate and leader of the Human Dimensions Research Unit at Cornell University and a research faculty member of the College of Agriculture and Life Sciences. He received his master's degree in natural resource-based recreation from the University of Minnesota. Tommy has also completed additional coursework in natural resource economics, statistics, and research methods at Cornell University. Tommy has over thirty-five years of experience as an outdoor recreation and human dimensions researcher. He has been principal investigator on seven studies dealing with recreation access and published in four hundred career publications.

SUSAN J. BUCK is associate professor of political science at the University of North Carolina at Greensboro. Since 1999, she has been director of the Environmental Studies Program. She has worked at the Florida pesticide research laboratory in Gainesville and as laboratory supervisor of the Wetlands Research Laboratory at the Virginia Institute of Marine Science. She is the author of numerous books and articles. In 1996, she was a Fulbright Research Scholar at the Robert Gordon University in Aberdeen, Scotland.

ISABEL BUECHSEL is actively involved in campaign design and research for wildlife conservation projects and sustainable development in Central America. She worked with the Wildlife Conservation Society's Public Research and Evaluation Program in 2007. She is candidate for a master's degree in public policy at Erfurt University's School of Public Policy in Thuringia, Germany.

SHAUNA B. BURNSILVER is a human ecologist, working currently as a research associate at the Natural Resource Ecology Laboratory and adjunct faculty in the Department of Anthropology at Colorado State University. Shauna's research interests include issues of land tenure, resource fragmentation, and socioeconomic change in East African and Asian pastoral systems.

LEN H. CARPENTER is a past president of the Wildlife Society. Len recently retired after twelve years as the southwest field representative for the Wildlife Management

Institute (WMI), he worked daily with agencies, managers, and universities, dealing with a myriad of contemporary challenges in wildlife management. He earned a doctorate in range science at Colorado State University. Before his duties at WMI, he worked for twenty-three years in research and management roles for the Colorado Division of Wildlife.

PETER COPPOLILLO is an ecologist who directs the Rungwa-Ruaha Living Landscapes Program for the Wildlife Conservation Society. He coauthored *Conservation: Linking Ecology, Economics, and Culture* (Princeton University Press, 2004) and has helped to develop protected area strategies in Bolivia, Ecuador, Argentina, Congo, the United States, and Cambodia.

DANIEL J. DECKER is a professor of human dimensions of wildlife management and co-leader of the Human Dimensions Research Unit in the Department of Natural Resources at Cornell University, where he has been a member of the staff since 1976. He has served as department extension leader, department chair, associate dean of the College of Agriculture and Life Sciences (CALS), and director of Cornell University Agricultural Experiment Station. He is currently director of the Office of Land Grant Affairs and senior advisor to the CALS dean. Dan's research interests include discovery and integration of human dimensions insights into wildlife policy, management, program planning and evaluation, and professional practice.

MARK DAMIAN DUDA is executive director of Responsive Management, a survey research firm specializing in natural resource and outdoor recreation issues. He holds a master's degree from Yale University in natural resource policy and planning and has directed more than five hundred quantitative surveys and hundreds of focus groups on natural resource and outdoor recreation issues. He is the author of three books about wildlife. His research has been featured in numerous journals, magazines, and major media, including CNN, the *New York Times*, the *Wall Street Journal*, and the front pages of both the *Washington Post* and *USA Today*.

ESTHER A. DUKE is coordinator for the Human Dimensions of Natural Resources Department at Colorado State University (CSU) where she is also pursuing her master's degree. Her professional experience includes development and community outreach for the Larimer Humane Society, contract grant writing, and program development/grant writing for Educo: Outdoor Adventure and Leadership School. She has worked and studied in both Japan and Costa Rica. At CSU Esther assists with departmental training and outreach projects. She is currently coordinating the international conference and training "Pathways to Success 2008: Integrating Human Dimensions into Fish and Wildlife Management."

HEATHER E. EVES is a wildlife biologist with a focus on socioeconomics and policy sciences related to wildlife management in Africa. She has a doctorate in Forestry and Environmental Studies from Yale University. She worked for ten years in education and conservation field research in East and Central Africa. Since 2000 she has led the Bushmeat Crisis Task Force (BCTF), a thirty-five-plus-member conservation collaborative in Washington, DC. As BCTF director she has led a professional team in building information management systems to inform policy, encourage funding, provide training and capacity building, and raise awareness about the bushmeat trade in Africa.

TULA G. FANG is interested in the conservation of wildlife, the Peruvian Amazon, and the well-being of rural people in local communities. She has a master's degree in conservation biology from the Durrell Institute of Conservation and Ecology. She is currently working in the wildlife management program of Fundamazonia.

JOHN FRASER is a conservation psychologist and architect concerned with how social group identities influence conservation behaviors and activism. He is currently Director of the Institute for Learning Innovation's New York office. He is also an adjunct professor at Hunter College of City University New York and Antioch University New England and a CERC scientist at Columbia University. He was Director of the Wildlife Conservation Society's Public Research and Evaluation program while writing for this book.

KATHLEEN A. GALVIN is professor and chair of the Department of Anthropology and senior research scientist at the Natural Resource Ecology Laboratory at Colorado State University (CSU), where she is also an advising faculty member for the Department of Sociology and the Graduate Degree Program in Ecology at CSU. She received her doctorate from State University of New York (SUNY) , Binghamton. Trained as a biological anthropologist, she has conducted interdisciplinary human ecological research in Africa for the past twenty years. Kathleen has been a member of a National Academy of Science/National Research Council (NAS/NRC) and was a panel member of the NAS/NRC Human Dimensions of Seasonal-to-Interannual Climate Variability group. She served on the National Science Foundation, Cultural Anthropology Program Panel. She was an Aldo Leopold Fellow in 2001.

LARRY M. GIGLIOTTI is planning coordinator/human dimensions specialist for the Division of Wildlife, South Dakota, Game, Fish and Parks. Larry is also an adjunct professor at South Dakota State University, Department of Wildlife and Fisheries Sciences and at Colorado University, Human Dimensions of Natural Resources. He received his graduate degrees from Michigan State University. Larry is a Certified Fisheries Scientist and a Certified Wildlife Biologist and has been a member of the Wildlife Society since 1976 and a member of the American Fisheries Society since 1987. He was a recent president (2005-06) of the Organization of Wildlife Planners and his primary research interest is human dimensions. His present projects and duties include development, coordination, and staff training for a comprehensive planning effort for the Division of Wildlife; incorporation of public involvement and human dimensions into Division of Wildlife activities; and staff training in TQM, leadership, public involvement, and human dimensions. Larry has conducted over one hundred human dimension surveys.

SCOTT GURTIN has worked in wildlife management for sixteen years, eleven of which in the Arizona Game and Fish Department. Scott has worked as a research biologist and endangered species recovery coordinator. Scott worked as a resources consultant for the department and served as the department's human dimensions specialist (2005–2006) and is now Hatchery Supervisor.

ABOUT THE CONTRIBUTORS

JOHN HADIDIAN is director of the Urban Wildlife Programs at the Humane Society of the United States (HSUS). He received his doctorate from Pennsylvania State University. John has been a member of the Harmony Institute's Community Action Board since 2001 and has served on the U.S. Department of State's Man and the Biosphere Program as a member of the Human Dominated Systems Directorate. He has also been associate editor for the journal *Urban Ecosystems*, chair of the Wildlife Society's Urban Wildlife Working Group, and member of the U.S. Department of Agriculture's National Wildlife Services Advisory Committee. He is the principal editor of the book *Wild Neighbors: The Humane Approach to Living with Wildlife.* He is currently an adjunct instructor in the Natural Resources Program at Virginia Tech's Northern Virginia campus.

CATHERINE M. HILL is reader in anthropology at Oxford Brookes University. She currently teaches courses in human ecology and human wildlife conflict issues to students in anthropology and primate conservation. Catherine's research ultimately relates to the inclusion of human stakeholder needs and perspectives within conservation policy and practice. Currently, her research team is working on different aspects of people-wildlife interactions in Africa, Indonesia, and South America, developing conflict mitigation tools and looking at how external factors such as rural economies, degree of control over and access to natural resources, and the impact of colonial conservation policies influence farmers' tolerance of and perceptions of wildlife, and their relationships with their natural world. She has also collaborated on research projects into different aspects of people-wildlife conflict in Nigeria, Japan, and Canada.

MICHAEL HUTCHINS is executive director/CEO of the Wildlife Society, an international, nonprofit scientific and educational organization serving and representing wildlife professionals in all areas of wildlife conservation and resource management. TWS's goal is to promote excellence in wildlife stewardship through science and education. Trained as a behavioral ecologist, Michael is also an adjunct associate professor in the graduate program in conservation biology and sustainable development at the University of Maryland and senior fellow at the Georgia Institute of Technology's Center for Behavior and Conservation.

DOUGLAS B. INKLEY is senior science advisor for the National Wildlife Federation (NWF). Previously director of NWF's Fish and Wildlife Resources Division in Washington, DC, Doug facilitated NWF's lobbying activities on a variety of conservation issues. Doug has testified numerous times in both House and Senate hearings, in addition to speaking throughout the country on many conservation issues. His current emphasis is on global climate change. In Washington, DC, Doug served as the chairperson of the Wetlands Working Group of the Clean Water Network. Doug was a founding member of the Steering Committee for the Teaming with Wildlife coalition, which secured new annual appropriations of more than $50 million for conservation by the state fish and wildlife agencies.

SUSAN K. JACOBSON is a professor in the Department of Wildlife Ecology and Conservation and the director of the Program for Studies in Tropical Conservation at the University of Florida. She teaches and conducts research on environmental communications and the human dimensions of wildlife conservation. She earned her doctorate in resource ecology at Duke University and has published over a hundred articles and reports dealing with environmental management education and natural resource conservation in the United States, Latin America, Africa, and Southeast Asia. She is the author/editor of several books, including *Communication Skills for Conservation Professionals* and *Conservation Education and Outreach Techniques*.

KIRSTEN M. LEONG is human dimensions program leader for the Biological Resource Management Division of the National Park Service (NPS). She received her doctorate from Cornell University. During her graduate studies she was a SCEP biologist with the NPS in Fort Collins, Colorado, and graduate research assistant on research related to human dimensions of deer issues in national parks in the northeastern United States, in collaboration with the Biological Resource Management Division of the NPS. Kirsten also was a research associate with Disney's Animal Kingdom, Lake Buena Vista, Florida, and served as a technical advisor to Parks and Wildlife Management, Isalo National Park, Madagascar, where she collaborated with Malagasy National Park Service (ANGAP) on a park management plan and flora and fauna inventories.

MICHAEL J. MANFREDO is a professor and head of the Human Dimensions of Natural Resources Department. He is founder and co-leader of the Human Dimensions in Natural Resources Unit at Colorado State University. Michael's research, teaching, and outreach activities focus on the role of social science in natural resource management. His theoretical focus is on applying attitude and value theory to natural resource issues. He has published over seventy peer-reviewed articles in a wide variety of natural resource journals and several books. Professor Manfredo has been principal investigator on over seventy-five research projects. He is the founding coeditor of the journal *Human Dimensions of Wildlife*.

STEPHEN F. McCOOL is a professor emeritus of wildland recreation management in the Department of Society and Conservation at the University of Montana. He has held special assignment positions with the USDA Forest Service Northern Region office, the Supervisor's Office of the Flathead National Forest, and the Interior Columbia Basin Ecosystem Management Project. He has authored and edited several books. In 2005, the USDA Forest Service recognized Stephen with the Excellence in Wilderness Stewardship Research award. The Wild Foundation and editors of the *International Journal of Wilderness* also recognized him in 2005 for lifetime achievements in wilderness research. The University of Idaho recognized him in 2006 with its Celebration Natural Resources award for demonstrating excellence in integrated natural resource management.

MALLORY D. McDUFF teaches environmental education and community organizing at Warren Wilson College in Asheville, North Carolina. Her research currently focuses on connecting local schools with local food and enhancing the role of faith communities in sustainability. She is the coauthor of *Conservation Education and Outreach Techniques* (Oxford University Press, 2006).

ROAN BALAS McNAB is director of the Wildlife Conservation Society's Guatemala Program where he has worked since 1996. He seeks to promote the development of synergies between community-based conservation efforts and national parks within the Maya Biosphere Reserve through programs that promote the conservation and sustainable use of resources.

TERRY A. MESSMER is Quinney Professor for Wildlife Conflict Management, Associate Director for Outreach at the Jack H. Berryman Institute, and extension wildlife specialist in the Department of Wildland Resources at Utah State University. His research, teaching, and extension/outreach programs engage stakeholders in identifying, implementing, and evaluating the effects of new conservation and management strategies and technologies on sustaining local community socio-economics and natural resources conservation.

CRISTINA GOETTSCH MITTERMEIER is a biochemical engineer specializing in fisheries and aquaculture and a photographer and writer. Cristina has coedited eight books, including a series published with Conservation International and Cemex. Cristina serves as executive director of the International League of Conservation Photographers (ILCP), a prestigious group of photographers that she founded in 2005. She is also senior director of Visual Resources at Conservation International (CI). From the popular to the scientific, her work has appeared in major magazines around the world. Cristina serves on the Advisory Board of *Nature's Best Magazine* and is a board member of the WILD Foundation. Christina was born and raised in Mexico.

RUTH S. MUSGRAVE is founder and director of the Center for Wildlife Law at the Institute of Public Law. She has authored and coauthored numerous articles and books on state and federal wildlife law. Ruth is editor of the *Wildlife Law News Quarterly* and the online "Wildlife Law News Weekly Alerts." She has been an adjunct professor and a visiting associate professor at the University of New Mexico School of Law. Ruth serves on the board of trustees of national and international wildlife nonprofit organizations. She is the trustee of the Frances V. R. Seebe Charitable Trust. She was law clerk to Chief Judge Oliver Seth of the U.S. Tenth Circuit Court of Appeals, an assistant United States attorney for the District of New Mexico, and in private practice for almost ten years before founding the Center for Wildlife Law.

MARK D. NEEDHAM is assistant professor in the Department of Forest Ecosystems and Society at Oregon State University. Mark has extensive research experience investigating human dimensions of wildlife, recreation resource management, and nature-based tourism. He also has expertise in survey methodology and quantitative analysis. He has conducted research for various federal, state, and provincial agencies, the results of which have been published in over thirty-five journal articles and conference proceedings in outlets such as *Human Dimensions of Wildlife, Wildlife Society Bulletin, Journal of Wildlife Management, Journal of Leisure Research,* and *Tourism Management*. Mark is Associate Editor of the journal *Human Dimensions of Wildlife.*

JOSEPH T. O'LEARY is dean of the Warner College of Natural Resources at Colorado State University. He was formerly professor and department head in the Department of Recreation, Park and Tourism Sciences at Texas A&M University. He is a member of the Academy of Leisure Sciences, the American Academy of Park and Recreation Administration, and the IUCN World Commission on Protected Areas (North American section) and chair of the Marco Polo Society on Tourism Statistics in the International Statistical Association. He received the prestigious Franklin D. and Theodore Roosevelt Excellence in Recreation and Park Research Award from the National Recreation and Park Association. His research has involved knowledge management and analysis of large national and international studies of travel and recreation behavior.

JOHN F. ORGAN is chief of Wildlife and Sport Fish Restoration for the Northeast Region U.S. Fish and Wildlife Service and adjunct associate professor of wildlife ecology at the University of Massachusetts, Amherst. He is past president of the Wildlife Society and a certified wildlife biologist. John's professional background has involved work in wetlands conservation, National Wildlife Refuge management, carnivore ecology, furbearer management, human dimensions of wildlife, and wildlife policy.

R. LILIAN E. PAINTER is a wildlife ecologist with a particular interest in protected areas and indigenous territorial management. Her career has focused on applied wildlife research, conservation strategic planning, and institutional strengthening through engagement with government agencies and grassroots organizations at community and supracommunal scales. She currently directs the Wildlife Conservation Society's Bolivia Program.

PABLO PUERTAS is a wildlife biologist and has worked on community-based wildlife management in northeastern Peru for more than twenty years. He is currently the Loreto program coordinator of the Wildlife Conservation Society and the president of the management committee of the Pacaya-Samiria National Reserve in northeastern Peru.

SHAWN J. RILEY is an associate professor in the Department of Fisheries and Wildlife at Michigan State University. His interests include human-wildlife interactions, systems modeling, and integration of ecological and social science in decision making. In the twelve years between his studies at Montana State University, where he received his master's degree, and Cornell University, where he received his doctorate, he was a wildlife biologist for Montana Fish, Wildlife and Parks.

IRENE RING joined the Helmholtz Centre for Environmental Research-UFZ in Leipzig, Germany, in 1992, where she contributed to the establishment of the emerging research field of ecological economics. In 2002, she became head of the newly founded Social Sciences Working Group on the Conservation of Nature and Biodiversity; in 2004, she became deputy head of the Department of Economics at UFZ. She also serves as a member on the Committee on Sciences of the German UNESCO-Commission and on the National Scientific Committee of DIVERSITAS Germany. Her current research focuses on biodiversity conflict reconciliation and on environmental policy instruments, mainly within the context of interdisciplinary and applied projects.

BRENT A. RUDOLPH coordinates the deer research program for the Michigan Department of Natural Resources (DNR) and is also a doctoral student at Michigan State University. He has previously served as a regional habitat biologist and acting species and habitat management section leader of Michigan DNR. His professional interests focus on addressing both the biological and sociological challenges to managing wildlife on increasingly human-dominated landscapes.

MICHAEL A. SCHUETT is an associate professor in the Department of Recreation, Park and Tourism Sciences and the Texas AgriLife Extension Service at Texas A&M University. He serves as Director of the Center for Socioeconomic Research and Education. His research focuses on the human dimensions of natural resources, concentrating on planning, visitor behavior, demographic change affecting public lands, and the use of secondary data in recreation, parks, and tourism. He has been working as a practitioner and academic for over twenty years.

DAVID SCOTT is an associate professor in the Recreation, Park and Tourism Sciences Department at Texas A&M University. He is also editor of the *Journal of Leisure Research.* His area of expertise is the sociology of leisure and community parks and recreation. He won the American Academy of Park and Recreation Administration's Willard E. Sutherland award in 1994 for his paper "Time Scarcity and Its Implications for Leisure Behavior and Leisure Delivery" (*Journal of Park and Recreation Administration*); the 1995–1996 Center of Teaching Excellence Scholar award from the College of Agriculture and Life Sciences, Texas A&M University; and the Partners in Learning Award of Excellence, Department of Student Life, Services for Students with Disabilities, Texas A&M University.

LORI B. SHELBY is an assistant professor in the School of Recreation, Health, and Tourism at George Mason University. Lori is also an Associate Editor of the journal *Human Dimensions of Wildlife.* She has research experience investigating human dimensions of natural resources, recreation resource management, tourism, and related survey and statistical methodology. Her research has been published in *Human Dimensions of Wildlife, Wildlife Society Bulletin, Tourism Management, Annals of Tourism Research,* and *Advances in Hospitality & Leisure.*

DUANE L. SHROUFE served as director of the Arizona Game and Fish Department from 1989 to 2008. He served two terms as president of the Western Association of Fish and Wildlife Agencies and recently served as chairman of the North American Wetlands Conservation Council. Duane has also chaired many committees for the Association of Fish and Wildlife Agencies, including the Human Dimensions Committee. After a career spanning forty years in wildlife management, Duane retired in March 2008.

WILLIAM F. SIEMER is a research specialist and PhD candidate with the Human Dimensions Research Unit at Cornell University. His research and outreach activities have focused on understanding wildlife-related attitudes and activity involvement, evaluating stakeholder engagement and stewardship education programs, and working with managers to integrate human dimensions considerations into management decisions. He is a certified wildlife biologist and a coeditor of *Human Dimensions of Wildlife Management in North America.*

AMANDA C. STAUDT is a climate scientist at the National Wildlife Federation, where she has focussed on how global warming will affect aquatic habitats in California, the Chesapeake Bay, and flooding in the Midwest. Previously she worked for the National Academies as a key liaison between the scientific community and the federal agencies that support climate change research. She directed the National Academics Climate Research Committee and helped author more than a dozen reports on topics including the U.S. strategy for supporting climate change research, radiative forcing of climate, past records of surface temperature, how climate and weather affect transportation, and practices for effective global change assessments.

ABOUT THE CONTRIBUTORS

TARA L. TEEL is an assistant professor in the Department of Human Dimensions of Natural Resources at Colorado State University. Tara's research interests are in human dimensions of natural resources, specifically in the application of social science theory and methods to natural resource–related issues. She works closely with wildlife and other natural resource agencies in collection and application of social science data to inform their planning, management, and communication efforts. In addition to research, Tara teaches courses at both the undergraduate and graduate levels in the areas of natural resources tourism, human dimensions and recreation behavior theory, and human dimensions research methods and statistical analysis.

PHILIP K. THORNTON is a systems analyst working in livestock in international development. Much of his work revolves around integrated modeling and impact assessment. He is a senior scientist at the International Livestock Research Institute in Nairobi, Kenya, and a research fellow in the Institute of Atmospheric and Environmental Sciences, University of Edinburgh, Scotland.

ADRIAN TREVES is assistant professor of Environmental Studies at the University of Wisconsin-Madison Nelson Institute for Environmental Studies. He specializes in research on human dimensions of wildlife management and conservation particularly focusing on carnivore damage to property (e.g., predation on livestock, attacks on people). Over six years in the international biodiversity nonprofit sector, he also facilitated-participatory planning exercises for conservation efforts in East Africa and the tropical Andes. Adrian has been first author or coauthor on twenty-seven peer-reviewed publications and twenty-four book chapters or edited pieces relating to ecology or conservation.

JERRY J. VASKE is a professor in the Department of Human Dimensions of Natural Resource at Colorado State University (CSU). Since his arrival at CSU in 1992, he has developed and taught the undergraduate and graduate courses in research methodology/ statistics, as well as theory courses in social psychology. For the last thirty years, Dr. Vaske's research has focused on the application of social psychological theories (e.g., norms, crowding, risk analysis) to managerial concerns and problems. He has authored or coauthored five books and over one hundred peer-reviewed articles. He is the founding coeditor of the journal *Human Dimensions of Wildlife*.

ROBERT WALLACE works on a wide range of conservation interventions, including applied research and conservation planning, natural resource management, local institutional strengthening, and sustainable conservation finance. He is a conservationist for the Wildlife Conservation Society and directs the Greater Madidi Landscape Conservation Program in Bolivia.

DAVID WILKIE is a wildlife ecologist with a particular interest in the human dimensions of conservation and has over twenty years of experience working with indigenous communities in Africa and Latin America. He is director of the TransLinks and Living Landscapes Programs at the Wildlife Conservation Society.

PETER ZAHLER is the assistant director of the Wildlife Conservation Society's Asia Program and is responsible for programs or projects in Iran, Russia, China,

Kazakhstan, Kyrgyzstan, Tajikistan, and Papua New Guinea. He has over twenty-five years of experience in conservation biology and started WCS programs in Pakistan, Mongolia, and Afghanistan.

HARRY C. ZINN is a faculty member of the Pennsylvania State University's Department of Recreation, Park and Tourism Management, where his teaching focuses on the psychology of human interaction with nature, environmental history, and management of resource-based recreation and tourism. He has conducted research with many state and federal wildlife and natural resource agencies, as well as municipal resource managers and private organizations. With colleagues in Taiwan, Hong Kong, and the United States, he is currently developing a study of domestic and international visitors in Taiwan's National Parks. Harry's research results have been published in a variety of journals.

Index

Italicized page numbers refer to figures and tables.

Island Press | Board of Directors